Envisioning Empire

Envisioning Empire

The New British World from 1763 to 1773

Edited by
Robert A. Olwell and James M. Vaughn

BLOOMSBURY ACADEMIC
LONDON • NEW YORK • OXFORD • NEW DELHI • SYDNEY

BLOOMSBURY ACADEMIC
Bloomsbury Publishing Plc
50 Bedford Square, London, WC1B 3DP, UK
1385 Broadway, New York, NY 10018, USA

BLOOMSBURY, BLOOMSBURY ACADEMIC and the Diana logo
are trademarks of Bloomsbury Publishing Plc

First published in Great Britain 2020

ISBN: HB: 978-1-3501-0996-4
         ePDF: 978-1-3501-0993-3
         eBook: 978-1-3501-0994-0

Typeset by Integra Software Services Pvt. Ltd.
Printed and bound in Great Britain

To find out more about our authors and books visit www.bloomsbury.com
and sign up for our newsletters.

Contents

List of Figures

Acknowledgments

Some of Hannah Weiss Muller's chapter, "Forging the Laws of Subjected after 1763," has been adapted from material that was originally published in: Hannah Weiss Muller, *Subjects and Sovereign: Bonds of Belonging in the Eighteenth-Century British Empire* (New York: Oxford University Press, 2017). We thank Oxford University Press for permission to use this material here.

A previous version of P. J. Marshall's chapter, "The East India Company's 'Ancient Form of Government' and the Exigencies of Empire: Bengal 1765 to 1773," was published as: P. J. Marshall, "The Shaping of the New Colonial Regime in Bengal," in *Bangladesh: History, Politics, Economy, Society and Culture—Essays in Honour of Professor Alamgir Muhammad Serajuddin*, ed. Mahmudul Huque (Dhaka: The University Press Limited, 2016), 15–40. We thank the University Press Limited for permission to print an altered version here.

List of Contributors

Christopher Leslie Brown is Professor of history at Columbia University and the author of *Moral Capital: Foundations of British Abolitionism* (Chapel Hill, NC: Omohundro Institute of Early American History and Culture, University of North Carolina Press, 2006).

Jessica L. Harland-Jacobs is Associate Professor of history at the University of Florida and the author of *Builders of Empire: Freemasonry and British Imperialism, 1717–1927* (Chapel Hill, NC: University of North Carolina Press, 2007).

P. J. Marshall is Emeritus Rhodes Professor of Imperial History at King's College London and the author of *The Making and Unmaking of Empires: Britain, India, and America, c. 1750–1783* (Oxford: Oxford University Press, 2005) and *Remaking the British Atlantic: The United States and the British Empire after American Independence* (Oxford: Oxford University Press, 2012).

Robert A. Olwell is Associate Professor of history at the University of Texas at Austin and the author of *Masters, Slaves, and Subjects: The Culture of Power in the South Carolina Low Country, 1740–1790* (Ithaca, NY: Cornell University Press, 1998).

David L. Preston is Westvaco Professor of National Security Studies at the Citadel Military College of South Carolina and the author of *Braddock's Defeat: The Battle of the Monongahela and the Road to Revolution* (Oxford: Oxford University Press, 2015).

Sudipta Sen is Professor of history at the University of California-Davis and the author of *A Distant Sovereignty: National Imperialism and the Origins of British India* (New York: Routledge, 2002) and *Ganges: The Many Pasts of an Indian River* (New Haven, CT: Yale University Press, 2019).

James M. Vaughn is Assistant Professor of history at the University of Texas at Austin and the author of *The Politics of Empire at the Accession of George III: The East India Company and the Crisis and Transformation of Britain's Imperial State* (New Haven, CT: Yale University Press, 2019).

Hannah Weiss Muller is Assistant Professor of history at Brandeis University and the author of *Subjects and Sovereign: Bonds of Belonging in the Eighteenth-Century British Empire* (Oxford: Oxford University Press, 2017).

Introduction: The Spirit of 1763

Robert A. Olwell

Imperial conceptions

On Wednesday, the sixth of July 1763, Connecticut Yankees gathered at the meetinghouse in Wethersfield to proclaim their "trust ... in our Mother Country," to express a "sincere and Heart-felt Gratitude" to "our wise Counsellors and Politicians, our Heroic Chiefs and Commanders, and our brave Soldiers," and to give thanks to God for delivering them from the menace of "*Gallic* chains and *Popish* superstition." Parson James Lockwood accorded most of the glory for the triumph of "our Fleets and Armies" in the recent war to the Almighty, but he also lauded "the *Patriot Pitt*" and "the gallant *Wolf*" for the parts they played in defeating the French and their Native American allies ("the Savages of the Wilderness"). Before calling upon his flock to demonstrate a pious appreciation for divine aid by repenting of their sins, Lockwood drew attention to the terms of the peace treaty, "by which we have acquired a mighty enlargement of Dominion and Territory ... peculiarly favourable and advantageous to us, in America."[1]

To us, such declarations of British patriotism and fealty to King George III are rich with irony for we know that in thirteen years colonial Americans would make another declaration with a quite different intent. In fact, prominent participants in that futurity sat among Parson Lockwood's congregation on that July day. Silas Deane, an up-and-coming young attorney, would one day help negotiate France's entry into the war for American independence. Now, he was enraptured, not by Parson Lockwood's oratory, but by the sight of Mehitable Webb, the wealthy widow he would marry that fall.[2] Mrs. Webb's nine-year-old son Samuel, pulling on the pigtails of his sister Sally, would, a dozen years hence, find another outlet for his violent impulses. Young Samuel would depart with the Wethersfield militia company for Boston immediately after Lexington and Concord. He would remain in the Continental Army until the war's end, and eventually rise to the rank of Brigadier General.[3]

Even the Wethersfield Meeting House was destined to play a small role in the downfall of Britain's American Empire. On the evening of May 21, 1781, George Washington and the Comte de Rochambeau, commander of the troops sent by France to help Americans against their common British enemy, attended a concert by the church's choir. The two men were meeting at Wethersfield to plan the campaign that would culminate that fall with the surrender of the British army at Yorktown, Virginia.[4] When news of this event reached London, it brought down Lord North's government. The new ministry of Lord Rockingham determined to end the war even if the price of peace was accepting American independence. By the time another Treaty of Paris that conceded this was signed in the spring of 1783, the world had turned upside down in ways that Parson Lockwood and his flock could not possibly have imagined twenty years earlier.

While such twists of fortune are fascinating, this volume is not concerned with retelling the familiar story of how British-Americans metamorphosed from loyal subjects into revolutionary citizens. Instead of the revolutionary "spirit of 1776," our focus is on what might be called "the spirit of 1763," or the "spirit of imperialism," that was running at flood tide throughout the anglophone world in the wake of the Seven Years' War.[5] Rather than view the decade that followed through the teleological prism of what was to come, that is, as the prelude to the downfall of the British Empire in the West or its concurrent rise in the East, our starting premise is that this era constitutes a discrete moment in the history of "Greater Britain" (as we might term the area of the globe that came under British rule in 1763) that deserves to be studied in its own right.[6]

To this end, the contributors to this volume were challenged to lower their historical horizons and to focus their gaze upon the events that took place and the expectations that were expressed in the decade immediately after 1763, and to disregard, as much as possible, more distant consequences. However, in directing our interpretive lens away from what happened after 1773, we do not aim to conjure an alternative history in which neither the American Revolution, nor the British Raj occurred. Instead, we merely seek to give the period immediately after the Seven Years' War its due, and to incorporate into our analysis the obvious fact that the people living in 1763, like the Yankees who attended to Parson Lockwood's sermon, could not have foreseen (and likely would never have predicted) their future. By temporally separating the years that lie between the signing of the Treaty of Paris and passage of the Tea Act from the portentous events that followed and lifting from their shoulders the enormous weight of inevitability, perhaps we might be able to better perceive (and appreciate) the various plans and possibilities that were being advocated, implemented, or merely imagined for the new, post-1763, British world before they were all swept away by the "course of human events," as Thomas Jefferson famously described the forces of historical causality in the Declaration of Independence.

February 10, 1763, was an epochal date not only for Britain itself, but also for that part of the world that now found itself under British rule. The terms of the treaty ratified in Paris on that day "securely established" Britain's new "imperial status."[7] The effects of this newfound power and influence were soon felt not only in the world outside of Britain, but also at home. As recent scholarship has demonstrated, the changes wrought by the outcome of the war and the terms of the peace profoundly affected the attitudes of both the British establishment and the British public regarding the nature and purpose of their newly won empire and their own national identity. The end of the long conflict meant that nagging questions such as how the enormous national debt incurred during the war could be carried (much less paid off), and how (or if) the diverse peoples who now fell under British rule could somehow be made into British subjects, must now be addressed.

A treaty written in blood and ink

The magnitude of the war and of Britain's triumph over her European rivals could be read in the terms of the concluding peace. A contemporary printed version of the treaty's twenty-seven articles required forty-eight pages (in parallel columns of French and English) to describe all of the negotiations and details required to conclude a "long and bloody War" that began in the forests of North America and "spread Troubles in the Four Parts of the World" before it ended.[8] After a century of European wars fought for limited purposes and with limited results, the war that began in May 1754 and ended in February 1763 was unprecedented in terms of its scale, its geographic scope, and the decisive character of its outcome.

The conflict was extremely complex; even its nomenclature is contentious. Its usual name in European history, "the Seven Years' War," belies the fact that fighting started in North America two years before war was formally declared in Europe. Perhaps for this reason, in anglophone America the conflict was and is more commonly called "the French and Indian War." But while this term avoids the mathematical error, and has the advantage of being used by British colonists during the war itself, it is not unproblematic. For one, it adopts an Anglocentric perspective. In Quebec, the preferred term for the conflict is the "*Guerre de la Conquête*" (War of the Conquest). In addition, if the global expanse of the struggle is taken into account, the list of Britain's foes must expand to include Austrians, Canadians, Cubans, Filipinos, Russians, Sardinians, Saxons, South Asians, Spaniards, Swedes, and the Army of the Holy Roman Empire.[9]

In the mid-twentieth century, two alternative names for the conflict were proposed in an effort to better comprehend its purpose and global character. Lawrence Henry Gipson, in his opus, *The British Empire before the American Revolution*, suggested the "Great War for Empire," while Winston Churchill, in historian mode, entitled his chapter on the conflict: "The First World War."[10] But neither of these suggestions has gained wide acceptance. Most recently, the term "Seven Years' War" has been used to signify the entire global conflict from 1754 to 1763, disregarding its literal meaning and chronological imprecision.[11] It is in this figurative sense that it is used in this volume.

The treaty's first order of business was to formally bring an end to hostilities. A "universal, and perpetual Peace" was proclaimed between "their Britannick, Most Christian, Catholick, and Most Faithful Majesties" (Britain, France, Spain, and Portugal) and their subjects. Previous international agreements going back to 1648 were reaffirmed and the belligerents promised to return any prisoners of war in their custody.

After this, the negotiators rolled out a map of North America and got to work. This was a fitting place to start because, as was noted above, the conflict had begun as a clandestine struggle between Britain and France for control of the "forks" of the Ohio River (the site of modern Pittsburgh). The first shots were fired in May 1754 in a skirmish inadvertently sparked by a hapless young lieutenant colonel of

Virginia militia named George Washington.[12] In the North American theater of the war, the British (with colonial auxiliaries and Indian allies) overcame initial defeats to not only displace the French at the head of the Ohio, but also to capture the great fortress of Louisbourg on Cape Breton Island, and finally, in 1759, the greatest prize of them all: the fortified city of Quebec. By the war's end, British soldiers gained possession of Montreal and the remaining French outposts in the Great Lakes basin.

The fourth article of the treaty must have thrilled Parson Lockwood's congregation in Wethersfield and every inhabitant of New England: "His Most Christian Majesty cedes and guaranties to his said Britannick Majesty, in full right, Canada, with all its dependencies, as well as the island of Cape Breton, and all the other islands and coasts in the gulph and river of St. Lawrence." What the euphoric Yankees may have failed to recognize was that as a consequence of the annexation of Canada, their ancient "Gallic" and "Popish" foes, the approximately seventy thousand Québécois, now became fellow British subjects.

But France's retreat from North America was not finished. By the treaty's seventh article, the French also ceded to Britain the eastern half of "Louisiana" (a term that then denoted the entire Mississippi River watershed) "from its [as yet unknown] source" southward to the Gulf of Mexico. Moreover, although their outposts of Fort Condé on Mobile Bay and Fort Toulouse on the Alabama River had not been attacked in the war, the French threw them in for good measure along with their territorial claims in that region.

What the text of the Treaty of Paris did not reveal, and what the British would not learn of for another year, was that on the same day that the peace preliminaries were signed at Fontainebleau, a private agreement had been concluded by which King Louis XV of France ceded the western half of Louisiana and the "island of New Orleans" to his "very dear and well-beloved brother and cousin," King Charles III of Spain.[13] Consequently, after February 10, 1763, the territorial extent of "New France," which seven years before had included the St. Lawrence, Great Lakes, Mississippi, and Alabama River watersheds (an area more than six times larger than France itself), was reduced to two tiny islands off the coast of Newfoundland which France was given as "a shelter to French fishermen."

Apart from the fighting in western Pennsylvania and in the Anglo-Cherokee war of 1758 to 1761 (which the Cherokee, in their own language, remembered as "the war with those in the red coats"), the trans-Appalachian region had not been the scene of combat.[14] Its native inhabitants, who thought of themselves as allies rather than subjects of the French, did not consider themselves a defeated or conquered people. They were therefore astonished to learn that by the terms of a treaty signed on the opposite side of the Atlantic, their lands had been passed from the king of France to the king of Britain. The natives' anger at the treaty (and British arrogance in implementing it) provoked Indians to attack Britain's western outposts in the late spring of 1763. The need to win the cooperation of the natives eventually induced the British crown to issue a royal proclamation in October in which the king offered "protection" (from encroaching settlers among other things) as well as lavish "presents" of manufactured goods to his new American Indian subjects.

The negotiators next looked to the Caribbean. By the end of 1759, the Royal Navy had asserted its supremacy over the *Marine Royale*. This spared Britain from the threat of invasion and left France's overseas possessions at the mercy of British sea power. Like apples plucked from a tree, French islands in the lesser Antilles—Guadeloupe, Martinique, and Grenada—fell into British hands. Now, apart from Grenada, this harvest was to be returned. The treaty also shared out four islands that had been declared "neutral" (i.e., left unclaimed) by the terms of the Treaty of Aix-la-Chapelle in 1748. Of these, Britain received the lion's share: Saint Vincent, Dominica, and Tobago, while France was compensated for the loss of Grenada by being allowed to claim Saint Lucia. In the Royal Proclamation issued by the British in October 1763, the four "ceded islands" were organized into the new colony of Grenada, the population of which included perhaps seven thousand free French Catholics, as well as four times as many enslaved Africans. But, quite unlike their withdrawal from the North American mainland, France's diplomats had managed to reverse the effects of military defeat in the Caribbean and to substantially restore the French Empire in the region to its pre-war status.

On the other side of the Atlantic, the commissioners agreed to divvy up two small African islands that the Royal Navy had captured during the war. The island of Gorée, off Cape Verde, was returned to France, while Île-Saint-Louis, in the mouth of the Senegal River, was ceded to Britain (along with exclusive trading rights along that river). In 1765, Île-Saint-Louis would be combined with Fort St. James (an island in the Gambia River) to form the new colony of Senegambia, Britain's first territorial footstep into sub-Saharan Africa.

Spinning the globe at Fontainebleau, the negotiators set their fingers upon South Asia where the British and French East India Companies had engaged in a hot and cold war, often in league with native princes, for almost twenty years. The course and outcome of the most recent round of this contest paralleled the war in North America in that the British Company, reinforced by naval and land forces from Britain and assisted by Indian allies, overcame early setbacks to obtain a commanding advantage. By 1763, British (or Company) forces had taken possession of all their French rival's posts in the subcontinent, including its headquarters at Pondicherry (Puducherry).[15]

If the terms of the treaty were simply read in terms of forts and flags, it might seem that the commissioners sought to return the pieces on the South Asian chessboard back to where they had been "at the beginning of 1749." Each company was to return any conquests it had taken from the other in the intervening fourteen years. On the diplomatic front, the treaty also proposed something of a quid pro quo. Perhaps in an effort to disentangle themselves from the internecine political struggles on the subcontinent, each company agreed to recognize one of the other's princely allies. Thus, as in the Caribbean, the treaty's terms regarding India might at first glance appear to restore the French to their pre-war position.

But looks were deceiving. For one, and unbeknownst to the men meeting in Fontainebleau, the political situation in central India had altered. The man the French had chosen to throw their support behind was Salabat Jung, Nizam of Hyderabad. Before the war, he had been a "French Protégé," and they no doubt planned to continue this close relationship after the war.[16] But, in July 1762, Salabat Jung was deposed.

(News of the event would not reach Europe until after the peace preliminaries were signed.) Rather than remained tied to the French, the new nizam, Asaf Jah II, began to "think coolly of his own interests," as one British official approvingly noted. Asaf Jah II decided that the British were better equipped to furnish him with the military supplies he desired to wage war against the Maratha Empire.[17] The loss of a reliable ally in Hyderabad greatly diminished French influence throughout the Deccan.

The balance of European power in India was tipped further by a clause in the treaty that dramatically altered the postwar situation in Bengal. The crucial detail lay at the end of a sentence otherwise concerned with restoring British trading factories in Sumatra captured in 1760.[18] However, after a semicolon, in a seeming non sequitur, the French also agreed "not to erect fortifications, or to keep troops in any part of the dominions of the Subah of Bengal." This restriction effectively prevented the French from exerting any future military or political influence in a region, which, in terms of its size, population, and wealth, was likened by a member of Parliament to "the whole kingdom of France."[19]

That the war's concluding treaty would place the British East India Company in the dominant position in Bengal would have seemed most unlikely when the conflict commenced, for its first act in South Asia had been the Company's humiliating expulsion from the region. In June of 1756, the nawab of Bengal, Siraj ud-Daulah, demanded that the company cease strengthening the defenses of Fort William, the citadel of its entrepôt at Calcutta (Kolkata). Company officials demurred, claiming that the new guns were aimed not at the nawab but at their French rival. (War had already been declared in Europe, although news of it would not reach India for months.) However, the nawab knew that cannon, once emplaced, would fortify the company against his authority just as well as against the French, and dispatched troops to occupy both the city and fort before the works were complete. Most of the resident Britons fled, but the death of a number confined in an overcrowded prison cell, the infamous "Black Hole of Calcutta," became a cause célèbre used for the next two centuries to justify British rule in India.[20]

In early 1757, the East India Company dispatched a military force (reinforced by ships from the Royal Navy and several hundred British soldiers) to retake Calcutta. The expedition was commanded by Robert Clive, a country lawyer's son from Shropshire who had come to India a dozen years earlier as a clerk but who found his true calling in the Company's army. Word of war with France having by now arrived, Clive next seized the French East India Company's trading post at nearby Chandernagore (Chandannagar). Although an uneasy truce had been negotiated with the nawab, Company officials feared that Siraj ud-Daulah might seek to ally with the French. To preempt this possibility, Clive marched upon the nawab's court in Murshidabad.

On the morning of June 23, 1757, two armies deployed at Plassey for what appeared a very unequal encounter. Clive's force consisted of 3,000 men: 900 British soldiers and 2,100 "sepoys" (European armed and trained natives). The nawab's army contained perhaps 50,000 soldiers (all natives apart from fifty French artillerymen who had escaped from Chandernagore). The outcome of the ensuing battle owed something to superior European firepower and military discipline, perhaps more to the sudden rain shower that soaked the gunpowder of the nawab's cannon, but was mostly due to treachery (or, to put it more politely, diplomacy).

Clive had left Calcutta with an ace up his sleeve. During negotiations with the nawab, Company officials noted the dissension and discontent rife in his court. Before marching to Plassey, Clive had conspired with three of Siraj ud-Daulah's four commanders to keep their troops out of the ensuing battle. Now, the Company's little army, strongly posted in a mango grove and defended by artillerymen who had kept their powder dry, repelled attacks by the loyal rump of the nawab's army. Meanwhile, Clive nervously peered through his spyglass at the majority of the nawab's army that was standing idly by to see what they would do. In the end, despite the nawab's desperate entreaties, they did nothing. As the sun set, the Company's soldiers advanced and drove Siraj ud-Daulah and his dispirited followers from the field.[21]

The next morning, Clive rewarded the nawab's principal lieutenant, Mir Jafar, for his betrayal by installing him as the new ruler of Bengal. The death of Siraj ud-Dualah at the hands of Mir Jafar's son a few days later completed "this great revolution, so happily brought about," as Clive reported to the Company's directors.[22] It is this political *coup d'etat*, rather than the somewhat perfunctory battle itself, that gives Plassey its place among the decisive engagements of world history. The East India Company had previously made alliances with Indian princes. But this was the first time the Company had acted to replace an Indian ruler with someone who was more to their liking. The practice, once begun, quickly became a habit. Three years after Plassey, the Company deposed Mir Jafar, who was now deemed unsatisfactory, and replaced him with his son-in-law, Mir Qasim.

Thus, although the Treaty of Paris allowed the French East India Company to reopen its trading factory at Chandernagore, the prohibition on garrisoning or fortifying the outpost left their merchants there at the mercy of both the nawab in Murshidabad and their British rivals in Calcutta. Conversely, the British East India Company was free to flex its mercantile, political, and military muscles throughout Bengal without interference from either the French or, in the aftermath of Plassey, from the "puppet" nawabs they had placed upon the *musnud* (cushioned throne) in Murshidabad.[23] After 1763, the fortunes of the British and French East India Companies moved in opposite directions. While the British corporation began to transform itself into a political–military "state," its Gallic counterpart shrank back to its original form as a purely mercantile enterprise.[24] The French state was largely reduced to playing the role of spoiler on a subcontinent that increasingly fell under British sway.

Articles twelve through fifteen of the treaty put European affairs back in order. In military terms, this was the war's main event (i.e., the scene of the largest battles), but, in strategic terms, it was a side show. At most, the French hoped to make territorial gains in Europe that could be used to counterbalance overseas losses. Therefore, a strategic stalemate in Europe was, in British eyes, almost equal to a victory. One month before war was declared, the French captured the western Mediterranean island of Minorca (which the British had possessed since 1713). However, this conquest was later counterbalanced by the British capture of Belle-Île, off the southern coast of Brittany. At Fountainbleau, it was agreed to simply return the two islands. Elsewhere, the treaty also sought to restore the European status quo ante-bellum. For example, fortifications constructed at the French port of Dunkirk to facilitate its use as a staging point for a projected invasion of Britain were to be demolished and the city returned to its previous, defenseless, condition.

In Germany, the belligerents had spent six years engaged in a bloody but inconclusive combat. At the war's start, the French outmaneuvered the duke of Cumberland and threatened the Electorate of Hanover, still the domain of the Hanoverian kings of Britain. The duke (King George II's son) negotiated a convention to spare the electorate from the ravages of war which the British public (and his father) deemed a humiliation. When William Pitt took charge of the war effort, he revoked the agreement and raised a new military force: "His Brittanick Majesty's Army in Germany," comprised of soldiers from Britain, Hanover, and other north German states (all financed by the British treasury). Britain's "German" army, commanded by Prince Ferdinand of Brunswick, "liberated" Hanover and, in a series of hard-fought campaigns, kept larger French forces at bay for the rest of the war.[25]

It was not until the treaty's sixteenth article that the commissioners turned to brokering peace between Britain and Spain. This belated attention reflected "His Catholick Majesty's" late entry into the conflict. In the fall of 1759, as the fortunes of the war began to turn against France, the Spanish court sought to mediate a cessation of hostilities on the basis of a return to the pre-war status quo. Following General Wolfe's conquest of Quebec, Spain warned Britain that it "could not regard with indifference" any change in the "balance of power in America."[26] (This was an interesting application of a European concept to the western side of the Atlantic.) But Pitt rebuffed Spain's hardly impartial offer to adjudicate the conflict and instead proposed a general congress of all belligerents, which, as he expected, came to nothing.

Two years later, as France's losses began to mount, Versailles and Madrid raised the stakes. In August 1761, they drew up a "family compact," one Bourbon monarch with another, by which Charles III promised his French cousin that if a favorable peace had not been negotiated with Britain by May 1, 1762, Spain would join the conflict on the French side. In that event, Louis XV promised his Spanish cousin that Versailles would not end the war without Madrid's approval. The threat of Spain's entry into the war (in particular, the prospect that the combined Spanish and French navies could reopen the war at sea) was a trump card that France was to play at the negotiating table to get better terms.

However, by the fall of 1761 the military situation had turned so decisively in Britain's favor that when Pitt learned of the family compact he regarded it not as a threat but as an invitation to conquer some of Spain's colonial possessions. Rather than wait until May 1762 to see what Spain would do, Pitt called for an immediate attack upon the Spanish Empire. When the new king, George III, and his advisor, Lord Bute, refused to endorse a preemptive strike (and a widening of the war), Pitt impetuously resigned. However, the bellicose clamor in the popular press and in Parliament proved irresistible, and war was declared against Spain a few months later in January 1762.

In March, a British expedition sailed for Havana, the third largest city (after Mexico City and Lima) and most important port in all of the Americas. The ships reached their destination by early June and, after a two-month siege, the city was taken.[27] Meanwhile, on the other side of the world, officials of the British East India Company engaged in "corporate raiding" in a very literal sense by attacking the city of Manila, in the Philippines. When a fleet of Royal Navy and Company ships carrying British soldiers and Indian sepoys appeared in Manila harbor in late September, the inhabitants had no idea that Britain and Spain were at war. The city was captured and ruthlessly sacked. News of the event would not reach Europe until two months after the final peace treaty was signed.[28]

The Spanish had assumed that in the event of war they would easily be able to invade their neighbor, and Britain's old ally, Portugal. The Portuguese were still recovering from the fiscal aftershocks of the great Lisbon earthquake of seven years before. Their border defenses were in bad repair; and the small Portuguese army was no match for that of their Franco-Spanish opponent. But the British rushed reinforcements to the peninsula, and, over the summer and fall of 1762, the spirited resistance of the Portuguese people, combined with the skillful maneuvers of the count of Schaumburg-Lippe, commander of the Luso-British army, inflicted heavy losses on the invaders and frustrated their plans. In Portugal, the conflict is remembered as the "*Guerra Fantástica*" (Fantastic War).[29]

By November 1762, less than a year after Britain had declared war, and only fifteen months after the signing of the family compact, Spain could claim a few small territorial gains in South America, but the costly invasion of Portugal had achieved little, and Havana, the keystone of the Spanish-American Empire, had been lost (the capture of Manila, as noted above, would not be known of until the spring). The war had gone no better at sea. Twelve ships of the line, a quarter of the entire Spanish battle fleet, were trapped in Havana harbor by the sudden arrival of the British and surrendered with the city. Most of Spain's remaining warships stayed in port to avoid the same fate.

France, by now financially and militarily exhausted, was desperate to end the war at almost any cost. But Versailles could not make peace without Madrid's consent, and the Spanish would not agree to end the war if this meant accepting the loss of Havana. On the British side, Prime Minister Bute and the new king also wanted to conclude the "bloody and expensive war," but for reasons of domestic politics, could not return Havana without recompense. To break the impasse, France's negotiators put together a diplomatic triple play by which Britain would restore Havana to Spain in exchange for Florida, and simultaneously, to persuade the Spanish to sign the treaty, and thus end the war, the French, by the terms of a separate Treaty of Fontainebleau, would cede the western half of Louisiana and the "island" of New Orleans to Spain.

The rest of the treaty was a simply matter of tying up loose ends. The French and Spanish agreed to return the border forts they still held in Portugal in "the same condition they were in when conquered." Deadlines for the evacuation of forces, exchange of prisoners, and the transfer of territories were set according to the time thought necessary for news of the treaty to travel across the world: six weeks from the date of signing for Europe, three months for America and Africa, and six months for India. Because the attack upon Manila was known of but not its outcome, the twenty-third article of the treaty stipulated that "all territories, which may have been conquered in whatsoever part of the world … which are not included in the present treaty … shall be restored without difficulty, and without requiring any compensations." (Thus, aside from the stupendous amount of loot they stole before departing in 1764, the East Company's speculative military venture was inconsequential.)

The peace preliminaries were endorsed on November 3, 1762, and the treaty was submitted to the respective governments for approval. When it was brought before the British House of Commons in early December, there was a heated debate. It was impossible to separate the terms of the peace from Britain's domestic political divisions and factions. Pitt, the victorious wartime leader who now sat in the front bench of the opposition, denounced the treaty as far too generous to France and Spain. Bute's opponents accused him of giving away at the negotiating table much of what had been won on the battlefield. In the vigorous "press war" that ensued, John Wilkes, an ardent Pitt supporter and anti-government gadfly, waggishly compared the treaty to the "Peace of God," because it "passeth all understanding."[30]

However, when the question was finally called, the Commons voted in favor of the treaty by a margin of almost five to one.[31] The large majority was due in part to the ferocity of the government whip, and perhaps, as the opposition claimed, to the efficacy of bribes and the associated levers of the "old corruption," but it also accurately reflected the war weariness of the British public, and the fact that by the terms of the treaty Britain would gain substantial and valuable new territories, particularly, as Reverend Lockwood would note from his pulpit in July, in North America.

On the evening of February 10, 1763, diplomats arrived at the Paris residence of the British ambassador. Both the site of the meeting and the décor of the meeting room (dominated by a life-sized portrait of King George III) underscored the outcome of the war.[32] One by one, the delegates for Britain, France, and Spain each signed four copies of the treaty, one for each of the monarchs mentioned in the document.[33] (Although not represented in the negotiations, King Jose I of Portugal was "included therein as a contracting party ... [just] as if he had expressly signed.") Beneath their names, the diplomats pressed their signet rings into blobs of molten red wax joined together by ribbons (red on the British copy, blue on the French), and, with that, it was "done."[34]

1763 and all that

Almost a century ago, Charles McLean Andrews, one of the "inventors" of the field of Colonial American History, denoted "the year 1763" as "a great turning point" in British and British-American relations.[35] Since then, most scholars of Colonial America have followed Andrews's lead and have used this year to draw a line between the "Colonial Period of American History," per se, and an era usually described as constituting the "origins" of the American Revolution.[36] However, in the spring of 1763, the first shots of the revolution were still a dozen years away, so the "turning point" that Andrews and others have discerned was a subtle change of direction rather than a violent about-face. The first sign of a "turn" in colonial policy, or British–colonial relations, came at the year's end when colonial Americans read the text of the Royal Proclamation that had been issued by the crown in October.[37] Along with organizing the new colonies of Quebec, East and West Florida, and Grenada from the territories acquired by the treaty, the proclamation's most important article was its prohibition upon any future settlements or land claims between the crest of the Appalachian Mountains and the Mississippi River. Instead, this vast area was "reserved" to the two hundred thousand or so indigenous peoples who resided in the region (many of them were the king's enemies in the late war and as recently as in "Pontiac's Rebellion" of May and June). As they set aside (at least for the moment) the real estate schemes they had been hatching for the Ohio Valley, prominent colonials like George Washington and Benjamin Franklin realized, with something of a shock, that the British ministry had its own, quite different, plans for the future of Britain's American Empire.[38]

To Andrews, the proclamation was a symptom rather than a cause of the imperial crisis that would soon break over the British-American Empire. He traced the origins of the ministry's new colonial policy to a transformation that occurred in the wake of the Treaty of Paris in how Britons conceived of their empire, and of themselves as an imperial people. "In the past," he wrote, when Britons "had spoken of 'empire,' … [they had meant] the self-sufficient empire of the mercantilists rather than a thing of territory, centralization, maintenance, and authority …. After the global acquisitions of 1763, however, territorial empire came into real and visible existence, and writers, both British and colonial, became aware that 'imperialism' meant something more than commerce and colonies." Andrews argued that after Britons' realization that they now possessed a global empire, "a new issue, that of territorial imperialism, emerged to perplex the souls of British statesmen."[39] In short, having won an empire, British ministers sought to conduct themselves like emperors.

In an empire that the sun never set upon, twilight on one side of the world coincided with dawn on the other. Similarly, the post-1763 gloom that began to darken Britain's relations with the North American colonies was matched by the first rays of an imperial sunrise in the East. For scholars of India, the events of the Seven Years' War and the terms of the Treaty of Paris signaled the first steps down a path that would end with the establishment of the "Raj," or Britain's direct political rule over the subcontinent. Clive's victory at Plassey in 1757 is often cited as the start of the process by which the East India Company was transformed "from trader to sovereign," or from company to state.[40] But in concrete terms, the change actually began to occur eight years later, when, by the terms of the treaty of Allahabad, Emperor Shah Alam II granted the Company the power to collect taxes in his provinces of Bengal, Bihar, and Orissa.

While these dramatic events were unfolding on the opposite sides of the world, the domestic situation in Britain was also becoming unsettled. The Whig political machine built and managed by Robert Walpole, and, after his resignation, by the Pelham brothers, Henry and Thomas (the Duke of Newcastle), had directed the government for almost four decades when King George III took the throne in October 1760. Three years earlier, the disastrous start of the Seven Years' War had forced the Whig leadership to invite William Pitt, a leading opposition member, into the cabinet as Secretary of State (but in reality, as the leading figure in the government). The Pitt–Newcastle partnership led the country to victory, but it was always something of a forced marriage. By early 1760, military success had made Pitt politically expendable; the death of King George II that fall made his resignation, one year later, inevitable.

The new king, George III, an immature bachelor of twenty-two, had been taught by his tutor, John Stuart, the Earl of Bute, that his grandfather and great-grandfather (George II and George I) had allowed themselves to be dominated by their ministers. From 1715 to 1760, this view supposed, the leaders of the Whig party had steered the ship of state from behind the throne while the king had been reduced to a largely ceremonial role. George III, advised by Bute, was determined to take an active, if not leading, role in government. The new king's ambition to rule as well as reign was bound to conflict with the headstrong Pitt. But it also was certain to create instability in a political system long accustomed to Whig party management.[41]

For a time, Pitt was shielded by the king's inexperience and by his own enormous popularity both with the British public and in the House of Commons. But, in the eighteenth century, a successful minister needed to please (or at least placate) two constituencies: the Parliament and the crown. Faced with an increasingly hostile and jealous court, Pitt's position gradually eroded. His resignation in the fall of 1761, ostensibly on the issue of war with Spain, ended a relationship with the king (and Bute) that had become unworkable. With Pitt gone, Newcastle's days were numbered. When he resigned in May 1762, George III was at last free to make his "favourite," Bute, also his first minister.

Bute had the king's support, of course, and could draw upon the considerable resources of royal patronage, but his short and turbulent government demonstrated that a prime minister also needed to have (or win) the support of Parliament. Bute was despised in the Commons (where he had never been a member) for his part in driving Pitt from office. He attempted to build a party of "King's Friends" by offering or withholding patronage, and sought to curry favor with the British public through the use of a subsidized press. But these ham-fisted efforts backfired. For a time, Bute became the most hated (and vilified) man in Britain.[42] In April 1763, only two months after the Treaty of Paris was ratified, he abruptly resigned.

Over the course of the next seven years, Britain would have five governments. In each case, a ministry's unpopularity with either the Commons or the Court (or both) rendered it politically weak and produced a fickle and ineffectual colonial policy. Yet, as we have seen, these were the very years in which great changes were brewing in both the American and Asian sides of the empire. Perhaps a more stable and confident administration in London might have been willing and able to make the difficult decisions and compromises required to solve the crisis with the American colonies, or to successfully rein in the East India Company.

It was not until January 1770, when the king asked Lord North to form a government, that a minister emerged from the political scrum able to manage both the Commons and the king. However, the fact that North, whose administration lasted until 1782, presided over both the loss of the American colonies and the Parliament's failure to restrain the excesses of Company rule in India suggests that the size, complexity, and conundrums of the post-1763 empire may have grown beyond any Westminster-based government's ability to comprehend, let alone control.

The history of empires

For reasons perhaps as much ideological and professional as chronological or geographical, it has long been customary to divide the history of the British Empire in two.[43] The first, or "old," empire borders the North Atlantic. Besides the British Isles, it includes eastern North America (including, after 1763, northeastern Canada, and Florida), as well as the islands of Bermuda, the British possessions in the Caribbean, and the coastal forts leased by the Royal African Company (after 1752, the Company of Merchants Trading to Africa) from which to manage the slave trade. The origins of this "old colonial system," which, until recently, most historians usually did not even denote with the word "empire," date back to the start of the seventeenth century.[44]

The primary orientation of the British-Atlantic Empire was entrepreneurial and commercial. Most of the early colonies were created as joint-stock corporations or were owned by proprietors whose goal was to establish a profitable trans-Atlantic trade, or, to attract quit rent-paying settlers by offering them land on liberal terms. Exceptions might be made for the "Puritan" colonies of New England and Providence Island in the Caribbean, which, although chartered as corporations, were conceived of as socio-religious experiments, and for Jamaica, captured by an English military expedition in 1655 as part of Oliver Cromwell's "Western Design" of striking at the Spanish Empire.[45] But the Providence Island colony quickly failed, and within a generation of their founding, both New England and Jamaica had become commercial cogs in the larger network of colonial trade.

Likewise, although proposals were made and limited efforts undertaken to "reduce" the natives to subjection in the mode of the Spanish, the great majority of the subjects of the first empire were either immigrants from Europe (especially Britain), enslaved people from Africa, or their creole descendants. Hence, the first empire is often described as based on colonies of "settlement" rather than of conquest. The question as to whether enslaved Africans, or those indigenous peoples who lived among colonial settlers, were to be considered as British subjects or merely as subject to British rule, was a vexed one, but gradually from the early seventeenth to the mid-eighteenth century, both legal theory and practice were increasingly inclined toward the more inclusive view.

Before 1763, the basic characteristics of Britain's "old colonial system" have been described as "Protestant, commercial, maritime, and free."[46] When this formulation is confined to the colonial ruling class it is not inappropriate. Colonial political elites were Protestants by law and most were engaged in producing commodities to be exchanged via overseas trade (hence "commercial and maritime"). Within their colonies they enjoyed a large measure of local autonomy and self-government (i.e., "freedom"). However, it must be noted that the great majority of people who lived in the first empire, whether women, children, property-less men, subjugated Indians, or African slaves, lacked the full "rights of Englishmen" (or any rights at all). Enslaved Africans, both as commodities and as an involuntary labor force, were the engine that drove the entire system. Even regions like New England, where slaves were few, found a place in the Atlantic trading system shipping foodstuffs and lumber to the sugar plantations, bringing back the by-product of sugar refining, molasses, to distill into rum.[47] Thus, to many people who lived under the union jack in 1750, the boastful refrain of "Rule Britannia" that "Britons never will be slaves" struck a sour note.

Britain's "second empire" differs from the first in terms of its image and defining attributes as well as its geography. Centered in Asia and Africa, and bordering the Indian Ocean more than the Atlantic, this imperial system was delineated more by race than by religion, was tributary and territorial rather than commercial and maritime, and, perhaps above all, was inherently unequal and unfree. All but a tiny percentage of the inhabitants of the second empire were indigenous inhabitants rather than immigrants who had traveled across the sea from Britain or Africa. (Thus, these were colonies of "conquest" and not of "settlement.") The huge native majority was kept in subjection by a relatively tiny number of migrants from Britain, most of whom were temporary sojourners rather than permanent settlers. But, in many ways, the most distinguishing characteristic of the second empire was its fixation with race. Beginning in the latter half of the eighteenth century, and with increasing political, intellectual, and scientific vigor through the century that followed, the British justified their rule over the vast native populations of the empire by asserting (often violently) a military, cultural and, above all, racial, superiority.

After the British government assumed direct rule over India in 1858, the peoples of the subcontinent became Queen Victoria's, or, after 1876, Empress Victoria's, subjects. But by the late nineteenth century, it was accepted that the liberties possessed by Victoria's many subjects depended upon both where they lived and the color of their skin. A distinction was made between the rights and role of the "British" or "white" people who lived in or originated from the metropole, and the non-British, "dark-skinned," population of the imperial periphery. The former was born to command and the latter to obey. Rudyard Kipling's 1899 poem inviting the United States (in the aftermath of the American seizure of the Philippines from Spain) to join with Britain in bearing "the White Man's Burden" of bringing order and the benefits of Western civilization to the "wild … sullen peoples, Half devil and half child" of Africa and Asia may mark the epitome, or perhaps nadir, of this racialized concept of imperialism.[48]

Of course, as with any conceptual paradigm, no sooner were categories defined but complications and anomalies emerged. For example, even as the empire's peoples were being divided by race, the children of interracial unions appeared to complicate the picture. Similarly, upon closer examination, the distinctions drawn between the two "empires" are far less distinct in reality than they seem in theory. For one, the "second" empire was actually just as old as, and, in fact, slightly older than the "first." The East India Company received its charter in 1600, six years before that of the Virginia Company, and for its first 150 years it operated primarily as a trading enterprise.

Given the enormous distance from Britain, and the long time it took for messages to travel from London to Calcutta, the East India Company was granted the means to defend itself. But, until the mid-eighteenth century, the East India Company largely deployed its soldiers and warships to defend its trading entrepôts and merchantmen and negotiated commercial rather than territorial (or tax-collecting) concessions.[49] Moreover, it is often forgotten that the Virginia Company's charter also granted it military powers and local political authority. Most of the "settlers" sent to Jamestown in its first decade were soldiers. In the seventeenth century, most overseas trading companies exercised powers that today seem to lie beyond the jurisdiction of a purely commercial entity.[50]

As with any conceptual paradigm, anomalies to the two empires model were treated either as exceptions that somehow "prove the rule," or were placed in a new, special, category. For instance, although sexual relations between Europeans and Africans quickly blurred the ideological (and legal) distinction between "white" and "black," the trope of the "tragic mulatto," trapped in the no-man's land between the color lines, served to reinforce rather than challenge the racial binary.[51] Likewise, Victorian conceptualizations of the second British Empire as being divided between a free, "white" (or British), core and an unfree, non-white, periphery had to contend with the existence of Canada, Australia, and New Zealand (largely settled by "white" immigrants from Britain and, by the late nineteenth century, largely self-governing). This might be accomplished by differentiating between colonies of settlement or conquest, as we have seen. But in the late nineteenth and early twentieth centuries it was perhaps more common to define them not as colonies at all but as "white dominions" (thus, reinforcing the racial distinction made between "white" Britons capable of ruling themselves, and "dark" colonial peoples who had to be ruled).[52]

During the first century or so of British imperial historiography, the first and second British Empires were usually depicted as separate and sequential. The multivolume *Cambridge History of the British Empire*, which began to be published in 1929, dated the end of the first empire and the birth of the second to the same year: 1783. But the series divided their histories into distinct volumes. Volume 1 covered the "old empire," that is, the American colonies, and spanned from "the beginnings to 1783." Volume 2, entitled, "The New Empire," began in 1783 and continued on to 1870.[53] Thus, by propitious timing, just as the curtain fell on the first empire, it rose upon the second. Somehow, Britain managed to pass the imperial torch from one hemisphere (and empire) to another without allowing the flame to go out but also without allowing any contact between the first empire and its successor.[54]

But this conceptual quarantine has long since been breached. At least since the publication of Vincent T. Harlow's *The Founding of the Second British Empire* in 1952, the birth of the second empire has been moved earlier so that its rise was concurrent with, rather than subsequent to, the downfall of the first.[55] Moreover, Harlow insisted that this coincidence was also consequential. "For rather more than twenty years," he wrote, "the two processes overlapped, and of course, reacted upon each other."[56] Eschewing metaphors such as ships passing in the night, or trains traveling along "parallel tracks," Harlow argued that, during these two decades, "the two conceptions of empire" must have "converged and collided."[57]

However, although he laid out the conceptual knitting, Harlow did little to actually weave the two sides of the empire together. In the two volumes of the *Founding of the Second British Empire*, his treatment of "the Argument about North America," that is, a history of the American crisis and American Revolution from 1760 to 1783, spans almost three hundred and fifty pages and constitutes something of a book within the book.[58] But nowhere in his otherwise competent and thorough study of this subject did Harlow refer to the events happening simultaneously in India. Likewise, in the almost seven hundred and fifty pages that he devoted to events in India and Asia, Harlow never stole so much as a sideways glance at what was then happening in North America.

Only in a brief conclusion after two volumes and over fourteen hundred pages, did Harlow attempt to sew a few speculative stitches between the two imperial histories. First, he boldly declared that "the line drawn across the ledger, between the First and Second British Empires" by earlier historians was "a division of convenience rather than of substance." Yet Harlow also argued, in keeping with the older interpretation, that the loss of the American colonies had little effect on subsequent imperial policy, because the "swing to the East" had begun before the American Revolution had started, and the foundations for the second empire were substantially in place before Parliament finally conceded American independence in 1783.[59]

Given this, Harlow only devoted a few tentative paragraphs to the question of how events in the two halves of the empire may have "converged and collided" between 1760 and 1783. The common thread, he suggested, led back to Whitehall and the policies undertaken by British ministers in the decade following the Seven Years' War. Sounding remarkably like Charles Andrews, Harlow described the "attempt of Crown and Parliament to impose uniform and centralized reforms" upon the empire in the aftermath of the Seven Years' War. However, these "new tasks" proved to be "complex and detailed beyond the knowledge of cabinet ministers and confused and remote beyond the comprehension of their departmental clerks." Harlow acknowledged that "to rule an empire from London required a feat of constitutional and administrative engineering beyond the skill of that (or any) generation." Induced by postwar fiscal concerns to "search for financial aid from its dependencies" in America, Ireland, and India, British ministers instead inadvertently provoked the resistance of American "Sons of Liberty, Anglo-Irish squires, and parvenu 'nabobs'" both in Calcutta and in the corridors of London's East India House.[60]

By the time the *Oxford History of the British Empire* was published at the end of the twentieth century, Harlow's concept of concurrent, converging, and colliding imperial systems had become the new orthodoxy.[61] Consequently, the organization of the Oxford series was strictly chronological, with one volume each on the seventeenth, eighteenth, nineteenth, and twentieth centuries along with a fifth historiographical volume at the end. Each volume also included contributions that focused upon the metropole as well as America, Asia, or Africa (although the preponderance of "colonial" essays shows a marked "swing to the East" in the later volumes). Moreover, with a few exceptions, the majority of the contributors dealt only with one part of the empire (according to each author's expertise) rather than try to integrate them into a whole. Thus, the net effect of the collection was to foreground the complexity and richness of contemporary scholarship on the British Empire rather than to formulate a coherent or comprehensive new schema, unless complexity itself can be called a new paradigm.

Among the few essays in the *Oxford History* that took up Harlow's challenge to investigate how the two sides of the empire may have influenced each other was Jack Greene's contribution to the second volume.[62] A year earlier, an important journal article by T.H. Breen had explored a similar track.[63] In their essays, both authors drew upon recent work by Benedict Anderson and Linda Colley on the emergence of British "national identity" in the eighteenth century to cast new light on the causes and nature of the imperial crisis of the 1760s. For Anderson, the most significant force behind the creation of nationalism in this period was the ability of the market linked to the emergence of a popular press, what he called "print capitalism," to construct a fictive community.[64] For Linda Colley, war was a crucible that forged British national identity.[65] These two interpretations are complementary, and perhaps are even mutually dependent, as accounts of battles and campaigns, the exploits of military heroes, and the menace posed by foreign enemies were favorite themes in the mid-eighteenth-century British popular press.[66]

Of course, the construction of an "imagined" national identity requires a process of exclusion as well as inclusion.[67] There cannot be an "us" unless there is also a "them." According to Colley, the "other" against which most Britons came to define themselves were the French and Spanish Catholics. Conveniently, for the purpose of popular prejudice and propaganda, both hostile kingdoms were ruled throughout most of the eighteenth century by branches of the same family, and so might be thought of as a single multi-headed beast (additional heads could also be added for the Pope and the Jacobite pretender).[68] For half of the seventy-five years between 1688 and 1763, Britain was at war with either France, Spain, or both. The same characteristics that supposedly defined the pre-1763 British Empire: "Protestant, maritime, commercial, and free" could also serve to differentiate Britain itself from its Catholic, terrestrial, tributary, and absolutist rivals. During war with France in the 1740s, English newspapers printed the slogans: "No Popery," "No Arbitrary Power," and "No Wooden Shoes" (Catholicism was also linked to poverty, and Protestantism to prosperity) on the front page of each issue to remind their readers of what they were fighting for (or against).[69]

Before 1763, British-American colonists had shared in this process of self-definition by exclusion. New Englanders had long demonized the "papist" French in Canada and their "savage" allies as frightening bogeymen who stole out of the forest to burn and kill.[70] Participating in imperial wars allowed colonists to stake a claim to inclusion in a larger, trans-Atlantic, British nation. After serving as a volunteer in the British attack on Cartagena in 1741, Lawrence Washington returned to Virginia and renamed his estate "Mount Vernon" in honor of the expedition's commander, Admiral Edward Vernon, and in memory of his own service to his king. No war did more to encourage Colonial Americans' sense of themselves as fully fledged British subjects than the Seven Years' War.

But the effects of the Seven Years' War and the terms of the Treaty of Paris pulled in opposing directions. The huge expense of blood and treasure the war demanded, the extensive coverage devoted to the military campaigns and commanders in the press (in both Britain and the American colonies), and the victorious results (nothing builds enthusiasm like success) helped create a shared identity among Englishmen, Welsh, Scots, and British-Americans. However, the huge territorial acquisitions made in America, Africa, and India by the terms of the Treaty of Paris also encouraged these newly forged "Britons" to begin to conceive of themselves as an imperial people, possessed of a global empire populated by subjects who were decidedly not British.

Although the British "nation" and the British "empire" were being constructed concurrently in the mid-eighteenth century, the two concepts operated in quite different, indeed almost opposite, ways. If the credo of nationalism is *e pluribus unum*—to make one people from a diverse population, the governing principle of empire is *dīvide et imperā*—divide and rule. Enlightened ministers, who tended to view religious differences as mere matters of opinion, were reluctant to use the confessional as a tool with which to sort the new empire. Instead, emerging "scientific" theories regarding racial difference and the affinity between climates and cultures provided a "scientific" taxonomy that could be deployed do the job. Thus, even as the pull of nationalism was melting the diverse peoples of Great Britain into "Britons," the push of imperialism was also starting to separate white, free, "Britons" from their darker-skinned, unfree, and unBritish, colonial subjects.

As both Breen and Greene noted in their essays, the alternating push and pull of these centripetal and centrifugal forces put British-Americans in a very awkward predicament. Colonial elites had long assumed and asserted that they possessed the "rights of Englishmen." Protestant, English-speaking, and (mostly) ethnically British, they thought of themselves as one of the various peoples: Scots, English, Welsh, and Protestant Irish, that made up the trans-Atlantic British "nation." The Royal Proclamation of October 1763, with its roughly drawn equivalence between British-Americans and Native Americans as "subjects" equally deserving of the king's "protection," was their first inkling that they stood on the wrong side of an ideological wall that was being built to separate the imperial center from the periphery and the rulers from the ruled. In many ways, the central question of the imperial crisis that tore apart the British-Atlantic Empire in the decade after 1763 was whether or not the colonists were British (with the "rights of Englishmen"), or something other (and inferior). Until July 1776, it was usually the colonists who insisted on their Britishness, and Britons who argued that while the colonists' forebears may indeed have come from Britain, their descendants had long since "degenerated" into a new type of imperial subject called "American."

In 2005, P. J. Marshall became the first scholar since Harlow to endeavor to combine the history of the British Empire in America, India, and Britain in the latter half of the eighteenth century.[71] Marshall started his study a decade earlier (1750 rather than 1760) than Harlow, made excellent use of the intervening fifty years of scholarship, and accomplished the task in only one-fourth as many pages. However, in other ways, Marshall's approach closely resembles Harlow's. Apart from two chapters at the start, and one at the end, the core of Marshall's book consists of pairs of chapters that each separately examines simultaneous developments in either North American or South Asia. The result therefore is less a fully integrated analysis than it is an extended work of comparative history whose focus alternately shifts between the two sides of the empire.

Where Marshall does discern a common thread, his conclusions support those tentatively advanced by Harlow, or by Charles Andrews long before. Like them, Marshall's trail leads him back to Whitehall. He concludes that after the end of the Seven Years' War, the British establishment evinced an "increasing determination to exert an effective sovereign authority over British possessions overseas."[72] However, the centralizing imperial program that was enacted was less the product of Andrews's triumphant "spirit of imperialism," than it was a result of the postwar ministries' anxious and fretful efforts to avoid bankruptcy, disorder, and decline. The problem with gaining an empire, it seems, is that it then becomes possible to imagine losing one.

In the last few years, other scholars have expanded on this theme and have greatly enhanced our knowledge of the cultural and political interconnections between the British metropolis and the two sides of the empire in the decade of the 1760s. Studies by Eliga Gould, Steven Pincus, Jonathan Eacott, and Justin DuRivage suggest some of the ways in which policies and programs being concocted in Britain were inspired by events, ideas, or commodities imported from the colonial periphery and also how post-1763 metropolitan aspirations and ambitions were being simultaneously deployed in the Western and Eastern hemispheres.[73] Similarly, Emma Rothschild and Patrick Griffin have focused on prominent families engaged in various aspects of the business of empire. The insights gained by this approach suggest, somewhat contrarily, that perhaps the best way to comprehend the vastness of the British Empire and the nature of the British imperial project in the 1760s may be through the small-scale lens of biography and micro-history.[74] They also serve as a salutary reminder that the British Empire, and indeed all history, is formed from a composite of individual experiences.

Another version of empire

The essays here are largely focused on the "new empire," that is, the territories acquired by the terms of the Treaty of Paris or, in its immediate aftermath. We believe that these regions are particularly fruitful places to study because they seemed to promise British policymakers a blank page on which to draw their design for the new empire. Of course, as many of the essays here amply demonstrate, the newly minted British subjects who lived in these areas had their own goals and expectations regarding the process and nature of the subjugation. Far from being putty in the hands of British ministers, new subjects often resisted or accommodated British colonial policies based on their preexisting customs and traditions. In the new, post-1763 territories, British ministers and Company officials confronted the challenges posed by the incorporation of non-British subjects most directly, but also conversely, in the absence of established colonial elites or practices, they may have felt more able to impose or create the new imperial order.

Some parts of this new empire would not stand the test of time. At the end of the American Revolutionary war and the ratification of a second treaty of Paris, both of the two Florida colonies, as well as the colony of Senegambia in West Africa ceased to be part of the British Empire (the Floridas were returned to Spain, Senegambia was dissolved and divided between Britain and France). As imperial false steps, or dead ends, these colonies may seem to have little historical significance (an impression reinforced by their historiographical neglect). But since our focus is upon the decade of the 1760s, an examination of British plans and projects for these "lost colonies" can be just as revealing as those that took place in regions that would be of much greater importance in the post-1773 empire.

If the British colonial conceptions in Florida and West Africa in the 1760s although abortive, can still be instructive, other aspects of British imperial enterprise in this era were still too embryonic to be of much analytical value. In the exploration of the Pacific that began in this era, science, as was also the case in Florida, was often the handmaiden of empire. In 1768, James Cook departed on the first of his three famous exploratory expeditions. Among the passengers on board the HMS *Endeavour* was a botanist, Joseph Banks, and an astronomer, Charles Green (brought along to observe the 1769 transit of Venus from Tahiti).[75] On this same voyage, Cook would claim New Zealand and Australia for Britain. The "discovery" of these new lands and peoples caused considerable excitement in Europe. They inspired the Enlightenment imagination, but not as yet any colonial projects.[76] The first seeds of Britain's empire in the Pacific would not be planted until the first fleet dropped anchor in Botany Bay in 1788.

Each of the chapters that follow examines a different aspect of the world that the Treaty of Paris made (or promised) for the British ruling class, for Britain's old and new subjects, and for those people who suddenly found themselves subject to British authority. The first essay, by James Vaughn, sets Britain's imperial turn in the wake of the Seven Years' War in the context of British domestic politics and the profound challenge that "Pitt and Patriotism" posed to the persistence of the Whig old guard. Vaughn argues that the post-1763 British world offered George Grenville a political and economic solution to his fiscal and political predicament. What Vaughn terms "illiberal imperialism" was a new vision of empire (or a vision for the new empire) that relied upon taxation and tribute more than trade, and which was open to incorporating new, non-Britons (as tax- or tribute-paying subjects), but which did not envision granting them the full "rights of Englishmen."

The next two essays, by Hannah Weiss Muller and Jessica Harland-Jacobs, examine the post-1763 debates and disputes over how the diverse peoples brought under British rule by virtue of the Treaty of Paris might best be incorporated into the British Empire, if not the British state. Weiss Muller's subject is the legal questions of sovereignty and subjecthood raised by the Treaty of Paris. From "Calvin's Case" at the beginning of the seventeenth century (and at the start of English colonization) to the Quebec Act of 1774, she describes how these issues were settled through a dialogue between written statutes (including treaties and proclamations) and more pragmatic judicial decisions. Harland-Jacob's essay challenges the assertion made by Linda Colley and others that Protestantism and virulent anti-Catholicism lay at the heart of emerging concepts of British identity in the eighteenth century. She shows that sixty-six years before Parliament passed the Catholic Emancipation Act, some enlightened British ministers and officials were willing to embrace the possibility of loyal "Roman Catholic subjects" who might, in certain circumstances, be granted political rights and even hold office.

Christopher Brown's essay on the origins of British Africa offers a model of Atlantic (or imperial, or even global) history. He demonstrates that the impetus behind the Royal Navy's capture of the French West African outposts of Île-Saint-Louis and Île de Gorée during the Seven Years' War came from a pair of English textile manufacturers, who even helped pay some of the cost of the expedition. Their aim was not, as we might expect, to gain access to slaves that could be sold to the sugar plantations, but rather to corner the market for "gum-arabic," a tree resin highly valued in the making of textile prints and dyes. In Brown's hands, the brief history of the colony of Senegambia illustrates both the beginnings of British ambitions in the African continent and its eighteenth-century limits.

The next three essays, by Sudipta Sen, Robert Olwell, and P. J. Marshall, investigate aspects of Britain's relations with its new "Indian" subjects, both in South Asia and North America. Sen demonstrates that Mir Qasim, a "puppet nawab" installed by the officials of the British East India Company in 1760, found himself in a very awkward situation. Beholden for his throne to a private corporation that was itself (somehow) beholden to the British state, was he the anointed ruler of the wealthiest province of the

Mughal Empire, or, as American colonists described their predicament in the face of Parliament's claims to wield authority over them "in all cases whatsoever," merely the "subjects of subjects?"[77] The similar strategies and contrasting tactics undertaken by British officials regarding their new Indian subjects on each side of the empire informs Robert Olwell's essay. In South Asia, East India Company officials sought to take the reins of power behind the façade of the old regime, while in American Indian Country, the British designed and implemented a project of "nation-building" among the natives in order to create a political framework through which they could be governed.

P. J. Marshall focuses on the same problem from the British perspective. Company officials, he argues, first endeavored to pour the new wine of their post Allahabad political and fiscal authority into the old bottle of Bengal's "ancient form of government." But, just as the scriptures had foretold, the resulting vessel was bursting with corruption and inefficiency. The passage of the Regulating Act in 1773, Marshall concludes, ushered in a "new system of British-Indian governance" that swept aside the "ancient" forms of rule in Bengal and which set a precedent for the system what would eventually spread across the subcontinent.

Finally, David Preston's essay on Charles Lee offers a micro-history of the post-1763 "imperial moment" through an examination of the life and writings of one individual. Lee's career as a military officer took him from the forests of America, to the hills of Portugal, to the Polish court, and, finally, elevated him to a rank second only to Washington in the American Revolutionary army. Along the way, Lee's extensive letters and political writings allow us to trace his transformation from an ardent British patriot in 1763, to a disillusioned and embittered English radical in the latter 1760s, to a soldier in the American cause by 1775, and finally to disgrace and possible treason on both sides of the Atlantic. George Washington, as Preston notes, followed a similar (but far less distinguished) path in the 1760s to arrive at a very different destination. Although Lee's life story extends beyond the chronological and conceptual parameters of our volume (one of the hazards of biography), his acts and writings during the revolution (and in particular his newspaper debate in 1775 with General Burgoyne) offer an insight into why and how the inclusive and expansive vision of empire that seemed possible in 1763 and in the decade that followed (and which had informed the "patriotism" of both Charles Lee and Parson Lockwood in 1763) proved to be nothing but a fleeting dream.

Notes

1   James Lockwood, *A Sermon Preached at Wethersfield, July 6, 1763. Being the day appointed by authority for a public thanksgiving, on account of the peace, concluded with France and Spain* (New Haven, 1763).

2   In 1775, Deane was one of Connecticut's delegates to the Continental Congress; in March 1776, he sailed for France to join the American delegation at Versailles; see Lisa Wilson, *A History of Stepfamilies in Early America* (Chapel Hill: University of North Carolina Press, 2014), 26–44; and George Larkin Clark, *Silas Deane: A Connecticut Leader in the American Revolution* (New York: G.P. Putnam's Sons, 1913).

3   For Samuel Webb's military career, see Worthington Chauncey Ford, ed.,
     Correspondence and Journals of Samuel Blachley Webb, 1772–1783 (3 volumes, New
     York: Wickersham Press, 1893–1894), I: xxvii–xxviii; Deane and the Webbs were
     members of Lockwood's congregation, but their presence in the church on July 6,
     1763 is a conjecture on my part; young Samuel's mistreatment of his sister is pure
     poetic license.

4   For the "Wethersfield Conference," see Richard M. Ketchum, *Victory at Yorktown:
     The Campaign That Won the Revolution* (New York: Henry Holt, 2004), 138–139; the
     meetinghouse still stands and bears a plaque describing the meeting of Washington
     and Rochambeau.

5   For "spirit of imperialism," see Charles M. Andrews, *The Colonial Background of the
     American Revolution* (New Haven, CT: Yale University Press, 1924), 143.

6   The definition of "Greater Britain" used here expands upon earlier uses of the term;
     the term was coined by J. R. Seeley in his book: *The Expansion of England, Two
     Courses of Lectures* (London: Macmillan, 1883) to describe those parts of the British
     Empire primarily inhabited by British immigrants (i.e., the "white dominions");
     To David Armitage, more than a century later, it denoted the early modern British
     Atlantic (including metropolitan Britain and Ireland as well as British Colonial
     America); for a history of the concept, see David Armitage, "Greater Britain:
     A Useful Category of Analysis?" *American Historical Review* 104 (April, 1999):
     427–445.

7   Andrews, *Colonial Background of the American Revolution,* 122.

8   In Britain, the treaty was translated and published as *The Definitive Treaty of
     Peace and Friendship, Between His Brittanick Majesty, the Most Christian King, and
     the King of Spain: Concluded at Paris, the 10th Day of February 1763. To Which,
     the King of Portugal Acceded on the Same Day* (London, 1763), unless otherwise
     noted, all the quotes and references to the treaty terms and text are taken from this
     version.

9   Fred Anderson notes contemporary British colonists' use of the term "French and
     Indian War," and discusses the debate over what to name the conflict in his epic
     history of it; see Fred Anderson, *The Crucible of War: The Seven Years' War and the
     Fate of Empire in British North America, 1754–1766* (New York: Knopf, 2000), 747
     (chapter 1, note 1); see also Matt Schumann and Karl Schweizer, eds., *The Seven Years
     War: A Transatlantic History* (New York: Routledge, 2008), 157–226.

10   Lawrence Henry Gipson, *The British Empire before the American Revolution* (15
     volumes, New York: Knopf, 1936–70), volume 6: *The Great War for Empire: The Years
     of Defeat, 1754–1757* and volume VII: *The Great War for Empire: The Victorious
     Years, 1758–1760*; Winston Churchill, *History of the English Speaking Peoples*
     (4 volumes, London: Cassell and Company, 1956–1958), volume 3: *The Age of
     Revolutions*, chapter 5.

11   A few examples: Anderson, *Crucible of War*; Schumann and Schweizer, *The Seven
     Years War*; Daniel Baugh, *The Global Seven Years War, 1754–1763* (London:
     Longman Pearson, 2011); Mark H. Danley and Patrick J. Speelman, eds., *The Seven
     Years' War: Global Views* (Leiden: Brill, 2012); and Frans De Bruyn and Shaun
     Regan, eds., *The Culture of the Seven Years' War: Empire, Identity, and the Arts in the
     Eighteenth-Century Atlantic World* (Toronto: University of Toronto Press, 2014); as
     the above list suggests, the apostrophe question is hardly settled.

12   A wonderful treatment of the first shots of the war can be found in Anderson,
     Crucible of War, 42–73.

13 By placing New Orleans on an "island" in the mouth of the Mississippi, the negotiators excluded it from the treaty's cession of the entire "left side" of the river to Britain; the quotes are taken from a translation of the "Treaty of Fontainebleau" printed in *Register of Debates in Congress, Comprising the Leading Debates and Incidents of the Second Session of the Twenty-Fourth Congress* 13 (Washington: Gales & Seaton, 1837), 226; for a discussion of France's motives for offering, and Spain's for accepting, this cession, see Paul W. Mapp, *The Elusive West and the Contest for Empire, 1713–1763* (Chapel Hill: Omohundro Institute for Early American History and Culture, University of North Carolina Press, 2011), 359–412.

14 Kimberly G. Weiser, *Back to the Blanket: Recovered Rhetorics and Literacies in American Indian Studies* (Norman: University of Oklahoma Press, 2017), 211 (note 20); for a history of the Anglo-Cherokee war, see Tom Hatley, *Dividing Paths: Cherokees and South Carolinians through the Revolutionary Era* (New York: Oxford University Press, 1995).

15 For accounts of the war in India, see Baugh, *The Global Seven Years War,* 282–297 and 462–483; G. J. Bryant, "The War in the Carnatic," in *The Seven Years' War: Global Views*, ed. Danley and Speelman, 73–106; and P. J. Marshall, "The British in Asia: Trade to Dominion, 1700–1765," in *The Oxford History of the British Empire: Volume Two, The Eighteenth-Century*, ed. P. J. Marshall (New York: Oxford University Press, 1998), 487–507.

16 Salabat Jung was installed as Nizam of Hyderabad by the French in 1751; see Claude Markovitz, ed., *A History of Modern India, 1480–1950*, trans. Nisha George and Maggie Hendry (London: Anthem Press, 2002), 219–221.

17 See Sarojini Regani, *Nizam-British Relations, 1724–1857* (New Delhi: Concept Publishing, 1963), 124–133; quote (from Robert Clive) 132; while Asaf Jah II proved a fickle friend, and occasionally an enemy to the British, he was a wily strategist who ruled Hyderabad until his death in 1803.

18 These were "Nattal and Tapanoully, in the island of Sumatra" (Natal and Tapanuli); in 1824, the British traded their "Bencoolen" territory to the Dutch in exchange for undisputed possession of Singapore; see James Stuart Olsen and Robert Shadle, eds., *Historical Dictionary of the British Empire* (Volume 1, Westport, CT: Greenwood, 1996), 124–125.

19 Edmund Burke, cited in P. J. Marshall, "Empire and Opportunity in Britain, 1763–1783" [the Prothero Lecture], in *The Royal Society Transactions* (6th Series, 5, Cambridge, UK: Cambridge University Press, 1995), 111–128 (quote on 112).

20 See Partha Chatterjee, *The Black Hole of Empire: History of a Global Practice of Power* (Princeton, NJ: Princeton University Press, 2012), 1–32.

21 See Baugh, *The Global Seven Years War,* 294–295.

22 Quoted in Malcolm, *The Life of Robert, Lord Clive* (3 volumes, London: John Murray, 1836), 1: 271.

23 For the origin of the term "puppet nawab," see Sudipta Sen's chapter in this volume.

24 See Donald Wellington, *French East India Companies: An Historical Account and Record of Trade* (Lanham, MD: Hamilton Books, 2006), 83–94.

25 For details of the campaign in Germany, see Baugh, *The Global Seven Years War,* 242–248, 275–280, 311–313, 443–445, 495–499, 519–520, 532–535, 574.

26 Ibid., 456.

27 Ibid., 598–609.

28 Ibid., 633–635; see also Nicholas Tracey, *Manila Ransomed: The British Assault on Manila in the Seven Years War* (Exeter: University of Exeter Press, 1995).

29   Larrie D. Ferreiro, *Brothers at Arms: American Independence and the Men of France and Spain Who Saved It* (New York: Knopf, 2016), 12; for an account of the campaign, see Baugh, *Global Seven Years War*, 590–598.

30   Quoted in Arthur Cash, *John Wilkes: The Scandalous Father of Civil Liberty* (New Haven, CT: Yale University Press, 2006), 93.

31   The actual vote was 319 in favor, 65 opposed; *The Parliamentary History of England* (London: Hansard, 1813). Volume 15 (1753–1765): 1271.

32   The signing ceremony is described in Ferreiro, *Brothers at Arms,* 3.

33   The signatories were John Russell, fourth Duke of Bedford for Britain, César Gabriel de Choiseul, Duc de Praslin for France, and Pablo Jerónimo Grimaldi y Pallavicini, Marqués y Duque de Grimaldi, for Spain.

34   The last words of the treaty were: "done at Paris the tenth day of February, 1763;" in 2013, to mark the 250th anniversary, the original British and French copies of the treaty were exhibited in Boston and Quebec, respectively.

35   For Andrew's background, see Richard R. Johnson, "Charles McLean Andrews and the Invention of American Colonial History," *William & Mary Quarterly*, 3rd Series, 43 (October, 1986): 519–541; the quoted passage is from his best-known work: Andrews, *The Colonial Background of the American Revolution*, 122.

36   Books written on Colonial American history or the American Revolution commonly use 1763 as either their ending or starting point; recent examples include Richard Middleton and Anne Lombard, *Colonial America: A History to 1763* (New York: Wiley-Blackwell, 2011); Paul Gilje, *The Making of the American Republic, 1763–1815* (New York: Prentice Hall, 2005); and Francis D. Cogliano, *Revolutionary America, 1763–1815: A Political History* (New York: Routledge, 2000).

37   For instance, the text of the proclamation was first published in the *Boston Newsletter* on December 9, 1763.

38   For colonial speculation in the Ohio Valley in this era, see Alfred P. James, *The Ohio Company: Its Inner History* (Pittsburgh, PA: University of Pittsburgh Press, 1959).

39   Andrews, *The Colonial Background of the American Revolution*, 123.

40   Gipson, *The British Empire before the American Revolution* Volume IX, *The Triumphant Empire: New Responsibilities within the Enlarged Empire, 1763–1766* (New York: Knopf, 1956), 345.

41   Recent work has revised our understanding of the alleged passivity of George II, and the supposed "Patriot" program of George III; see John L. Bullion, "'George, Be a King!' The Relationship between Princess Augusta and George III," in *Hanoverian Britain and Empire: Essays in Memory of Philip Lawson*, ed. Stephen Taylor, Richard Connors, and Clyve James (Woodbridge: Boydell & Brewer, 1998), 177–197; and Karl W. Schweitzer, "The Myth of Lord Bute's Secret Influence," in *Lord Bute: Essays in Reinterpretation*, ed. Karl Schweitzer (Leicester, UK: Leicester University Press, 1988).

42   For the "Press-War," see John Brewer, "The Misfortunes of Lord Bute: A Case Study in Eighteenth-Century Political Argument and Public Opinion," *Historical Journal* 16 (March 1973): 3–43.

43   For discussion of the historiography of the "First" and "Second" empires, and the debate over the boundaries between them see: P. J. Marshall, "The First British Empire," and C. A. Bayley, "The Second British Empire," both in *The Oxford History of the British Empire*, Volume V [Historiography], ed. Robin W. Winks and Alaine Low (New York: Oxford University Press, 1999), 43–72.

44   The term "old Colonial system" was coined by J. R. Seeley in 1883, but its most famous elaboration was made by George Louis Beer thirty years later; see Seeley, *The*

Expansion of England, 56; and George Louis Beer, *The Old Colonial System, 1660–1754*, 2 volumes (New York: Macmillan, 1912).

45 For New England, see Perry Miller, *Errand into the Wilderness* (Cambridge, MA: Harvard University Press, 1956), 1–15; for Providence Island, see Karen Kupperman, *Providence Island, 1630–1641: The Other Puritan Colony* (Cambridge, UK: Cambridge University Press, 1993); for Jamaica, see Carla Gardina Pestana, *The English Conquest of Jamaica: Oliver Cromwell's Bid for Empire* (Cambridge, MA: Harvard University Press, 2017).

46 See David Armitage, *The Ideological Origins of the British Empire* (Cambridge, UK: Cambridge University Press, 2000).

47 See Wendy Warren, *New England Bound: Slavery and Colonialism in Early America* (New York: Liverlight Publishing, 2016).

48 See Patrick Brantlinger, *Taming Cannibals: Race and the Victorians* (Ithaca, NY: Cornell University Press, 2011), 203–226; and also Anne Mcclintock, *Imperial Leather: Race, Sex, and Gender in the Imperial Contest* (New York: Routledge, 1995).

49 For the commercial focus of the East India Company prior to 1757, see Emily Erikson, *Between Monopoly and Free Trade: The English East India Company, 1600–1757* (Princeton, NJ: Princeton University Press, 2014).

50 See Philip J. Stern, *The Company-State: Corporate Sovereignty and the Early Modern Origins of the British Empire in India* (New York: Oxford University Press, 2011).

51 See Werner Sollors, *Neither Black nor White yet Both: Thematic Explorations of Interracial Literature* (Cambridge, MA: Harvard University Press, 1997), 220–245.

52 See John Darwin, *The Empire Project: The Rise and Fall of the British World System, 1930–1970* (Cambridge, UK: Cambridge University Press, 2009), 288.

53 An additional volume (number four) was later published to cover the history of India from the arrival of Vasco De Gama in 1497 to the Great Mutiny of 1857, thus preserving the historiographical separation between the two empires despite acknowledging a long chronological overlap.

54 John Holland Rose, A. P. Newton, and Ernest Alfred Bennians, eds., *The Cambridge History of the British Empire* (9 volumes, Cambridge, UK: Cambridge University Press, 1929–1959); the "white dominions": South Africa and Rhodesia, Canada, Australia, and New Zealand each received their own volumes, thus achieving a racial, as well as a geographical and chronological segregation.

55 Vincent T. Harlow, *The Founding of the Second British Empire, 1763–1783* (2 volumes, London: Longmans Green, 1952).

56 Ibid., 1: 198.

57 Ibid.

58 Ibid., 1: chapters five through nine, pages 146–492.

59 The phrase "Swing to the East," which Harlow used for the second section of his first volume (covering events in Asia post 1763), is probably the best remembered and most often quoted line in the entire book.

60 Ibid., 2: 796.

61 Wm. Roger Louis, editor in chief, *The Oxford History of the British Empire* (5 volumes, New York: Oxford University Press, 1998–1999).

62 Jack P. Greene, "Empire and Identity from the Glorious Revolution to the American Revolution," in *The Oxford History of the British Empire: The Eighteenth Century [Volume 2]*, ed. P. J. Marshall (New York: Oxford University Press, 1998), 2: 208–230.

63   T. H. Breen, "Ideology and Nationalism on the Eve of the American Revolution: Revisions Once More in Need of Revising," *The Journal of American History* 86 (June 1997): 13–39.

64   Benedict Anderson, *Imagined Communities: Reflections on the Origin and Spread of Nationalism* (London: Verso, 1983).

65   Linda Colley, *Britons: Forging the Nation, 1707–1837* (New Haven, CT: Yale University Press, 1992).

66   Kathleen Wilson, *The Sense of the People: Politics, Culture and Imperialism in England 1715–1785* (Cambridge, UK: Cambridge University Press, 1995).

67   See, for example, David Waldstreicher, *In the Midst of Perpetual Fetes: The Making of American Nationalism, 1776–1820* (Chapel Hill: Omohundro Institute of Early American History and Culture, University of North Carolina Press, 1997).

68   Both Louis XV of France and Charles III of Spain were the great-grand children of Louis XIV.

69   Cited in Hannah Barker, *Newspapers and English Society, 1695–1855* (New York: Routledge, 2014), 132.

70   See Peter Silver, *Our Savage Neighbors: How Indian War Transformed Early America* (New York: Norton, 2008).

71   P. J. Marshall, *The Making and Unmaking of Empires: Britain, India, and America, c. 1750–1783* (New York: Oxford University Press, 2005).

72   Ibid., 5, 9.

73   Eliga Gould, *Among the Powers of the Earth: The American Revolution and the Making of a New World Empire* (Cambridge, MA: Harvard University Press, 2012); Steven Pincus, *The Heart of the Declaration: The Founders' Case for an Activist Government* (New Haven, CT: Yale University Press, 2016); Justin DuRivage, *Revolution against Empire: Taxes, Politics, and the Origins of American Independence* (New Haven, CT: Yale University Press, 2017); Jonathan Eacott, *Selling Empire: India in the Making of Britain and America, 1600–1830* (Chapel Hill: Omohundro Institute of Early American History and Culture, University of North Carolina Press, 2017).

74   Emma Rothschild, *The Inner Life of Empires: An Eighteenth-Century History* (Princeton, NJ: Princeton University Press, 2011); Patrick Griffin, *The Townshend Moment: The Making of Empire and Revolution in the Eighteenth-Century* (New Haven, CT: Yale University Press, 2017).

75   See Andrea Wulf, *Chasing Venus: The Race to Measure the Heavens* (New York: Knopf, 2012).

76   See John Gascoigne, *Encountering the Pacific in the Age of Enlightenment* (Port Melbourne: Cambridge University Press, 2014).

77   John Philip Reid, *Constitutional History of the American Revolution* (Madison: University of Wisconsin Press, 2003), 77–82.

2

The Ideological Origins of Illiberal Imperialism: Metropolitan Politics and the Post-1763 Transformation of the British Empire

James M. Vaughn

On the fall and rise of empires

At the close of 1759, Great Britain stood victorious against France across the overseas theaters of the Seven Years' War, from Cape Breton to the Ohio Valley in North America, in the Caribbean and West Africa, and along India's Coromandel Coast. In Europe, the forces of King George II's chief ally, Frederick the Great of Prussia, heavily subsidized by the British taxpayer and assisted by Prince Ferdinand of Brunswick's Anglo-German army, effectively held their own against the armies of France, Austria, Russia, and Sweden, preventing King Louis XV from making significant gains that could be used to recover French colonial losses at the eventual peace conference. "Never was there such a series of happy and glorious events," exclaimed the Patriot politician and poet Sir George Lyttelton to his brother with regard to the key British victories won in 1759, "Guadaloupe conquered, just before a reinforcement arrived; our East Indies saved when the Company themselves had despaired of their safety; the battle of Minden won … the King of Prussia on the point of repelling all his enemies … the French and Canadian army beat, and Quebec taken by Wolfe."[1] Horace Walpole boasted that the empires of antiquity paled in comparison to the worldwide extent of Britain's victories and conquests. "Our last three campaigns had overrun more world than [the Romans] conquered in a century," he mused, "and for the Grecians, their story were a pretty theme if the town of St Albans were waging war with that of Brentford."[2] Congratulating the government on the "glorious and unbounded success of his Majesty's arms, in every part of the globe," Britain's ambassador to Berlin, Sir Andrew Mitchell, contended that the war's outcome "cannot fail to transmit to posterity the King and his ministers in the fairest and most amiable lights."[3]

The British state had not merely managed to defend its possessions but had unexpectedly triumphed in what Winston Churchill later famously described as "the first world war." The final terms of the Treaty of Paris, signed in February 1763, sealed the victory and confirmed Britain's position as Europe's and indeed the world's leading commercial and colonial power. The island kingdom's victory in the Seven Years' War was in an important respect the fulfillment of the Glorious Revolution of 1688. The Revolution defeated Stuart absolutism, committed England to the European struggle against King Louis XIV's hegemonic ambitions, and led to the creation of a parliamentary state that commanded an effective and sophisticated machinery of public credit. By the end of the Seven Years' War, that parliamentary state and its financial machinery had rolled back the imperial frontiers of Bourbon absolutism, upheld the balance of power in Europe, and established Britain's global supremacy. While contemporary Britons boasted that their commercial and maritime "empire of liberty" had successfully extended to the farthest reaches of the globe, the war left the French imperial state, as well as that of its Spanish ally, tottering on the brink of fiscal and military ruin, badly in need of reform in order to prevent collapse.

But, while defeat left Bourbon France in disrepair, the weight of heavy indebtedness and taxation, administrative and fiscal reorganization, and political crisis would not come crashing down in Paris until 1789. Instead, fourteen years before the revolutionary drama took the stage at Versailles, it debuted in the British Atlantic world with the imperial crisis and the outbreak of the War of American Independence. For Britain's massive victory in the Seven Years' War did not lead to imperial stability but rather undermined it. Governing vast new territories, struggling to come to terms with a national debt that had nearly doubled during the war, and bearing the burden of the highest tax rates in Europe, British policymakers believed that a general reformation of the Empire was necessary in the wake of 1763. They put in place new forms of imperial administration, commercial regulation, and taxation that were designed to exercise stronger metropolitan control over, to maintain a peacetime standing army in, and to raise revenue from the American colonies.[4] These measures provoked widespread colonial resistance and instigated an imperial crisis that eventually led to a violent rebellion. The American Revolution tore the British Atlantic apart and brought about the downfall of what has been called the First British Empire.

Meanwhile, in the other half of Britain's empire, the successful outcome of the British East India Company's military and political conflicts with European and South Asian rivals had transformed the commercial corporation into an imperial power, with dominion over extensive territory in northeastern India and its own revenue-collecting bureaucracy and standing army.[5] In 1765, by the terms of the Treaty of Allahabad concluded with the Mughal Emperor Shah Alam II, the Company was granted the *diwani* for Bengal, Bihar, and Orissa, which gave it the right to collect revenue in provinces with approximately twenty million inhabitants. This acquisition laid the foundation for the British Raj, the rule of which eventually extended over the entire subcontinent. The Company's state was an autocratic regime that departed significantly from the political order in Britain and its Atlantic empire. While the Crown ruled through Parliament in Britain and royal governors ruled in cooperation with colonial leaders in councils and elected assemblies in British America, the Company's territorial empire in India was a bureaucratic and military despotism.

These two nearly simultaneous processes—the loss of thirteen North American colonies and the beginnings of a vast territorial empire in the East—transformed British overseas expansion.[6] After 1783, Britain's gaze and ambition shifted from an Atlantic-centered system based largely upon trade and colonial settlement to its Asian and, by the later nineteenth century, African empire characterized by territorial conquest and autocratic rule over large native populations. Thus, the two decades following the Seven Years' War witnessed not only the crackup of the First British Empire but also the beginning of the so-called Second British Empire, which lasted well into the twentieth century.

But merely describing these events begs the question of why Britain's parliamentary classes—heirs to seventeenth-century England's anti-absolutist, libertarian political upheavals—countenanced the creation of an autocratic garrison empire in South Asia and implemented new measures in the American colonies designed to maintain a standing army and to greatly strengthen the power of the imperial executive, effectively removing royal officials from the reach of colonial assemblies. This chapter examines why Britain's parliamentary state supported the East India Company's assumption of autocratic rule in India and attempted to establish such a rule for itself in North America by directly taxing the colonies and using the revenue raised to support the Crown's officials and policies, thus circumventing local assemblies and the populations they represented. How could proud boasts regarding Britain's commercial and colonial "empire of liberty" so quickly give way after the Seven Years' War to support for the creation of an autocratic, military-driven, and revenue-extracting empire? What were the ideological origins of this "illiberal imperialism"?

Any adequate answer to these questions must first deal with the statesmen and policymakers that implemented and supported the new authoritarian imperialism. The key measures were put in place by a group of politicians, administrators, and advisors who came to power following the accession of King George III, and who steered the British ship of state through the conclusion of the Seven Years' War and during the immediate postwar years. As Daniel Baugh argues, this group of men "were strongly, not resignedly or reluctantly, disposed toward imperial intervention."[7] While in power under the successive ministries of the Earl of Bute and George Grenville between 1762 and 1765, these politicians and policymakers planned and implemented the Atlantic imperial reorganization, which included employing the Royal Navy in colonial waters to strictly enforce trade and navigation laws and to increase customs collection; garrisoning a large peacetime standing army in America without seeking any cooperation or input from colonial assemblies; issuing the Proclamation of 1763 restricting colonial settlement west of the Appalachians; raising revenue to pay for the American army by imposing new restrictions and duties on colonial trade with the passage of the Sugar Act in April 1764; and directly taxing the colonies with the passage of the Stamp Act in March 1765.[8] The passage of the stamp tax did more than any other act to provoke the widespread colonial resistance that eventually led to the American Revolution.

The same circle of political elites that implemented the key Atlantic imperial reforms intervened in the elections to the East India Company's Court of Directors in 1764 and helped to replace a corporate leadership that was hesitant to pursue territorial empire in Bengal with a group of directors and major shareholders that strongly backed Robert Clive, the famed military commander who had advocated the creation of such an empire since the later 1750s.[9] Through their combined actions and influence, these political elites ensured not only Clive's takeover of the Company but also that he sailed for Calcutta armed with extraordinary civilian and military powers to deal with the crisis engulfing the British presence there. After arriving in Bengal, Clive accepted the *diwani* from the Mughal emperor on the Company's behalf and transformed the commercial corporation into an imperial state collecting land revenue and maintaining a standing army on the conflict-ridden subcontinent.

Why did the circle of political elites in power during the Bute and Grenville ministries pursue this authoritarian imperialism? The remainder of this chapter lays out the case for a new interpretation of why British statesmen and administrators acted as they did in the period following the Seven Years' War. My central claim is that the reasons for the postwar policy changes lay neither exclusively nor primarily in events occurring in the far corners of the Empire but rather, to an important degree not recognized in existing scholarship, in the political and ideological conflicts taking place in the metropole. More specifically, this chapter argues that both the imperial reforms unsuccessfully imposed on the American colonies and the successful consolidation of an autocratic and tributary empire in Bengal were the offspring of a conservative–reactionary political project that emerged in response to upheavals taking place in Britain as much as in the Empire during and following the Seven Years' War. A key element in these upheavals was the emergence of a robust and popular political movement in Britain, a new radical Whiggism, which resonated throughout the Empire. This radical Whiggism consisted of Patriot Whigs, Pittites, and Wilkesites who sought fundamental parliamentary and political–economic reform. This movement was ideologically motivated by a bourgeois radicalism that viewed Britain's political system as inadequate for the more commercial, manufacturing-based, and urban society that had developed since the later seventeenth century.

The illiberal imperialism emanating from Britain's political establishment after 1760 was part of a conservative–reactionary political project supported by authoritarian Whigs, King George III's closest allies, and Tories.[10] This political project sought to master the upheavals in Britain and the Empire, to contain or confound the rising tide of radicalism, and to assert the imperial supremacy of Britain over its colonies. This conservative–reactionary politics, buttressed by an ideology of King-in-Parliament absolutism, defended the existing parliamentary system against all challenges, domestic and colonial, supported and reinvigorated the authority of the Crown's officials at home and abroad, upheld the power of the landed and moneyed oligarchy that governed Britain, and subordinated the Empire to the metropole.

As the radical Whiggism of the third quarter of the eighteenth century was an important predecessor of the Radicalism that challenged Britain's political status quo during the later eighteenth and nineteenth centuries, so too the conservative–reactionary project that defended the existing political system in the era of the imperial crisis played a vital role in the emergence of the new conservatism that held sway in British political life from William Pitt the Younger to Lord Liverpool and that gave rise to the Tory Party of the early nineteenth century. The conflict between these radical and conservative–reactionary forces wracked British political culture following 1760. As a result, the Court Whiggism that was predominant in the governments of Robert Walpole, Henry Pelham, and the Duke of Newcastle was dislodged from the halls of power, leaving the Whig faction led by the Marquis of Rockingham as both the principal defender of the policies of the pre-war Whig establishment and the charterer of a new course for a moderate Whiggism that steered clear of the radical Scylla and the reactionary Charybdis.[11]

This chapter contends that both the fall of the First Empire and the origins and early formation of the Second Empire were deeply informed by the conflict between these radical and conservative–reactionary political projects. More specifically, it argues that the illiberal imperialism that emanated from the metropole immediately following the Seven Years' War, supporting the East India Company's territorial empire and provoking the Atlantic imperial crisis and, eventually, the American Revolution, is best understood as one aspect of a conservative–reactionary politics concerned with developments in Britain as much as in the Empire. The fall of the First Empire and the origins of the Second Empire lay, to an important degree not previously understood, in metropolitan political conflicts and dynamics.[12]

The emergence of radical Whiggism

The turning of the tide of the Seven Years' War against Bourbon France in every theater of conflict was the major achievement of the Newcastle–Pitt ministry, an alliance of convenience (or, perhaps, of desperation) forged in 1757 during the darkest days of the war between the leader of the Whig establishment, the Duke of Newcastle, and a prominent voice of the Patriot opposition, William Pitt the Elder. Once forged, this coalition was most formidable. Newcastle was backed by George II, closely allied with leading Whig magnates such as the Earl of Hardwicke and the Duke of Devonshire, and commanded vast reserves of patronage, while Pitt drew support from Patriot Whigs and Tories among the parliamentary opposition as well as from the popular press. Together, the two ministers were able to unite the political nation and win victory after victory following 1757.

Though wartime unity dampened political conflict, it did not eliminate the fundamental disagreements on which such conflict was based. In January 1760, Lord Barrington warned that the prevailing mood of national unity did not arise "from any improvement made by our countrymen either in wisdom or in virtue" but "solely from this—no man who can raise any sort of disturbance finds it either convenient or agreeable to be out of humour at this time."[13] What's more, Britain's accumulated military victories generated new sources of political disagreement that made such unity short-lived. It "was in this year of unanimity and victory," the radical Whig publisher John Almon observed with regard to the *annus mirabilis* of 1759, "that the seeds were sown of those divisions which appeared soon after the accession of George the Third."[14] Leading politicians and opinion-makers began to spar over how much longer the conflict should continue, whether or not the public finances were exhausted, which conquered territories should be kept and which bargained away at the peace table, and what the shape of final victory might look like. Central to these developing disagreements were the increasing debt and tax burdens necessary for prosecuting the conflict. The public debt nearly doubled during the war, expanding from £74 to £133 million between 1756 and 1763.[15] Its growth preoccupied the minds of policymakers and pamphleteers and, from 1760, generated an increasingly vigorous and virulent debate over the public finances. "Since *Jacobite* or *arbitrary* principles have been exploded ... what has been the source of fear and apprehension to considerate men? What has afforded colour to party clamours and contention?" queried one writer, "What (I would be glad to know) but *the national debt*, its concomitants, and apprehended consequences?"[16] Many voices in the political nation fretted over how, or even if, this enormous obligation could be met. Meeting the interest payments alone would swallow up half of the pre-war annual tax revenue.

The immense costs of the conflict partly stemmed from Pitt's rise to power and his strategic commitment to wage war in every theater of combat across the globe and to deliver a crushing defeat to Bourbon France. In December 1756, George II placed Pitt in office alongside the Duke of Devonshire and put him in charge of the war effort in order to restore public confidence when the conflict was going poorly for Britain, with defeats in North America and, worse yet, the loss of Minorca. The Devonshire–Pitt ministry was ultimately undermined by George II's dislike of the "Great Commoner" and by the political maneuverings of the king's son, the Duke of Cumberland, and his wily ally Henry Fox.[17] Although George II dismissed Pitt from office in April 1757, the overwhelming tide of public opinion in Pitt's favor, as well as the inability of leading politicians to assemble a stable ministry without him, forced the king to bring him back into power, this time alongside Newcastle, less than three months later in June.[18] Newcastle served as the First Lord of the Treasury, managing Parliament and the public finances, while Pitt served as the Secretary of State for the Southern Department, commanding the war effort and foreign policy more broadly.

Pitt's direction of the conflict was transformative for Britain and its overseas possessions. Earlier in his career, he evinced the standard hostility of the Patriot opposition to continental warfare and Hanoverian interests. However, after Pitt took control of Britain's military effort during the Seven Years' War, he concluded that fighting France in Central Europe was crucial to his strategy for a crushing global victory.[19] Thus, despite the huge costs, Pitt supported both subsidizing Prussia to enable Frederick the Great to keep his armies in the field against France, Austria, Russia, and Sweden and subsidizing and supplying British troops to the Hanoverian Army of Observation, which was raised to defend the Electorate and to assist Prussia in its western military theater. But Pitt was adamant that such continental measures and expenses, however great, were always secondary to the struggle Britain waged against France in the rest of the world.[20] "Pitt's strategic choices showed that it was never his wish ... to try to win the war in Germany[,]" Baugh remarks. "His strategy there was to help Prince Ferdinand fight a defensive war, both to consume French resources and to limit France's conquests ... [which] did not mean that he had ceased to give priority to the navy, overseas trade and colonial possessions."[21] Pitt's belief that the war would decide whether Britain or France became the leading global power, with a lasting superiority in maritime trade and manufacturing exports, led him to commit unprecedented levels of manpower and materiel to fighting overseas, particularly in North America—in 1759, Britain deployed 20,000 royal troops there and paid for 25,000 colonial troops[22]—but also in the West Indies and South Asia.

Pitt's ambition to deliver a crushing global victory over Bourbon France began to be realized in 1758 and 1759. British forces captured the French settlements at Saint-Louis and Gorée in West Africa, successfully laid siege to the fortress of Louisbourg on Cape Breton Island in Canada and defeated the French siege of Madras on the Coromandel Coast of India, captured the island of Guadeloupe in the Caribbean, won the Battle of Lagos off the coasts of Portugal and Spain, and captured Quebec. In November 1759, the Royal Navy's decisive defeat of the French Atlantic fleet at Quiberon Bay gave Britain a virtual free hand against France's overseas empire. Pitt's main strategic goal throughout the war was to secure and extend Britain's commercial and maritime "empire of liberty." This, he believed, would allow for the free flow of British trade and manufactures throughout the world, unfettered by the military and political obstacles put in place by rival European monarchies. Pitt rose to political prominence as a Patriot Whig in the mid- to late 1730s, strongly advocating the defense and expansion of Britain's commercial and maritime empire against the encroachments of the Bourbon monarchies of France and Spain in opposition to the imperial and foreign policies of Robert Walpole. "When trade is at stake, it is your last retrenchment; you must defend it, or perish," Pitt declared before the House of Commons in 1738 when, along with his fellow Patriot Whigs, pressing for war with Spain over transatlantic conflicts and trade interference. He described "the rights and trade" of Britain as "the first law of nature" and the "highest and sacred point" to be secured in any conflict or negotiation.[23] By the end of 1760, after over three years of directing Britain's conflict against Bourbon France, Pitt seemed close to fulfilling his long-standing ambition of establishing his country as the preeminent commercial and colonial power, thus securing its ability to trade unhindered throughout the world.

In advocating and pursuing a global war for markets and colonies, Pitt was not only backed by the popular press but also by politicized tradesmen, artisans, shopkeepers, middling merchants, and petty manufacturers who lived in London and in the provincial cities and towns.[24] The urban middling sort included approximately one million people in a total population of seven million,[25] and the politicized and increasingly radical elements among them formed a popular phalanx of support for Pitt.

For many among the middling sort, Pitt's leadership of the war had restored their faith in the government and roused their patriotic spirit. One pamphleteer recalled that "the genius of Britain seemed to rise on his elevation, and a new soul diffused itself through all ranks of persons. From diffident, disconsolate, and desponding, they became easy, chearful, and assured. Their hearts burned with resentment to wipe out past disgraces, to restore the glory, the honour, the true character of their country, and their purses opened equal to the benevolence of their hearts."[26] Members of the mercantile community viewed Pitt as representing their needs and interests in opposition to the Whig establishment that dominated the country's political life during the Walpole and Pelham governments, and which drew its support from the aristocracy, the greater gentry, and the commercial and financial *haute bourgeoisie* of the City of London.[27] The urban middling sort were elated with the Great Commoner's rejection of the long-standing notion that commercial and industrial wealth were inferior to landed property, and they swelled with pride when he proclaimed to the Commons in 1758 "that he would be prouder of being an alderman of London than a peer of the realm."[28]

More than any previous prime minister, Pitt appealed to a larger public beyond Parliament and the Court. He consulted with overseas merchants while planning military campaigns, such as the one launched against French settlements in West Africa, and worked with the broader mercantile community, particularly in London, in pursuit of his strategic objective of achieving Britain's commercial and colonial supremacy.[29] This community shared Pitt's desire to establish a vast maritime empire that would extend Britain's commercial reach, and saw the expenses of the war—which led to heavy public indebtedness—as an investment that would eventually pay for itself by increasing prosperity, economic activity, and tax revenues.[30] A war that protected and expanded Britain's maritime traffic, access to markets, and colonies would lead to booming trade and manufacturing, which would generate more revenue for the purpose of defending and expanding the Empire. As news of each victory reached the metropole between 1758 and 1760, the support for Pitt and his policies in the extra-parliamentary political culture of the cities and towns, in which the middling sort were predominant, grew in strength. Newcastle responded to George II's complaints about Pitt's grand-standing style of leadership by asking "His Majesty whether he thought that this war, at this immense expense, could have been carried on without the unanimity of the people … which was entirely owing to Mr. Pitt[.]"[31] Military success "made Pitt what he had long claimed to be, the tribune of the people," Paul Langford observes. "It also made him the most powerful figure in British political life."[32]

However, with the renewal and intensification of political conflict in the halls of power following the death of George II in October 1760, it was clear that Pitt's combination of military victory and popularity out of doors did not make him politically invincible. Following the accession of King George III, differences in the cabinet over how best to proceed in the geopolitical arena soon came to the fore. The main dispute centered on the question of peace or war. The two leading disputants were Pitt, who sought to extend the war, and the new king's closest advisor, Lord Bute, who wanted to bring the war to an end sooner rather than later.

Despite the financial and military exhaustion of all the combatants, Pitt was doubtful of France's readiness to make peace in 1761. Furthermore, he was strongly committed to significantly curbing French power overseas and to extending Britain's commercial and maritime "empire of liberty" as far as possible.[33] As Baugh argues, Pitt's aim was "to create a world in which Great Britain might be permanently secure."[34] During the summer of 1761, Pitt increased the pressure upon Versailles by sending an amphibious expedition to capture Belle-Île, a large island off the coast of Brittany.

In August 1761, Louis XV of France concluded the third Bourbon Family Compact with the king of Spain, Carlos III, in which the two countries agreed to negotiate their disputes with Britain together and not separately. The Family Compact included a secret convention in which Spain promised to enter the war against Britain if the conflict was not over by May 1762. The British government learned of the agreement between the Bourbon powers in early September and intercepted a letter from the Marquis de Grimaldi, Spain's ambassador in Paris, which suggested that Spain was making preparations for hostilities with Britain but would not enter the war as France's ally until after the New World treasure fleet arrived and it was prepared to fight.[35]

With typical belligerence, Pitt saw the Bourbon Family Compact not as a threat—France had been defeated across the globe and Spain was ill prepared for war—but as an opportunity to attack the Spanish Empire and add the choicest of its colonies to the French possessions that Britain had already taken. As Richard Middleton observes, the Great Commoner "wanted to inflict on Spain the same mortal blow he was seeking to give France. The present crisis was a golden opportunity to crush both branches of the Bourbon dynasty."[36] Pitt strongly urged declaring war against and striking Spain before it was prepared to enter the conflict at cabinet meetings from mid-September to early October but, beyond his radical ally and brother-in-law Earl Temple, he received little support. Bute and his allies, already disturbed by Pittite ideas and ambitions, were strongly opposed to expanding the war. Newcastle and other ministers were troubled by a recent financial crisis in the City and believed that the conflict was fast approaching Britain's fiscal limits for fighting it. The Earl of Hardwicke believed that war with Spain was not inevitable and, thus, that Pitt's plan risked creating an enemy where there was none.[37]

It was clear that nearly the entire ministry as well as George III was opposed to declaring war against Spain. At the cabinet meeting on October 2, Pitt gave up the ghost. He informed his fellow ministers that he could not assume responsibility for a war effort that he no longer controlled, then withdrew from the room and resigned three days later. Before departing, the Great Commoner reminded the cabinet that he had assumed office and taken control over the war in 1757 because he was asked to "by his Sovereign, and he might say, in some degree by the voice of the People, to assist the State, when others had *abdicated* the service of it."[38]

Although the main points in dispute between Pitt and his emerging rival Bute in the summer and fall of 1761 were over the pursuit of peace with France and a potential war with Spain, the two statesmen also differed considerably over fiscal policy. They disputed whether Britain could afford to continue (or widen) the war and thus further stretch the already greatly expanded national debt. But, beneath all of these issues, their most fundamental disagreements were political and ideological. Both statesmen recognized that Pitt's imperial project had profound domestic ramifications.

According to the Pittites, the *rentier* oligarchy that had governed the country for decades was limited both in terms of the resources that it could contribute in support of British overseas interests and in terms of its narrow goals in that regard. Pittites wanted to enlist the urban middling sort to support commercial and colonial expansion on a far greater scale. Where conservative Patriot and Tory politicians such as Bute, as well as establishment Whigs such as Newcastle and Hardwicke, viewed the middling social strata as little more than a problem to be managed—i.e., as a sub-political strata whose only role was to pay their taxes without difficulty or delay—Pitt and his radical supporters saw them as political allies and their wealth as a vast economic potential. When Newcastle and other leaders in the political establishment pointed out that the costs of the war were straining the fiscal-military regime inherited from the Glorious Revolution to the breaking point, Pitt and his allies expressed little concern.[39]

By protecting and expanding trade and colonial enterprise, the Pittite war machine would encourage domestic commercial and industrial expansion as Britain's manufactures and re-exports flooded the globe. The costs of maritime imperial expansion would therefore be recuperated by its success. As new markets for British goods were permanently opened up, customs and excise revenues would flow into the coffers of the Treasury, paying down the debt and providing the funds for future hostilities. Pitt and his allies argued that this was in fact already happening. "If you are afraid you are not able to carry on the War, enquire of the Merchants what are your Imports what are your Exports," Pitt's radical ally William Beckford thundered in the House of Commons in 1761, "Look into the Customhouse books—Your Manufactures are not sufficient for your demands. There is nothing the Parliament & King can't do hand in hand [and] the Nation never was in so comfortable a State."[40] The radical Whig John Almon remarked retrospectively that "commerce gave copiously, but circuitously … and, as Lord Chatham said, carried us triumphantly through the great seven years war[.]"[41]

The king, Bute, and their conservative and Tory allies were not the only political elites troubled by Pitt's desire to continue and expand the war with the aim of achieving a maximum victory over Bourbon France. The Whig establishment worried that the stupendous war-driven growth of the national debt was outstripping the state's ability to raise taxes and to meet interest payments on loans.[42] Although many establishment Whigs had praised Pitt's spirited conduct in the early years of the war, they became increasingly troubled by his expansive military and radical political commitments. They feared that they had unleashed a monster. "Mr. Pitt, on entering administration, had found the nation at the lowest ebb in point of power and reputation," Horace Walpole remarked, and had "roused us from this ignoble lethargy." But not content with obtaining an ordinary, limited victory, "he went farther, and perhaps too far. He staked our revenues … as if we could never have another war to wage, or as if he meant, which was impracticable, that his administration should decide which alone should exist as a nation, Britain or France, [and] he lavished the last treasures of this country with a prodigality beyond example and beyond excuse."[43] The Duke of Bedford, a leading authoritarian Whig and a fierce opponent of Pitt's military and foreign policy, argued that Pitt was dangerously pursuing the same hegemony that Louis XIV sought decades earlier and, similar to the Bourbon monarch, was likely to alienate all the powers of Europe.[44]

Bute was ascendant in the cabinet after Pitt's resignation in October 1761, finally becoming prime minister upon Newcastle's resignation in May 1762. The main aim of Bute and George III was to bring the war to a close as quickly as possible in order to reduce expenditures, stabilize the domestic political scene, and take command of the oligarchic state away from the Whig establishment. They were willing to go to remarkable lengths in pursuit of peace. Following Pitt's departure, Britain was not able to resolve outstanding issues with France and relations with Spain continued to deteriorate until war was finally declared between the two powers in January 1762. Despite this general situation and the highly advantageous military position in which Britain found itself, Bute negotiated with the Bourbon powers through secret channels, offering in late 1761 to conclude peace terms before the result of the British expedition to capture Martinique from France was known and, again, offering in 1762 to conclude peace terms before the result of the British expedition to capture Havana from Spain was known.[45] Throughout late 1761 and 1762, Bute and the king pursued, as Baugh remarks, "a process that came very close to begging for peace"—a process that entailed the inverse of typical wartime diplomacy: "The usual diplomatic pattern, of course, was and is for the side enjoying military advantage to await word of a probable military success before concluding a settlement. Under Bute's direction the British government proceeded in reverse order."[46]

Ascendant in the cabinet by late 1761, Bute not only abandoned Pitt's goal of winning a crushing global victory over France but also moved against the continental commitment that had been so crucial to the Newcastle–Pitt ministry's strategy for winning the war.[47] At a meeting in January 1762, Bute proposed that the cabinet consider abandoning the German war altogether, withdrawing British troops and funds from Ferdinand of Brunswick's forces. The following month, Bedford, a close ally of Bute and George III, made a motion along similar lines in the House of Lords. Although these proposals for an immediate end to the German war were not realized, Bute and his ally Grenville worked to undermine the conflict's financing and reopened the question of withdrawing British troops from Ferdinand's army that spring.

At the same time that Bute and the king were offering generous peace terms to the Bourbon monarchies and questioning the continuation of the German war, they were also distancing themselves from Britain's most important ally, Frederick the Great. In early 1762, Bute put considerable diplomatic pressure on Frederick to make peace with Austria and suspended the annual subsidy of £670,000 to Prussia, which was a key aspect of the alliance between the two countries dating back to 1758. The subsidy was canceled altogether that spring and the Anglo-Prussian alliance subsequently dissolved. It was in this context—the efforts by Bute, Grenville, and their political allies, with the backing of George III, to erode the German war and the alliance with Prussia—that Newcastle realized his power in the cabinet was vanishing and eventually decided to resign as prime minister in late May 1762.

Bute became prime minister and, with Pitt and Newcastle out of government and the Prussian alliance at an end, pursued peace with France and Spain without considerable political interference. With the king's full support, Bute dispensed with both major aims of the Pittite war effort—to win a crushing global victory over France and to expand Britain's commercial and colonial "empire of liberty" to the furthest extent possible— and sought to end the conflict as quickly as possible despite the considerable triumphs of Britain and its allies over France in the New World, Asia, and Europe throughout 1762. Bute was willing to make significant concessions to France, returning territories that had been taken with considerable loss of life and treasure, and appointed the pro-French and stridently anti-Pittite Bedford as an ambassador to Paris responsible for concluding the peace terms. It is no surprise that the peace preliminaries agreed in November 1762 were generous to France despite its much reduced geopolitical and military position. As Baugh observes, although Louis XV's ministers were undoubtedly deft at diplomacy, "it was not hard to look like a negotiating genius when dealing with an opponent so eager to please."[48]

Pitt (now in opposition) and his supporters decried the peace negotiations and measures as a betrayal of the complete and transformative victory that, they believed, Britain had been on the brink of attaining before he left office. Radical opinion was deeply hostile to Britain's ongoing negotiations with France and Spain during the summer and fall of 1762, especially as it became clear what kind of peace terms the Bute ministry aimed to achieve. *The Monitor*, a newspaper founded by William Beckford's brother, Richard, claimed:

> There was a sudden change in the countenance of [the] country, from an universal mirth and joy, spread over the whole island, at the success of our arms over her enemies, and the increase and security of our strength and trade, to the most dismal sorrow and disconsolate murmurings, at the publication of such conditions of peace, as would leave us in the sad situation of Tyre, disabled by sea and land; deprived of the richest branches of our trade; rendered contemptible in all nations, and reduced to submit to the dictates of Bourbon.[49]

This newspaper and John Wilkes's *The North Briton*, two pillars of radical Whiggism in the public sphere, waged a press war against the peace provisions in late 1762 and early 1763. "War is more desirable than a peace, which by the continual alarms of hostile preparations, obliges us to lie always upon our arms," *The Monitor* declared in November 1762. Instead of accepting such a treaty (and temporary peace), the newspaper argued in true Pittite fashion that Britain "ought to proceed in the way of arms, till [it] shall deprive them of their resources to raise and pay fleets and armies for those mischievous purposes: and then there is no doubt of making the most ambitious, revengeful, and obstinate nation a harmless, inoffensive people, even against their will."[50]

As these remarks suggest, the political energies that had surged around Pitt and his imperial project during the war did not suddenly dissipate when he resigned from office or even after the Treaty of Paris was signed in February 1763. The Pittite program itself was part of a larger political movement and transformation that began before the war and grew in strength during the 1760s. In the course of this transformation, the urban and radical elements within the Patriot opposition separated from the conservative Tories that they had been in alliance with against the Whig establishment since the late 1720s.[51] This change was itself bound up with the middling sort's growing resentment of the landed elite's near monopoly on political power. The shopkeepers, tradesmen, and middling merchants who found in Pitt both a voice and a hero sought not only to secure and extend Britain's commercial and maritime "empire of liberty" but also to change the domestic political order. The connection between Pitt's imperial project and the wider growth of this radicalism lay in a strident commercial expansionism that underpinned both Pitt's war aims and the radical Whig critique of Britain's existing political system.[52] The campaign for political reform that emerged in the 1760s was largely centered on the imbalance between taxation and representation—i.e., the fact that the segment of society that bore the brunt of the former was being denied its fair share of the latter.[53]

After signing the Treaty of Paris, Lord Bute announced that not only could the government not afford to reduce the high wartime taxes but also there was to be an additional excise tax levied upon cider. The public particularly disliked the new tax for the wide-ranging powers of search and seizure it granted excise officers and the fact that accused tax offenders were not granted jury trials.[54] There were widespread and angry protests in the cider-producing West Country as well as in London.[55] The radical press, fresh from decrying the terms of the peace, happily joined in. "A duty is imposed upon our very apples," proclaimed Wilkes's *North Briton*, "and I confess that great sums of *money* may be raised by the tax, as well as great murmurings." Wilkes rejoiced in the "general alarm, which has spread not only through the capital, but likewise through the whole kingdom, from a well-grounded terror of fatal consequences so justly apprehended from the next tax on *cyder*."[56]

Having enlisted as participants in the political nation with the ascent of Pitt, the middling sort were reluctant to simply return to passive obedience. When the cider bill successfully made it through the House of Lords, the sheriffs of London approached George III and urged him not to sign it. "What times do we not live in," the king wrote to Bute shortly before adding his name to the bill, "when a parcel of low shopkeepers pretend to direct the whole Legislature."[57] Bute, increasingly attacked with both rhetorical and literal brickbats (an assault was made on his London house by an anti-tax mob and its windows were smashed), resigned shortly after the passage of the cider excise in April 1763. Grenville, who assumed the premiership with Bute's support, took office amply warned of the dangers of raising any further taxes on Britons.

Although no one likes to pay taxes, the ordinary British taxpayer of 1763 was perhaps right to feel himself particularly hard done by. At this time, the British tax burden amounted to approximately "20 percent of the nation's commodity output[,]" a level that was about twice the rate in France.[58] Moreover, during the previous half century, the government had gradually shifted the tax burden from landowners to manufacturers and consumers. At the beginning of the century, the land tax was the Treasury's largest single revenue stream, accounting for 40 percent of all tax income. During the next several decades, the public revenue derived from excise taxes far surpassed that drawn from landed wealth. By 1763, while the total amount of taxes collected had more than doubled, the share of all public revenue contributed by landowners had fallen to 25 percent. The balance was laid on consumers and producers. In terms of actual pounds and pence, the yield of the land tax had increased in these decades by 40 percent, while the harvest the Treasury reaped from excise taxes placed on domestic production (like cider making) had increased 450 percent.[59]

The regressive character of this taxation was a chief target of the radical opinion-makers who loudly called for tax reform. "When I consider the enormous load of taxes under which this wretched kingdom labours, and how unequally they are borne by different members of it," averred one radical Whig, "I do not wonder at that murmuring and discontent, which prevails amongst the lower order of people, who contribute more than their proportion to the expences of government." This radical writer contended that

> in a country like this, which depends for its strength and riches on its manufactures, the necessaries of life should escape as free as possible from taxation, because they are common to the poor and to the rich, in almost the same proportion; and it is impossible they should be taxed without increasing the price of labour, which it is for the benefit of commerce to be kept moderate and reasonable.

He advocated that the tax burden be shifted on to luxury consumer goods and reduced upon necessities. "Every duty that is contrived to fall principally on the lower or middling part, which is the bulk of the nation, is unjust, iniquitous, and execrable," the radical Whig averred, arguing that "all the superfluities, elegancies, and luxuries of life be taxed and retaxed over and over: Double or triple the duty upon *plate* and *coaches*, as well as upon *dice* and *cards*: It is not fit that vanity and vice should be free and unrestrained, while the most galling shackles are imposed upon labour and industry."[60]

In addition to tax reform, the radical Whigs were concerned with gaining better access to government and, ultimately, better political representation (largely for the middling sort). They no longer sought merely to eliminate ministerial corruption and to remove pensioners and placemen from the legislature. They now wanted to transform the very basis of parliamentary representation in order to provide a more adequate institutional framework for Britain's commercializing and urbanizing society. Upon his election as MP from London in 1761, Beckford declared that "our Constitution is deficient in only one Point, and that is, that little pitiful Boroughs send Members to Parliament equal to Great Cities; and it is contrary to the Maxim, that Power should follow Property."[61] Unlike Viscount Bolingbroke and his Tory literary circle earlier in the century, the radical Whig critics of the aristocratic-oligarchic state in the 1760s did not look backward to a traditional agrarian order but forward to a more commercialized and urbanized polity. As John Brewer notes, "The attack on the state of representation marked, as it were, the urbanisation of country party ideology."[62]

During the early 1760s, the supporters of "Pitt and Patriotism" in the extra-parliamentary arena—i.e., the politically radicalized sections of the urban middling sort and plebeian classes—abandoned conservative notions of reform in favor of a full-blown radical Whiggism. This transformation was nowhere more apparent than in London, where many of the city's merchants and shopkeepers began to articulate their own radical ideas and expansive interests.[63] The emergence of domestic radicalism in turn induced many Tory squires to leave their traditional place in the political opposition and rally around the embattled Court and ministry. In effect, the old Patriot coalition was ripped in half. While the Tories were increasingly critical of the new urban-based radicalism, the radical Whigs began to take aim at the landed classes as a whole. In October 1762, *The Monitor* observed that "all ranks of people" were in support of continuing the war "except for a few miserable wretches, that disgrace their immense patrimonies by grudging the out-goings of land tax."[64] It was in this context that Alderman Beckford abandoned his Tory political allies and became, as George Rudé observes, the "champion of the commercial and 'middling' classes against the aristocracy."[65]

A new ideological division had supplanted the decades-old political conflict between the Whig establishment and the Patriot opposition. Radical Whigs denounced their opponents as "Tories" regardless of their actual party labels because they supported the powers of the government against the participation of "the people." In the spring of 1764, *The Monitor* claimed that "the distinction which formerly had been between *country gentlemen and courtiers*, was now betwixt *the friends of liberty*, and *the slaves of power*."[66] While the radical Whigs viewed their opponents as the harbingers of a return to seventeenth-century Toryism and Stuart absolutism, Bute, Grenville, and members of George III's inner circle viewed the strident opposition and reform demands of the radical Whigs as an anarchic threat to political stability. Believing themselves to be the only "true Patriots," both sides accused the other of wanting to undo the revolutionary settlement of 1688.

The making of the New Toryism

Since Walpole, the ruling Whig oligarchy had been concerned with diffusing and suppressing popular discontents with the post-1688 British regime. Government ministers and officials frequently discussed the threat that disaffected Britons at either end of the political spectrum, whether motivated by Jacobite counter-revolutionary or Commonwealthman republican principles, might pose to the regime. Any and all political opposition, regardless of circumstances and ideological character, was quickly tarred with one (or both) of these brushes. Pitt, who had cut his political teeth as a member of the Patriot opposition, was hardly immune to such suspicions. Before the Duke of Newcastle (very reluctantly) offered Pitt high office in 1757, the establishment Whig magnate was warned of "the spirit of Jacobitism and Rebellion, [which was] so propagated (in its new disguise) [as] to Varnish a man ... of yet unknown benefits," and might serve "to make Proselytes of the more unthinking." Such appeals, Newcastle's correspondent continued, might prove particularly persuasive "amongst the tribes of the City, that so Idolizes the man in question."[67] Subsequently, the reckless manner in which Pitt continued and expanded the Seven Years' War despite the strain it placed on the state's fiscal-military machinery astonished Newcastle and his allies.[68]

Beyond the establishment Whigs, much of the ruling class was troubled by Pitt's policies and views as well as by the political developments of the period. Taking note of the ideas and opinions expressed by Pitt's allies and supporters in London and the provincial urban centers, as well as Pitt's own views regarding the unlimited fiscal potential of British commercial and manufacturing expansion, Bute, Grenville, Bedford, the Earl of Egremont, and others concluded that Pitt was waging war against the domestic sociopolitical order as much as he was against Bourbon despotism. Indeed, drawing attention to the Great Commoner's popularity among Britain's middling and lower ranks, one writer declared that Pitt embodied the frightening prospect of popular rule: "The voice of the multitude, like a swelling stream, covered all [his] actions, concealed the false, unequal bottom of the channel it flowed in, and rapidly carried away all reason and argument before it."[69] Troubled by what they perceived to be the dangerous agenda of political transformation advocated by Pittite and radical Whigs, and concerned with the links between the progress of the war and political radicalization in Britain, George III, Bute, Grenville, and their allies desired to end the war and conclude a peace from domestic and political as much as from international and fiscal motives.[70] "Mr. Grenville considered the opinion we enter[tain]ed of the late war, and the value we set on our conquests, as the effect of popular madness," one writer asserted in 1765, "in all his speeches, and those of his faction, it was always spoken of under the appellation the *unfortunate war*."[71]

In the circles surrounding George III, an illiberal political movement began to coalesce that allied Tories and more conservative Patriot oppositionists with elements within the Whig establishment. Although once bitter enemies, these forces now found common cause in a shared desire to stave off the looming threat to the political order posed by the emergence of radical Whiggism as personified in Wilkes and his supporters, who called themselves "the friends of liberty." Embracing a more authoritarian political style, these men rejected reformist calls for public oversight of government policy and sought to preserve the aristocratic–oligarchic character of the post-1688 British state. To do so, they were prepared to use the powers of the Crown and to invoke the absolute sovereignty of Parliament in order to achieve a due measure of popular subordination.

Typical of this group was the Solicitor General and future Lord Chancellor Alexander Wedderburn. A good Scottish Whig upon his arrival in London in the 1750s, Wedderburn was deeply committed to the Hanoverian Settlement and firmly opposed to the illiberal character of much Tory political thought. Nevertheless, his growing concern with the depth and extent of post-1760 radicalism led him to reconsider his political views. By 1762, Wedderburn believed "that the right of the people to interfere in the affairs of government had been pushed to an inconvenient length" and that "the time was come when popular licentiousness might be repressed, and the people, ever incapable of governing themselves, might be governed by the prerogative which, for their benefit, God had bestowed upon his viceregent the King."[72] Alarmed by the increasingly mass-based and radical character of politics, Wedderburn penned an angry letter to his close ally Grenville in 1768 decrying the

> Great Bedlam under the dominion of a beggarly, idle, & intoxicated mob without Keepers, actuated solely by the word Wilkes which they use as Better Savages do a War Mosh to incite them in their Attempts to insult Government, & trample upon Law … The Mob has been made sensible of its own importance, & the pleasure which the Rich & Powerful feel in governing those whom fate has made their Inferiors, is not half so strong; as that which the Indigent & worthless feel in subverting Property, defying Law, & lording It over those whom they used to respect.[73]

In many of the writings of these illiberal and anti-radical circles, the word "licentiousness" was used as a shorthand for a kind of popular liberty that was incapable of recognizing its proper limits, leading to the subversion of political order and social hierarchy. Examples of such licentious behavior ranged from smuggling networks on the Isle of Man to rioting sailors demanding higher wages in Newcastle to the propaganda activities of radical agitators such as Wilkes. Grenville averred that such popular licentiousness "may [if not curbed] tear up the Constitution by the Roots & shake the Palace of the King himself."[74]

Shared fears of anarchy and revolution led many supporters of the long-standing Whig establishment—conservative and moderate Hanoverian Whigs—and their old political foes, the Tories, to make common cause with the Court of George III in defense of the existing order. Despite their factional and personal differences, politicians and officials such as Bute, Charles Jenkinson, the Earl of Halifax, Grenville, William Knox, Thomas Whateley, Bedford, the Earl of Sandwich, Charles Townshend, and Lord

North shared a coherent ideological response to the perceived crisis in British political affairs. As Charles Ritcheson argues, this conservative rapprochement and the political alliances it spawned would eventually become "the seedbed of a new Tory party."[75] This politico-ideological formation, although only in its early stages in the 1760s, is what I refer to as the New Toryism.

The New Tories rejected the concept of popular sovereignty and recoiled at radical notions of parliamentary reform. Their ultimate goal was to consolidate a strong parliamentary state that upheld the principle of unqualified parliamentary sovereignty and preserved the political hegemony of the landed classes. The New Toryism sought to unify the political elite around a governing ideology of King-in-Parliament absolutism, in which the unreformed parliamentary system "virtually represented" the domestic population as well as colonial populations overseas.[76] Lord Mansfield articulated a key ideological plank of the New Toryism when he opined in the House of Lords in February 1766 that "the British legislature, as to the power of making laws, represents the whole British empire, and has the authority to bind every part and every subject without the least distinction, whether such subjects have a right to vote or not, or whether the law binds places within the realm or without."[77]

The New Tories—including Whigs such as Grenville, Tories such as Samuel Johnson, and conservative Patriots such as the Earl of Egmont—shared an increasingly authoritarian political ideology according to which radical Whiggism did not represent new social groups and economic interests seeking incorporation into the political settlement achieved at the Glorious Revolution but rather a dangerous and growing tumor in the body politic. They viewed this tumor as an unfortunate product of Britain's advanced commercial society. Conservative commentators expressed anxiety about both the flood tide of consumer goods that was spreading throughout British society and the selfishness and decadence that such items were thought to invariably produce. They thought the situation was dire: "Luxury emasculates our minds, and makes us regardless of every thing but what relates to the gratification of its incessant and insatiable demands … and that corruption, its natural attendant, spreads its baneful infection so wide, as to threaten the undermining our constitution and the downfall of our state."[78]

According to the New Toryism, an advanced commercial society inevitably degenerated into a culture of luxury and a politics of licentiousness. In 1756, the Anglican parson John Brown published his enormously influential diatribe against luxury and effeminacy entitled *An Estimate of the Manners and Principles of the Times*. In this treatise, Brown sought to refute those political economists who emphasized the advantages of overseas trade, asserting that such maxims may have held true in the first and second stage of commercial expansion but no longer applied for societies such as Britain and the Netherlands that had long since entered the third stage. According to Brown, the deep political divisions in Britain stemmed from "luxurious and effeminate manners in the higher ranks" that were the inevitable byproduct of the growth of trade and wealth. "And this national disunion," the parson concluded, "besides it's proper and immediate effects, being founded in avarice for the ends of dissipation, hath again weakened the small remainder of publick capacity and defence[.]"[79] Writing under the name of Aurelius, another pamphleteer declared that contemporary ills were the result of the overabundance of consumer goods as "a little rational consideration will enable us to discover the kindred links between luxury, rapine, meanness, extravagance, misery, idleness, vice and guilt."[80] From the ideological standpoint of the New Toryism, the reckless pursuit of self-interest generated by commercial and industrial advance would ultimately undermine the sociopolitical order.

Bitter imperial medicine: Bengal as a model patient[81]

As Grenville cast his eye over the world from his perch atop the government in the spring of 1763, Britain and its newly won empire appeared to exist more on the paper of newly printed maps than in reality. Across the globe, British claims to imperial authority appeared to be honored more in the breach than in the observance. Smuggling flourished in the ports on both sides of the Atlantic, depriving the Customs of much needed revenue.[82] In the North American interior, the king's new Indian subjects had risen in rebellion. Even soldiers of the army, so recently victorious over the French, had mutinied against a cut in pay in several American garrisons. In Britain itself, the embers of the cider tax riots still smoldered in the West Country, while in London Wilkes's printed attacks on the character and policies of the country's leaders had made him into a popular hero.

Grenville saw disobedience and disorder everywhere he looked. Undaunted, the new premier promised the king that he would act with resolution to stem the tide of anarchic political and economic freedoms that threatened the imperial peace. George III, who had accepted Bute's resignation with reluctance, agreed with Grenville "that it was necessary to restrain the licentiousness of the times." The king was adamant that "a remedy should be found to these evils, for that if he suffered force to be put upon him by the Opposition, the mob would try to govern him next."[83] For all of their personality differences and conflicts, the king and his prime minister concurred on the urgent need to curb both the licentiousness that threatened to transform British liberty into anarchy and the concomitant popular politics of radical Whiggism. They both believed that domestic political authority must be vigorously upheld and that the vastly expanded empire overseas must be reorganized, with its populations duly subordinated to metropolitan authority.

Grenville, backed by George III and supported by allies in the cabinet and in Parliament, sought to implement a new and more authoritarian imperial policy in the Atlantic colonies. Likewise, the prime minister wanted the crisis in the East India Company's affairs in Bengal resolved decisively. The Company was the country's largest overseas trading corporation, its leading investors and shareholders were among the City of London's business elite and the kingdom's political elite, and the corporation itself was a pillar of the fiscal-military state that made possible Britain's rise to global preeminence.[84]

A key ally in Grenville's effort to stabilize the Company's affairs was Robert Clive, the man who, through his victory over the nawab of Bengal, Siraj ud-Daulah, at the Battle of Plassey in 1757, personally embodied the restoration of British fortunes in the East after the potentially fatal setback of the capture of Calcutta by the nawab's forces. Upon his return to Britain in 1760, Clive was lionized in the press as a national hero and granted an Irish peerage (as Baron Clive of Plassey). But he had no thought of resting on his laurels. Clive quickly secured a seat in Parliament from where he sought to influence the government's India policy, and also joined a campaign waged in 1763 by malcontented directors, shareholders, and former employees to wrest control of the East India Company away from its leading figure, Laurence Sulivan.

Clive was a bitter rival of Sulivan. They initially came into conflict over the income from Clive's *jagir*, a grant of yearly land revenue from Mir Jafar, the new nawab of Bengal whom Clive helped put in power following Plassey, but their competing visions regarding the Company's position overseas widened into a broader rivalry for leadership of Indian affairs in Britain. Unlike Clive, who had advocated creating a British territorial empire in Bengal since the late 1750s, Sulivan was staunchly opposed to acquiring political dominion over extensive territory on the Indian subcontinent. Rather, he thought the Company's interests were best served by remaining true to its original commercial purpose as a joint-stock trading corporation purchasing lucrative Asian goods, above all Indian textiles, for sale in Britain and re-export in European and Atlantic markets.

Clive and his allies were finally able to wrest control of the Company away from Sulivan by winning the election to its Court of Directors in April 1764. While the strong backing of the Grenville ministry in the election played a key role in securing Clive's victory, it was a crisis in Bengal that shifted circumstances decisively in his favor. In 1763, armed conflict broke out in Bengal between the Company and the man it had made the nawab, Mir Qasim, after deposing his predecessor, Mir Jafar, in 1760. Mir Qasim sought to curb the expansion of the duty-free private trade conducted by the Company's servants throughout his territory. The disputes that arose led to open warfare and, eventually, to Mir Qasim joining his forces with those of the Nawab of Awadh Shuja ud-Daulah and the Mughal Emperor Shah Alam II in an effort to check the growth of British power in northern India. When news of the conflict reached Britain in early 1764, demands for Clive's return to Bengal to stabilize the situation spread throughout the newspapers and boardrooms of London, greatly strengthening his hand against Sulivan and allowing his allies to win control of the Company's Court of Directors in the election of April 1764. Now in control, Clive's backers returned him to India in June 1764 with extraordinary civilian and military powers as the Governor of Bengal and the Commander-in-Chief of the Company's forces.

Clive and Grenville had consulted closely during 1763 and 1764, and they agreed that a strong hand and determined policy were needed to secure the Company's affairs in Bengal. Grenville and his political circle backed the Baron of Plassey's takeover of the Company and return to Bengal with quasi-autocratic power for the same reasons they supported a more authoritarian form of imperial rule in North America: the licentiousness of the Company's servants in Bengal and the difficulties of fortifying Britain's imperial position in Asia, like the licentiousness of American colonists and the difficulties of fortifying the British Empire in North America, required a strong imperial state that ruled above local civil society and checked its excesses. "The Scenes of Corruption on the one Hand & Licentiousness on the other which have been opened in the East Indies," Grenville later wrote to Clive in Calcutta, "have been at least as notorious in the other Parts of His Majesty's Dominions, & will I much fear be

Attended with the same unhappy Consequences in all."[85] Many in Britain viewed Clive's return to Bengal with unprecedented powers as one step in a grand struggle to master the tide of licentiousness generated by an advanced commercial society. Indeed, as one of Clive's correspondents enthused during his return trip to India in December 1764:

> I am in great hopes, to See you appear as remarkable by fixing affaires on a Solid foundation, in India, by preventing our being ruined by the Covetousness of the Companys Servts … tho Indeed, that Selfish Spirit is So fashionable at home, that it is No wonder It finds its way to India. Ld chesterfield observes, that there is a Triumvirate, by which nations Rise, viz, Industry, virtue, and Liberty, and that they are ruined by another Triumvirate, viz Luxury, want of publick Spirits and Slavery, and Indeed one of your Lordships turn of mind, preferring Dangers, and Serving the publick to Luxury and private Interest, Is a Phenix, which Scarce appears once in an age[.][86]

Many political elites and opinion-makers in Britain hoped Clive's second governorship of Bengal would accomplish for the British Empire in the East what the Grenville ministry aimed to do for it in the Atlantic world.

Clive's decision to establish a territorial empire for the Company in Bengal upon his return there in 1765, achieved with his acquisition of the *diwani*, was deeply informed by the illiberal imperial vision he shared with Grenville. According to the Baron of Plassey, it was the immense riches that accrued to the Company's employees in Bengal during the Seven Years' War and afterwards, largely as a result of the expansion of British private trade in the province, that led to a profound transformation of their conduct. In the past, the Company's corporate hierarchy had kept in check the ambitions of its servants and of independent British merchants. However, Clive argued, the sudden and vast accumulation of wealth in Bengal during the late 1750s and early 1760s had swept away these barriers in a deluge of self-interest and avarice. "The sudden, and among many, the unwarrantable acquisition of riches, had introduced luxury in almost every shape, and in its most pernicious excess," Clive wrote to the Company's Court of Directors from Calcutta in the fall of 1765. "The evil was contagious, and spread among the civil and military, down to the writer, the ensign, and the free merchant," he concluded.[87] With each man pursuing only his own selfish interests, the greater public interests of the Company and of the British state were entirely neglected. "If I was to give You an Account of all our Proceedings in Bengal, Volumes would not suffice," Clive observed to one correspondent, "I shall only observe, that upon my Arrival in [Calcutta], I found it overwhelmed with Luxury & Corruption, the Company's Affairs totally neglected, & their Orders from Home set at Defiance … to the great Detriment of the Company, & the Dishonor of the Nation."[88]

The licentiousness of the Company's employees undermined established authority, as the lure of wealth overwhelmed notions of hierarchy and subordination among the British population in Bengal. "Anarchy, & Confusion, Bribery, & Corruption, have extended themselves over the 3 rich Provinces of Bengal, Bahar, & Orissa," Clive averred to Grenville's ally in the City, Joseph Salvador, "in short the Gentlemen [the Company's servants] having the Revenues of the Country amounting to upwards 3 Million [per] Annum at their Command, were making such strides towards Independency, that in two Years time, I am persuaded the Company would not have had one Servant upon the Establishment above the Rank of a Writer [i.e., a clerk]."[89] Clive's September 1765 report to the Company's directors on the situation in Bengal reads almost as if it was written by one of the royal governors in North America reporting to Whitehall about the colonists' resistance to the Stamp Act that same month:

> From hence arose that forward spirit of independancy which in a manner set all your orders at defiance, and dictated a total contempt of them as often as obedience was found incompatible with private interest. At the time of my arrival, I saw nothing that bore the form or appearance of Government. The authority and pre-eminence of the Governor, were leveled with those of the Councillors; every Councillor was as much a Governor as he who bore the name, and distinction of rank … was no longer to be found in the whole settlement.

The Baron of Plassey contended that the rising "spirit of independency" of the Company servants led them not only to treat the corporation's rules with contempt but also to disregard and disdain the lines of authority connecting the Company to local South Asian rulers (like Mir Qasim). The result was confusion and chaos. "Notwithstanding a special order from the Court of Directors … that all correspondence with the country powers should be carried on solely in the Governor's name," lamented Clive, "I found, that our whole correspondence with the Great Mogul, *the subahs*, nabobs, and rajahs, had been of late carried on by and in the name of the whole Board, and that every servant and free merchant corresponded with whom they pleased."[90]

Although the Company was a commercial corporation and profit-making enterprise, its business before the Seven Years' War had always been conducted within a framework of chartered rights and historical privileges that were extended to it by the British state. Furthermore, the corporation's long-established hierarchy had previously controlled and shaped the ambitions and interests of its employees. The Company had defeated its European and South Asian rivals during the course of the war, but, according to Clive and his allies, a new threat to order and regularity emerged from within its own ranks. In a telling resort to military metaphors, Clive warned the directors in London that "all is not safe; danger still subsists from more formidable enemies within; luxury, corruption, avarice, rapacity, there have the possession of your principal posts, and are ready to betray your citadel."[91]

The ideological framework within which Clive, Grenville, and their supporters comprehended events in Bengal also provided the basis for their solutions to the Company's problems. Whereas Sulivan and the previous leadership viewed the British corporation primarily as a commercial enterprise, and sought primarily mercantile remedies for its woes, Clive and his allies pursued a military and political solution. Central to that solution was the creation of a political dominion over extensive territory in northeastern India, and, with it, the Company's transformation from a commercial corporation into an imperial state.

En route to Calcutta in April 1765 with his new commission in hand, Clive wrote to Thomas Rous, a key ally who had been elected Company Chairman the year before, giving full vent to his ambitions and expectations:

Can it then be doubted that a large Army of Europeans would effectually preserve
to us the Sovereignty, as I may call it, not only by keeping in Awe the Ambition
of any Country Prince, but by rendering us so truly formidable, that no French,
Dutch, or other Enemy could ever dare to molest us? ... We must indeed become
the Nabobs ourselves in Fact, if not in Name, perhaps totally so without Disguise,
but on this Subject I cannot be positive until my arrival at Bengal. Let us, and
without delay, compleat our three European Regiments to one thousand each. Such
an Army together with five hundred light Horse, 3 or 4 Companies of Artillery,
and the Troops of the Country will absolutely render us invincible. In short, if
Riches and Stability are the Objects of the Company, this is the Method, the only
Method we now have for attaining and securing them.[92]

For Clive, the *diwani* and the revenue it promised were vital to fund the "large Army of
Europeans" that he envisaged and thought necessary for the defense of the Company
against both internal and external threats. "With regard to the Latitude of our
Possessions, be not staggered," Clive wrote to the Company's Deputy Chairman George
Dudley one month after acquiring the *diwani*, "assure Yourself that the Company
must either [accept these new responsibilities] ... or be annihilated." He contended
that there was "no alternative, for in a more moderate [i.e., limited] State, though the
Power might still be preserved, Corruption, and frequent Revolutions, must in the end
overset Us."[93] From Clive's standpoint, the establishment of the Company's territorial
empire and the autocratic state governing it were necessary to curb the licentiousness
of its servants and to fortify its position in northeastern India.

An essential step in Clive's founding of a militarized imperial state was his "Plan of
Reformation" for the Bengal presidency's civil department. "Rapacity and Luxury; the
unreasonable desire of many to acquire in an Instant, what only a few can, or ought to
possess[,]" were, he contended, the reigning vices plaguing the corporation's Calcutta
administration. It was, he noted, the ambition of everyone "[to] be rich without the
Merits of long Service and from this incessant Competition undoubtedly springs
that Disorder to which we must apply a Remedy, or be undone, for it is not only
malignant but contagious."[94] With the extraordinary civilian and military powers at his
disposal, Clive purged the Company's Calcutta presidency of this contagious disease.
"I do declare, by that Great Being who is the searcher of all hearts," he averred, "that
I am come out with a mind superior to all corruption, and that I am determined to
destroy those great and growing evils, or perish in the attempt."[95] He implemented a
series of measures designed to create a disciplined corps of salaried administrators
and officers. By removing "corrupt" and "degenerate" members of the corporation's
civil service from office, Clive hoped to change the Company's post-Plassey culture of
rapacious individualism to one of disinterested imperial service. The success of this
transformation depended on the Company recruiting its officials from a different social
background than previously. "The Court of Directors must supply the Settlement with
young men [who are] more moderate, or less eager in their pursuit of Wealth," Clive
informed Rous in April 1765. Rather than dispatching men from Britain of modest
means who went to India to make their fortunes, Clive now asked the Company's
directors to "do all in your Power to send out proper Gentlemen."[96]

Clive's second governorship only lasted from 1765 to 1767, but before he returned to Britain he was able to lay several of the bureaucratic and military foundations of the autocratic and extractive state that governed Bengal, and eventually much of India, until direct Crown rule was established in 1858. The same imperial state largely remained in place until Indian independence in 1947 finally brought about its end.

The defeat and success of illiberal imperialism

By contrast, Britain's empire in most of North America lasted barely eleven years after the Grenville ministry's passage of the Stamp Act in March 1765. However, the vastly different outcomes on each side of the post-1763 British Empire should not obscure the fact that both the new imperial reforms imposed on the American colonists and Clive's consolidation of an imperial state in Bengal stemmed from the same metropolitan political impulse and the same circle of like-minded ministers and officials. In this new imperial design, India was not to become, and America was not to continue as, part of a commercial and maritime "empire of liberty" of the kind that Britons had celebrated before the Seven Years' War. Rather, the overseas periphery, both in the East and the West, was to be governed by a militarized imperium largely paid for by revenues extracted from local subjects via taxation (without representation). The rampant commercial expansionism and licentiousness that were seen as threatening Britain's domestic and overseas establishments were to be restrained by an unreformed parliamentary state and its autocratic imperial administrations.

In addition to their ideological purpose in reining in what the New Tories viewed to be a rampant and dangerous spirit of radicalism that demanded ever-larger and -freer markets and political reform, the measures implemented in North America and South Asia in the years between 1763 and 1767 were also undertaken to help resolve the crisis of Britain's fiscal-military state following the Seven Years' War. According to the New Tories, revenues raised in America and India via taxation or tribute would eventually help to reduce Britain's immense public debt and to ease the tax burden on its population. The more the costs of empire, including maintaining peacetime standing armies, could be "outsourced" to the imperial periphery, the less need for metropolitan ministers to tax the middling and lower orders and, thus, potentially further the cause of radical Whiggism among them.

The solution to Britain's domestic problems, both political and fiscal, lay overseas, not in trade and manufacturing exports as the radical Whigs envisioned but rather in taxation and tribute. As William Knox, Georgia's colonial agent and a consigliere to Grenville on imperial affairs, advised British ministers in 1763, "The circumstances of England require that her burdens should be lightened by distributing them amongst the several Members of her Empire."[97] Clive made much the same point with regard to northeastern India when he wrote two years after Plassey that "an income yearly upwards two millions sterling [gained] with the possession of three provinces abounding in the most valuable productions of nature and of art … would prove an immense wealth to the kingdom, and might in time be appropriated in part as a fund towards diminishing the heavy load of debt under which we at present labor."[98] Later, after returning to India and acquiring the *diwani*, Clive reminded Grenville of "some discourse we had together about the [East India] Company's affairs" before he left Britain in 1764. "I have now the particular Satisfaction of seeing the great Object of my Wishes nearly accomplished," the Baron of Plassey proudly wrote. "I hope by the Years Conveyance to send you a particular Account of the Revenues of these Provinces which ... cannot fall short of 4 Million per Annum," he added boastfully in what proved to be a wildly exaggerated calculation. Such a sum, the equivalent of more than 30 percent of all the tax revenue collected in Britain that year, might, Clive hoped, "in times of Distress and Necessity, contribute towards lessening the Debt of the Nation."[99] With the establishment of the Company's territorial empire, a pillar of the City of London and the fiscal-military state had been saved from internal decay and external threats. What's more, the post-*diwani* corporation was in a better position to assist the fiscally strapped British government both directly by providing vast patronage resources and indirectly by providing loans from its leading shareholders.

Whether acquired by the Crown-appointed tax collectors in the American colonies or by the Company's administrators in Bengal, these new revenue streams were intended in part to support an imperial officialdom that ruled above civil society instead of through it. Local elites and institutions throughout the Empire would not have to be overthrown; they would simply be bypassed. A necessary step in this plan was to maintain among the local population a "large Army of Europeans ... to effectually preserve to us the Sovereignty," as Clive called for in Bengal. In peacetime, these troops were to act as imperial policemen, upholding authority, protecting property, and discouraging disorder. Knox and the other advisors who helped design the new imperial policy for America argued that the proposed peacetime standing army of ten thousand men (to be paid in part from the revenue raised by the Stamp Act) would not only deter the French and Spanish from attacking but would also help in "securing the Dependence of the Colonys on Great Britain."[100] Imperial administrations that ruled above their subjects rather than through negotiation with local institutions and representatives required a strong military component.

As this chapter demonstrates, valuable insights can be gained by looking at the simultaneous plans being proposed and implemented on both sides of the British Empire, in India and America, in the years immediately following the Seven Years' War. These insights are multiplied when they are viewed through the prism of the metropole, and the perspective and intentions of the British ministers and officials who devised the plans and set them in motion. By their actions, the New Tories provoked the American Revolution and laid the foundation for the British Raj. In Britain itself, their vigorous defense of the existing political system successfully saw off the challenge posed by radical Whiggism and parliamentary reform. While the return of political radicalism in Britain after its suppression in the era of the French Revolutionary and Napoleonic Wars eventually led to the passage of the Great Reform Act in 1832, the Second British Empire, with the Raj at its heart, proved far less susceptible to reform.

Notes

1   Sir George Lyttelton to William Lyttelton, December 4, 1759, in *Memoirs and Correspondence of George, Lord Lyttelton, from 1734 to 1773*, ed. Robert Phillimore (London: J. Ridgway, 1845), 2: 619–620.

2   Horace Walpole, *Memoirs of King George II*, ed. John Brooke (New Haven, CT: Yale University Press, 1985), 3: 80.

3   Sir Andrew Mitchell to William Pitt, January 15, 1760, in *Correspondence of William Pitt, Earl of Chatham*, ed. William Stanhope Taylor and Captain John Henry Pringle (London: John Murray, 1839), 2: 14–15.

4   For a good overview of these reforms, and their objective of raising revenue from the colonies, see Charles R. Ritcheson, "The Preparation of the Stamp Act," *William & Mary Quarterly,* 3rd Series, 10 (October 1953): 543–559. On the plan to station ten thousand regular soldiers in British North America, see John L. Bullion, "Security and Economy: The Bute Administration's Plans for the American Army and Revenue, 1762–1763," *William & Mary Quarterly,* 3rd Series, 45 (July 1988): 499–509; and John L. Bullion, "'The Ten Thousand in America': More Light on the Decision on the American Army, 1762–1763," *William & Mary Quarterly,* 3rd Series, 43 (October 1986): 646–657.

5   For an excellent overview of this transformation, see P. J. Marshall, *The Making and Unmaking of Empires: Britain, India, and America, c. 1750–1783* (New York: Oxford University Press, 2005), 119–157.

6   Ibid., 1–12.

7   Daniel A. Baugh, "Maritime Strength and Atlantic Commerce: The Uses of 'A Grand Marine Empire,'" in *An Imperial State at War: Britain from 1689 to 1815*, ed. Lawrence Stone (London: Routledge, 1994), 210.

8   The best overview of this Atlantic imperial reorganization remains Bernhard Knollenberg, *Origin of the American Revolution: 1759–1766*, ed. Bernard W. Sheehan (Indianapolis, IN: Liberty Fund, 2002), 76–94, 116–145, 157–173, and 210–216.

9   James M. Vaughn, *The Politics of Empire at the Accession of George III: The East India Company and the Crisis and Transformation of Britain's Imperial State* (New Haven, CT: Yale University Press, 2019), 131–164.

10 By "authoritarian Whigs," I mean those members of the long-standing Whig establishment who, especially after 1760, embraced a more conservative and autocratic form of politics in reaction to the developing radicalism of the period.

11 For an important analysis of the ideological commitments of the Whig establishment that governed the country in the decades preceding the accession of George III, see Reed Browning, *Political and Constitutional Ideas of the Court Whigs* (Baton Rouge, LA: Louisiana State University Press, 1982).

12 The political and ideological developments analyzed in this chapter can be read as the pan-imperial counterpart to the developments analyzed in Bernard Bailyn, *The Ideological Origins of the American Revolution* (Cambridge, MA: Harvard University Press, 1967).

13 Lord William Wildman Barrington to Sir Andrew Mitchell, January 14, 1760, quoted in *Correspondence of William Pitt*, 2: 14, note 1.

14 John Almon, *Anecdotes of the Life of the Right Honourable William Pitt, Earl of Chatham* (London, 1778), 340.

15 John Brewer, *The Sinews of Power: War, Money and the English State, 1688–1783* (New York: Knopf, 1989), 114.

16   "On the necessity of raising supplies within the year," and "The Same Subject
     Continued," in *A New and Impartial Collection of Interesting Letters, from the Public
     Papers* (London: J. Almon, 1767), 1: 5–6.
17   Daniel Baugh, *The Global Seven Years War, 1754–1763: Britain and France in a Great
     Power Contest* (Harlow: Pearson, 2011), 219 and 237. Baugh's magisterial tome
     provides the best account of the formation of military policy and strategy by both
     leading combatants.
18   Ibid., 238–240.
19   Brendan Simms, *Three Victories and a Defeat: The Rise and Fall of the First British
     Empire, 1714–1783* (New York: Basic Books, 2008), 462.
20   Nicholas Rogers, *Whigs and Cities: Popular Politics in the Age of Walpole and Pitt*
     (Oxford: Oxford University Press, 1989), 109–110.
21   Baugh, *The Global Seven Years War,* 26–27.
22   Williamson Murray, "Grand Strategy, Alliances, and the Anglo-American Way of
     War," in *Grand Strategy and Military Alliances*, ed. Peter R. Mansoor and Williamson
     Murray (Cambridge: Cambridge University Press, 2016), 29.
23   "Pitt's Speech on the Convention with Spain, 1738," in *The Modern Orator* (London:
     Aylott and Jones, 1847), 5–8.
24   George Rudé, *Hanoverian London, 1714–1808* (Stroud: Sutton Publishing, 2003),
     163–164.
25   John Brewer, "Commercialization and Politics," in *The Birth of a Consumer Society:
     The Commercialization of Eighteenth-Century England*, ed. Neil McKendrick, John
     Brewer, and J. H. Plumb (London: Hutchinson, 1983), 197.
26   *A Political Analysis of the War: The Principles of the Present Political Parties Examined*
     (London: Tho. Payne, 1762), 11.
27   Kate Hotblack, *Chatham's Colonial Policy: A Study in the Fiscal and Economic
     Implications of the Colonial Policy of the Elder Pitt* (Philadelphia, PA: Porcupine Press,
     1980), 11–27.
28   Linda Colley, *Britons: Forging the Nation, 1707–1837* (New Haven, CT: Yale
     University Press, 1992), 61.
29   Hotblack, *Chatham's Colonial Policy*, 17–18; Rogers, *Whigs and Cities,* 111–112.
30   As Kate Hotblack argues: "The merchants recognized that the government was
     pledged to carry on a war for and upon trade, and determined that trade should
     support the war … When the Great Commoner returned to office [in 1757] he knew
     that the cities of England were with him, and was confident that with their aid he
     would eventually win the King's support[.]" Hotblack, *Chatham's Colonial Policy,*
     15–16.
31   Quoted in ibid., 18.
32   Paul Langford, *A Polite and Commercial People: England, 1727–1783* (Oxford:
     Clarendon Press, 1989), 340.
33   For a retrospective account of the radical imperial project pursued by Pitt at this
     time, see *The Monitor, or British Freeholder,* No. 381, November 6, 1762.
34   Daniel A. Baugh, "Great Britain's 'Blue-Water' Policy, 1689–1815," *International
     History Review* 10, no. 1 (February 1988): 58.
35   Fred Anderson, *Crucible of War: The Seven Years' War and the Fate of Empire in
     British North America, 1754–1766* (New York: Knopf, 2000), 484; Richard Middleton,
     *The Bells of Victory: The Pitt-Newcastle Ministry and the Conduct of the Seven Years'
     War, 1757–1762* (Cambridge: Cambridge University Press, 1985), 192–193.
36   Middleton, *The Bells of Victory,* 193.

37   Baugh, *The Global Seven Years War,* 551–554; Middleton, *The Bells of Victory,* 192–197.
38   Quoted in Middleton, *The Bells of Victory,* 196.
39   Rogers, *Whigs and Cities,* 114–116.
40   "Beckford on the Address, 1761," British Library (BL), Additional MS. 38334, ff. 30v–31r.
41   John Almon, *Biographical, Literary, and Political Anecdotes, of Several of the Most Eminent Persons of the Present Age* (London: T. N. Longman and L. B. Seeley, 1797), 2: 85.
42   Brewer, *The Sinews of Power,* 124.
43   Walpole, *Memoirs of King George II,* 3: 51–52.
44   Anderson, *Crucible of War,* 484.
45   Baugh, *The Global Seven Years War,* 559–560.
46   Ibid., 559 and 560.
47   See the excellent discussions of this in Anderson, *Crucible of War,* 490–496; and Baugh, *The Global Seven Years War,* 565–574.
48   Baugh, *The Global Seven Years War,* 560.
49   *The Monitor, or British Freeholder,* No. 373, September 11, 1762.
50   *The Monitor, or British Freeholder,* No. 382, November 27, 1762.
51   For an example of this protracted process of ideological radicalization, see Marie Peters, "The 'Monitor' on the Constitution, 1755–1765: New Light on the Ideological Origins of English Radicalism," *English Historical Review* 86, no. 341 (October 1971): 706–727.
52   For an example of the evolution of this radical commercial expansionism into a vigorous, wide-ranging critique of British politics, see *The Monitor, or British Freeholder,* No. 369, August 14, 1762; No. 370, August 21, 1762; No. 375, September 25, 1762; No. 383, December 4, 1762; No. 384, December 11, 1762; No. 385, December 18, 1762; No. 386, December 25, 1762; No. 387, January 1, 1763; No. 388, January 8, 1763; No. 389, January 15, 1763.
53   Rogers, *Whigs and Cities,* 93–106.
54   John Brewer, "English Radicalism in the Age of George III," in *Three British Revolutions: 1641, 1688, 1776,* ed. J. G. A. Pocock (Princeton, NJ: Princeton University Press, 1980), 339.
55   Rogers, *Whigs and Cities,* 124; Peter D. G. Thomas, *George III: King and Politicians, 1760–1770* (Manchester: Manchester University Press, 2002), 85–86.
56   John Wilkes, *The North Briton,* No. 43, March 26, 1763.
57   King George III to the Earl of Bute, March 30, 1763, in *Letters from George III to Lord Bute, 1756–1766,* ed. Romney Sedgwick (London: Macmillan and Co., Ltd., 1939), 207–208.
58   Brewer, "English Radicalism in the Age of George III," 338.
59   Brewer, *The Sinews of Power,* 90–100.
60   "Oppressive Duty upon Beer Considered," in *A New and Impartial Collection of Interesting Letters,* 2: 153–154.
61   *The London Evening-Post,* No. 5216, April 4–7, 1761.
62   John Brewer, *Party Ideology and Popular Politics at the Accession of George III* (Cambridge: Cambridge University Press, 1976), 206.
63   Rudé, *Hanoverian London,* 162; Lucy Sutherland, "The City of London in Eighteenth-Century Politics," in Lucy Sutherland, *Politics and Finance in the Eighteenth Century,* ed. Aubrey Newman (London: Hambledon Press, 1984), 41–66.

64 *The Monitor, or British Freeholder,* No. 376, October 2, 1762.

65 Rudé, *Hanoverian London,* 164.

66 *The Monitor, or British Freeholder,* No. 458, May 12, 1764.

67 John Gordon to the Duke of Newcastle, April 6, 1756, BL, Additional MS. 32889, ff. 388r–v.

68 Rogers, *Whigs and Cities,* 114–116.

69 "To Isaac Buckhorse, Esq.; from the E. of C.," in *A New and Impartial Collection of Interesting Letters,* 2: 264.

70 While Bute was anxious to bring the war to a conclusion as quickly as possible, and thus was willing to return territories won from France in order to do so, Grenville took a much tougher negotiating position, seeking greater concessions from France at the peace table. Nevertheless, they were both severely critical of Pitt's war aims and viewed achieving peace as necessary for the restoration of stability and the defense of the political order.

71 "Letters on behalf of the Administration, in answer to Anti-Sejanus," in *A New and Impartial Collection of Interesting Letters,* 2: 84.

72 John Lord Campbell, *The Lives of the Lord Chancellors and Keepers of the Great Seal of England,* 3rd Series (Philadelphia, PA: Lea and Blanchard, 1848), 6: 73.

73 Alexander Wedderburn to George Grenville, April 3, 1768, BL, Additional MS. 42086, ff. 10v–11r.

74 "Speeches in the House of Commons," BL, Stowe MS. 372, f. 41v.

75 Charles R. Ritcheson, *British Politics and the American Revolution* (Norman, OK: University of Oklahoma Press, 1954), 31.

76 For my conceptualization of post-1760 New Toryism, I am heavily indebted to the work of Paul Langford on British political ideology in the era of the American Revolution. For the development of concepts of parliamentary absolutism in the 1760s and 1770s, see Paul Langford, "Old Whigs, Old Tories, and the American Revolution," in *The British Atlantic Empire before the American Revolution,* ed. Peter Marshall and Glyn Williams (London: Cass, 1980), 106–128.

77 "Speech by Lord Mansfield in the House of Lords on the right of Parliament to tax the colonies, February 10, 1766," in *English Historical Documents,* 10: 1714–1783, ed. D. B. Horn and Mary Ransome (London: Eyre & Spottiswoode, 1957), 753.

78 *London Magazine,* January 1756, 15.

79 John Brown, *An Estimate of the Manners and Principles of the Times* (London: L. Davis and C. Reymers, 1757), 181–182.

80 *London Magazine,* December 1764, 620.

81 The interpretation provided in this section is based on Vaughn, *The Politics of Empire at the Accession of George III,* 131–200.

82 By 1763, the Treasury was fully aware of the depth and extent to which colonial American commerce extended beyond the legal boundaries set by the laws of trade and navigation. Ritcheson, *British Politics and the American Revolution,* 16–18.

83 George Grenville, "Some Account of the Memorable Transactions since the Death of Lord Egremont," in *The Grenville Papers,* ed. William James Smith (London: J. Murray, 1852), 2: 193.

84 Brewer, *The Sinews of Power,* 114–126; Philip Lawson, *The East India Company: A History* (Harlow: Longman, 1993), 73–79.

85 George Grenville to Robert Clive, November 22, 1766, BL, Additional MS. 42084, f. 213v.

86   Hugh Baillie to Robert Clive, December 30, 1764, BL, Oriental and India Office Collections, India Office Library, Eur. Mss. G 37, Box 32, f. 2r.
87   Robert Clive to the Directors of the East India Company, September 30, 1765, in *Fort William–India House Correspondence* [*FWIHC*], 4: 1764–1766, ed. C. S. Srinivasachari (Delhi: National Archives of India, 1962), 330.
88   Robert Clive to Rev. Dr. Adams, September 29, 1765, National Library of Wales (NLW), Clive MS. CR3/1, 27.
89   Robert Clive to Joseph Salvador, September 29, 1765, NLW, Clive MS. CR3/1, 23.
90   Robert Clive to the Directors of the East India Company, September 30, 1765, in *FWIHC,* 4: 331.
91   Ibid., 339–340.
92   Robert Clive to Thomas Rous, April 17, 1765, quoted in Sir George Forrest, *The Life of Lord Clive* (London: Cassell, 1918), 2: 256–257.
93   Robert Clive to George Dudley, September 29, 1765, NLW, Clive MS. CR3/1 and 3.
94   Robert Clive to Thomas Rous, April 17, 1765, quoted in Forrest, *The Life of Lord Clive,* 2: 257.
95   Robert Clive to John Carnac, May 6, 1765, quoted in John Malcolm, *The Life of Robert, Lord Clive* (London: J. Murray, 1836), 2: 322.
96   Robert Clive to Thomas Rous, April 17, 1765, quoted in Forrest, *The Life of Lord Clive,* 2: 257.
97   Thomas C. Barrow, "A Project for Imperial Reform: 'Hints Respecting the Settlement for our American Provinces,' 1763," *William & Mary Quarterly*, 3rd Series, 24 (January 1967): 122.
98   Robert Clive to William Pitt, January 7, 1759, quoted in Forrest, *The Life of Lord Clive*, 2: Appendix, 413–414.
99   Robert Clive to George Grenville, September 30, 1765, BL Microfilm, RP/460, 1, Letters from Robert Clive to George Grenville, 1763–1769.
100   Barrow, "A Project for Imperial Reform," 122.

3

Forging the Laws of Subjecthood after 1763

Hannah Weiss Muller

"Our loving subjects"

When the Treaty of Paris brought an end to global conflict in February 1763, it also foreshadowed the central role that subjecthood would play in the decade after the Seven Years' War. Explicitly framing the agreement as one between monarchs, their "Britannick, Most Christian, Catholick, and Most Faithful Majesties" vowed that no articles would be "infringed" upon by their "respective subjects." Most importantly, George III pledged to protect freedom of worship for "his new Roman Catholic subjects," acknowledging the transfer of subjecthood from one king to another.[1] The Royal Proclamation, issued in October 1763, similarly acknowledged this vast new community of British subjects, as the king established guidelines for the "speedy settling" of new governments and addressed "our loving subjects" living throughout them.[2] Signed within seven months of each other, both the Treaty of Paris and the Royal Proclamation brought peoples of innumerable backgrounds under the aegis of British subjecthood, even as each largely failed to clarify the limits and rights associated with this newfound status.

In the decade following the publication of these influential documents, many contemporaries therefore found themselves grappling with the legal status of the populations added to the British Empire in 1763 and with the implications of subjecthood more generally. Alexander Wedderburn, who opined on the legal system in the Province of Quebec in his capacity as England's Solicitor General, observed:

> In more civilized times, when the object of war is dominion, when *subjects* and not slaves are the fruits of victory, no other right can be founded on conquest but that of regulating the political and civil government of the country, leaving to the individuals the enjoyment of their property, and all privileges not inconsistent with the security of conquest.[3]

Some of this chapter has been adapted from material that was originally published in Hannah Weiss Muller, *Subjects and Sovereign: Bonds of Belonging in the Eighteenth-Century British Empire* (New York: Oxford University Press, 2017), and is used here with permission of Oxford University Press.

His even better-known contemporary, William Murray, Lord Mansfield, had made several sweeping generalizations about new subjects in Quebec when corresponding with the prime minister a few years earlier, commenting on the injustice of abolishing the laws and customs of a conquered people.[4] Moreover, by 1774, when he was serving as Chief Justice of King's Bench, Mansfield outlined the rights of conquered peoples in a case originating in the ceded colony of Grenada. Mansfield ruled, among other things, that "conquered inhabitants once received into the conqueror's protection become subjects" and that the laws of the conquered country continued in force until they were altered by the conqueror.[5]

In their observations, both men suggested that the post-1763 British Empire differed fundamentally from its predecessor—this enlarged empire now possessed a range of new subjects whose laws and rights, however defined, merited protection. Their reflections furthermore reveal that concerns about subject status became widespread during this period and that the definition of subjecthood itself was contested. Whereas scholars have noted that the early-eighteenth-century empire was conceived of as being predominantly Protestant, commercial, maritime, and free, the British Empire of the 1760s, as Peter Marshall has observed, now also included "subject populations of Native Americans, French Canadians, and Indians, none of whom were Protestant, British, or free, according to 'British notions of freedom.'"[6] Many legal queries that arose in the 1760s and 1770s therefore related to non-British, non-Protestant, and non-white populations who had been transformed into British subjects with the territorial acquisitions of 1763. Questions about their status, duties, and precise privileges, which remained unanswered by the Treaty of Paris, only became increasingly pressing as colonial administrators sought to integrate and exercise jurisdiction over populations regarding whom there were few legal precedents.[7]

Above all, the various opinions offered by Wedderburn and Mansfield remind us that to reconstruct legal understandings of subjecthood after 1763, we must consult an array of sources. Wedderburn's observations made in his capacity as solicitor general and Mansfield's private correspondence with the prime minister are as relevant to considering subject status during this period as Mansfield's official opinion published in the *English Law Reports*. Indeed, questions about how subject status was attained and about what rights it entailed in the new colonies were frequently raised—and regularly answered—across a range of forums. Many colonial administrators joined legal practitioners in determining who was or was not a British subject and in responding to conflicts that involved subjects' rights, both of which were inherently legal and constitutional questions; their voices and interpretations often affected local outcomes far more than did the holdings of case law or the opinions of judges.

Traditional analyses of subjecthood, which have relied largely on distinctions drawn from case law alone, cannot capture the diversity of ideas that circulated relating to subject status and its associated rights. Instead, we must identify definitions that surfaced both in London and in the colonies themselves, that emerged both within and without the formal systems of courts, and that were shaped both by those familiar and unfamiliar with case law. By tracing discussions of subject status that took place outside the walls of the common law courts in the 1760s and early 1770s, we can see that the law of subjecthood was less a coherent doctrine and more a body of often-conflicting ideas and practices by which administrators sought to resolve a series of complex questions. We are able to document how the integration of new territories and peoples after 1763 simultaneously provoked an array of legal questions and was made possible by legal multiplicity.

Moreover, the presence of diverse new peoples often merely highlighted the problematic ambiguities of existing case law. Because so much about subject status remained uncertain in case law and because many legal experts and colonial administrators often operated far from the oversight of common law courts in the metropole, a range of additional interpretations of subjecthood emerged. As administrators in the far-flung colonies confronted demands made by their constituents, they were more apt to consult the treaties or instructions they had in their possession, to seek guidance from law officers of the crown who communicated with the Board of Trade,[8] or to rely on their own sense of judgment and equity, than they were to wait for cases to be brought in the courts. Through these other extra-judicial sources, we can identify some of the more practical approaches to subjecthood that operated alongside the more theoretical formulations detailed by the central judiciary. Subjecthood in the British Empire was as much justice "on the spot" as it was a body of decisions preserved in case law. And only by considering the expansive conceptions of subjecthood found in these additional avenues of law, can we begin to fully understand how colonial administrators were able to extend subjecthood to a vast range of conquered peoples.

That legal understandings of subjecthood were plural will come as no surprise to the many historians who have documented the practices of law across empires or who have traced the variety of legal arguments wielded by imperial agents in justifying their actions.[9] Indeed, legal history has helped redefine "law" so that it is not merely what is recorded in statutes and court decisions, but also includes the contributions of people who were not officially part of the legal hierarchy, the set of social struggles that often precipitated legal change, and the meanings of law in individuals' lives. Law is as much a "cacophony of many voices," an "arena of conflict within which alternative social visions contend," and a multiplicity of practices, as it is a received doctrine.[10] Legal history, when it assesses these many contexts of law, can also take into account the range of individuals who shape legal thinking and who disseminate and interpret legal doctrine.

This chapter therefore begins with an analysis of subjecthood as defined by case law and then considers both the other sources to which colonial administrators turned for legal guidance and the numerous legal ideas that shaped discussions relating to subject status. Only by broadening our conceptions of what constituted "law" during this period and by consulting the documents used, cited, and written by colonial administrators, can we accurately parse the many ideas about subject status actually in operation in the decade following the Treaty of Paris. This was an empire administered by a vast array of corporations, assemblies, governors, and secretaries of state. It was characterized by few clear lines of authority, by overlapping jurisdictions, and by extensive space for local administrators to interpret their instructions. Recent studies have detailed the stunning cultural and institutional diversity of this post-1763 empire, but few have examined the multivalent nature of its legal world, the complexity of its legal culture, or the space it allowed for competing legal opinions. By uncovering the rich legal history of subjecthood that existed at the interstices of legal rulings and everyday experience, this chapter also suggests that it was administrators' ability to recognize so many new peoples as subjects that ultimately underpinned the period's relative inclusiveness.

The silences of the law

Although the boundaries of British subjecthood were widely debated in the decade after 1763, judicial ruminations on the matter had a far longer history. Where case law was concerned, the judiciary had attempted to define subject status and to clarify the rights of subjects since at least the early seventeenth century, when the ruling handed down in *Calvin v. Smith* (1608) provided a legal basis for distinguishing between subjects and aliens. Most analyses of subjecthood begin with "Calvin's Case," as it is better known, in large part because so many subsequent legal opinions cite it as precedent. Despite my contention that critical legal discussions flourished outside the realm of case law, this landmark case nonetheless remains essential to understanding how and why multiple legal understandings of subjecthood came to coexist. Precisely because it established an inclusive but unspecific definition of subjecthood, *Calvin v. Smith* ensured that uncertainties about new subjects would prevail for centuries to come and that competing ideas about subjecthood would proliferate. More particularly, the definition of subjecthood first enunciated in 1608 was critical for two reasons after 1763: first, it lent a certain legitimacy to inclusive definitions of subjecthood that were proposed in many of the conquered and ceded colonies; and second, its failure to establish any clear rights for subjects left room for administrators in those territories to interpret subjects' rights as they saw fit. In short, Calvin's Case provided future generations with a vocabulary and set of ideas that could be wielded for radically varied purposes.

Like many court rulings, *Calvin v. Smith* formalized categories of persons that had been emerging over the centuries. Terms such as "natural-born" and "naturalized" subjects, "aliens," and "denizens" regularly appeared in both printed works and legal practice in the decades preceding Calvin's Case, but they gained significant traction only in 1608. By the early sixteenth century, for example, the alien status of foreign merchants was recognized and aliens' inability to inherit lands in England had been repeatedly confirmed.[11] Within a century, John Cowell's 1607 law dictionary defined an alien as "one born in a strange country." A subject, by contrast, was "a man born out of the land, so it be within the limits of the king's obedience, beyond the seas, or of English parents, out of the king's obedience (so the parents at the time of the birth, be of the king's allegiance) is no alien in account, but a subject to the king."[12]

The notion that subjects and aliens were both differentiated by birthplace and allegiance and defined by reference to one another was becoming more familiar to educated audiences in the years before *Calvin v. Smith*. When Coke noted that "denizens" had "acquired allegiance" and been granted privileges by the king, he referenced an already well-established procedure for denization and naturalization. Denization was granted by the monarch through letters patent and allowed the denizen to hold but not to inherit property. Only an act of Parliament, however, could naturalize a subject, putting him "in exactly the same state as if he had been born in the king's ligeance; except only that he is incapable, as well as a denizen, of being a member of the privy council, or parliament."[13] By the start of the seventeenth century, there were thus several statuses used to categorize those who owed allegiance to the monarch of England, but it was Calvin's Case that ensured that they were widely recognized and that they became part of legal precedent.

Furthermore, by the early seventeenth century, the judiciary had available several interpretations of how subjecthood was acquired. Just as the geographical boundaries of the English king's territories had changed throughout the wars of the medieval period, so too had the populations subject to the king and the legislation regarding them. By 1351, a statute known as *De Natis Ultra Mare* recognized that many English subjects might find themselves living abroad in an increasingly mobile world, and extended subjecthood to their offspring. Seventeen years later, another statute stipulated that persons born in any of the king's territories were actually subjects in England. Although still inchoate, these laws indicate that understandings of *jus sanguinis* ("right of blood") and *jus soli* ("right of soil") had emerged and begun to coexist by the mid-fourteenth century. Indeed, an earlier medieval judicial tradition of recognizing the subject status of all those born in the king's diverse dominions would be referred to in the various published reports of *Calvin v. Smith*, alongside examples of subjecthood conferred on individuals born overseas of parents who were subjects. Coke's report, in particular, noted that "the Laws of England" regarding the subject's relationship to the king were "copious," and he was keen to establish continuity with earlier statutes.[14]

Calvin v. Smith was intimately connected to lingering political and legal questions that remained unanswered in the aftermath of the Union of Crowns (1603). When Elizabeth I died without heirs, her cousin, James VI of Scotland, ascended the English throne as James I. Two kingdoms composed of separate legislatures, court systems, and established churches came to share one monarch. In the years immediately following that union, several separate committees grappled with the legal status of James's Scottish subjects, but ultimately failed to resolve the issue.[15] Many in Parliament remained bitterly divided over both whether James's Scottish subjects needed to be naturalized and whether legislative action for naturalization was even desirable. Several accounts suggest that the suits initiated in 1607 were contrived by the crown to remove the question of naturalization from Parliament and to place it in the hands of the judiciary, where a number of leading figures had already shown themselves to be sympathetic to naturalizing James's Scottish subjects.[16]

Regardless, in 1607, John and William Parkinson initiated civil suits in both the Court of King's Bench and Court of Chancery for two separate estates in England. They claimed that their charge, Robert Calvin, an infant born in Scotland after the union of the crowns, had been unjustly dispossessed of lands in England. The defendants responded that Calvin's plea was inadmissible because he was an alien and, as such, could not own freeholds in England. The defendants' plea resuscitated a fundamental legal and political question that had been contested for several years: were the *postnati*, or those born in Scotland after the English throne had descended to James, aliens or subjects? The answer to this question would then determine whether they were eligible to bring real or personal actions before the royal courts for lands within the realm of England.

As published reports of the case indicated, the matter was recognized as one of "great import and consequence," and both suits were adjourned to the Exchequer Chamber, where the Lord Chancellor and fourteen judges from the common-law courts of King's Bench, Common Pleas, and Exchequer might together consider them "according to the ancient and ordinary course of the law."[17] All but two of the fourteen justices assembled eventually concluded that the *postnati* were natural-born subjects of the king of England, meaning that they were entitled to hold property in England, a right denied to aliens, or non-subjects.[18] Sir Edward Coke's opinion in this case became the definitive statement of the applicable law, and it was repeatedly published and cited as the authoritative source of ideas about subjecthood in the centuries that followed.[19] For many legal scholars, Calvin's Case also came to represent the "first comprehensive statement in England of the law of naturalization."[20]

Perhaps more importantly, Calvin's Case offered three holdings that would enable jurists and administrators to accommodate the many new peoples and places added to the empire in 1763. First, allegiance, defined most simply as the "true and faithful obedience of the subject due to his sovereign," was declared to be an immutable birthright, one that could not be taken from him since it was an "incident inseparable to every subject." Allegiance and subjecthood were therefore available to all born within the king's dominions—regardless of religion, race, or ancestry.[21] Second, allegiance was owed to the king as a person rather than to the king as representative of the body politic. As Coke's report stated, allegiance was "due to the natural Person of the King … and it is not due to the Politick Capacity only."[22] This meant that allegiance, and correspondingly subjecthood, were not territorially bounded and were not restricted to those living within a specific kingdom. Instead, they could extend to those living in territories lying beyond the realm that were nevertheless a part of the king's dominions. This decision inaugurated a broad and inclusive definition of subjecthood: anyone born within the various dominions of the monarch of England was a natural-born subject of the king. Third, because the bond between sovereign and subjects predated the enactment of local laws and because allegiance was due to the sovereign "by law of nature," there might be a "union of ligeance" without a corresponding "union of laws."[23] Subjects did not have to be born within the ambit of the common law, and individuals who lived under a wide variety of laws might still be subject to the same monarch. This holding laid the groundwork for an allegiance and subjecthood that could transcend and embrace multiple systems of law. Calvin's Case thus established the idea that subjects of the same king might not only be spread across different political units but might also live under different systems of law.

In the century and a half following 1608, *Calvin v. Smith* and its more inclusive tenets became the sine qua non for rulings on subject status and initiated a tradition of juridical rulings on naturalization. Moreover, cases tried before the Courts of King's Bench, Exchequer, and Common Pleas, or resolved by appeals to the House of Lords and Privy Council, revealed that subject status in the expanding British Empire repeatedly surfaced as a topic of concern. In *Dutton v. Howell* (1693), for example, the judiciary insisted that when British subjects settled in the "uninhabited country" of Barbados, they carried with them the common law of England.[24] By contrast, in the cases of *Blankard v. Galdy* (1694) and *Smith v. Brown and Cooper* (1702), the courts ruled that in the "conquered territories" of both Jamaica and Virginia, the English statutes and law did not apply. British subjects who inhabited those colonies might live under laws that were not necessarily English.[25] Still other cases, like *Anonymous* (1722) and *Rex v. Cowle* (1759), which explored the differences between "conquered" and "settled" colonies, including the town of Berwick, also dealt, to some extent, with the status and rights of subjects in the overseas territories. In fact, the ruling in 1722 stated that law was the "birthright of every subject."[26] Although, as Jack Greene has noted, the question of whether common law and English law more generally followed the subject was never really resolved in the extended polities of the British Empire, the many cases that addressed these questions in the seventeenth and eighteenth centuries indicate that the judiciary consistently addressed matters of law and subjecthood.[27]

Furthermore, several well-known cases, initiated by individuals residing in the more recently added colonies, reinforced Coke's earlier notions of expansive allegiance and multiplicity of law. In *Craw v. Ramsey* (1681), the Court of King's Bench was asked whether a naturalization in Ireland would also naturalize a person in England. In its ruling, the Court affirmed the various ways in which men "born out of England may inherit in England" even if they were not the children of subjects; these included birth in one of the king's dominions, naturalization by act of Parliament, birth in the territories of a prince who held those territories as a liegeman to the monarch of England, and birth in territories controlled by the king's armies. The report concluded: "A subject born in any dominion belonging to the Crown of England is inheritable in England as well as native Englishmen. So the natural born subjects of Ireland, Guernsey, Jersey, Berwick, and all the English plantations inherit … they are born liege-men to the same king."[28] While *Craw v. Ramsey* distinguished between natural-born and naturalized subjects across the empire, the case also suggested that there were many potential paths to subjecthood available at the time. And by upholding the idea that British subjects included all those who were born in the monarch's diverse dominions, it effectively transferred Coke's ruling for England and Scotland to other territories of the expanding empire.

Another case, *Fabrigas v. Mostyn*, tried nearly a century later, extended these understandings of subjecthood to the British Mediterranean. In 1773, Anthony Fabrigas, a native of Minorca, brought an action against Lieutenant-General Mostyn in the Court of Common Pleas for having arrested, imprisoned, and deported him to Spain without proper trial. Mostyn maintained that he was justified in his actions against the seditious Fabrigas by the "ancient laws of Minorca" which had been granted to the Minorcans in 1713 despite the British conquest. The plaintiff, however, argued that he was entitled to the protection of the laws of England given that he was a "free-born subject of England." In its ruling, the Court of Common Pleas repeatedly stated that inhabitants of Minorca, "being born in Minorca since its subjection to the crown of England," were natural-born subjects. The court affirmed the principle, initially elaborated in *Calvin v. Smith*, that subject status was conferred by birth in any of the king's dominions, whether conquered or settled. The judges determined that even if British subjects lived under laws different from those in force in England—in this case "the usages and customs of Spain"—they were still allowed to sue for damages inflicted by colonial administrators in English courts and still due the broader protections of

English law.[29] Together, cases like *Craw v. Ramsey* and *Fabrigas v. Mostyn* helped to perpetuate notions of inclusive subjecthood, confirming two notable precedents set by Calvin's Case—first, that subject status was conferred by birth within the dominions and protection of the monarch of England and that its conferral did not require birth within the kingdom of England; and second, that subjects might live under a range of laws. Each of these was critical to accommodating the growing number of imperial subjects in the eighteenth century, most of whom were born outside the kingdom of England but within dominions of the crown.

As legal historians have noted, because it welcomed as subjects even those individuals born in overseas dominions of the king, Coke's conception of subjecthood, subsequently developed by other cases, gradually facilitated the idea of subjects spread across an expanding empire.[30] The definition of subjecthood in *Calvin v. Smith* theoretically permitted multiple local identities to coexist within a larger polity. Whether or not this was the intention of the justices in 1608, they had provided the intellectual and legal foundations for an empire in which *all* peoples born within the king's allegiance and dominions could claim subject status. Perhaps this is why assessments of British citizenship and nationality have often emphasized its historically inclusive tendencies.[31] Defining subjecthood based on a personal relationship to the monarch allows inhabitants who do not share common blood or culture to be legally accepted as subjects. Rieko Karatani notes, for example, that "British formal membership has always been granted in such a way as to encompass inhabitants of the global institution, that is the British Empire and Commonwealth," though she contrasts this inclusive formal membership with a less inclusive cultural sense of Britishness.[32] Even if they may identify and be identified as British subjects, these varied individuals often maintain numerous other identities. Subjects can therefore be "British subjects" in legal terms without necessarily being accepted as truly "British."

But while the inclusive holdings of *Calvin v. Smith* continued to shape understandings of subjecthood, the many questions it left unanswered were more critical to shaping the legal world after 1763. Indeed, the ambiguities of both Calvin's Case and subsequent case law encouraged many colonial officials to look elsewhere for legal clarification and provided opportunities for the emergence of divergent understandings of subjecthood in the empire. Largely the product of a specific historical moment surrounding the Union of the Crowns of Scotland and England, Calvin's Case focused on answering certain limited questions relating to the status of those born in Scotland after that union and about their rights to hold land within the kingdom of England.

As Daniel Hulsebosch makes clear, the case was more concerned with the rights of people entering England than with the rights of Englishmen emigrating elsewhere.[33] The case was largely uninterested in issues of subjecthood outside of England, not least because the overseas empire was still in its infancy in 1608, Jamestown having hardly survived its first year. Although Calvin's Case may have made possible an expansive, even imperial, definition of subjecthood, the ruling itself was relatively silent as far as the empire was concerned.[34] The judges who presided in Calvin's Case and in other cases could not, or did not, anticipate the various dilemmas that would arise as new territories were added to the empire, nor did they attempt to delineate a set of rights due what was becoming an increasingly diverse group of subjects.

More specifically, the decision in Calvin's Case left several issues unresolved that encouraged concerned parties to seek legal guidance outside the confines of the common law courts. To begin, Calvin's Case addressed the status of the *postnati*, or people born in Scotland after the Union of the Crowns, but it provided no definitive direction about the status of the *antenati*, or those Scots born before 1603. In other words, despite insisting that those born in territories that were part of the king's dominions or born within the king's allegiance were British subjects, Calvin's Case said little about the status of individuals born in territories before they had become part of the king's dominions. Did such individuals have to be formally naturalized or might naturalization occur with the cession or conquest of territory? Might this happen by treaty? Because Calvin's Case and subsequent cases were concerned with particular matters at hand, rather than with the ramifications of subjecthood for the British Empire more generally, the guidance they could provide was limited, particularly regarding the status of individuals added to the empire in 1763.

In addition, the ruling in *Calvin v. Smith* had insisted that subject status was indissoluble and permanent. The tie between subject and king was personal, due to the "natural body" of the king upon birth, and it therefore could not be severed if a territory fell into enemy hands. Coke noted that "naturalization due and vested by Birth-right, cannot by any Separation of the Crown afterward be taken away: nor he that was by Judgment of Law a natural Subject at the Time of his Birth, become an Alien by such a Matter ex post facto."[35] Whereas generations of scholars have viewed Calvin's Case as instrumental in institutionalizing a territorially expansive definition of subjecthood, the narrow focus of the 1608 ruling on the status of the *postnati* and on a population whose allegiance was unchanging, meant that it was not always relevant to questions of subject status in the territories added to the empire after 1763. If Coke's argument in *Calvin v. Smith* was applied universally to other monarchies and empires, then subjects of one king could never become subjects of another. However, the reality in the eighteenth century, as in other eras, was that territories and subjects were regularly traded between the European powers. French or Spanish subjects became British, as happened at the cession of Grenada or Florida to Britain in 1763. Nominally British subjects suddenly became French or Spanish, as was the case in 1763 when Guadeloupe and Cuba, both briefly British territories, were returned to France and Spain, respectively. There was thus a fundamental difference between case law and international diplomatic practice, and, as soon became evident, administrators needed legal guidance attuned to the realities of the postwar empire, which they often sought beyond the judiciary.

Perhaps most significantly, neither Calvin's Case nor the cases that followed substantially addressed the question of privileges due British subjects. Most of the court decisions considered here dealt with specific issues raised by individual cases, and, though the justices might opine on subjecthood, they resisted establishing any extensive set of rights possessed by British subjects residing in far-flung colonies. The rights to own freeholds in England and to sue before the English courts were affirmed in Calvin's Case and subsequently, but these were rights centered on England that were at best marginally relevant to many inhabitants of the empire.[36] Only *Christian v. Corren* (1716), which originated as an appeal from a decree in the Isle of Man, addressed the issue of additional rights for subjects residing outside England. In that case, the court confirmed that it was the "right of subjects to appeal to the sovereign to redress a wrong done to them in any court of justice"—a right of subjects that had actually already been confirmed by statute on several occasions.[37] Much as it was the subject's right to apply for justice, so too was it the "right, inseparable from the Crown, to distribute justice among his subjects," allowing them to petition even if they resided across the seas.[38]

Even when put together, these were hardly very extensive or specific rights, and none of these rulings helped clarify what subjects' rights might be in the dominions beyond the realm. Were subjects entitled to English common law and to English courts even when residing overseas? Were they required to live under a Protestant ascendancy and to subscribe to the Test, or declaration against transubstantiation, before standing for election? Were they owed any economic privileges? Were they entitled to redemption from captivity? Case law had not anticipated what would become increasingly pressing questions in the empire, and the issue of subjects' rights remained open to interpretation. Overall, evidence from the common law courts suggests that although questions of subject status were becoming decidedly imperial, identifying the unalienable rights of subjects was proving surprisingly elusive.

Requests for clarification on these contested points of law became increasingly frequent after huge swaths of territory were added to the British Empire after 1763. The incorporation of diverse new peoples and colonies meant that administrators repeatedly faced problems relating to their new subjects' rights for which there appeared to be no clear answers in case law. British governors in Grenada and Quebec were unsure, for example, of what rights to grant their so-called "new subjects"—the French Catholics who chose to remain in these territories after they were ceded to Britain and who made urgent demands about participating in local elections. Their peers in Minorca and Gibraltar repeatedly inquired as to whether they could grant protective Mediterranean Passes—generally reserved for "British subjects"—to mariners who lived in Minorca and Gibraltar and who regularly sought them. On the opposite side of the globe, judges in the Calcutta Supreme Court of Judicature wrestled with the question of whether continental European, Hindu, and Muslim inhabitants were also British subjects in the eyes of the law.[39] Case law and the ruminations of common law judges did not provide adequate guidance.

In many ways, then, case law provided the *raison d'être* for additional legal opinions about subject status. Seventeenth- and eighteenth-century law favored an expansive approach to subjecthood—marking as subjects anyone born within the king's dominions, whether within the British Isles or across the seas, and unified by their common allegiance to the English monarch. Such a definition was, in theory, favorable to accommodating the new peoples of the empire. But because the definition of subjecthood found in case law was both broad and imprecise, it could not provide adequate guidance when territories and peoples were dramatically reconfigured in 1763. Consequently, different legal understandings of subjecthood proliferated. Responding to both these absences in case law and also to questions provoked by diverse new populations, eighteenth-century officials often turned elsewhere for answers. Put simply, the ambiguities of case law left significant room for individual interpretation, and a focus on court decisions alone would obscure the many understandings of subjecthood that came to coexist after the Treaty of Paris. Only by considering the range of additional interpretations that emerged to fill the judiciary's silences is it possible to fully analyze the multivalent legal understandings of subjecthood that coexisted after 1763.

Other avenues of legal opinion

In the decade following the Seven Years' War, the common law courts continued to review cases that hinged on subject status, affirming the precedents set by Calvin's Case. Cases like *Fabrigas v. Mostyn* (1773) suggest that case law could prove to be an appropriate forum for handling questions of significance to particular colonies and that judges were sometimes well-positioned to consider the local circumstances of an outpost like Minorca. More often than not, however, colonial secretaries of state and governors could not wait for the decisions of the courts and sought more immediate and specific resolutions to the everyday problems arising in their variegated territories. Perhaps there was not necessarily a plaintiff willing to bring suit in the English courts. Perhaps the legal forum provided by the common law courts seemed too removed from the realities of day-to-day colonial life for administrators who were thousands of miles away. Regardless, eighteenth-century officials often looked beyond case law for answers, and accepted that they had significant room to interpret legal matters themselves. They turned for advice to the Board of Trade or to secretaries of state, who in turn might rely on treaties or the opinions of law officers of the crown for guidance. In these other layers of legal opinion, additional and at times more expansive perspectives on subject status emerged and were communicated to colonial governors and consuls. And it was the existence of these wide-ranging and often broadly encompassing extra-judicial interpretations that enabled colonial administrators to recognize so many of their new peoples as subjects and to accommodate their demands in the period after 1763.

The first such layer comprised international treaty articles and official instructions sent to colonial administrators from London. Because the Treaty of Paris was central to framing discussions about subject status and subjects' rights in the new territories, it deserves recognition as a key source for the evolving understandings of subjecthood in the British Empire. Copies of the Treaty of Paris were sent to administrators throughout the British world and were often cited in explaining royal concern for the "new subjects."[40] As Secretary of State Lord Egremont wrote to Governor James Murray of Quebec, "You will have seen by the Definitive Treaty, which has been already transmitted to you from my office, the particular care the King has taken of the interests of His Canadian Subjects."[41] Excerpts from the treaty were frequently enclosed with routine correspondence.[42] Governors might be instructed to apprise the inhabitants under their purview of the contents of treaty articles.[43] Likewise, many of the instructions sent to governors referenced the Treaty of Paris and reiterated its specific articles, indicating the central role the document played in governing the postwar territories and in guiding administrative practice.[44]

Administrators were not alone in relying on this treaty when contemplating the possibilities of subjecthood. Inhabitants themselves evoked it as they made claims of their monarch. The French Catholics of Grenada, for example, asserted that they were entitled to "the enjoyment of every privilege and indulgence stipulated by Capitulation and by Treaty." Several of the British Protestants on the island concurred with this statement, arguing that "by Capitulation and by Treaty," the French Catholics were entitled to "the name and to the immunities of British subjects."[45] Even letters sent to colonial governors reflected the notion that those who remained in the conquered and ceded territories had done so with the expectation of certain rights being forthcoming. In Grenada, Governor Robert Melvill was instructed that it was only "justice and sound policy" that a limited number of French Catholic subjects should be allowed to sit in the assembly and council given that they had chosen to remain in Grenada "under the faith of the Treaty of Paris, and professing the religion of the Church of Rome, the free Exercise of which is allowed by the said Treaty."[46] Because the Treaty of Paris and official instructions accompanying it were central to framing discussions about subject status and subjects' rights in the new territories, they represented a key source in the development of legal understandings of subjecthood.

Similarly, correspondence that passed between British colonial administrators throughout the Mediterranean reveals that many of them relied on royal commissions, official instructions, and treaty agreements in order to make decisions about the status of inhabitants in the outposts of Minorca and Gibraltar. The earliest instructions regarding the conquered island of Minorca, stating that the "People and Inhabitants of Our Island of Minorca are now to be looked upon as Our Natural born Subjects … and to enjoy all the benefits thereof as well as the rest of Our Subjects in Our other Dominions," were issued in 1713, and several clauses were reprinted throughout the century.[47] Moreover, the second article of the treaty concluded between Britain and Algiers in October 1716 confirmed that the inhabitants of both Minorca and Gibraltar were to be "looked upon as His Majesty's subjects in the same manner as if they had been born in any other part of Great Britain."[48] Over the course of the eighteenth century, when consuls and governors explained their decisions regarding subjecthood, they regularly cited this treaty article, among others, as a critical determinant. In his communications with the secretary of state, for example, Governor Eliott of Gibraltar enclosed copies of treaties concluded in 1716, 1751, and 1760, all of which addressed the question of whether foreigners residing in the territory should be viewed as British subjects for the purposes of trade.[49] In the hands of many administrators, then, royal instructions and treaty articles came to provide essential guidance to those making legal determinations about subject status.

A second source of legal opinions after 1763 was the reports of law officers of the crown. When colonial governors sought the advice of the Board of Trade on legal matters, their queries were often forwarded to law officers of the crown rather than to legal personnel affiliated with the common law courts. Answers to these queries came in the form of reports from advocates, attorneys, and solicitors general, which represented another important sphere for the development of ideas and references relating to subjecthood. Since the crown's law officers were responding to particular questions posed by specific colonial administrations rather than to legal cases that might present several entangled questions, they were typically better positioned to weigh the needs of a diverse empire than were the law courts. Unlike the more famous *English Law Reports*, these reports were rarely published, though the author who compiled them in 1814 noted that these opinions could be deemed of "little less authority than decided law" when they had been presented to the king or his council.[50] In these internal legal memoranda, new and at times even more expansive ideas about subject status emerged, many of which were communicated to governors and consuls and came to represent another important source for legal ideas about subjecthood after 1763.

Colonial administrators often anticipated the issues posed by unclarified status well before they became debates in the individual colonies and well before cases could have been initiated in the common law courts. At the end of 1763, several years before conflicts between British-born Protestant subjects and French-speaking Catholic subjects had reached a boiling point in Grenada, the Lords Commissioners for Trade and Plantations preemptively sought the attorney general's advice on precisely how the inhabitants of newly acquired territories were to be viewed and treated.[51] Noting that they had been born out of the allegiance of the king, the board wondered whether the French and Spanish inhabitants of Canada, Florida, and Grenada were to be considered as subjects or strangers. In 1764, the attorney general determined that these new inhabitants, "having intituled themselves to the Benefits thereof by taking the Oaths, etc., are not to be considered in the light of Aliens," and that they were entitled to the rights promised them under the Treaty.[52] The 1764 report suggested that birth within the dominions of the king, so important in Calvin's Case, was not the only criteria for determining subject status, but that choosing to remain in conquered territories and swearing oaths of allegiance might provide other paths to subjecthood.[53]

In addition, on several occasions, law officers of the crown were consulted on the particular position of Roman Catholics in the territories added to the empire in 1763. In 1765, the attorney and solicitor general jointly opined that the "Roman Catholick Subjects, residing in the Countries, ceded to his Majesty, in America, by the Definitive Treaty of Peace, are not Subject, in those Colonies, to the incapacities, disabilities, and penalties to which Roman Catholics in the Kingdom, are Subject by the Laws thereof."[54] Thus, inhabitants of the ceded colonies were classified as subjects, possessed of rights denied their co-religionists in England. A second report submitted by the king's advocate, attorney general, and solicitor general to the Privy Council in 1768 confirmed this earlier report, noting that "the several Acts of Parliament which impose disabilities and penalties upon the publick exercise of the Roman Catholicks do not extend to Canada."[55] Both of these reports conceded that the Test, a requirement for all occupants of public office in England since the 1670s and designed to render Catholics ineligible for offices of trust, was not to be extended to the colonies added in 1763. In their decisions, law officers of the crown thus proposed a differing and increasingly flexible interpretation of subjects' rights from those found in case law, even suggesting that new subjects in Grenada and Quebec had a set of rights that varied from those of subjects within the British Isles.

Occasionally, these legal opinions also addressed the related issue of what recognizing individuals as subjects might mean for administrators across the empire.

For example, in 1766, James Marriott, the advocate general, was approached to determine whether the king, consistent with the Treaty of Paris signed with Spain in 1763, might establish any kind of civil government or jurisdiction over the British subjects residing in the Bay of Honduras. He responded by explaining that if Spain's right to territory in the Bay of Honduras were sole and absolute, then the persons residing there would be Spanish subjects and could not possibly be considered British subjects. Because Spain had acknowledged by treaty that some of the inhabitants were British subjects, however, Spain's right could not be absolute. Since "such as the subject is such is the jurisdiction," British inhabitants of the region were entitled to have civil regulations made for them according to the laws of Great Britain.[56] According to Marriott, the bodies of subjects served as a kind of territorial and jurisdictional marker even in territory that had been ceded to the crown of Spain.[57] He even hinted that colonial administrators could extend the sphere of British authority and jurisdiction by acknowledging that diverse peoples were British subjects. In this particular example, the advocate general's report revealed an attention to the imperatives of colonial rule that did not have parallels in case law.

A third and final arena for the development of eighteenth-century understandings of subjecthood centered on the actions and interpretations of numerous administrators, who often operated far from metropolitan oversight and had significant latitude in making decisions about subject status. The period after the Seven Years' War, which was characterized by the rapid addition of territories and peoples without a universally accepted legal ruling about their status, was a period when local actors were particularly dynamic in generating novel interpretations of subject status. Governors and consuls, among others, often sought guidance about subjecthood, making repeated requests for copies of instructions regarding the colonies under their command and for basic information about the individuals in these territories. Occasionally, they received directions from superiors as to who was or was not a bona fide British subject. Sometimes they were given specific instructions about the rights of those under their purview. Nonetheless, the discrepancy between the information they required and that which they received was striking.[58] Frequently without handbooks or relevant precedents at hand, and often waiting to little avail for answers from London, many administrators simply took matters into their own hands, using their personal judgment about what defined subjecthood and the rights of subjects in the new territories.

In the absence of formal educational institutions or training for imperial servants in the eighteenth century and lacking clearly delineated instructions on such matters, the individual backgrounds, experiences, and biases of administrators were especially likely to shape their interpretations of subject status, just as the pressures they faced on the ground might affect their willingness to grant certain privileges to subjects. In the Atlantic colonies of Grenada and Quebec, governors were often notably receptive to the claims made by French Catholics for religious freedoms and for legal and constitutional privileges. Their reliance on these majority Catholic populations in developing and protecting these ceded colonies certainly shaped their more expansive views of subject status and of Catholics' rights. However, it is also possible that their overwhelmingly Scottish backgrounds and more intimate familiarity with the relative success of allowing the Scots to maintain their own church and laws in the aftermath of the Act of Union (1707) between England and Scotland may have shaped their relative openness to the French Catholics under their commands.

In the Mediterranean, consuls were routinely responsible for determining which individuals should be redeemed from captivity as British subjects. They frequently sent officials in London a list of individuals they had reclaimed, explaining that they had made such determinations based upon subjective factors such as who "looked" or "sounded" British, which no doubt seemed like the most equitable way to make such calculations.[59] Their decisions often had little to do with an individual's place of birth or allegiance. Moreover, the personal opinion of particular administrators might determine whether or not they chose to grant an individual the status of a bona fide British subject, as became clear in the cases of many deserters, whom not all officials felt should be redeemed from captivity. Some governors insisted on reclaiming these renegades, whereas others, perhaps feeling personally betrayed, believed that deserters had renounced their subjecthood and were no longer entitled to protections.[60] Particularly during the decade after 1763, a range of administrators drew on generally accessible but often imprecise legal ideas about subjecthood. Although many of them may have intended to uphold tenets of case and common law, they also proposed and applied new definitions of subject status, often thereby facilitating increasingly expansive and flexible notions of subjecthood.

The indeterminate legal nature of subjecthood merely enabled the ordinary biases and maneuverings of individual administrators, just as it led inhabitants throughout the empire to propose their own ideas about subjecthood. French Catholic inhabitants would assert that they were loyal British subjects throughout the 1760s, entitled to the rights of representative government and ancient laws in Grenada and Quebec, respectively. Mariners throughout the Mediterranean would write to British governors in Minorca and Gibraltar, insisting that they were subjects of the king and entitled to free trade or redemption from captivity.[61] Groups of subjects in Bengal would appeal to Parliament, arguing, among other things, that they "humbly conceived" trial by jury to be their indefeasible birthright as British subjects.[62] Throughout these colonies, various residents drew on myriad legal ideas about subject status to justify their arguments, just as administrators relied on their own sense of what constituted fair practice to formulate their policies. As both administrators and inhabitants wielded these diverse understandings of subjecthood at the local level, they were operating in an empire where the laws of subjecthood actually in effect often differed dramatically from the law of subjecthood expounded by judges.

Divergent definitions of subjecthood

In our analysis of Calvin's Case, we have seen that case law had offered an inclusive interpretation of subjecthood for all those born within the king's dominions and allegiance since the early seventeenth century. However, the British Empire that emerged from the Treaty of Paris—an empire that now included Grenada, Quebec, East and West Florida, and a growing number of provinces in India, and that referred to Native Americans, Minorcans, and Québécois as "fellow-subjects"—was shaped by legal understandings generated both within and without the courts. Despite the fact that the rulings of the central common law courts had a more recognized "force of law," it is really only by examining international treaties and official instructions, reports from attorneys and solicitors general, and the decisions of individual administrators, that we begin to understand how several divergent understandings of subjecthood emerged and were upheld across the British Empire. Indeed, outside the common law courts, subjecthood was defined even more expansively and inclusively than it had been in case law. This section therefore identifies three of the ways in which subjecthood was reimagined in these other avenues of legal opinion, suggesting that each was essential to the British Empire forged after 1763 and had important implications for administrators' abilities to legally recognize diverse populations in the new colonies.

First, unlike case law, neither treaty articles nor the opinions of law officers of the crown defined subjecthood or its privileges based exclusively on birth within the king's dominions or allegiance. In *Fabrigas v. Mostyn* (1773), judges had recognized as subjects only natives of Minorca born after the conquest of the island. This was actually a limiting ruling, and it did not unilaterally grant subject status to all inhabitants of Minorca. By contrast, treaty articles and instructions extended subject status to inhabitants who chose to remain in a territory after its conquest. In 1763, for example, inhabitants of Grenada and Quebec were allowed either to sell their estates and depart within a space of eighteen months or to remain as "new Roman Catholic subjects."[63] Indeed, the broader construction of treaties signed for Gibraltar, Minorca, Grenada, and Quebec over the course of the eighteenth century was that they granted subject status to all inhabitants, whether they had been born before or after the conquest by Britain. Because Minorca and Grenada, in particular, changed hands so frequently in the eighteenth century, and because their inhabitants repeatedly went from being foreign to British subjects, documents like treaties and royal instructions, which endorsed definitions of subjecthood that were expansive and inclusive, provided solutions not otherwise available. In these extra-judicial sources of law, where birth was not construed as the only path to belonging, British subjecthood was defined broadly such that it could accommodate the many peoples added to the continually expanding empire.

Second, although legal scholars have argued that *Calvin v. Smith* conferred a uniform subject status across the king's dominions, several of the law officers' reports challenged these assumptions and articulated a contrasting idea that British subjects' rights might vary between territories.[64] The reports drafted by the attorneys and solicitors general in both 1765 and 1768 concurred that Catholic subjects in the conquered and ceded colonies were not liable to the same penalties as Catholics elsewhere. If inhabitants of the empire were classified as subjects, they were nonetheless subjects whose rights varied from those of their co-religionists in England. The king's legal servants thus formulated a definition of subjecthood that allowed for differential rather than uniform rights: British subjects in England might have one set of rights whereas British subjects in the ceded colonies might have another. As administrators would discover, differential rights were essential to accommodating the diverse peoples of the empire. They allowed administrators to reward some inhabitants with specific privileges without worrying that these would be extended throughout the globe or constructed as the rights of subjects more universally.

Third, and perhaps most significantly in a century dominated by global war, the understanding of subjecthood that emerged outside the judiciary acknowledged that subject status might be transient. This contrasted directly with Calvin's Case, for example, which had determined that subject status was unalienable and perpetual. In the colonies, where French subjects often became British, and British subjects sometimes became Spanish, other ideas about the impermanence of subjecthood gained traction. In 1756, for example, Consul Hyde Parker indicated that Minorcans, once identified as subjects, should not be reclaimed as such since their countrymen had failed to support the British during the French capture of Minorca that same year.[65] His opinion would never have held sway had the tenets of case law been paramount. Similarly, in Calcutta, the judges of the Supreme Court determined on any number of occasions that defendants were "only temporary subjects of the King." They endorsed notions of a subjecthood that evaporated as soon as a foreign inhabitant left the settlement of Calcutta.[66] The circumstances of the empire thus prompted new assertions about subjecthood: in some territories, subjects could lose their status; in others, subjects could never renounce their allegiances. Because they could draw on a range of other legal sources, colonial administrators often ignored Cokeian notions of "indelible" subjecthood, defining subject status instead as temporary and embracing as subjects many who had once been aliens. These approaches were more attuned to the circumstances of the eighteenth-century overseas empires—where territories and peoples moved in and out of various monarchs' allegiances—and were more responsive to the realities of subject status as experienced by individuals in the British colonies.

The fact that *Calvin v. Smith* and much of subsequent case law failed adequately to explain the processes for attaining subjecthood and neglected to establish definitive rights for imperial subjects opened up possibilities. Unable to respond to many questions regarding subject status by referring to case law, administrators often looked elsewhere for legal opinions, a practice which encouraged the emergence of other, more inclusive ideas about subjecthood in the British Empire. In treaty articles, reports of law officers, and the practices of governors and consuls, subjecthood became increasingly flexible and expansive, accommodating inhabitants in the conquered and ceded territories as well as those born within the king's dominions. Coexisting, sometimes even conflicting, legal interpretations of subjecthood in turn enabled a wide range of individuals to seek recognition as British subjects. Just as many shaped legal understandings of subjecthood in the eighteenth century, so, too, would many become a legal part of the post-1763 empire.

Conclusion

By the 1760s and early 1770s, colonial administrators and individuals throughout the British Empire derived their understanding of "British subject" from a vast and sometimes contradictory array of cases, treatises, opinions, and ideas generated across the many arms of officialdom. There was not one unitary law of subjecthood for the entire British Empire. There was no uniform understanding of subjecthood passed down from the judges who ruled in *Calvin v. Smith* to subsequent generations without alteration, just as there was no centralized court or office whose determinations about subject status were effectuated systematically. Legal understandings of subjecthood were drawn from both the decisions of the central common law courts and the determinations made by individual officials across the colonies. Indeed, the wide range of interpretations touched upon here points to an empire where local administrators and judges established many different laws of subjecthood.

Both Alexander Wedderburn and Lord Mansfield recognized that subjects were the fruit of Britain's triumph in 1763. What neither man necessarily discerned at the time was that the variety of issues provoked by the transfers of territories and peoples to British control would also profoundly shape the postwar legal universe, encouraging an efflorescence of legal opinions. The inclusive definition of subjecthood found in seventeenth- and eighteenth-century cases, combined with the inadequacies and ambiguities of case law more generally, pushed many administrators to seek clarifications from sources outside the traditional judiciary. Among these other actors, many better positioned to respond to local circumstances in the colonies than were common law adjudicators in England, new and at times even more inclusive definitions of subjecthood emerged. The empire became a space where numerous ideas, practices, and individual conceptions of justice shaped the development of law. Subjecthood, rather than being unequivocally defined after 1763, remained imprecise and malleable, allowing it to be easily extended to the empire created at that time. In turn, the multivalence of its law served to accommodate the many peoples and places of this expanding empire, and ultimately helped to shape its very identity.

Notes

1   For an easily accessible published copy of the Treaty of Paris, see Adam Shortt and Arthur G. Doughty, eds., *Documents Relating to the Constitutional History of Canada, 1759–1791* (Ottawa: Printed by J. de L. Taché, 1918), 113–122. The Treaty of Paris drew on capitulations signed in Quebec, Montreal, and Grenada, among others, that pledged to regard the French Catholic inhabitants who remained as "Subjects of the King" and were viewed as legally binding. See Carolee Ruth Pollock, "His Majesty's Subjects: Political Legitimacy in Quebec, 1764–1791" (PhD diss., University of Alberta, 1996), 32, 171.

2   For a published copy of the Royal Proclamation, see Shortt and Doughty, eds., *Documents Relating to the Constitutional History of Canada*, 163–168.

3   As quoted in Philip Lawson, *The Imperial Challenge: Quebec and Britain in the Age of the American Revolution* (Buffalo: McGill-Queen's University Press, 1989), 121.

4   As quoted in Lawson, *The Imperial Challenge*, 58.

5   For an accessible version of Mansfield's decision in *Campbell v. Hall* (1774) and his propositions at large, see Shortt and Doughty, eds., *Documents Relating to the Constitutional History of Canada*, 525–526.

6   For the early-eighteenth-century conceptions of the empire, see, among others, David Armitage, *The Ideological Origins of the British Empire* (New York: Cambridge University Press, 2000). For the 1760s, see Peter Marshall, *The Making and Unmaking of Empires: Britain, India, and America, c. 1750–1783* (New York: Oxford University Press, 2005), 6–7.

7   For "The Treaty of Paris," see Shortt and Doughty, eds., *Documents Relating to the Constitutional History of Canada,* 113–122. In the eyes of many, the Treaty of Paris seemed to establish an inclusive definition of subjecthood for the inhabitants of new territories. This same agreement, however, was remarkably silent where several critical issues were concerned. Among other things, the treaty failed to clarify which laws were in effect in the new colonies and which rights, other than religious freedom, were to be accorded the conquered peoples who had become subjects.

8   The law officers of the crown included the attorney general (who was traditionally the primary representative of the sovereign in the courts), the solicitor general (who was the attorney general's deputy and assistant in all responsibilities), and the advocate general (who served as a standing advisor to the government on matters relating to questions of international, maritime, and ecclesiastical law). When the Board of Trade was established, it was allowed, by a special clause in its first commission, to call for the advice and aid of the law officers, and the attorneys, solicitors, and advocates general continued to be consulted on regular occasions. In general, the crown tapped its law officers for a range of services, from legal opinions on domestic and international law, to decisions about litigation, to advice in drafting bills proposed to Parliament. This led to the emergence of a body of legal opinions whose exact relationship to case law was not clear but whose purpose was generally to represent and protect the rights of the monarch as well as the rights of the public. See: George Chalmers, *Opinions of Eminent Lawyers on Various Points of English Jurisprudence, Chiefly Concerning the Colonies, Fisheries, and Commerce of Great Britain* (London, 1814); J. Edwards, *The Law Officers of the Crown* (London: Sweet & Maxwell, 1964); and James Oldham, *English Common Law in the Age of Mansfield* (Chapel Hill: University of North Carolina Press, 2004).

9   See, most recently, Lauren Benton and Lisa Ford, *Rage for Order: The British Empire and the Origins of International Law* (Cambridge, MA: Harvard University Press, 2016) and Tamar Herzog, *Frontiers of Possession: Spain and Portugal in Europe and the Americas* (Cambridge, MA: Harvard University Press, 2015). For the importance of local actors and imperial agents in shaping the "law" that developed in the empire, see also influential arguments made by Douglas Hay and Paul Craven, *Masters, Servants, and Magistrates in Britain and the Empire, 1562–1955* (Chapel Hill: University of North Carolina Press, 2004); and Daniel Hulsebosch, *Constituting Empire: New York and the Transformation of Constitutionalism in the Atlantic World, 1664–1830* (Chapel Hill: University of North Carolina Press, 2005).

10   For these foundational arguments, see William E. Forbath, Hendrik Hartog, and Martha Minow, "Introduction: Legal Histories from Below," *Wisconsin Law Review* 4 (1985): 765; Hendrik Hartog, "Pigs and Positivism," ibid., 934. For other important pieces, see Laura Edwards, *The People and Their Peace: Legal Culture and the Transformation of Inequality in the Post-Revolutionary South* (Chapel Hill: University of North Carolina Press, 2009); Amy Louise Erickson, "Common Law versus Common Practice: The Use of Marriage Settlements in Early Modern England," *Economic History Review* 43, no. 1 (1990): 21–39; Robert W. Gordon, "Critical Legal Histories," *Stanford Law Review* 36, nos. 1–2 (1984): 57–125; Robert W. Gordon, "Introduction: J. Willard Hurst and the Common Law Tradition in American Legal Historiography," *Law & Society Review* X, no. 1 (1975): 9–55; John Phillip Reid, *Law for the Elephant* (San Marino, CA: Huntington Library, 1997); Austin Sarat and Thomas R. Kearns, eds., *Law in Everyday Life* (Ann Arbor: University of Michigan Press, 1993); and Christopher L. Tomlins and Bruce H. Mann, *The Many Legalities of Early America* (Chapel Hill: University of North Carolina Press, 2001).

11   Keechang Kim, *Aliens in Medieval Law: The Origins of Modern Citizenship*
      (Cambridge: Cambridge University Press, 2000); Polly J. Price, "Natural Law
      and Birthright Citizenship in Calvin's Case (1608)," *Yale Journal of Law and the
      Humanities* 9 (1997): 93.
12   John Cowell, *The Interpreter: or Booke containing the signification of words wherein
      is set foorth the true meaning of all, or the most part of such words and termes, as are
      mentioned in the lawe writers, or statutes of this victorious and renowned kingdome,
      requiring any exposition or interpretation* (Cambridge: John Legate, 1607). The same
      definitions persisted in editions of *The Interpreter* that were being published well into
      the eighteenth century.
13   William Blackstone, *Commentaries on the Laws of England*, ed. Stanley N. Katz
      (Chicago, IL: University of Chicago Press, 1979), 362. Blackstone also described a
      "denizen" as a kind of "middle state" between alien and natural-born subject.
14   Sir Edward Coke, *The Seventh Part of the Reports of Sir Edward Coke* (London, 1738),
      4. Henry de Bracton's thirteenth-century treatise, which linked subject status to
      an individual's allegiance, was cited in this report. In addition, the defendants and
      plaintiffs themselves referred to Sir Thomas Littleton and to the statute of 1351.
15   Both the Commissioners of Union appointed by James I and a separate parliamentary
      committee wrestled with the legal status of James's Scottish subjects, mulling over
      various proposals for naturalization. Whereas the Commissioners declared that Scots
      born after the union, or *postnati*, ought to be considered subjects, and that Scots born
      before the union, or *antenati*, ought to be formally naturalized, a committee drawn
      from both houses of Parliament debated the issue in 1606 and decided that subjects of
      one kingdom were not necessarily subjects of the other. Perhaps in large part because
      many in Parliament were unsympathetic to a full legal union between England and
      Scotland and feared the influx of Scottish migrants, the issue remained unresolved for
      several years. For details of the commission convened, the parliamentary debates, and
      the reports produced, see Keechang Kim, "Calvin's Case (1608) and the Law of Alien
      Status," 17 (1996): 155–171; Daniel J. Hulsebosch, "The Ancient Constitution and the
      Expanding Empire: Sir Edward Coke's British Jurisprudence," *Law and History Review*
      21, no. 3 (2003): 443–445; and Price, "Natural Law and Birthright Citizenship."
16   In the account of Calvin's Case in *A Complete Collection of State Trials* (London:
      T. C. Hansard, 1816), T. B. Howell reported that after the House of Commons
      challenged the Commissioners' proposals, a decision was made to settle the point
      out of Parliament by bringing two suits. In "Natural Law and Birthright Citizenship,"
      Price asserts that most scholars agree that the case was contrived (81), just as
      Kim argues in "Calvin's Case (1608)" that the case was brought as an attempt to
      bypass Parliament (156). Price also insists that scholars should revisit the 1606
      parliamentary debates regarding naturalization because many of the ideas associated
      with 1608 were initially voiced there. Bacon, Coke, and Ellesmere had shown
      themselves willing to naturalize well before 1608 and many of the arguments they
      later published first appeared in parliamentary discussions. See "Case of the Union of
      the Realm of Scotland with England," in Howell, *A Complete Collection of State Trials*.
17   Sir Thomas Egerton, *The Speech of the Lord Chancellor of England, in the Exchequer
      Chamber, touching the Post-nati* (London: Societie of Stationers, 1609); "Speech
      of Lord Bacon as Counsel for Calvin, in the Exchequer Chamber," in Howell, *A
      Complete Collection of State Trials*, or in James Spedding, ed., *The Letters and the Life
      of Francis Bacon, including all his occasional works* (1868), 3 and 4; Coke, *The Seventh
      Part of the Reports of Sir Edward Coke*.

18 For details of the commission convened and the reports produced, see Kim, "Calvin's Case (1608)"; and Price, "Natural Law and Birthright Citizenship."

19 James H. Kettner, *The Development of American Citizenship, 1608–1870* (Chapel Hill: University of North Carolina Press, 1978), 17.

20 Price, "Natural Law and Birthright Citizenship," 83.

21 *The Seventh Part of the Reports of Sir Edward Coke,* 5. For a more recent and sustained analysis of concepts of allegiance, protection, and obedience in *Calvin v. Smith*, see Muller, *Subjects and Sovereign,* 21–28.

22 *The Seventh Part of the Reports of Sir Edward Coke,* 10. For a more detailed analysis of Calvin's Case and the theory of the king's "two bodies," see Price, "Natural Law and Birthright Citizenship." The classic study of the king's "two bodies" remains Ernst Kantorowicz, *The King's Two Bodies: A Study in Mediaeval Political Theology* (Princeton, NJ: Princeton University Press, 1957).

23 Ibid., 13–15.

24 See *Dutton v. Howell* (1693), Shower 24, 1 *English Reports* 17. Judges decided that Barbados was a "plantation or new Settlement of Englishmen by the King's Consent in an uninhabited country," which meant that settlers must abide by the same laws as England. In a non-conquered country, the common law was deemed the "birthright" of subjects who "no more abandoned the English laws than they did their Natural Allegiance, which they did not." The idea that Barbados was "uninhabited" was, of course, problematic, but based on understandings of settlement patterns at the time. When English ships reached Barbados in 1625, they found an uninhabited island. Colonists arrived shortly thereafter in 1627 to establish a settlement. The island had, however, been inhabited by various Amerindian populations in previous centuries. Many fell victim to Spanish slave-raiding expeditions or to disease (which may help explain why Spanish writers noted that the island had no indigenous peoples in the sixteenth century). See Hilary D. Beckles, *A History of Barbados: From Amerindian Settlement to Nation State* (New York: Cambridge University Press, 1990); Larry Gragg, *Englishmen Transplanted: The English Colonization of Barbados, 1627–1660* (New York: Oxford University Press, 2003); F. A. Hoyos, *Barbados: A History from the Amerindian to Independence* (London: Macmillan, 1978).

25 See *Blankard v. Galdy* (1694) 4 Mod. 222, 87 *English Reports* 359 and *Smith v. Brown and Cooper* (1702) 2 Salkeld 666, 91 *English Reports* 566. In *Smith v. Brown and Cooper*, judges, for example, determined that the laws of England did "not extend to Virginia, being a conquered country their law is what the king pleases." This then allowed the court to rule that "negroes, by the laws and statutes of Virginia, are saleable as chattels."

26 See *Anonymous* (1722) 2 P. Wms 75, 24 *English Reports* 646 and *Rex v. Cowle* (1759) 2 Burr. 834, 97 *English Reports* 587. More specifically, in 1722, the Privy Council decided that in an "uninhabited country newly found out, and inhabited by the English," subjects were to be governed by the laws of England since law is the "birthright of every subject."

27 Jack P. Greene, *Peripheries and Center: Constitutional Development in the Extended Polities of the British Empire and the United States, 1607–1788* (New York: W.W. Norton & Company, 1986).

28 *Craw v. Ramsey*, Vaughan 274, 124 *English Reports* 1072.

29 T. B. Howell, *A Complete Collection of State Trials*, 20 (London: 1816): 82–238.

30 In "The Ancient Constitution," Daniel Hulsebosch asserts that Sir Edward Coke "was on the verge of recognizing a new kind of imperial subjectship (466)." A. F. Madden demonstrates that coexisting legal systems across Gascony, Ireland, Scotland, Man, Anjou, Jersey, and Wales furnished the jurists of 1608 with precedents for discussing the rights of king and subjects and for envisioning a kind of "union in diversity." See A. F. Madden, "1066, 1776, and All That: The Relevance of Medieval Experience of 'Empire' to Later Imperial Constitutional Issues," in *Perspectives of Empire*, 9, ed. J. Flint and G. Williams (New York: Barnes and Noble Books, 1973), 19. Keechang Kim believes that the lawyers in 1608 acted deliberately and mindfully to liberate allegiance from the boundaries of the kingdom of England and its law. In "Calvin's Case (1608)," he argues that Sir Francis Bacon, then the crown's solicitor general, sought a definition of allegiance that was appropriate "for a warlike and magnanimous nation fit for empire" and that could extend the king's power beyond the shores of England (158).

31 In *Subjects, Citizens, Aliens and Others: Nationality and Immigration Law* (London: Weidenfeld & Nicolson, 1990), Ann Dummett and Andrew Nicol assert that English law's reliance on *jus soli* ("right of soil") in addition to *jus sanguinis* ("right of blood") to determine subject status is in many respects more assimilative of foreigners than laws that emphasize only *jus sanguinis*. They further claim that although there have always been "separate nationalities within the British empire there was only one name for them all: the British subject" (77).

32 Rieko Karatani, *Defining British Citizenship: Empire, Commonwealth, and Modern Britain* (Portland, OR: Frank Cass, 2003), 4.

33 Hulsebosch, *Constituting Empire*; Hulsebosch, "Ancient Constitution." England was envisioned as an "importer" rather than an "exporter" of people. The case did encourage mobility, however, because it allowed a subject born in the king's overseas territories to migrate to England and secure certain limited rights to freeholds and to sue in the common law courts when there.

34 Indeed, Coke, who had been involved with drafting the Virginia Company's original charter, made no mention of North America in his report. And although Coke mentioned Ireland, Berwick, and the Norman provinces, he did so briefly, simply noting that "all men know that they [those born in Ireland] are natural-born subjects, and capable of and inheritable to lands in England." Given that these were the early years of a renewed and intensified English settlement in Ireland, Coke's neglect of Ireland is even more striking. This was a case centered on the particular matter at hand and the repercussions of subjecthood within England rather than on the ramifications of subjecthood throughout the empire.

35 *The Seventh Part of the Reports of Sir Edward Coke*, 28.

36 This is a point made by Daniel Hulsebosch in *Constituting Empire*; see supra 34.

37 In the seventeenth century, statutes such as the 1661 Tumultuous Petitioning Act were passed, which put limits on petitions but which nonetheless confirmed the subject's right to petition. In 1689, the Bill of Rights confirmed that the subject was entitled to petition the monarch for redress.

38 *Christian v. Corren* (1716) 1 P. Wms. 329, 24 *English Reports*, 411.

39 For more on these particular cases, see Muller, *Subjects and Sovereign*.

40 As Colin Calloway notes, however, a copy of the treaty signed on February 10, 1763, did not reach the British commander-in-chief in North America until May 1763. See Colin Calloway, *The Scratch of a Pen: 1763 and the Transformation of North America* (New York: Oxford University Press, 2006), 19.

41 Letter from Egremont to Murray dated May 21, 1763, National Archives, Kew, UK (NA) CO/42/24.

42 Letter from Egremont to the commanding officer at St. Vincent dated August 13, 1763, NA CO/101/9; Egremont wrote to instruct the commanding officer of the "nullity" of certain purchases from the departing French inhabitants there, inclosing the "9th Article of the Definitive Treaty."

43 In his General Instructions dated November 3, 1763, Robert Melvill was ordered to "signify to Our Subjects under Your Government the Purport and Intent" of two articles from a seventeenth-century treaty, NA CO/102/1.

44 See, for example, the additional instructions sent to Robert Melvill and dated October 6, 1768, NA CO/102/1; Melvill is reminded that the "new subjects" in Grenada, "remaining in the said Islands, under the Faith of the Treaty of Paris … should be admitted in certain proportions … to a participation in the Executive as well as Legislative Offices of Government there."

45 Memorial of His Majesty's Adopted Subjects and Memorial of His Majesty's Natural Born Subjects attested February 14, 1766, NA CO/101/1.

46 Additional Instructions to Robert Melvill dated October 6, 1768, NA CO/102/1.

47 Instructions for our trusty and welbeloved Sr. James Wishart given at Our Court at St. James's on February 28, 1713, NA CO/389/54.

48 Copy of the Second Article of the Treaty of Peace and Commerce concluded between Great Britain and Algiers dated October 29, 1716, NA CO/91/31.

49 Letter from Eliott to Sydney dated June 25, 1784, NA CO/91/31.

50 Chalmers, *Opinions of Eminent Lawyers,* xxi–xxii.

51 I am referring here to the virulent debates that occurred in the 1760s about whether French Catholics might vote for assembly members. In 1768, the Privy Council ruled that two members of the French Catholic community might sit in the assembly and local council in an attempt to resolve the matter. This decision, however, did not stop British Protestant members from walking out of council meetings, nor did it stop the flow of angry petitions against Catholic representation and participation. For more on these debates, see Muller, *Subjects and Sovereign,* 135–151.

52 See Report of His Majesty's Attorney General dated July 27, 1764, NA CO/323/18/1, on the question whether those Subjects of the crowns of France and Spain, who remain in the ceded Countries in America, are to be considered as Aliens.

53 These were indeed widespread understandings in the 1760s. In Grenada, many inhabitants would argue that because French Catholic planters had taken oaths of allegiance, they were entitled to the rights of subjects. The Memorial of His Majesty's Adopted Subjects in the Island of Grenada attested February 14, 1766, and The Memorial of Several of His Majesty's Natural Born Subjects attested February 14, 1766, NA CO/101/1; Moreover, one of the main reasons given for removing the Acadians from Nova Scotia in 1755 had been that they had refused to swear unqualified oaths of allegiance and were not, therefore, British subjects. For more on this, see John Bartlett Brebner, *New England's Outpost: Acadia before the Conquest of Canada* (New York: Columbia, 1927); N. E. S. Griffiths, *From Migrant to Acadian: A North American Border People, 1604–1755* (Ithaca, NY: McGill-Queen's University Press, 2005); Christopher Hodson, *The Acadian Diaspora: An Eighteenth-Century History* (New York: Oxford University Press, 2012); Geoffrey Plank, *An Unsettled Conquest: The British Campaign against the Peoples of Acadia* (Philadelphia: University of Pennsylvania Press, 2001). By contrast, judges in the Calcutta Supreme Court of Judicature would argue that having taken the oaths of allegiance did not,

in fact, confer subjecthood. In the case against Francois Fairie in 1783, his attorney argued that taking the oath of allegiance did not make Fairie a British subject "for if it did, the statutes which are yearly passed to make persons denizens would never be applied for, because it would be much easier to take the oaths." The Court agreed and determined that Fairie was not a British subject. See Hyde Papers, Microfilm, National Library, Calcutta, India (HP), Reel 2—March 17, 1783. Thus, although many believed that the oaths of allegiance conferred subjecthood, this was not a universally accepted legal understanding.

54 Letter to the Lords Commissioners for Trade & Plantations dated Lincoln's Inn, June 10, 1765, signed Norton and de Grey, NA CO/42/2; this report is reproduced in many other locations, including Short and Doughty, eds., *Documents Relating to the Constitutional History of Canada.*

55 Report from Marriott to the Privy Council dated January 18, 1768, NA CO/42/7.

56 Letter from James Marriott to John Pownall in response to April 21, 1766, NA CO/123/1; letter referred to His Majesty's Advocate General from the Lords of Trade and Plantations. I am grateful to Peter Silver for having referred me to this volume of correspondence.

57 As Elizabeth Mancke has noted, the polities of Europe were often "dependent on the bodies of subjects establishing and perpetuating claims." See Elizabeth Mancke, "Sites of Sovereignty: The Body of the Subject and the Creation of Britain's Overseas Empire" (paper presented at the University of Chicago Early Modern Workshop, February 21, 2005).

58 There are, of course, many reasons for this, some related to the distance between metropole and colony, some related to the fact that other issues often preoccupied administrators in London, some related no doubt to administrative overload. Additionally, because the colonial offices themselves were not very professionally managed, gaps in knowledge were significant between administrators. The work of secretaries of state and their ability to communicate with their subordinates suffered from the fact that the correspondence of their predecessors had been treated as private and therefore not part of the administrative archive until George III ended this detrimental practice. See Hulsebosch, *Constituting Empire*, 132–136.

59 See Report of the Transactions at Algiers between the Dey & Regency & Sir Roger Curtis dated November 20, 1783, NA FO/113/3; when Sir Roger Curtis personally determined that one captive spoke English well enough to make him a legitimate object of redemption and therefore judged it "proper to require this man."

60 For example, Governor Tyrawley argued that deserters and men who had entered the foreign service were "all born the King's Subjects, though bad ones," and that regardless of their service abroad, the king did "not lose his right over them." See Letter from Tyrawley to Barrington dated February 18, 1757, NA CO/91/12; By contrast, Charles O'Hara, later appointed lieutenant-governor of Gibraltar, categorically expressed his opinion that deserters should not be redeemed from captivity. He wrote to one consul, stating that he hoped they would not be obliged to claim certain deserters, it being his opinion "that deserters should never be re-incorporated into the King's Troops, and as there is still less prospect of their becoming useful members of society in any other line of life, I think it most adviseable leaving them to their fate in foreign service, or slavery, as an example to deter others from such gross villainy and Infidelity to their legal sovereign." It is not hard to imagine that this vehement response might have been shaped by his own years of loyal military service and that he might have failed to intervene

to assist enslaved deserters despite arguments by his predecessors that deserters remained subjects of the king. See Letter from O'Hara to Logie dated November 28, 1787, Government of Gibraltar Archives, Gibraltar (GGA), Letters to Consuls and Ambassadors.

61 See, for example, Memorial of Salvador Cosino to William Blakeley dated January 31, 1754, NA CO/174/16.

62 See *The Several petitions of the British Inhabitants of Bengal, of the Governor-General and Council, and of the Court of Directors of the East India Company to Parliament* (London, 1780).

63 See Articles IV and IX of "The Treaty of Paris" in Shortt and Doughty, eds., *Documents Relating to the Constitutional History of Canada,* 113–122.

64 See, for example, William Searle Holdsworth, *A History of English Law,* 9 (London: Methuen, 1922), 80. The author summarizes: "The result of the decision was to make a uniform status for natural-born subjects, not only in England and Scotland, but also in the many lands which, in the succeeding centuries, were added to the king's dominions."

65 Letter from Parker dated August 25, 1756, NA SP/71/20.

66 See HP R4074—Volume 26—July 27, 1789; HP R4074—Volume 33—April 28, 1791; and HP R4071—Volume 13—March 22, 1792.

4

Multi-Confessional Governance: Incorporating Catholics in the British Empire, 1713–1783

Jessica L. Harland-Jacobs

The conqueror's lessons

On the night before Christmas, 1764, Lord Mansfield, the Chief Justice of England and Wales, dashed off a letter to the prime minister, George Grenville. Mansfield had just received intelligence that the government planned to introduce anti-Catholic penal laws in Quebec, which Britain had acquired by the terms of the Treaty of Paris, the year before. "Is it possible," he incredulously demanded, "that we have abolished their laws, and customs, and forms of judicature all at once, a thing never to be attempted or wished? The history of the world don't furnish an instance of so rash and unjust an act by any conqueror whatsoever: much less by the Crown of England." Mansfield drew Grenville's attention to the fact that the Mediterranean island of Minorca, ceded to Britain fifty years earlier, still retained its own laws. He apologized for interrupting the prime minister's Christmas eve dinner, but continued: "I am so startled … that I cannot help writing to you," he exclaimed. "For God's sake learn the truth of the case, and think of a speedy remedy."[1]

Two significant points are immediately apparent from Mansfield's letter. First, he clearly perceived that the British body politic was faced with a serious problem, and although he did not offer any prescription, he discerned the need for a "speedy remedy." Second, although the acquisition of Quebec and other territories in 1763 was, in terms of scale, unprecedented, Mansfield nonetheless thought it important to consult past precedents. He specifically referred Grenville to the example of Minorca and indirectly referred to Ireland, where penal laws, described by Edmund Burke as a "machine of wise and elaborate contrivance" that were designed to oppress, impoverish, and degrade the majority Catholic population, had been in place for more than seventy years, since King William III's victory over his rival, King James II, at the battle of the Boyne in 1690.[2]

Following Mansfield's lead, this chapter explores the ways in which 1763 marked an important moment in the history of British attitudes and policies regarding the king's Catholic subjects. It examines some of the experiments that were conducted and the "remedies" that were devised as the British faced the challenge of what I call "multi-confessional governance," or, the imperial acceptance of religious diversity, on an unprecedented scale. It does so in accord with Mansfield's plea to attend to both precedents—how the attitudes and policies adopted after 1763 both built on and departed from previous approaches—and future implications—how policies adopted to suit one part of the empire could reverberate in the metropole and across the entire imperial system.[3]

In the past two decades most scholars have accepted the argument advanced by Linda Colley that anti-Catholicism lay at the very root of how British identity was forged in the eighteenth century. Whether discussing policies of state, cultural constructions of nationalism, or the religious characteristics of the empire, the prevailing orthodoxy views Catholics as the foil against which Britons defined, understood, and conducted themselves.[4] What would happen, then, when a hundred thousand Catholic "new subjects" became a part of the British Empire in the aftermath of the Seven Years' War? Were these Catholics, only recently the loyal subjects of Britain's arch enemies France and Spain, to be exiled, assimilated, or accommodated? In short, could the Catholic ever become a loyal Briton?

To fully appreciate the extent to which 1763 marked a turning point, we must first examine how the British had dealt with the problem of governing Catholics earlier in the century not only in Ireland, but also in Minorca and Nova Scotia (both ceded to Britain in 1713). Minorca in particular offers an important, understudied, case of how a Protestant empire might govern Catholic subjects.[5] The second section of the chapter turns to the challenge of multi-confessional governance after 1763, first by analyzing changing developments in the British Isles and Minorca and then by focusing on two of the new colonies that entered the empire as a result of the Treaty of Paris: Quebec and Grenada. The final section of the chapter will briefly look at all of these sites in the period of the American War of Independence, which in some ways presented an opportunity for the empire's Catholic subjects to press for greater concessions from the government, but also was seen by contemporaries as a test of their mettle as loyal Britons.

My principal argument is that anti-Catholicism, while strong among ordinary Britons and colonists seeking to advance themselves and ensure their own rights during a turbulent era, was not as prevalent in the official mind of empire, as scholars have commonly assumed. Indeed, in the period between 1763 and 1783, British ministers generally sought to accommodate Catholics and the practices, functions, and personnel of their church (the focus of this chapter) in order to increase the empire's stability and productivity. In response to the increasingly complex "politics of difference" that resulted from imperial expansion in this period, religious accommodation became an important tool in Britain's "repertoire of imperial power," one that was gradually adopted to the strategic and commercial needs of the empire.[6]

Governing Catholics before 1763

While all Catholics in the British Isles labored under significant disabilities during the early eighteenth century, it was in Ireland where anti-Catholicism was most institutionalized and affected the largest number of people. After the Williamite conquest in 1691, the victorious Protestant Ascendancy erected a comprehensive set of Penal Laws designed to deny Catholics religious, political, and economic equality and keep them in their place as suspect, second-class, subjects. Recent studies of the Penal Laws have demonstrated that in practice they were unevenly enforced and that many Catholics were able to work around them. Indeed, despite the legal constraints placed upon them, a relatively prosperous and influential Catholic middling class emerged in the course of the century, particularly in fields such as medicine and trade.[7] But the fact remains that all Irish Catholics, even the prosperous, suffered disabilities and discriminations. They could not receive a Catholic education, bear arms, marry Protestants, practice law, or vote. Their priests were closely monitored and restricted in their movements and required to take the Oath of Abjuration.[8] Oath requirements (in the Test Act) were also deployed to exclude Catholics from holding public office and, as will be seen, became a tool used widely if ineffectively to manage Catholic subjects and their priests in the ceded colonies. Finally, laws that barred Catholics from buying rural property or from practicing primogeniture effectively finished the job, begun with the plantations of the previous centuries, of transferring the island's real estate into Protestant hands. By 1774, Catholics, two-thirds of the island's people, possessed only 5 percent of its land.[9]

After Ireland, the biggest population of Catholics in the early-eighteenth-century British Empire resided in Minorca. The British had captured the western Mediterranean island from Spain during the War of the Spanish Succession in 1707 and retained possession by the terms of the Treaty of Utrecht six years later. In the eighteenth century, the island was home to a population of over 16,000; they enjoyed an unusual form of elective local self-government, whose preservation was guaranteed by the terms of the treaty. Municipal councils, or "universities," were responsible primarily for regulating the island's economy, but also had the power to tax the population, petition the governor, determine quarantine regulations, and supply the garrison.[10] From 1716 on, successive British governors, who did not appreciate the challenge this system posed to their authority, would struggle constantly with the universities over a wide range of issues.

The postwar religious settlement of the island was equally complex and challenging for the British. The eleventh clause of the Treaty guaranteed Catholics in Minorca a significant degree of religious freedom, much more than that experienced by their contemporary co-religionists in Ireland. Queen Anne agreed:

> She will take care, that all the inhabitants of the said island, both ecclesiastical and secular, shall safely and peaceably enjoy all their estates and honors, and the free use of the Roman Catholic religion shall be permitted: and measures shall be taken for preserving the aforesaid religion in that island, provided the same be consistent with the civil government and laws of Great Britain.[11]

Adhering to this article, early British governors made no attempt to meddle with Minorcans' religious doctrines and practices.

The clause, however, was ambiguous when it came to church–state relations and the governance of the Minorcan Church. The Minorcans interpreted the clause to mean that they maintained their "ancient privileges" and could conduct church affairs as they had always done. Meanwhile, the British operated under the assumption that the phrase "consistent with the civil government and laws of Great Britain" (known as the "restricting clause") meant that, as in Britain, the king had final say over church affairs. William Wake, the archbishop of Canterbury at the time of Minorca's cession, recognized the ambiguity of the clause, expressing doubt about "whether by the said words of the Treaty is understood an Establishment of the Popish Religion in that Island; or only a Toleration of it."[12] When Minorcan expectations of a fully established Catholic church met with British intentions of merely tolerating Catholicism, a great deal of conflict and frustration ensued.

At first, the actual goal of British policy was not to tolerate Roman Catholicism indefinitely. In the early years of the occupation, hopes ran high that Minorcans, inspired by the example of British industry, prosperity, and morality, would willingly adopt Protestantism.[13] Archbishop Wake proposed that the government build two new Anglican churches, staffed with well-paid ministers, and a school to educate both the children of the garrison and native children in the ways of Protestantism and Britishness. He also urged the governor to demand the highest standards of conduct on the part of British soldiers, so that they might set an example for the Minorcans to emulate.[14] Meanwhile, Lieutenant Governor Richard Kane, an Ulster Presbyterian who had fought for William's Protestant cause against both James and Louis XIV before being assigned to Minorca, took steps to banish foreign priests and friars, whom he suspected of secretly conspiring with Spain.[15]

Bringing about a Minorcan reformation was clearly a strategy for the long term; in the meantime, successive British governors attempted to exert control over church governance. To do so, they necessarily challenged the authority of the Bishop of Majorca, who had overseen the Minorcan Church since the thirteenth century. For decades, the British pressed for the establishment of a separate see for Minorca, which would free the Minorcan Church from Spanish oversight.[16] Until this happened, British authorities closely monitored the Spanish bishop and his appointed vicar general on the island. Kane ordered the vicar general to submit for his approval a list of Minorcan preachers; he also required priests to take an unqualified oath of loyalty and pray in public for the royal family. When the vicar general, under the bishop's instructions, refused to abide by these regulations, Kane banished him. The governor explained that he would "serve in like manner" any remaining priests who "give uneasiness to the State," and he subsequently denied a request from the bishop himself to visit the island.[17]

Not surprisingly, this approach created an atmosphere of mutual suspicion, resentment, and confusion about who ultimately was in charge of the church. In 1721, Kane attempted to regularize church-state relations by issuing a set of decrees, based on recommendations Wake had developed at the request of the secretary of state in 1718 and Kane's own orders of 1714. The "Seventeen Decrees" obligated all priests to take the oath of allegiance, banished foreign clergy, required the superiors of religious houses to be natives of the island, restricted the powers of church courts, abolished the right to sanctuary and the Inquisition, and forbade Catholic clergy from interfering with British troops. Recalcitrant clergy were subject to banishment.[18] The Minorcan clergy refused to accept the decrees, leading to a long and bitter standoff between Kane and Catholic leaders. Meanwhile, a state of general disquiet prevailed among the people due not only to the Seventeen Articles, but also to rumors circulating that the British intended to take drastic measures to anglicize the island.[19] An impasse reached, the Minorcans sent deputies to Vienna and Rome, and the matter of Minorca's religious settlement became an issue of European diplomacy at the highest levels. The British were able to assure the Catholic powers that they did not intend to breach the eleventh article, and meanwhile the Privy Council cleared Kane of the various charges levelled against him. Yet, despite all the time it spent deliberating on Minorcan issues, it neither formally approved Kane's regulations nor instructed him to be more accommodating, leaving the matter unsettled.[20]

Relations between the British and the Minorcan Church remained acrimonious through the mid-eighteenth century, and the authorities in London basically bungled along without a clearly defined policy. It was not until 1753 that the Privy Council took decisive action on the matter of church–state relations. That year, in the wake of several ugly, public disputes between successive governors and various religious houses on the island, the Privy Council issued a ruling that expanded the governor's power over both the universities and the clergy.[21] When the Minorcans complained, Thomas Robinson, the secretary of state, reasserted the king's authority over the church and told the clergy they should be grateful for the liberties they enjoyed.[22] Meanwhile, the Minorcan Church and universities became increasingly distressed by the encouragement that both the governor and the Privy Council were giving to Orthodox Greeks who were settling on the island.[23] In the decades leading up to the Seven Years' War, therefore, if British policy toward Minorcan Catholics was one of reluctant toleration, Minorcans' own experience of the British Empire was one of frustrated expectations and constant negotiation.

On the other side of the empire, in far North America, British imperial officials encountered another sizeable Catholic population in Acadia, also ceded to Britain in 1713. Populated by nearly 2,000 descendants of seventeenth-century French settlers as well as approximately 4,600 indigenous Americans (primarily Mi'kmaq), Acadia was a complex crossroads of French, British, and native American activity during the eighteenth century.[24] Like many other colonies, it became a pawn in the struggle between the century's great powers. They competed not only for the strategically and economically important territory (it was the gateway to New France and boasted a lucrative fishery), but also for the loyalty of the French-speaking, Catholicism-practicing Acadians.

To discourage the Acadians from migrating to French territory on the other side of the Bay of Fundy, the British first adopted a stance of toleration. The Acadians were valued as they provided Nova Scotia with a much-needed European population base, an established economy, and local knowledge (especially in dyke-building). The Treaty of Utrecht guaranteed the Acadians, like the Minorcans, the free practice of their religion. Early British governors allowed priests to attend to their duties, but because they viewed them as a profound threat to their authority, they attempted to control them through the same strategies applied to priests in Ireland and Minorca (requiring oaths, keeping registries, and sending recalcitrant priests into exile).[25] Oath taking became a major bone of contention between colonial administrators and not only Catholic priests (as it was in Minorca), but also with the Acadian population as a whole. For five decades, British governors repeatedly attempted to convince or cajole the Acadians into signing an unconditional oath of allegiance, but they never achieved the level of response they desired. For their part, most Acadians preferred to maintain a position of neutrality. They fully realized their precarious position and anticipated they might once again find themselves the subjects of France. Because British authority in the region remained tentative, the Acadians had little incentive to declare themselves. Thus, as Elizabeth Mancke observes, "the conquest of Acadia proved to be an ambiguous, contested, and repeatedly renegotiated achievement."[26]

Meanwhile, the early decades of British rule in Nova Scotia were characterized, on the one hand, by rapid population growth and economic prosperity and, on the other, unresolved communal tensions. By the 1740s, the Acadian population had grown to almost 10,000 (fewer than 500 British soldiers and settlers resided permanently in the colony at this point). A primary source of produce and livestock for the region, Acadia was also experiencing significant economic growth from the 1730s.[27] While this expansion seemed to bode well for the colony's future, tensions with both the Mi'kmaq and the French remained high and regularly led to armed conflict. The close proximity of British, French, Acadians, and aboriginal peoples, each with a different vision for the future of the region, meant that peace was never fully achieved after Utrecht.[28] Indeed, when war between Britain and France broke out again in 1744, the French went on the offensive, attacking the primary settlements of Canso and Annapolis Royal. As a key imperial prize in the American theater of the War of the Austrian Succession, Acadia was plunged, once again, into war. Fighting between the British and the French, with the Acadians anxiously stuck in the middle, lasted until 1748; intermittent conflict between the British and the Mi'kmaq would continue for the next two and a half decades.[29]

British policy toward the Catholic community of Acadia underwent a decided shift toward anglicization in the years following the war. First, the British began to build a counterweight to Fortress Louisbourg, which the French had constructed on Cape Breton Island after 1713 in an attempt to check British territorial claims. The British treasury spent lavishly to establish a naval base and settlement at Halifax, in Chebucto Bay on the Atlantic coast of Nova Scotia. Governor Edward Cornwallis heavily fortified the town to protect the thousands of new British and foreign Protestant settlers who arrived in the 1750s and help to extend British authority through the region. Second, anglicization motivated the crown's policies to the colony's ecclesiastical settlement and the Acadians. The instructions issued to Cornwallis concerning religion and relations between Catholic Acadians and Protestant settlers were extensive and specific: he must refuse to allow the Bishop of Quebec to visit the colony and to exercise episcopal authority (especially his practice of excommunicating Catholics who married Protestants); he was to allot land to every Anglican schoolteacher and clergyman sent by London, as well as to Acadians who converted; and he must "give all possible encouragement" to educating Catholic children in Protestant schools and intermarriage between the French inhabitants and Protestants.[30]

British implementation of the plan to populate the colony with Protestant settlers and assimilate the Acadian population coincided with heightening concerns over the colony's security and a decreased willingness to tolerate the Acadians. Local British authorities increasingly viewed the Acadians, who continued to refuse the oath and to trade with Native Americans, as hostile actors, and they became alarmed by French military preparations and outreach to both the Acadians and the Mi'kmaq. Thus, as Britain and France drifted once again toward a full-scale war in the summer of 1755, an atmosphere of intense suspicion and competition prevailed. It was in this context that British policy toward the Catholic Acadians turned suddenly from toleration and assimilation to persecution and removal. Governor Charles Lawrence issued orders to round up and expel the colony's entire Acadian population of 14,000 men, women, and children. In late 1755 alone, almost half of the Acadians were driven from their homes and put on ships bound for British-American colonies. Other Acadians fled to French territory before they could be banished. By the war's end in 1763, only 1,500 Acadians remained in Nova Scotia. Lawrence and his contemporaries justified their action on the grounds that the Acadians by, once again, refusing to take the oath of allegiance had forfeited any claims to British subjecthood.[31]

In the aftermath of the expulsion, the British quickly erected the institutions and laws necessary to put the colony on a firmly Protestant foundation. The first legislative assembly was summoned in 1757; Catholics were refused the franchise and the ability to sit in the assembly. The assembly got to work erecting an anti-Catholic penal code: Catholics could not own land, Catholic priests were banished, and individuals who harbored priests were subject to heavy fines.[32] Meanwhile, the Church of England became the colony's officially established religion, although dissenters were given "free Liberty of Conscience" and released from taxes collected to support the established church. Catholics, on the other hand, were specifically excluded from the religious freedom the colony was then touting to attract settlers. Describing the situation in Nova Scotia on the eve of the Seven Years' War, Stephen Patterson observes that the region, "given the plural society developing in it, badly needed a cultural or intellectual framework based on accommodation and toleration, [but] neither the materials nor the creative intelligence had yet emerged to forge it."[33] This was true not only for Nova Scotia, but all parts of the growing empire.

During the first half of the eighteenth century, Catholics in both the British Isles and across the empire lived under significant legal disabilities and faced both official and popular discrimination. In some places, despite this, they might have room to maneuver and even prosper, as evidenced by the emergent Catholic middle class in Ireland and Acadia's dynamic growth during the years between 1713 and 1750. Moreover, the British tolerated the practice of Catholicism and the presence of priests, whom they monitored closely. But the prevailing attitude toward the empire's Catholics was that they were not in the king's trust: they should be restricted in their rights, kept on a very tight rein, and, if necessary, could be forcibly expelled from their lands.

Accommodating Catholics after 1763

Following the Treaty of Paris in 1763, the Catholic question acquired a new urgency as the size of the empire's Catholic population expanded significantly. George III gained about eighty thousand Catholic subjects in the ceded Caribbean islands and New France.

At the same time, the population of Ireland was beginning to grow dramatically.[34] Britain had won the war, but now it had to win the peace. In order to preserve the expanded empire and enable it to realize its full productive and commercial potential, it had to secure its possessions, both old and new. Doing so involved governing huge swaths of territory, strengthening defenses, increasing revenue, encouraging trade and settlement, and incorporating new subjects.[35] How could Britain ensure that its new Catholic subjects would not become a dangerous fifth column that might aid Louis XV, smarting from defeat, in any effort to recoup his losses? Could these new subjects become loyal, productive Britons, capable of being in the king's trust? The expanding numbers of Irish Catholics represented an untapped well of men who could fight Britain's wars, but only if they could be trusted with arms. Addressing such problems and possibilities in the wake of 1763 warranted some new thinking on the part of ministers, politicians, and colonial administrators.

The Seven Years' War marked an important turning point in the history of Irish Catholics, whose potential for loyalty was contemplated and asserted for the first time in decades.[36] Ireland had remained relatively quiet during the war. The French scuttled their invasion plans in 1759 and although gangs of "Whiteboys" had begun agitating against landlords, they neither called for nor instigated a widespread Catholic rebellion against British rule. Moreover, groups of Irish Catholics began working to redefine their community's historically antagonistic relationship with the British state. Some prominent Catholics sent addresses of loyalty to the king during the war.[37] In 1760, middle-class Catholics in Dublin formed the Catholic Committee to represent their interests and press for relief from the penal laws. The committee argued that, by restricting Catholic enterprise, the penal laws were harming the country's economy and that Catholics should "not be left incapable of promoting the general welfare and prosperity." The committee's overtures to the crown did not sit well with some of its higher-ranking members, who split off, and thereby weakened the organization. But it was periodically reactivated in subsequent decades with the goal of working within the framework of Hanoverian loyalism to improve Catholics' position.[38]

At the same time, there is evidence that domestic British attitudes toward Catholics were also changing. It had traditionally been assumed that the political loyalties of Irish Catholics lay not with the Hanoverians but with the exiled Stuarts and with Rome. By the 1760s however, the futility of the Jacobite cause was finally accepted. In 1766, upon the death of the Old Pretender, even the Vatican decided to acknowledge the legitimacy of the Hanoverian succession.[39] This made it possible not only for British Catholics to express their loyalty to the king but also for British politicians to think of them as loyal subjects. Indeed, historians have perceived a weakening of anti-Catholic sentiment on the part of English elites in this period. That British ministers and Irish Catholic leaders had begun to contemplate allowing Irish Catholics to serve openly in the army indicated a new willingness to acknowledge their credentials as loyal Britons.[40]

But while anti-Catholicism might have been ebbing among elites, it remained a potent force in British popular culture and continued to influence British ministers and governors as they developed plans for governing ceded colonies after the war. Indeed, two competing programs—accommodation and assimilation—were clearly at work, and the tension between them is evident in two key documents produced in 1763, the

Treaty of Paris and the Royal Proclamation. The treaty writers directly borrowed the ambiguous language of the Treaty of Utrecht concerning Catholic rights: George III would order "that his new Roman Catholic subjects may profess the worship of their religion according to the rites of the Roman church" assuming such worship was not repugnant to British law. The Privy Council included a similar clause in the instructions given to the governors who went out to administer the new colonies after the war and in so doing guaranteed Catholics a basic degree of toleration, if not full accommodation.[41]

Seven months later, the Royal Proclamation clearly demonstrated an impulse to anglicize the ceded colonies. The king hoped to "contribute to the speedy settling of our said new Governments" by informing his "loving Subjects" of his "Paternal Care" and his commitment to securing "the Liberties and Properties of those who are and shall become Inhabitants" of his new realms.[42] The document's establishment of a "Proclamation Line" and requirement that trade with the Native Americans be controlled from London, which caused great discontent among the colonists, are well known to students of British North American history. Somewhat less appreciated, but particularly relevant for present purposes, is the fact that the Proclamation provided for four new colonial governments to be ruled according to British custom and law. The aim of the Proclamation was to absorb and assimilate the ceded colonies into the British Empire. Whether the attempted assimilation was intended to proceed gradually, as in Minorca, or more drastically, as the Acadian precedent suggested, the goal remained an empire composed of anglicized (i.e., Protestant) colonies complete with English place names, settlement norms, legal systems, and institutions such as legislative assemblies and the established church.[43]

If an anglicized empire was the long-term vision in 1763, accommodation was the short-term strategy for governing the empire's Catholic new subjects in Minorca, Quebec, and Grenada. Indeed, in these colonies, Catholics enjoyed rights and protections that their co-religionists in the British Isles would acquire only gradually starting in the 1770s and not fully until 1829.[44] While the timing and nature of these concessions varied from colony to colony, and they were not always permanent, their formulation and implementation represent that, at least in official circles, more open conceptions of Britishness were at work after 1763.

Britain's postwar administration of Minorca got off to a rocky start, due not only to the unresolved issues that had plagued British–Minorcan relations during the first half of the century but also to the heavy-handed governing style of James Johnston.[45] With the restoration of British rule from the French in 1763, Johnston bluntly informed leaders of the universities and the church that the terms of the Treaty of Paris did not guarantee their privileges as the Treaty of Utrecht had done fifty years before, but, if they behaved well, he would consider restoring them nonetheless. Such an approach unsurprisingly prompted the Minorcans to complain to London (as well as to Madrid and Paris). The Grenville ministry's response was not to back Johnston, but rather to reprimand and order him to acknowledge to the Minorcans that the grant of privileges was unconditional and perpetual.[46] To ease Minorcans' suspicions, the Privy Council made further concessions to the universities, giving them control over quarantine policy and freedom from interference in their elections. Two years later, London was still ordering Johnston to be more conciliatory and "allay the heats that subsist at present."[47]

Johnston was also intent upon asserting his authority over the Minorcan Church, but metropolitan authorities consistently frustrated his plans and demanded he be more accommodating. Many of the privileges that Johnston had initially declared null and void pertained to the church. This naturally upset church leaders, members of the religious orders, and the laity and put them on their guard. One of Johnston's primary concerns was what he perceived as an alarming increase in the number of Catholic clergy. He proposed several ways to stop and even reverse this trend (his main target was the religious orders and especially the Franciscans), but successive secretaries of state ignored his suggestions, ordering instead that the "people [were] to be made easy by assurances that the Treaty of Utrecht will be observed with regard to Ecclesiasticks as well as Seculars."[48] Johnston also locked horns with Dr. Gabriel Roig, the vicar general who had been appointed during the French occupation and whom Johnston now sought to remove. The two men and their representatives became embroiled in bitter disputes: their battle over who controlled the island's religious infrastructure led at one point to British soldiers' forcibly occupying a church, and their contestation over church courts led Johnston to deny the request of a priest (who was suspected of robbery) for an ecclesiastical trial to avoid imprisonment in a government jail.[49]

By 1770, the Privy Council had heard enough (every time there was a dispute, both sides would appeal to London for redress), ruling that Johnston did not have the authority to interfere with the clergy's privileges. It also finally issued a decision on Johnston's overall conduct as governor. The Council did not find any wrongdoing on his part, but it did support the universities' claims to control over certain taxes and public health. Johnston, who had been recalled to London, returned to Minorca with revised orders and an urging from Secretary of State Weymouth that he would not exercise power hastily and rely instead on "Moderation, Affability & Gentleness."[50] Thus, by the early 1770s, the British had arrived at an accommodationist policy; an overzealous governor was frustrated in his intolerant policies, and the island's vested interests were assured that Minorcans' ancient rights and privileges would remain intact.

Though facing many challenges in Minorca, the colonial administration there did not confront a problem that plagued the other ceded colonies, namely, the arrival of hundreds of British-Americans who expected the colonies' new governments to follow the model of the established colonies, as per the Royal Proclamation. As "natural-born" Britons, they fully anticipated the establishment of elective legislative assemblies. But, in Grenada and especially Quebec, long-resident "new subjects" (French Canadian Catholics) vastly outnumbered the just-arrived (Anglo-Protestant) old subjects. If given the right to vote and hold office, Catholics would gain control over local governments, a prospect neither imperial officials nor old subjects were willing to countenance. Metropolitan authorities and colonial governors thus found themselves pulled in one direction by the Proclamation's and old subjects' vision of anglicized colonies and the Treaty's and the new subjects' expectation of religious accommodation and equality.

These conflicting drives were in full evidence in Quebec during, and in the years following, the war. British merchants had begun to arrive during the occupation and as their numbers increased, so did the pressure to institute English common law and representative government. The British hoped that the native French-speaking Catholic population would soon be outnumbered by a massive influx of anglophone

Protestant migrants from the South, so French-appointed judges were dismissed and the French colonial militia disbanded.[51] The requirement that all public officials subscribe to the Religious Test precluded French Canadians from holding public office. Such prohibitions caused fear and uneasiness on the part of the new subjects (and, as we have seen, of Chief Justice Mansfield, quoted above). "What would become of the general prosperity of the Colony," they asked in an address to the King in January 1765, "if those who form the principal section thereof, become incapable members of it through difference of Religion?" If they were barred from holding office, they continued, "instead of the favoured subjects of Your Majesty, we should become veritable Slaves."[52]

When the expected flood of Protestant migrants did not materialize, the British had to adapt their policy, and there was a decided shift away from efforts aimed at assimilation and proscription on the basis of religion. The shift was clearly evident in the administration of the colony's first civilian governor, James Murray. Rather than imposing English law across the board, he instituted a legal system that drew on both English and French traditions, and he permitted Catholics to serve on juries and act as barristers. He recognized French customary rights of inheritance. For fear the British mercantile interests would dominate an elected assembly, he refused to convene one, effectively keeping the colony under the martial law that had been in force since 1760, and he appointed councilors who were friendly to the French.[53]

The matter of Quebec's ecclesiastical settlement received some preliminary attention from metropolitan ministers in the years immediately following the war; political anti-Catholicism ran high among them, but imperial expansion demanded pragmatism.[54] While maintaining anglicization as the long-term goal, they realized the need for some immediate accommodation. Several memoranda in circulation demonstrate the recognition that the secular clergy would have "to continue on their usual Footing" but only under careful supervision by means of close vetting, the keeping of registries, and, if necessary, banishments.[55] As Egremont put it, the secular priests must be watched "very narrowly"; those who would "busy themselves in any civil matters" must be immediately removed.[56] While the secular clergy might be tolerated, the same memos urged an almost Henrician-style dissolution of the regular orders, or, at the very least, a gradual dying off of their numbers.[57] The same mix of accommodation and assimilation is evident in the "Plan for the Establishment of Ecclesiastical Affairs in Quebec," produced by the Board of Trade in 1765. Its strategy was to offer temporary accommodation of the Catholic Church while putting the Anglican Church on a firm foundation for the long term, thus gradually anglicizing the ecclesiastical landscape in Canada.[58]

On the ground in the colony, Murray opted for accommodation of the Catholic Church.[59] He protected and even rebuilt church property, much of which had been damaged during the war. He tolerated the male religious orders in the short term and ultimately preserved the female religious orders. Most significantly, he maintained the Catholic episcopate by agreeing, with the support of the Rockingham ministry, to allow the installation of Jean Olivier Briand as the new bishop of Quebec.[60] Such policies followed from Murray's plan to secure the loyalty of the "Ancient French," who if "indulged with a few privileges which the laws of England deny to Roman Catholics at home, would soon … become the most faithful and most useful set of men in this American empire."[61] But Murray's resistance to the anglicizing intentions of the Proclamation was unpopular with the British merchant community, who argued that by the terms of the Treaty of Paris, Catholicism was to be "only tolerated … so far as the Laws of Britain admit."[62] Murray's open-ended conception of Britishness allowed him to see Catholics as potentially loyal, and "useful" Britons, but he had gone too far in marginalizing the old subjects and was recalled to London in 1766. The status of the King's new French Canadian subjects would not be resolved for close to a decade.

As with their co-religionists to the north, King George III's new subjects on the island of Grenada were exposed to a degree of anglicization but on the whole experienced the postwar period as one of accommodation. Like Quebec, Grenada had long been a part of France's Atlantic Empire and after 1763 needed to be fit in with the new vision of an anglicized postwar British Empire. The small southern Caribbean island had a much smaller francophone population than that of New France: in 1762, Grenada contained only 3,500 white inhabitants and approximately 12,000 slaves.[63] Although the island was not as productive or developed as other French islands, Grenada's plantation economy exported lucrative commodities, and the British were eager to realize its full economic potential. The Board of Trade compiled a "Plan for the Speedy and Effectual Settling" and advertised the ceded islands to potential investors and settlers in North America and the British Isles. It did not take long for scores of old subjects to arrive on Grenada bringing their slaves with them. Even with the influx of old subjects and slaves, the island's economic future depended on the continued presence—and investment—of as many of the French new subjects as possible.[64] The terms of the island's surrender and the Treaty of Paris both allowed for the French inhabitants to remain on the island and become subjects of the British crown. Unhappy with the neglect and heavy taxes they had experienced under French rule, many accepted this invitation. They assured their new king that they were pleased to exchange the "despotic Government of France" for "the happiness and Excellence of the British Constitution" and asked him to grant them the favor "of enjoying, without distinction, every advantage of a British subject."[65]

Arriving in late 1764, the island's first civilian governor, Robert Melvill, oversaw a turbulent administration that navigated a rocky course between the conflicting imperatives of assimilation and accommodation. He followed the dictates of his instructions to form a government complete with an appointed Council and an elected House of Assembly. English became the official language of the colony, and the governor replaced all French parish, town, and street names with English ones. Like Murray in Canada and the early governors of Minorca, Melvill also optimistically believed that the new subjects wanted "to become British as far as possible" and, given time, would have no trouble subscribing to the Test. He even granted lands to some of the "poor and industrious" among them in the hope that they would bring up their children as Protestants.[66]

At the same time, Melvill instituted a rather remarkable accommodation of the Catholicism. Catholics could worship openly, and the state recognized the church's ceremonial and administrative functions (e.g., registrations of births and deaths). This meant that colonial administrators accepted the need for priests to go about their business. In the early years of the British administration, these included an Irish Dominican named Father Devenish who had gone to Grenada from St. Croix and

Father Benjamin Duhamel, a Capuchin from Martinique who had been accused of having pro-British sympathies during the war.[67] After the war, Vatican put the ceded islands under the jurisdiction of the Vicar Apostolic of London, Richard Challoner. Feeling overwhelmed by the scope of his responsibilities, he informed Rome that "we are entirely ignorant of the present state of the Catholic religion in them [the ceded islands], or what the ecclesiastical government is" and recommended that the Bishop of Quebec be given responsibility for all the English colonies in America.[68] Nevertheless, Challoner was put in charge and did what he could to oversee Duhamel, whom he appointed as his vicar general, and other priests in the ceded islands.[69] Reporting in 1778 on the death of Duhamel, he expressed frustration about the "truly deplorable" state of religion in Grenada. Yet, as deplorable as Challoner felt the condition of the Catholic Church in Grenada was, it was still in better shape than the Church of England. Melvill had attempted to follow his instructions to put it on a solid footing, but he could neither get the land commissioners to allot lands for glebes nor convince the assembly to pay ministers' salaries.[70]

Meanwhile, the assembly itself had emerged as a matter of profound communal struggle, bringing the tension between anglicization and accommodation into bold relief.[71] At issue was whether propertied new subjects enjoyed the franchise and could stand for election. The conflict dragged on for years, bedeviled the administrations of successive governors, and reached the highest levels of the British government. As Hannah Muller argues, the Grenada case presents a clear example of the emergence of "conflicting visions of subjecthood" in the aftermath of the war.[72] According to those old subjects who promoted exclusivist understandings of British subjecthood, giving Catholics the right to vote would strike "at the Root and Foundation" of the "Constitutional Law of the Mother Country."[73] Led by a Scottish planter, William Lucas, the exclusivists (or Protestant party) many of whom were also Scottish, portrayed the new subjects not as fellow Britons, but as "aliens." In their campaign to exclude them from both the franchise and the assembly, they sent petitions to London, obstructed the business of the assembly, and rejected all of Melvill's efforts to compromise. Meanwhile, the new subjects petitioned George III to confirm to them "the rights of British subjects." Presenting an inclusive conception of British subjecthood, they urged their new king "not to put much of a difference between the new and old subjects, giving them all rights, without distinction of English citizens."[74]

For their part, the empire's administrators appreciated the fact that incorporating Catholics was an empire-wide issue that required careful handling and generally supported "more flexible approaches to subjecthood."[75] On the island, Melville and his successors favored at least a limited accommodation of the new subjects. They were motivated by a desire to build the island's economy, to raise revenues, and to keep the new subjects loyal and contented. It was also necessary that Grenada's white minority present a united front against the island's huge and growing slave population.[76] Back in London, the crown lawyers who were consulted about the legal status of the new subjects observed that those in Grenada shared "the same predicament" as those in Quebec, restating a 1765 opinion that Catholics were "not subject, in those Colonies, to the Incapacities, disabilities, and Penalties, to which RCs in this Kingdom are subject by the Laws thereof."[77] And so, finally ruling on the

Grenada assembly controversy in 1768, the Privy Council recommitted to the policy of accommodating Grenada's Catholic new subjects, confirming their eligibility for election into the assembly and reserving two seats on the council and three in the assembly for Catholic representatives. Significantly, the order also exempted the new subjects from the Test; to assume "positions of trust in the island," they needed only to take an oath of allegiance to the king. (Meanwhile the governor was to tell the assembly that "a due attention ought to be had to the establishment and support of the Church of England.")[78] In a report the following year, the secretary of state described the policy of accommodation as "an essential part of … the foundation upon which the whole is built, and without which it must fall to the ground."[79]

As Melvill and his successors attempted to implement the accommodationist terms of the 1768 order in council, the battle between the two sides, and their competing conceptions of Britishness, intensified and spilled onto new fronts. Representatives of the exclusivist party protested by walking out of council meetings, resigning from judgeships and other offices, and boycotting the assembly. In their petitions and pamphlets, they attacked Catholic councilors and assemblymen arguing that "fatal consequences have resulted from the admission of French Roman Catholics into the legislature and magistracy." "Let the British constitution be restored," they pleaded; the only way to do so, they argued, was to require public officials to subscribe to the Test.[80] When the exclusivists opened a new line of attack—targeting the property and revenues of the Catholic Church on the island—the government recommitted to the policy of accommodation. In 1774 Father Duhamel and his parishioners sent memorials to the secretary of state, complaining that some Protestant tenants had begun refusing to pay their rents on glebe lands. Dartmouth ordered Governor Leybourne to look into the matter and made it clear that he would issue "necessary orders for their redress." That same year, a group of planters known as "the Scottish party" challenged the new subjects' right to their churches. They suggested that the six Catholic churches on the island be shared, appropriated, or even destroyed. Leybourne fended off this attack by sternly instructing the legislative assembly to follow the king's instructions and make provision for the construction of new Protestant churches.[81]

By 1775, as Britain's Atlantic Empire descended into disunion and war, the island's white inhabitants were not only deeply divided on the basis of religion, they also had to contend with a plague of red ants, the burning of the island's principal town of St. George, and the ever-present prospect of slave revolt. It was not at all clear whether, when their loyalty was put to the test, Grenada's Catholic new subjects would prove themselves to be true Britons or seek common cause with Britain's internal and external enemies.

Britain's difficulty, Catholics' opportunity: 1774–83

One of the many grievances the North American colonists expressed in their Declaration of Independence from Britain was the king's decision to abolish "the free System of English Laws in a neighbouring Province, establishing therein an Arbitrary government." The "neighbouring Province" to which they referred was Quebec, and the instrument by which the "tyrannical" George III had established arbitrary government there was the Quebec Act of 1774. The act built on the precedents set by Governor Murray and followed the recommendations of his successor, Guy Carleton, who was in England advising the crown on Canadian matters between 1770 and 1774. Carleton, like Murray, was not interested in catering to the colony's still small anglophone, Protestant community. Rather, keeping a close eye on wider imperial developments, and especially the prospect of conflict with the colonies to the south, he focused his energies on cultivating the loyalty of Quebec's French Catholic majority.

French Canadian elites, like their counterparts in Grenada, had expressed a willingness to become British (they too had felt abandoned by the French government after the Seven Years' War). In 1773, they sent a petition to London that demonstrated their own broad conception of Britishness, in contrast to those who believed that British and Catholic were almost a contradiction in terms. On the one hand, the new subjects humbly begged the king to reverse the anglicizing policies that had been in effect since the conquest. They asked for the re-institution of French law, landholding practices, and systems of governance, and a preservation of the position and property of the Catholic Church. But they sought more than a return to the old French colonial status quo. For they also entreated to king "to grant us, in common with your other subjects, the rights and privileges of citizens of England," including freedom of religion. To the exclusivist British merchants in Quebec, like the anglophone planters and merchants in Grenada, British subjecthood was defined by the very things the new subjects rejected: English common law, land tenure systems, mixed government, and especially Protestantism. But for the new subjects, it was the king's willingness to restore "our ancient laws, privileges, and customs" that would make them fully fledged, loyal Britons: "Then our fears will be removed, and we shall pass our lives in tranquility and happiness, and shall be always ready to sacrifice them for the glory of our prince and the good of our country."[82]

Their petition did not fall on deaf ears. As a result of growing support in the metropole for a policy of accommodation and the strategic imperative to secure Quebec as the situation in the colonies to the south grew increasingly unstable, the government worked out a modus vivendi with its new subjects and put the plan into effect via the Quebec Act. Most analysis of the act has focused on the politics behind its passage, its implications for westward expansion, the form of government (conciliar) and dual legal system it prescribed (English law for criminal matters and French civil law in other cases), or its negative reception in the southern colonies.[83] But in several other, less studied respects the Act had major implications for the status of the empire's Catholics, new and old, and for the politics of religion in the ceded colonies moving forward. First, in effect it recognized the "Religion of the Church of Rome" as the established church. In legalizing the Catholic clergy's ability to "enjoy their accustomed Dues and Rights," the Quebec Act went a step further than the treaties of Utrecht and Paris that had merely guaranteed Catholics the freedom to practice their religion under the terms of the restricting clause.[84] In this way the Quebec Act set a precedent for the colonial governments of ceded colonies that came into the empire during the Napoleonic period (e.g., Trinidad and Malta) that acknowledged the Catholic Church as the established church.[85]

Second, the Quebec Act was highly significant because it foreshadowed and set the precedent for the shift to crown colony government that would come to characterize the nineteenth-century empire. In fact, the only way the North ministry could justify Catholicism's legal establishment was to extend the state's control over the Church. It did so first by re-asserting the principle of the royal supremacy and, second, by strengthening the crown's authority (by concentrating power in the hands of the governor and his appointed council).[86] Royal instructions issued subsequently to Carleton ordered him to subordinate the bishop, control ordinations and appointments to benefices, and surveil religious communities. While Carleton, like Murray, chose a more lenient approach, he did possess ultimate authority over Quebec's ecclesiastical affairs. The Act thus instituted accommodation of Catholicism in Quebec, but it was a highly controlled and vigilant form of accommodation.[87]

Third, the legislation passed in 1774—not only for Quebec but also for Ireland— had major and lasting implications in its provision of a new oath for the King's Catholic subjects. The seventh clause of the Quebec Act states that no Catholic residing in Quebec would be required to take the oath specified in the Elizabethan Act of Supremacy. Instead, it provided a purely political oath of allegiance. Likewise, the Irish Parliament finally arrived at a way, as the title of the 1774 act put it, for "his Majesty's Subjects of whatever persuasion to testify their allegiance to him."[88] Catholics in both Ireland and Canada now had a mechanism by which they could demonstrate their loyalty and hold positions of trust. The provision of a new oath for the empire's Catholic subjects was a turning point: moving forward, as Britain incorporated more colonies with large Catholic populations during and after the Napoleonic Wars, the Quebec Act—and specifically its oath—became both a model and a frequent reference point.[89]

This groundbreaking experiment in religious accommodation in Quebec was launched at the same time that a policy of more gradual Catholic relief was being attempted in Ireland. While the pace of reform may have differed, the motivations were the same: to ensure the loyalty of a potentially rebellious Catholic population in time of war. As we have seen, Catholic relief in Ireland had been contemplated during the 1760s and the initial legislative foray toward accommodation took place with the very limited Bogland Act of 1772, but it was the exigencies of the American war that prompted substantive (if still limited) relief, not only in the form of a new oath for Catholics but also in laws affecting land ownership. The alliance of Catholic France with the rebellious American colonists, concluded in the spring of 1778, raised alarms about Ireland's strategic vulnerability (the French might invade or infiltrate Ireland in an effort to instigate a rebellion). That fall, citing Irish Catholics' "peaceful behaviour for a long series of years," the Irish Parliament passed a relief act that eased restrictions on inheritance and landholding.[90] Arguing that a hidden agenda lay behind the passage of these acts, Robert Donovan demonstrates that the need to make Catholics available for military service was a primary motivation behind the passage of relief in 1778. While the law did not explicitly legalize military service for Catholics, it targeted two groups—the clergy and landed elites—who could encourage Catholic enlistment.[91]

The proposal of a similar bill for Scotland's Catholics provoked the famous Gordon riots in London, which Linda Colley and others have cited as evidence of the persistent anti-Catholicism that characterized British identity. But while popular prejudice and outrage were no doubt significant (mobs raged uncontrolled in London for a week and the homes of the legislation's supporters, including Chief Justice Mansfield, were attacked), the Irish and English acts remained in force and set the stage for further reforms. Subsequent measures enacted by the Irish Parliament in 1782 allowed Catholics to purchase land, removed the penalties aimed at the Catholic clergy, and permitted the operation of schools by Catholics who had sworn allegiance to the crown. That said, the provision of relief stopped well short of fully emancipating Catholics—they still could not vote, practice law, attend Trinity College, establish a seminary, or hold public office. Restrictions on public Catholic worship remained in place. While a nearly total accommodation was deemed appropriate for Quebec's Catholics (who lived on the other side of the Atlantic and who vastly outnumbered the colony's Protestant old subjects), much more limited concessions were offered to Catholics in Ireland. They were enough to get Catholics into the army and keep them loyal, yet not too much to threaten the Ascendancy's hold on power.

But even while the tide was gradually turning toward accommodation in Ireland and Quebec, its course was reversed in Grenada, as Governor George Macartney would soon discover. A member of the Anglo-Irish gentry who had been educated at Trinity College and trained for the bar in London, Macartney had already served as envoy to Russia and Chief Secretary of Ireland. It did not take long after arriving in Grenada for him to realize the extreme divisiveness of the society in his charge. He was particularly appalled by the Protestant party's "rancorous … hatred against the Catholic religion" and especially its deep suspicion and fear of French-speaking, Catholic, free blacks. Like his predecessors, Macartney rejected their attempts to introduce anti-Catholic laws and policies.[92]

Given that he arrived on the island after the outbreak of war, Lord Macartney naturally made defense his first priority. But the island's defenses, not surprisingly, had long been a bone of contention. Governor Fitzmaurice had reported to Hillsborough in 1771 that "the new (French) subjects had not only declined to enter into Associations for their better security [militias], but even refused to concur with the English inhabitants in petitioning His Majesty for an augmentation of the garrison."[93] The feeling that the new subjects could not be trusted was widespread, especially among those who continued to hold narrow conceptions of Britishness. Macartney hoped that a militia composed of both old and new subjects would help ease confessional tensions, which he believed were especially aggravated by the island's Scottish planters. But his plan to use the militia "to reconcile the different parties to one another" did not work out as intended. In fact, it had the opposite effect. About 1,000 men responded to his summoning of the militia in December 1778 when he received intelligence of an imminent invasion. Macartney's encounters with the new subjects among them led him to the conclusion that "the French of every denomination and colour are totally disaffected and, according to the best of my observation, incapable of any sincere attachment to us."[94] In any case, it was too late. In July 1779, a French fleet under the command of the Comte d'Estaing landed the 2,000-man Irish brigade of the French Army upon the island. Macartney was captured and surrendered the island to the French.

Across the empire, James Murray, late of Quebec and now in charge of Minorca, was strengthening his island's defenses and desperately hoping the Catholic subjects in his charge would offer their support against Britain's enemies. Perhaps not surprisingly given Murray's approach to governing Quebec, he had developed a reputation for overindulging Catholic interests. According to historians of Minorca, he was "eager to use his experiences in Canada to try to conciliate the Minorcans"; he told Secretary of State Rochford he was working "to prevent future troubles and difficulties from arising" and before leaving England to go to Minorca had been encouraged by the king to reach a settlement with the universities.[95] For example, after ordering the relocation of a town for strategic reasons, he encouraged British and Hanoverian officers to raise the funds necessary to rebuild one of the churches on the island. He reported home that such "an instance of generosity" had made "a very happy impression on the minds of the Kings Minorqueen subjects."[96]

But Murray made little headway in this regard, and he was soon complaining about how difficult it was "for a soldier [himself] to combate [*sic*] with Ignorant People, assisted by the chicanery of Lawyers, & influenced by the Artifice of the Roman Catholic Preisthood [*sic*]." The only solution, he concluded, was to enact extensive reforms.[97] Metropolitan authorities might agree that the island desperately required constitutional reform and wish that they had greater control over the church, but they were not about to undertake this task in the midst of a war. Murray also became preoccupied by wartime exigencies. In order to fortify the island's defenses and ensure adequate supplies of oil and wood, he enacted emergency measures that met with resistance from Minorcans. The universities once again sent representatives to London, but the Privy Council backed Murray on the grounds that the island's defense trumped all other considerations. Thus, when the Spanish–French invasion finally came in 1781, the majority of Minorcans did little to assist the British and were ambivalent, if not grateful, when the island was granted to Spain by the terms of the peace treaty of 1783.[98]

True confessions

The policies of accommodation adopted in the wake of the Seven Years' War were maintained in some parts of the empire and abandoned in others, with important implications for subsequent developments. The case of Quebec presents an example of thorough and sustained, if vigilant accommodation. The policy was instituted because Catholics vastly outnumbered Protestants and the colony's first governors sought to keep the new subjects loyal to the empire, especially as relations with the colonies to the south deteriorated. The policy remained intact because the governor held the reins of power and Lord North's government had the temerity to pass a controversial law that many of its opponents argued established Popery and despotism in the midst of a Protestant empire of liberty. In the aftermath of the American War, additional legislation further solidified accommodation of Roman Catholicism in Quebec, and Catholics in Nova Scotia were granted relief in 1783.[99]

In Minorca, British policy generally trended toward accommodation, but anti-Catholicism was never very far beneath the surface, especially during Johnston's tenure as lieutenant governor. Tension resulting from conflicting interpretations of the 11th article of the Treaty of Utrecht prevented the island's complete and permanent incorporation into the empire. The Minorcan clergy expected the state to give the church its total support; the British, while instituting a policy of tolerating multiple religious communities and taking many measures to preserve the Catholic Church, stopped short of complete establishment. In so doing, they failed to convince Minorcans that being British was in their best interest, and Britain's hold over the island, while lasting for much of the century, was in the end precarious. Minorca was ultimately returned to Spain in 1802 with little to no protest from the Minorcans themselves.

The cases of Ireland and Grenada suggest that the consequences of either delaying or abandoning accommodation could be, from the imperial perspective, disastrous. In Ireland, the 1778 Catholic Relief Act was followed by another relief act in 1792, passed once again in a time of war and seen as a way to keep Catholics quiet and hopefully help to swell the ranks of the army. Pitt viewed complete emancipation as a measure essential to the security of the realm and almost realized its passage, but was foiled by the king himself. Ultimately, the decision to defer full emancipation was one factor that helped radicalize Irish politics in the mid-1790s and led to the outbreak of the United Irish Rebellion in 1798. Though swiftly and effectively put down by the British, the rebellion rocked the kingdoms to their core and resulted in an entirely new constitutional arrangement between Britain and Ireland.[100]

Finally, in Grenada, the crown's experiment in accommodation was, in the period after the American War, abandoned. The 1780s witnessed a systematic campaign against Catholics. While in the past the governors had served as a check on the stridency of the anti-Catholic party, by this point, they aligned themselves with the old subjects and displayed little sympathy for the new. Likewise, the Privy Council, deciding in 1793 to return to the assimilationist dictates of the Royal Proclamation of 1763, "invalidated all subsequent concessions to new subjects." Notably, it argued that Catholics in Grenada should be treated as Catholics in Britain and not as in Canada.[101] The turn away from accommodation was a major cause of a rebellion that engulfed the island in 1795. Led by a free mulatto planter and Catholic, Julien Fédon, the rebels embraced the opportunity created by the turmoil of the French Revolution to take a stand against the old subjects.[102] Fédon and his co-conspirators captured and killed several British planters including the governor. It took a major show of force on the part of the British to regain control of the island.

Examining the intersecting histories of Catholics' experiences across the British Empire in the aftermath of 1763 suggests some important conclusions. First, while anti-Catholicism was certainly prevalent and powerful in the eighteenth-century empire, it was not all pervasive. Rather than over-emphasizing the anti-Catholic basis of the British state and British identity, we might more usefully think in terms of a spectrum of attitudes and policies toward Catholics. The spectrum ranged from complete accommodation (with an officially established church) to violent persecution (often resulting in loss of life and property).[103] In between the extremes was a complex intermixing of the two; it was this intermixture that characterized most Catholics' experience of life in the eighteenth-century British Empire.

Second, the period after 1763 witnessed a significant decline in official anti-Catholicism, as the British attempted various experiments in accommodation in the ceded colonies. Accommodation was, first and foremost, a policy adopted for reasons of pragmatism.[104] In a time of intense imperial rivalry, Catholic new subjects were accommodated in the hope that they would remain loyal to their new monarch and contribute to their adopted nation's security and prosperity. At times, especially in the immediate aftermath of the Seven Years' War, it was hoped that accommodation was a temporary policy; anglicization, whether by the new subjects' ultimately adopting superior British ways or by an overwhelming influx of old subjects, remained the long-term goal. In these cases, accommodationist policies could be based in anti-Catholicism. But eventually accommodation came to be seen as a rational end, and not just a pragmatic means, as it formed the basis of policies adopted to deal with the challenges of confessional governance in colonies like Trinidad gained after the Napoleonic Wars.

Third, examining the post-1763 Catholic "question" in multiple imperial sites reveals competing conceptions of Britishness, with varying degrees of anti-Catholicism, at work. In the 1760s and 1770s, as we have seen, more open conceptions of British citizenship on the part of officials butted up against popular, exclusivist conceptions of Britishness. Old subjects in Quebec and Grenada, jealously guarding their opportunities for wealth accumulation, argued that only natural-born, Protestant Britons could be trusted to carry on the trade and governance of the British Empire. Meanwhile, colonial officials, anxious about the departure of colonists and seeking stability after seven years of war, viewed Catholics as quite eligible for British citizenship, as did the new subjects themselves. In this view, confessional identity was less significant in defining citizenship in the colonies than one's willingness to express loyalty to the monarch and ability to contribute to the expansion of British wealth. Thus, it seems that for an increasing number of imperial Britons, the ideologies of patriotism and capitalism, not militant Protestantism, were fast becoming the "confessions" underlying national identity in this period.

Notes

1   Mansfield to Grenville, December 24, 1764, in Jane Samson ed., *The British Empire* (Oxford: Oxford University Press, 2001), 84–85.

2   *Edmund Burke: Selected Writings and Speeches*, ed. Peter J. Stanlis (New Brunswick, NJ: Transaction Publishers, 2009), 319.

3   Traditionally, historians have focused on Catholics and their governance in individual colonies. For recent exceptions that put this issue of the ceded colonies' incorporation into a broad imperial perspective, see P. J. Marshall, *The Making and Unmaking of Empires: Britain, India, and America, c. 1750–1783* (Oxford: Oxford University Press, 2005); Stephen Conway, "The Consequences of the Conquest: Quebec and British Politics, 1760–1774," in *Revisiting 1759: The Conquest of Canada in Historical Perspective*, ed. Phillip Buckner and John G. Reid (Toronto: University of Toronto Press, 2012), 141–165; Hannah Weiss Muller, *Subjects and Sovereign: Bonds of Belonging in the Eighteenth-Century Empire* (New York: Oxford University Press, 2017).

4   Linda Colley, *Britons: Forging the Nation, 1707–1837* (New Haven, CT: Yale
      University Press, 1992); David Armitage, *Ideological Origins of the British Empire*
      (Cambridge, UK: Cambridge University Press, 2000); Carla Gardina Pestana,
      Protestant Empire: Religion and the Making of the British Atlantic World (Philadelphia:
      University of Pennsylvania Press, 2009).

5   Minorca has been overlooked by most historians of the British Empire, except
      Desmond Gregory, *Minorca: The Illusory Prize* (Cranbury, NJ: Associated University
      Presses, 1990); Linda Colley, *Captives: Britain, Empire and the World, 1600–1850*
      (New York: Random House, 2004); and Muller, *Subjects and Sovereign.*

6   J. Burbank and F. Cooper, *Empires in World History* (Princeton, NJ: Princeton
      University Press, 2010), 12–13. The British did not maintain accommodation as
      a policy across the board during the Age of Revolution that followed the events
      examined here, but it did become a defining feature of the British Empire during
      and after the Napoleonic Wars. See Harland-Jacobs, "Incorporating the King's New
      Subjects: Accommodation and Anti-Catholicism in the British Empire, 1763–
      1815," *Journal of Religious History* 39, no. 2 (June 2015): 203–223.

7   For a recent assessment, see Thomas Bartlett, "The penal laws against Irish Catholics:
      were they too good for them?" in *Irish Catholic Identities,* ed. Oliver P. Rafferty
      (Manchester: Manchester University Press, 2013), 154–168.

8   The Act for Registering Popish Clergy (1703) required registration with the
      authorities and confined priests to specific counties while the "Amending Act" (1709)
      ordered registered priests to take oaths abjuring the Stuart claim.

9   R. F. Foster, *Modern Ireland* (New York: Penguin Press, 1989), 211. Anti-Catholic
      penal laws were also instituted in the Leeward Islands and in Nova Scotia during the
      eighteenth century (see below).

10   Gregory, *Minorca,* 45–47. See also David Donaldson, "Britain and Menorca in the
      Eighteenth Century" (PhD diss., Open University, 1994).

11   From the text of the Treaty of Utrecht, en.wikisource.org

12   Undated note, Papers of William Wake (hereafter: Wake Papers) Reel 35, Institute
      of Historical Research, University of London, London, UK. The term "restricting
      clause" was used at the time. See Paul Mascarene to Bishop of Quebec, December 2,
      1742 in Thomas Akins, ed., *Selections from the Public Documents of the Province of
      Nova Scotia* (Halifax: Charles Annand, 1869), 122–123.

13   Gregory, *Minorca,* 109.

14   William Wake, "The English Church in Minorca," n.d. [1718], Wake Papers, Reel
      35. Wake also recommended keeping a register of Catholic priests, not replacing
      them as they died, requiring all families to keep a copy of the New Testament and
      the Book of Common, in Spanish, in their homes, and banning various Catholic
      practices.

15   Orders Kane issued in 1714 banned foreign missionaries. In 1715 he expelled
      the rector of Mahon, whom he accused of being a "faithfull Agent" of Spain and
      subsequently "several Augustin Fryers," whom he described as "the plague of this
      place." Kane to Bubb, May 11 and 22, 1716, British Library, London, UK (BL)
      Egerton MS 2171 357. See Gregory, *Minorca,* 113–114, and Donaldson, "Britain and
      Menorca," 203–205.

16   Kane to Bubb, July 6, 1716, BL Egerton MS 2172 115.

17   Gregory, *Minorca,* 113–114; Kane to Bubb, July 6, 1716, BL Egerton MS 2172 115;
      Bruce Laurie, *Life of Richard Kane: Britain's First Lieutenant-Governor of Minorca*
      (Rutherford, NJ: Fairleigh Dickinson University Press, 1994), 202–203.

18   Memorial of Lord Carpenter and Lt Governor Kane to the King in Council [includes
     the 17 Articles and Wake's recommendations], 1730, BL Add MS 35885 161–163;
     Gregory, *Minorca*, 118–120; Kane to Vicar General, May 17, 1714, summarized in
     Donaldson, "Britain and Menorca," 203.
19   In December, Kane found it necessary to issue a series of proclamations that the king
     had no intention of obstructing the free exercise of the Catholic religion. See Kane to
     the King, December 1721, Wake Papers, Reel 35.
20   Gregory, *Minorca*, 118–121; Laurie, *Life of Richard Kane*, 218–223.
21   Order in Council, August 11, 1753, National Archives, Kew, UK (NA) CO/174/19
     2–5; Instructions to Tyrawley, October 8, 1753, NA CO/174/16 175, in Gregory,
     Minorca 128. For an analysis of Minorca's military governors as "powerful and
     uncompromising imperialists" in this period, see Geoffrey Plank, *Rebellion and
     Savagery: The Jacobite Rising of 1745 and the British Empire* (Philadelphia: University
     of Pennsylvania Press, 2015), chapter 5.
22   Brief Heads of the Conference between Robinson and the Agents of the Island of
     Minorca, 1754, NA CO/174/1 23–29.
23   F. H. Marshall, "A Greek Community in Minorca," *The Slavonic and East European
     Review* XI (July 1937), 100–107; Muller, *Subjects and Sovereign*, 89–90.
24   John Reid et al., *The "Conquest" of Acadia, 1710: Imperial, Colonial, and Aboriginal
     Constructions* (Toronto: University of Toronto Press, 2004), ix.
25   See for example, Armstrong correspondence and council minutes in Akins, ed.,
     Selections, 62–106, and *Calendar of State Papers, Colonial, America and West Indies*
     42 [1735–36] (London: Her Majesty's Stationary Office, 1953), 462. For the reasons
     behind British suspicions and the influence of priests on the Acadians, see Naomi
     Griffiths, *From Migrant to Acadian: A North American Border People, 1604–1755*
     (Montreal: McGill-Queens University Press, 2005), 329–331. For the status of
     the Catholic Church more generally, see also Peter Doll, *Revolution, Religion,
     and National Identity: Imperial Anglicanism in British North America, 1745–1795*
     (Madison, WI: Fairleigh Dickinson University Press, 2000), chapter 1.
26   Elizabeth Mancke, "Global Processes to Continental Strategies," in *Canada and the
     British Empire*, ed. Phillip Buckner (Oxford: Oxford University Press, 2010), 27.
27   George Rawlyk, "Cod, Louisbourg, and the Acadians," in *The Atlantic Region to
     Confederation*, ed. Phillip Buckner and John Reid (Toronto: University of Toronto
     Press, 1994), 108, 117–120.
28   Mancke, "Global Processes to Continental Strategies," 28. On communal interactions
     and the elusive nature of sovereignty in this period, see Jeffers Lennox, "A Time and
     a Place: The Geography of British, French, and Aboriginal Interactions in Early Nova
     Scotia, 1726–44," *The William & Mary Quarterly*, 3rd Series, 72 (July 2015): 423–460.
29   See Stephen Patterson, "Colonial Wars and Aboriginal Peoples," chapter 7 in Buckner
     and Reid, eds., *The Atlantic Region to Confederation*.
30   Leonard Labaree, ed., *Royal Instructions to British Colonial Governors, 1670–1776* (2
     volumes, New York: Octagon Books, 1967), 2: 498–499.
31   See J. M. Faragher, *A Great and Noble Scheme: The Tragic Story of the Expulsion of
     the French Acadians from Their American Homeland* (New York: Norton, 2005);
     Christopher Hodson, *The Acadian Diaspora: An Eighteenth-Century History* (New
     York: Oxford University Press, 2012); A. Vasquez-Parra, "Les empires français et
     anglais due xviie siècle face aux Acadiens," *Revue Historique* 1 (2018): 59–98.
32   Minute of Council, January 3, 1757, in Akins, *Selections*, 718–722; An Act for
     Confirming Titles to Land and Quieting Possessions; An Act for the Establishment

of Religious Publick Worship in this Province, and for Suppressing of Popery, NA CO/219/7.

33 Patterson, "Colonial Wars and Aboriginal Peoples," 154.

34 Ian Steele, "The Anointed, the Appointed, and the Elected," in *The Oxford History of the British Empire, The Eighteenth-Century* [Volume 2], ed. P. J. Marshall (New York: Oxford University Press, 2001), 122–123; Stuart Daultrey et. al., "Eighteenth-Century Irish Population: New Perspectives from Old Sources," *Journal of Economic History* 41 (September 1981): 624.

35 See Marshall, *The Making and Unmaking of Empires,* chapter 6.

36 For the reasons behind this shift, see Thomas Bartlett, *Ireland: A History* (Cambridge, UK: Cambridge University Press, 2010), 167–170.

37 James Kelly, entry for John Curry, in *Oxford Dictionary of National Biography* online edition.

38 S. J. Connolly, ed., *Oxford Companion to Irish History* (Oxford: Oxford University Press, 1998), 74; Kelly, entry for John Curry, *Oxford Dictionary of National Biography* online edition; petition quoted in R. B. McDowell, *Ireland in the Age of Imperialism and Revolution* (Oxford: Clarendon Press, 1979), 186.

39 For a recent argument on the "converging interests" of the papacy and the British in this period, see Stella Fletcher, *The Popes and Britain: A History of Rule, Rupture, and Reconciliation* (London: I. B. Tauris, 2017).

40 Colin Haydon, *Anti-Catholicism in Eighteenth-Century England* (Manchester: Manchester University Press, 1993), chapter 5; Stephen Conway, "War, Imperial Expansion and Religious Developments in Mid-Eighteenth-Century Britain and Ireland," *War in History* 11, no. 2 (2004): 134–139; Robert Kent Donovan, "The Military Origins of the Roman Catholic Relief Act Programme of 1778," *The Historical Journal* 28, no. 1 (1985): 92.

41 Text of the Treaty of Paris, February 1763, Avalon.yale.edu; Labaree, *Royal Instructions* 2: 496.

42 Text of the Royal Proclamation, October 7, 1763, Avalon.yale.edu

43 The impulse to assimilate the new colonies to British norms is also evidenced by the official encouragement given to the migration of British subjects. See "Plan for the speedy and effectual settlement of HMs Islands of Grenada," March 26, 1764, NA PC/2/110 335–46; Royal Proclamation, March 26, 1764, *The London Gazette*, March 24–27, 1764.

44 For evidence of accommodation in the colonies' surrender terms, the granting of rights of new subjects, and approaches to the Catholic hierarchy and religious orders, see Harland-Jacobs, "Incorporating," 208–212.

45 For details on the Johnston administration, see Gregory, *Minorca,* 75–84, 129–32 and Donaldson, "Britain and Menorca," 164–172, 241–246.

46 Johnston to Halifax, October 13, 1763, NA CO/174/19 7 and enclosures in Johnston to Halifax, December 16, 1763, CO 174/19 8; Halifax to Johnston, December 30, 1763, NA CO/174/19 13; "Points relating to Minorca," nd [1767], NA CO/174/1 49–64.

47 Order in Council, March 22, 1766, NA CO/174/4 15 and Shelburne to Johnston, July 8, 1768, NA CO/174/5 38, cited in Gregory, *Minorca,* 80–81.

48 Johnston to Halifax, November 24, 1763 NA CO/174/3 44–46; Halifax to Johnston, December 30, 1763, NA CO/174/19 13; Johnston to Halifax, March 12, 1767, NA CO/174/19 33–34.

49 For the dispute over churches, see Johnston to Halifax, April 28, 1764, NA CO/174/3 94–95 and Gregory, *Minorca,* 83. The priest was José Vilar; the case is described

in Donaldson, "Britain and Menorca," 244–245, and Gregory *Minorca*, 130–131. Johnston understood the matter as a test of the doctrine of royal supremacy. See Johnston to Vicar General, December 25, 1767, NA CO/174/1 177.

50   Privy Council ruling, April 7, 1770, NA CO/174/17 23; Weymouth to Johnston, March 7, 1770, NA CO/175/6 5 quoted in Gregory, *Minorca*, 84, and John Booker, *Maritime Quarantine: The British Experience, c. 1750–1900* (London: Routledge, 2016), 142.

51   Hilda Neatby, *The Quebec Act: Protest and Policy* (Scarborough: Prentice-Hall, 1972), 9.

52   Address of the Principal Inhabitants of Canada to the King, January 7, 1765 in Adam Shortt and Arthur Doughty, ed., *Documents on the Constitutional History of Canada, 1759–1791* (Ottawa: Dawson, 1907), 161–166.

53   G. P. Browne, "Murray, James," in *Dictionary of Canadian Biography*, 4 (Toronto: University of Toronto and Les Presses de l'université Laval, 2003).

54   On the forms of anti-Catholicism circulating in this period, see Haydon, *Anti-Catholicism*, 3–7.

55   "On the Subject of Religion with respect to Canada," May 31, 1763, Shelburne Papers, 64, 553–564; Verner Crane, "Notes and Documents: Hints Relative to the Division and Government of the Conquered and Newly Acquired Countries in America," *Mississippi Valley Historical Review* 8, no. 4 (1922): 367–373 (hereafter "Hints").

56   Egremont to Murray, August 13, 1763, NA CO/42/24 113–119.

57   Hints, 371. "On the Subject of Religion with respect to Canada" argued for the total abolition of both the male and the female orders. For the background and significance of this memo, see Philip Lawson, *The Imperial Challenge: Quebec and Britain in the Age of the American Revolution* (Kingston and Montreal: McGill-Queen's University Press, 1989), 45–47.

58   Board of Trade, "Heads of a Plan for the Establishment of Ecclesiastical Affairs in Quebec," May 30, 1765, W. L. Grant and J. Munro, ed., *Acts of the Privy Council, vol. VI The Unbound Papers* (London: Her Majesty's Stationary Office, 1912), 396–399; Doll, *Revolution, Religion, and National Identity*, 94.

59   For a recent assessment of Murray as "pro-Catholic—or rather, pro-tolerance," see Lawrence A. Uzzell, "James Murray: A Forgotten Champion of Religious Freedom," *The Catholic Historical Review* 104, no. 1 (2018): 57–91.

60   Harland-Jacobs, "Accommodation and Anti-Catholicism," 211–212. Notably, the Rockingham administration requested a copy of Bishop Gibson's "Recommendations on the Ecclesiastical Government of Minorca" written in 1720 as it formulated policy for Quebec in the 1760s; Doll, *Revolution, Religion, and National Identity*, 119.

61   Murray to the Board of Trade, October 29, 1764, in Shortt and Doughty, ed., *Documents on the Constitutional History of Canada*, 167.

62   Presentments of the Grand Jury, October 16, 1764, NA CO/42/25 169–175.

63   Steele, "The Anointed, the Appointed, and the Elected," in Marshall, ed., *The Oxford History of the British Empire, The Eighteenth-Century*, 122–123.

64   Muller, *Subjects and Sovereign*, 127–129.

65   *Annual Register for the Year 1765* (London, 1766), 269–270; Memorial of Adopted Subjects in Melville to the Board of Trade, March 1, 1766, NA CO/101/1 205–222.

66   Melvill to Board of Trade, February 7, 1765 and to Hillsborough, December 27, 1767, NA CO/101/12, quoted in Marshall, *The Making and Unmaking of Empires*, 188; Melvill to Board of Trade, April 19, 1766, NA CO/101/1 259.

67   R. Devas, *Conception Island or The Troubled Story of the Catholic Church in Grenada, B. W. I.* (London: Sands, 1932), 31–32; Challoner to Dr. C. Stonor, August 28, 1764, in Edwin Burton, *The Life and Times of Bishop Challoner* (2 volumes, London: Longmans, 1909), 2: 139–142.

68   Challoner to Propaganda, August 2, 1763 in Burton, *Life and Times of Challoner,* 2: 133–135.

69   Challoner expressed the suspicion that the authorities had intercepted his letters regarding the ceded islands, indicating their awareness of his appointment; they appear to have accepted it. See Challoner to Stonor, March 15, 1764 in ibid., 2: 136.

70   Melville to the Board, July 26, 1765, NA CO/101/1 309–312; Devas, *Conception Island,* 56–57. The first Anglican church would not be constructed until the nineteenth century.

71   The constitutional struggle in Grenada has recently been subject to rigorous analysis by Hannah Weiss Muller, who focuses on petitions, and Aaron Willis, who examines the pamphlet debate. Both argue that the incorporation of the new subjects led to a more flexible constitutional structure. See her essay in this volume and also Muller, *Subjects and Sovereign*, and Willis, "The Standing of New Subjects: Grenada and the Protestant Constitution after the Treaty of Paris," *Journal of Imperial and Commonwealth History* 42, no. 1 (2014): 1–21.

72   Muller, *Subjects and Sovereign,* 139.

73   Memorial of the undersigned British Protestant Inhabitants of the Island of Grenada to Melvill, February 14, 1766, NA CO/101/1 215.

74   Address of the King's new subjects in the Island of Grenada, 1767, NA CO/101/2 82–88.

75   Muller, *Subjects and Sovereign,* 124.

76   For the argument that whites needed to present a united front against the slaves, see Edward Cox, *Free Coloreds in the Slave Societies of St. Kitts and Grenada* (Knoxville: University of Tennessee Press, 1984), 81.

77   Clare et al. to the Privy Council, November 20, 1767, NA CO/102/1 286–288; crown lawyers' report, 1765, in Shortt and Doughty, ed., Documents on the Constitutional History of Canada, 171.

78   Order-in-Council, September 7, 1768, NA CO/101/3 1; Devas, *History of the Island of Grenada,* 71.

79   Hillsborough to Fitzmaurice, May 1, 1769, NA CO/101/3, 112.

80   *A Letter … on the Present Situation of Affairs in the Island of Gr-n-da* (London, 1769).

81   Dartmouth to Leybourne, December 10, 1774, NA CO/101/17 303–304; Beverly Steele, *Grenada: A History of Its People* (Oxford: Macmillan Caribbean, 2003), 78–79.

82   "Petition of divers of the Roman-Catholick Inhabitants of the Province of Quebeck to the King's Majesty, Dec 1773," in Shortt and Doughty, ed., *Documents on the Constitutional History of Canada,* 354–356.

83   The literature is extensive; key works include Neatby, *The Quebec Act*; Lawson, *The Imperial Challenge*; Phillip Buckner and John Reid, *Revisiting 1759: The Conquest of Canada in Historical Perspective* (Toronto: University of Toronto Press, 2012).

84   Text of the Quebec Act, October 7, 1774, Avalon.yale.edu. According to Leonard Levy, the Quebec Act in actuality set up a "dual establishment" (of Catholicism and Anglicanism). See Leonard Levy, *The Establishment Clause: Religion and the First Amendment* (Chapel Hill: University of North Carolina Press, 2017).

85   Harland-Jacobs, "Incorporating the King's New Subjects," 217–222.

86   Text of the Quebec Act; Doll, *Revolution, Religion, and National Identity*, chapter 4.

87   For the argument that the British ruled the Canadian Church with an iron fist,
        see Michel Brunet, *Les Canadiens après la Conquête* (Montreal: Fides, 1969), 140.
        For more recent interpretations that emphasize the complexities of church–state
        relations, especially given the personalities involved on both sides, see Lucien
        Lemieux, *Histoire du catholicisme québécois, Les XVIII et XIX siècles* (Montreal:
        Boreal, 1989) and Gilles Chaussé, "French Canada from the Conquest to 1840," in
        Concise History of Christianity in Canada, ed. Terrence Murphy and Roberto Perin
        (Oxford: Oxford University Press, 1996), 56–106.

88   See Patrick Fagan, *Divided Loyalties: The Question of the Oath for Irish Catholics in
        the Eighteenth Century* (Dublin: Four Courts Press, 1997).

89   For example, see Instructions of Robert Farquhar (Mauritius), April 4, 1811, NA
        CO/168/2 8–19.

90   Gardiner's Act granted Catholics the right to hold leases of up to 999 years and
        inherit land as Protestants did but prevented them from gaining freehold rights.

91   Donovan, "The Military Origins of the Roman Catholic Relief," 84. See also J.
        Hill, "Religious Toleration and the Relaxation of the Penal Laws: An Imperial
        Perspective," *Archivium Hibernicum* 44, no. 10 (1989): 98–109.

92   Roland Thorne, entry for George Macartney, *Oxford Dictionary of National
        Biography* online edition; John Barrow, *The Earl of Macartney* (London: T. Caddell
        and W. Davies, 1807), 52; Steele, *Grenada,* 79–80, 102.

93   Fitzmaurice to Hillsborough, April 6, 1771, NA CO/101/4 150.

94   Macartney to George Germain, April 10, 1778, NA CO/101/21 173; December 31,
        1778, NA CO/101/23 42; January 10, 1770, NA CO/101/23 58.

95   Gregory, *Minorca,* 89, citing Murdie; Murry to Rochford, April 22, 1775, NA CO/174/9 31.

96   Murray to Weymouth, January 15, 1777, NA CO/174/10 21.

97   Murray to Weymouth, August 11, 1777, NA CO/174/10 116. Murray accused
        the jurats of not appreciating "the happy advantages" of British subjecthood, told
        them that they "did not deserve to be treated as freemen," and chided them for not
        learning English. Murray to the jurats, July 4, 1777, NA CO/174/10, 132–133.

98   Gregory, *Minorca,* 89–92, 183–193.

99   Philip Girard, "Liberty, Order and Pluralism: The Canadian Experience," in
        Exclusionary Empire: English Liberty Overseas, ed. Jack P. Greene (Cambridge:
        Cambridge University Press, 2010), 169–172.

100   It was only in the context of a union, in which the power of elected Catholics was
        significantly diluted, that emancipation was acceptable and only as a result of a masterful
        politician, Daniel O'Connell, that official anti-Catholicism was ultimately dislodged.

101   Steele, *Grenada,* 98–104; Cox, *Free Coloreds in the Slave Societies of St. Kitts and
        Grenada,* 5.

102   For an analysis of the insurgents' program as a reclaiming of rights enjoyed in
        the decade after 1763, rather than "as an ideological extension of the Atlantic
        Revolutions," see Tessa Murphy, "A Reassertion of Rights: Fedon's Rebellion,
        Grenada, 1795–96," *La Révolution française* 14 (2018): 1–26.

103   Toleration is not a synonym for accommodation, though most scholars of the
        empire's politics of religion use it as such. Contemporaries often qualified the term
        toleration with "mere" or "only," using it in the sense of connivance.

104   For interpretations that emphasize pragmatism, see Marshall, *The Making and
        Unmaking of Empires,* 184, 189 and Douglas Fyson, "Les Canadiens et le Serment
        du Test," in *1763: Le Traite de Paris bouleverse l'Amerique*, ed. Sophie Imbeault
        (Quebec: Septenrion, 2013), 272–277.

5

1763 and the Genesis of British Africa

Christopher Leslie Brown

Trade and war on the West African coast

In some ways, 1763 was an unremarkable year in the history of the Atlantic slave trade. In that year, ships of all nations embarked almost 60,000 captive Africans for the Americas. Nearly 14 percent of them, more than 8,000 men, women, and children, died en route. These numbers match almost exactly the annual averages, both in terms of volume and in terms of mortality, for the forty-year span between the Treaty of Utrecht in 1713 and the beginning of the Seven Years' War in 1754.[1] Moreover, in 1763, as throughout the first half of the eighteenth-century, British and Portuguese merchants dominated; their ships combined to carry more than three-fourths of all the enslaved exported from Africa in that year.

The appearance of continuity between 1763 and the pre-war slave trade, though, is in other ways misleading. The Seven Years' War wrought profound changes on the slave trade during the war and caused subtle but important shifts in its aftermath. French participation in the trade, for example, came to a near total halt during the war. British merchants rushed in to fill the void. In the four years following the capture of Guadeloupe in 1759, British slave ships delivered more than 25,000 African captives to the island's French planters who were in need of laborers and eager to take advantage of the new and ultimately short-lived British market for their molasses and sugar. The British conquest of Havana in 1762 had similar if less dramatic consequences. British merchants imported more slaves to Cuba in 1763—nearly three thousand by current estimates—than the island had received directly from West Africa in any single previous year. Moreover, the disruptions in the trade that accompanied the war created a pent-up demand for enslaved workers that generated lucrative opportunities for all slave shippers in the war's immediate aftermath. North American slave traders, for example, and merchants from Rhode Island in particular, shipped more Africans to the Americas in 1763 than they ever had before, an intensified investment in the trade that would characterize all carriers in the dozen years between 1763 and the outbreak of the American War for Independence.[2]

So, 1763, in fact, marked a moment of transition in the Atlantic slave trade. From 1764 to 1775 slavers embarked an annual average of more than 90,000 African captives for the Americas, a nearly 20 percent increase above the annual average in the four years immediately preceding the Seven Years' War.[3] Because British ships accounted for more than two-thirds of this increase, the volume of the British slave trade grew by nearly 50 percent.[4] This growth in the British slave trade was driven by the new imperial acquisitions in the Caribbean and in North America that expanded the acreage available for sugar production (and the demand for slave labor) after the peace. Between the Seven Years' War and the American Revolution, British ships transported at least 125,000 captives, more than 10,000 a year, to Britain's new tropical colonies— Grenada, Dominica, St. Vincent's, Tobago, East Florida, and West Florida—places where before the war slavery had been either small-scale or nonexistent.[5] The British purchase of slaves increased everywhere on the coast of Atlantic Africa after 1763 but most dramatically in numerical terms in the Bight of Biafra, where the British slave trade long had thrived, and most spectacularly in percentage terms, along the Windward Coast and Sierra Leone, where the British slave trade, by contrast, had previously been comparatively small.[6]

The peace of 1763 also left Britain with new possessions on the West African coast. The same treaty that awarded Britain new colonies in the Caribbean and in North America also confirmed British control over Île-Saint-Louis, an island at the mouth of the Senegal River that had been captured from France in 1758, "as well as all the rights and dependencies of the said River." The provisions of the treaty not only expelled France from the fort and upriver factories critical to the Senegal trade, they also enabled a new kind of presence for Britain on the West African coast. Nowhere else in Atlantic Africa did Britain claim exclusive rights to trade. Although British merchants predominated throughout the coast south and east from the Gambia River to the Bight of Biafra, almost everywhere they faced competition from European rivals. The British slave trade had thrived most consistently in those places where peace prevailed on the coast, in the Bight of Biafara where British merchants developed intimate partnerships with the local merchant elite or in the Bight of Benin, the port of Ouidah, and then the kingdom of Dahomey which forbid European merchants from pursuing their feuds along their coast.[7] Elsewhere, there was fierce competition for access to African markets in time of peace and open season on rival ships and factories in time of war. The definitive treaty of peace, therefore, seemed to allow Britain, for the first time, monopoly control over a significant sector in the West African trade.

One hundred years of intermittent warfare brought Britain to this position. To attain prominence in the Africa trades, English merchants backed by the Royal Navy had fought their way in. There was first the seizure of Dutch West African trading forts on the Gold Coast during the second Anglo-Dutch war in the reign of Charles II. Even after the Royal Africa Company secured a foothold there and in the Gambia River during the last quarter of the seventeenth century, maintaining access to the Africa trade proved bloody and expensive. Four times during the Nine Years' War and the War of Spanish Succession, French ships took James Fort in the River Gambia, and each time agents of the Royal Africa Company returned to rebuild the outpost. If the English and the Dutch were allies against France in Europe at the close of the seventeenth century, on the Gold Coast they were at each other's throats, embroiled in what would be a long-running struggle for access to Fante markets and Fante exports that would extend through the American Revolution. Well into the eighteenth century, opening new African markets required trespassing into a rival's trading territory. In 1721, looking to open a new outpost for its operations, the Royal Africa Company constructed a fort at the port of Cabinda, near the mouth of the Congo River. It lasted only two years before the Portuguese, who thought of trade from the region as national property, reduced the fort to ruins. The conquest of Île-Saint-Louis concluded several decades of British interloping along the Atlantic coast of the Western Sahara, a region that French merchants regarded as their right to command.[8] Every war in Europe during the eighteenth century led to the destruction of forts and the seizure of ships in Atlantic Africa.[9] These were, in most instances, small-scale affairs. The British government rarely sent more than a half-dozen ships and several hundred men to sustain the nation's interests on the West African coast. The Royal Navy sustained a soft but sustained presence there, sufficient to keep trade open, discourage piracy, and discourage European rivals' intending to prey on British trade, but, until the Seven Years' War, insufficient for the assertion of imperial power on the West African coast.[10]

The acquisition of Île-Saint-Louis, therefore, seemed to award Britain sovereignty, for the first time, over an Atlantic African entrepôt. To secure that possession, Parliament established the Province of Senegambia in 1765. During its relatively short life from 1765 to 1783, it would be the first and only British colony on the West African coast, preceding by a generation the comparatively more successful and, to historians, more familiar settlement at Sierra Leone.[11] If Sierra Leone represented an early experiment in antislavery colonization, Senegambia marked the first attempt to bring West African territory anywhere, of any kind, under British imperial control. Parliament gave George III direct authority over the settlement after brief unsatisfactory experiments with garrison government (1759–64) and merchant rule (1764–5).

In no sense, of course, was there the founding of a second British Empire in Africa after the Seven Years' War, or for many decades afterwards. The important changes would come after 1807, after the abolition of the British slave trade and the creation of a colonial and naval infrastructure in Africa to enforce it.[12] The French conquest of that colony in 1779, during the American War for Independence, and its formal dissolution at the second Peace of Paris in 1783 put an end to those ambitions for a time. The venture itself, though, indicated a subtle but important shift in perceptions of the West African trade and how the imperial state might relate to it. As elsewhere in the British Empire, the demands of imperial rivalry in West Africa created for the British government after 1763 new imperatives, fostered new ambitions, and generated new problems. That transition becomes most apparent when considered alongside the more familiar institutional and strategic adjustments that followed the Seven Years' War in other parts of the British Empire.

The taking of Île-Saint-Louis and Gorée numbered among the first British victories against France in the Seven Years' War. In March of 1758, William Pitt sent a small squadron of six ships and two hundred soldiers to seize Île-Saint-Louis. Unprepared, suffering from the consequences of a prolonged drought, and betrayed by their Waalo allies, the French garrison capitulated as soon as the British squadron made its way across the bar between the Atlantic Ocean and the Senegal River. This expedition lacked the numbers required to take on the more formidable fortress of Gorée to the south.

Several months later, in the fall of 1758, Pitt dispatched a much larger fleet—more than twenty ships and seven hundred troops—to fulfill that objective. Within days of his arrival in December 1758, Admiral Augustus Keppel forced a surrender of the Gorée garrison and, thereby, eliminated French military and commercial power on the Upper Guinea coast. The following year, nine ships carried more than one thousand men to occupy Île-Saint-Louis and Gorée and to secure these new holdings for the crown.[13] At the time, it was the largest armed force that the British government had sent to West Africa in at least a half-century.

Back in Britain, news of these victories was celebrated widely, alongside other conquests in North America, the West Indies, and South Asia.[14] The political economist Malachy Postlethwayt thought that the new acquisitions would allow Britain to shutdown the French slave trade for good and, thereby, ruin the profitability of the French West Indies, expand the commercial prospects for the British West Indies, and open new markets in the Americas for British manufactured goods. While still in office, Pitt was enamored by the prospect of excluding France from the Upper Guinea coast completely. One may understand the disappointment that prevailed in some quarters, then, when his successor as prime minister, Lord Bute, instead chose to return Gorée to France at the Peace of Paris in 1763.[15]

Most accounts of this treaty emphasize Britain's decision to retain Canada and return Guadeloupe, a choice that had far-reaching consequences for the history of the Caribbean, of British North America, and the British Empire more generally.[16] Few scholars, though, have noted that, at the time, some thought the return of Gorée an equally egregious error.[17] Although the tiny island off the Upper Guinea coast played only a modest role in Atlantic trade, Gorée held considerable strategic value as a supply station and a naval base. Critics of Bute's peace worried that French agents in Gorée would conspire to overthrow the new British settlements along Senegal. They insisted that the Senegal factories could only have commercial value if Britain possessed Gorée too.[18]

Defenders of the treaty, by contrast, argued that Gorée scarcely figured in the Atlantic slave trade. They explained that denying France an outpost on the Upper Guinea coast would only encourage French merchants to establish trading posts elsewhere, such as along the Gold Coast, a far more important mart for the export of Africans, and a region where Britain already had to contend with Dutch competition, and, in the most recent decade, French incursions at Anomabu. Better, it was argued, to permit a foothold in a region where the French could do the least harm to the British slave trade, the apologists maintained.[19] In this respect, the defenders of the treaty were correct. During the first half of the eighteenth century, the Upper Guinea coast provided no more than 15 percent of the captives embarked on French slave ships. Far more significant for France was the trade from Whydah in the Bight of Benin—the Slave Coast as it was then known—and equally extensive markets for slaves at Cabinda, Loango, and Malemba in West Central Africa, as well as Anomabu on the Gold Coast. These regions, together, accounted for more than 70 percent of the French slave trade and would remain the most important sources of African slaves for the French plantations until the end of slavery. Gorée, by contrast, had only limited commercial value. On average, in the first half of the century, it provided less than five hundred captives a year to French slave ships.[20] Gorée's importance lay in its use as a fortress, naval base, and supply station. Nonetheless, it was precisely the island's capacity to command the Senegambia coast militarily that made Pitt and others nervous. The London *Annual Register* assessed the situation well: "The English ... seem to be the most advantageously situated for the trade in time of peace," and the French "for carrying away the whole of it in time of war."[21]

An empire of gum

Given the relative unimportance of the Atlantic slave trade from the region, what can explain the British determination to gain control of the Senegal trade in the first place? The answer lies in the traffic that later generations of Britons would come to describe as "legitimate commerce." Because of the obvious significance the Atlantic slave trade played in the history of the Americas and Western Europe, most non-Africanist historians have shown little interest in non-slave exports from West Africa in the early modern period. But historians of Africa have long recognized that until the end of the seventeenth-century European merchants sent ships to West Africa to acquire gold, ivory, woods, and spices as frequently as slaves. Prior to 1700, in fact, the export of non-slave commodities to Europe equaled the Atlantic slave trade to the Americas in value. It was only after the turn of the eighteenth century that slaves became the dominant export from Atlantic Africa.[22] The commodities trade, though, persisted everywhere along the coast throughout the eighteenth century, increasing in absolute terms even as its share of the total trade was eclipsed by the ever-increasing demand for slaves.[23] In Senegambia, uniquely, the trade in commodities continued to outweigh the slave trade in value for much of the eighteenth century.

One of these products, gum senegal, so increased in value during the course of the century that merchants in Britain and France believed it worth fighting for. Senegalese gums had a variety of uses in the eighteenth century: as ingredients in medicines, as a binder in the mixing of watercolors, and, most importantly, as thickeners in textile printing, especially in the dying of linens and silks. For European textile manufacturers trying to compete with printed cloth imports from South Asia, there was no suitable substitute for Senegalese gums. As a consequence, the growth of the textile industry in the eighteenth century was accompanied by an equally rapid growth in the demand for gum senegal, which in turn drove up its price, according to some accounts, by a factor of fifteen over the course of the century. That rapid escalation in value was due as much from the limits placed upon its supply in Africa as to the intensity of European demand. As far as European merchants knew, there was only one place in the world to acquire these gums—the Atlantic shore of present-day Mauritania and along the northern banks of the Senegal River. In both regions, the cultivation of the acacia trees that provided the gums lay under the control of two Berber emirates—the Trarza of the Atlantic coast and the Brakna of middle Senegal. These two groups determined both the volume and the price of gums sold in the local market. However, because these gums only could be purchased in or near the Senegal Valley, the European merchants who purchased them possessed in turn, a monopoly over its sale in Europe.[24]

In the first half of the eighteenth century, the French government ferociously defended its command of the Senegalese trade, a claim that originated with establishment of Île-Saint-Louis in 1659. The French *Compagnie des Indes* drove Dutch merchants from the coast of Senegal for good in the 1720s. It proved more difficult, however, to prevent British merchants from poaching on the trade in gum senegal, particularly at Portendick, a western Sahara Atlantic harbor one hundred and forty miles north of Île-Saint-Louis. At times, British merchant ships traveled in armed convoys when hoping to trade along the Mauritanian coast, where the Trarza attempted to circumvent the French monopoly. The British slaving stations along the Gambia River also provided British smugglers with a base of operations. To discourage British ambitions in Senegal, France negotiated a series of treaties with Britain in the early 1740s that ensured British merchants a fixed supply of gum Arabic, in the hope that a regulated trade under French control would satisfy British needs. Environmental and economic changes along the Western Sahel, however, made the arrangement unworkable. A drought and famine decimated the lower Senegal in the late 1740s and compelled the Brakna to shift their energies from the production of gum to the production of grains. Faced with a decline in supply, the French government in 1751 banned the sale of gum senegal to all foreign merchants. Because British manufacturers now could only acquire gum senegal by smuggling it out of France or through Dutch intermediaries, the price of both tripled in London between 1751 and 1754.[25] The primary purpose of the 1758 British attack on Île-Saint-Louis and Gorée, then, was not to undermine the French slave trade but to guarantee British manufacturers access to an ingredient that was essential to early textile industrialization.

Textile merchants conceived, organized, and financed the 1758 expedition to Senegal and Gorée. The scheme originated with Thomas Cumming, an entrepreneurial Scot and sometime Quaker, who, in 1754, had opened a private trade for gum Arabic with the Trarza at Portendick. He decided that the declaration of war with France presented an opportunity to break the French monopoly. Cumming brought the project to William Pitt, offering to lead the expedition personally, if Pitt would promise him a monopoly of trade from Senegal for fourteen years after the conquest. Cumming received authorization for the venture early in 1756 but the size of the force detached for the expedition fell well below his expectations. So Cumming turned for assistance to a merchant and financier: Samuel Touchet, one of the richest men in Manchester, who possessed extensive overseas interests in the import of raw cotton from the Levant and the West Indies, yarn from the Continent, and in the slave traffic. Touchet, who expected to profit handsomely from command of the gum trade, agreed to help underwrite the costs. He outfitted more than half of the ships for the expedition against Senegal on his own account at the expense of more than £6,000. The initial British conquest of Senegal, therefore, was in truth a private military venture licensed by the state but conducted by a middling merchant on the make and a Lancashire textile baron.[26]

Touchet had a special talent for locating opportunities to use state power for personal gain. In the mid-1740s, he had concocted an elaborate scheme to monopolize the supply of raw cotton and to finance and control the mechanization of cotton spinning. In 1749 he had joined a coalition of merchants hoping to secure exclusive control over the British trade to Labrador. Some years after the Senegal expedition, in 1772, he would fix on an ambitious scheme to acquire mineral rights in and about Lake Superior.[27] His desire for a monopoly of the Senegal trade was in character. Given the promise of proprietary rights that they had received from Pitt, Touchet and Cumming expected to be awarded exclusive possession and petitioned George III to grant them a commercial monopoly. But by the war's end, Pitt was no longer in office and other British textile merchants and manufacturers were eagerly anticipating that the cession of Île-Saint-Louis would increase the supply of gums and drive down prices. Continued dependence on a single supplier—even if that supplier was British—was unlikely to produce that result. As a consequence, a consortium of textile merchants and manufacturers petitioned against the proposed monopoly and in favor of a free trade in Senegalese gums. In their petition, the consortium argued that the 1758 expedition could not have succeeded without the assistance of the crown and therefore questioned whether the merchants who aided the state deserved an exclusive claim upon an entire branch of commerce. They also resented the secrecy with which the terms had been negotiated and, most particularly, denounced the principle of monopoly, "that canker of industry, that disease, under which no commerce can long survive."[28]

Granting Cummings and Touchet a monopoly in Senegal would not only place a valuable trade into the hands of two men, it also was contrary to a half-century of established and successful practice in Africa. The Royal Africa Company had lost its privileged position in the British slave trade in 1714 and Parliament had dissolved the corporation for good in 1752. Thereafter, management of the English slaving "factories" on the West African coast fell under the control of the Company of Merchants Trading to Africa, a consortium of independent merchants based in London, Liverpool, and Bristol. Since the demise of the Royal Africa Company, the British slave trade had grown to unprecedented heights, surpassing the Dutch, Portuguese, and French traffics. Following this precedent, Parliament in 1764 rejected Cumming and Touchet's petition for a monopoly and instead vested control of the new Senegal River trade in the Company of Merchants Trading to Africa, "in the same manner, and under the same Regulations and subject to the same Rules … as the other Forts and Settlements on the Coast of Africa are now vested in the said Company."[29]

Almost immediately, however, Parliament realized that this arrangement would not work, that the Senegal trade differed from the slave trade, not only because of the central importance of gums, but because of French jealousy toward British commercial privileges in the region. The 1763 treaty, and the 1764 commercial arrangement failed to provide peace and security on the Senegambia coast, just as some British opponents of the settlement, like William Pitt, had predicted. It also allowed individual merchants to establish their own individual trading concerns in the Senegal River, a development that promised to enrich a few but compromise the British government's new interest in the region. From their base at Gorée Island, French officials and merchants challenged British control of the Senegal trade at every opportunity. Despite British objections, the French constructed a new slave-trading fort on the River Gambia. They increased the size of the garrison at Gorée and transferred authority over the island from the *Compagnie Des Indes* to the crown. British critics of the independent merchants who conducted the Africa trade had long contended that the pursuit of private interest had not always served the public good. The merchants who outfitted ships to Africa, they explained, put their own needs first, with no concern for establishing a more lasting presence for Britain along the West African coast. A British army garrison had occupied Île-Saint-Louis from 1758 to 1764. When the troops departed, it quickly became apparent that the Company of Merchants Trading to Africa, who assumed authority for the post, were ill-equipped to assume the task (and expense) of maintaining it. Consequently, one year later, in 1765, the Lords Commissioners of Trade and Plantations—the Board of Trade— suggested a change of course. The Senegal forts, the Board concluded, "do essentially differ from the Establishments upon the other parts of the Coast of Africa, and do, we conceive, require a very different System of Management ... which a Committee of Merchants with very limited powers ... is in no respect qualified to establish or to carry into Execution." The Board, for this reason, thought it "absolutely necessary, both for the Preservation of this important part of your Majesty's Dominions, and for the Advancement and Improvement of its Commerce, that the districts of Senegal and Gambia should be taken out of the Hands of the Company of Merchants trading to Africa, and instead placed under Your Majesty's immediate direction," just as France had previously done.[30]

Placed in a broader view, this was an extraordinarily creative moment in the constitutional history of the British Empire. Parliament assigned to the new royal province of Senegambia a governor, council, courts, and constitution in the same years that it was also establishing new colonial governments in the Floridas, Quebec, and the Ceded Islands of the West Indies. The establishment of the Senegambia colony represents not only the first attempt at British rule in West Africa. It also represents a first experiment in Crown Colony government anywhere in the British Empire—a structure that would become increasingly common in the nineteenth century, but for which there was as yet few precedents. The British government made no attempt to populate its new African colony with British colonists, despite occasional enthusiasm for such a step by interested observers and officials. This was to be a colonial government without an elected colonial assembly. Parliament awarded the full authority to legislate to the Governor and his appointed Council. Public officials, justices, sheriffs, and constables would all be appointed by the Governor and Council, and the Anglican Church would be supported at public expense, at least in principle. The imperial state would also pay the costs of government, review legislation, and hear judicial appeals.[31] The institutional structure of the new Senegambia colony, therefore, reflected the more general impulse, as indicated throughout this volume, to consolidate authority in the empire in the decade after the Seven Years' War, to ensure that overseas enterprise would serve the overarching interests of the imperial state and, in particular, to guarantee the security of the new acquisitions. It anticipated the future distinction between colonies of British settlement that would be granted institutions of representative government and provinces dominated by Africans, Asians, or Indigenous peoples deemed unworthy of similar political rights.

An island in the river

When the British took up residence in Île-Saint-Louis in 1758, they placed themselves at the center of a society, economy, and culture they scarcely understood. The strategic importance of the island as a trading entrepôt made it a meeting point for a variety of peoples—Muslim traders from the Senegal hinterland, Trarza merchants from the southern shore of the Western Sahara, Waalo villagers from the mainland east and south of Senegal, as well as European visitors seeking tropical commodities. The three thousand inhabitants of Île-Saint-Louis were also a diverse lot. Most of the commercial elite were the mixed-race descendants of Portuguese and French traders and Waalo women. They conversed typically in French and Wolof and regarded themselves as Catholics. Several mixed-race women, the *signares* as they were known, numbered among the wealthiest traders on the island. For several generations they had served as brokers between European visitors and Muslim traders. The principal inhabitants owned and employed a large number of slaves, mainly Bambara captives from the upper Niger valley, whom they frequently rented to European merchants. In addition, there was the large number of *laptots*, Waalo boatmen who ferried peoples and goods to the island from the Senegalese mainland and up and down the Senegal River. In the last half of the eighteenth century, Île-Saint-Louis numbered among the most cosmopolitan port towns in Atlantic Africa, a place where a variety of languages (French, Wolof, and Arabic) and a variety of religions (including Islam and Catholicism) facilitated cross-cultural trade.[32]

French traders had learned to negotiate with and respect the authority of the Île-Saint-Louis elite over the previous half-century. From their arrival, however British officials in Île-Saint-Louis showed more concern with the dignity and power of their station than with coming to terms with local customs and laws. In 1758, for example, Lieutenant-Colonel Richard Worge, the commander of the 1758 expedition, refused to escort a Trarza leader from the mainland to the island. Worge was informed that "it had been a custom with the French for their Governor to go in person and conduct crowned heads" to Île-Saint-Louis. However, as Worge's aide explained to the offended nobleman, "the French were only a company of merchants and trading men—their Governor only a private person; whereas the English were the immediate servants of the King of Great Britain, and that therefore such condescension could by no means be complied with."[33]

British military officers and crown officials tended to think of the island as conquered and its inhabitants, therefore, as subject to British rule (if not precisely as British subjects), an inclination that the designation of Senegambia as a province of the British Empire in 1765 only reinforced. The Board of Trade ordered Colonel Charles O'Hara, the first governor of the colony, to establish British authority, construct fortifications, and facilitate the gum trade. They also forbade him from trading on his own account or trafficking in slaves.[34] O'Hara liked to build forts, but showed no interest in, or capacity for, the delicate work of governance or the facilitation of peaceful trade. Shortly after his arrival in Île-Saint-Louis, he became enamored with the prospect of building not just a colony but also an empire in the

Senegal River Valley. O'Hara predicted that, in time, Senegambia would become "one of the richest colonies, belonging to his Majesty," and that British colonists would eventually "extend over every part of this Continent that was worthwhile to settle." He clung to this vision even after his own experience in Île-Saint-Louis proved the folly of inland colonization, which, already, had produced hundreds of English deaths but no permanent settlement. In 1771, he started repairs on the deserted French fort at Podor, one hundred and thirty miles up the Senegal River in part because "the neighborhood," he explained, "abounds with a variety of different kinds of corn, likewise rice, tobacco, indigo, and cotton." It can "produce every kind of West India commodity in the greatest perfection."[35] For O'Hara, when thinking about the future of British enterprise in Africa, the American plantations provided the useful point of reference.

Île-Saint-Louis, though, was not St. Kitts, nor any of the other American settlements O'Hara seems to have had in mind. The Province of Senegambia could not support British plantations, for the actual reach of British authority in the "province" barely extended beyond their two island forts at the mouths of the Senegal and Gambia Rivers. O'Hara seems never to have understood, or at least would not accept, the fact that although he was technically in power he was, practically speaking, not in control. Frustration at his impotence led O'Hara to regard the people of Île-Saint-Louis with undisguised contempt. When the Board of Trade told him to incorporate African soldiers into the garrisons in his command as vacancies occurred, O'Hara refused the "impolitic" suggestion because it would "destroy that subordination" which he thought "the Negroes" were obliged to accept.[36] When the Damel of Cayor on the mainland blocked British access to the upper reaches of Senegal in 1771, O'Hara prohibited trade with his people entirely, severely restricting the supply of fresh food and water that reached the people of Île-Saint-Louis in the process. O'Hara's proposed solution to this self-created subsistence crisis was to seek to oppress rather than appease. He tried to snatch territory on the mainland, across from the river from Île-Saint-Louis, in order to secure his own food supply. When that failed, he asked the crown for "a King's sloop" to patrol the river which, he said, "would … so intimidate the Natives as to put an effectual stop to the many dangerous and distressing irregularities they are guilty of," which "would, by being able to burn and destroy their villages, … soon bring them to reason."[37]

O'Hara, and the other British men who came to Senegal, found it difficult to abandon the institutional models they knew best. British merchants delivered gum senegal to England in substantial quantities from 1759 to 1779,[38] but British merchants purchased slaves in Senegal too, and in much greater numbers than the French had done previously. In two decades, British merchants dispatched more than twice as many slave ships to Île-Saint-Louis as French merchants had sent in the previous century.[39] The sharp spike in slave exports from Senegal in the years of the British occupation suggests that British slave traders were so aggressive in identifying and capitalizing on new supplies of captives that they succeeded in creating a slave trade where one scarcely had existed before. To punish Waalo and promote the traffic in captives, O'Hara encouraged Trarza slave raids on the kingdom.[40] Those raids help account for the more than 8,000 captives shipped from Île-Saint-Louis between 1773 and 1775. This would be the largest number of enslaved men, women, and children shipped from the island in a three-year period in the island's long history of European occupation.

London merchants predominated in the new British slave trade from Senegal. They carried more than two-thirds of the slaves sent to the American colonies from Île-Saint-Louis between 1759 and 1776, and at a time when London ships carried less than one-fifth of the British slave trade as a whole. The opening of the Senegal trade, in fact, seems to have revived the London-based slave trade, which had declined to negligible levels in the decades before the Seven Years' War.[41] British ships scattered the men, women, and children they boarded into their holds at Île-Saint-Louis to every corner of the British-American Empire. No colonial port received more than a fraction of the total. But the newly acquired colonies (Grenada, Dominica, and St. Vincent) and the ports of mainland North America (particularly Charleston, South Carolina) predominated.[42] Those places received more than half of the Senegalese captives at a time when the British slave trade disembarked the majority of its human cargo at the older Caribbean islands of Jamaica, Barbados, Antigua, and St. Kitts. The new slave trade from Senegal, then, seems to have been created by new men entering the business, who in turn sold to new customers in the peripheries, rather than the core, of the British plantations.

The determination among British officials to make Île-Saint-Louis into something new—a colony subject to imperial rule that was also an important node in the Atlantic slave trade—helps explain the petition that the principal inhabitants delivered to the Board of Trade in 1775. Their indictment of O'Hara was long, detailed, and, in the end, decisive.[43] His failure to establish cordial relations with any of the local elite meant the trade and the region "were constantly in Disturbance," wrote the petitioners. O'Hara regarded the payment of tribute as beneath him and his office. As a consequence, the Damel of Cayor and the Trarza Moors, the chief suppliers of corn and beef to Île-Saint-Louis, refused to provision the island, a situation, in the words of the petitioners, "never known before." This left the residents increasingly dependent upon food imported from Europe, which always was in short supply. O'Hara was also accused of personal malfeasance and corruption. He not only encouraged the emerging slave trade, the petitioners reported, but also reserved to himself first preference for the slaves thus acquired. In violation of the 1758 capitulation agreement, he seized houses and yards "and gave them to whom he pleases." Previous customs had no standing with him, the petitioners complained. "Eight days after his arrival," O'Hara "broke the Counsel" of the Inhabitants put in place by his predecessors. He seized and shipped to the Americas the slaves of residents who displeased him. He appropriated their cattle, as well as their homes, and then incinerated the cattle even as famine threatened in order to demonstrate their utter-dependence on his will. O'Hara, in their telling, was an over-mighty subject who had taken for himself not only the property and persons of the island but the prerogatives of a despotic king.

The Île-Saint-Louis petitioners sought to put themselves under the protection of George III, and pled for relief as his majesty's royal subjects. In this way, they unknowingly participated in a broader effort across the expanding empire to use the authority of the crown against the ambitions of new British settlers.[44] The petitioners insisted upon their status as a free people. They derided O'Hara's tendency to treat them as subject peoples rather than subjects of the crown. Their rejection of the subordinate status that O'Hara tried to impose helps make sense of their frequent references to his insulting behavior, to his intermittent declarations that "he did not care anything about us," "that we may all goes to the Devil &c. for what he cares." O'Hara replied to appeals for justice with recommendations to leave Île-Saint-Louis, or with threats of enslavement. Reluctantly, some inhabitants had abandoned their homes on Île-Saint-Louis and sought sanctuary on the mainland. But they were still, the petitioners insisted, "subjects to his Majesty King of great Britain," and hoped, with his protection, "to return Back Again to our houses." In short, to regain the customary rights they had enjoyed under the French before 1758, the Île-Saint-Louis elite asserted their standing as British subjects. The era of British rule marked their emergence as a distinct political community with a self-conscious ethnic identity that separated them from both mainland rulers and European authorities.[45]

Imperial eclipse

The petition marked the beginning of the end for the colony of Senegambia. Secretary of State George Germain recalled O'Hara because he feared that further alienating the local elite would destroy British trade in Senegal. After a prolonged investigation, the Board of Trade sided with the Île-Saint-Louis petitioners. They found that O'Hara had "governed arbitrarily without the advice and consent of a Counsel," that "he had invaded the property rights of the inhabitants," that "he had distressed the inhabitants for want of fresh provisions," and that "he had engaged largely in private trade."[46] Germain relieved O'Hara of his office and recalled him to London. Meanwhile, in O'Hara's absence, the government of Senegambia lost what little authority it still possessed, as his successors charged each other with corruption and profiteering.[47]

In 1779, not long after France entered the war to assist the thirteen American colonies win their independence, a French naval squadron recaptured Île-Saint-Louis. There was no resistance offered, for the British garrison had already fallen to ruin. A yellow fever epidemic nearly wiped out the small British garrison even before the French arrived. The *habitants*, fully alienated from the British administration in the aftermath of O'Hara's rule, finished off the rest.[48] The same French expedition then destroyed Fort James on the Gambia, completing the conquest of the colony. Few in Britain mourned when the terms of the Treaty of Paris of 1783 included the return of Île-Saint-Louis to France.[49]

The lowering of the Union Jack in Île-Saint-Louis brought only a partial return to the practices that existed prior to the British arrival in 1758, and the establishment of the colony of Senegambia in 1765. A new trading monopoly funded by Le Havre merchants and chartered by the French crown to maximize Senegalese commerce continued to operate the slaving networks that British traders had stimulated there.[50] Before the Seven Years' War, French merchants had exported little more than three hundred men, women, and children each year from Île-Saint-Louis. In the eight years between the end of the American Revolution and the outbreak of the Saint-Domingue slave uprising (the Haitian Revolution), more than one thousand captives each year were shipped from the island. While this was still a only a minor branch in the Atlantic slave trade, the years of British occupation had clearly destabilized the Senegal River Valley and intensified the role of slaving in it.

The Seven Years' War and its aftermath, therefore, had consequences for peoples across the Upper Guinea coast, far from the principal theaters of action, and in ways, to this point, only partially understood. Many of the principal themes in this postwar historiography—problems of jurisdiction and governance, the threat of a French *revanche*, the difficulties of incorporating new peoples into the empire—apply to the Senegambians as well as they do to Canadians, the North American natives, or South Asians. Perhaps the short-lived history of those possessions that were gained in 1763 and lost in 1783—Senegambia, Tobago, and the two Floridas—might be better understood if they were considered together, as parts of a larger story about the limits of British expansionism in 1763.

The short life of the British province of Senegambia matters to the history of the Atlantic slave trade too, not because of its significance in either numerical or percentage terms, which remained small, but instead because its example illuminates revealing aspects of the Africa trades that are too frequently overlooked. Viewed from a macroscopic perspective, perhaps, the history of the Africa trade is the history of economics and demographics, first and foremost—a history of the movement of peoples across several centuries in the aggregate. From the perspective of the history of events, though, when viewed through the lens of particular moments of war and trade on the West African coast, the history of the Atlantic slave trade becomes something rather different—the history of everyday struggles to assert political authority, command territory, devise new modes of trade, and reckon with cultural difference. If the Seven Years' War brought the expansion of the British Empire, the historiography of that conflict now needs to extend our understanding of what is relevant to it.

Notes

1   The current estimate for the total embarked in 1763 is 59,890, with an estimated 8,264 (or 13.8 percent) perishing en route. The estimated average for captives embarked between 1713 and 1754 is 56,557 per year with an estimated mortality rate of 15.3 percent.

2   Robert Louis Stein, *The French Slave Trade in the Eighteenth Century: An Old Regime Business* (Madison: University of Wisconsin Press, 1979), 29–32; Richard Pares, *War and Trade in the West Indies, 1739–1763* (Oxford: Clarendon Press, 1936), 186–194, 481–482, 487, 491, 493, 565–566; Peggy K. Liss, *Atlantic Empires: The Network of Trade and Revolution, 1713–1826* (Baltimore, MD: Johns Hopkins University Press, 1983), 79–80; J. R. McNeill, *Atlantic Empires of France and Spain, 1700–1763* (Chapel Hill: University of North Carolina Press, 1985), 166–170; Elena Schneider, *The Occupation of Havana: War, Trade, and Slavery in the Atlantic World* (Chapel Hill: Omohundro Institute of Early American History and Culture, University of North Carolina Press, 2018), 82–84, 205–206, 270–275; Jay Coughtry, *The Notorious Triangle: Rhode Island and the African Slave Trade* (Philadelphia, PA:

Temple University Press, 1981), 30; James G. Lydon, "New York and the Slave Trade, 1700–1774," *William & Mary Quarterly*, 3rd Series, 35 (1978): 379–381; Johannes Postma, "A Reassessment of the Dutch Atlantic Slave Trade," 137; Johannes Postma, "Suriname and Its Atlantic Connections," 306–307; Eric William Van Der Oest, "The Forgotten Colonies of Essequibo and Demerara," 335, in *Riches from Atlantic Commerce: Dutch Transatlantic Trade and Shipping, 1585–1817*, ed. Johannes Postma and Victor Enthoven (Leiden: Brill, 2003); Joseph Miller, *Way of Death: Merchant Capitalism and the Angolan Slave Trade, 1730–1830* (Madison: University of Wisconsin Press, 1988), 570–597.

3   Current estimates suggest 91,126 African captives on average sent to the Americas from 1764 to 1775. From 1752 to 1755, by contrast, an estimated 74,855 slaves were sent to the Americas each year.

4   The estimated annual average of slaves shipped by British merchants rose from 27,496 between 1752 and 1755 to 40,233 from 1764 to 1775.

5   Richard B. Sheridan, *Sugar and Slavery: An Economic History of the British West Indies, 1763–1775* (Barbados: Caribbean Universities Press, 1974), 452–459; D. H. Murdoch, "Land Policy in the Eighteenth-Century British Empire: The Sale of Crown Lands in the Ceded Islands, 1763–1783," *Historical Journal* 27 (Fall 1984): 549–574; S. Max Edelson, *The New Map of Empire: How Britain Imagined America before Independence* (Cambridge, MA: Harvard University Press, 2017), 197–247, especially 241–242; Christopher Taylor, *The Black Carib Wars: Freedom, Survival, and the Making of the Garifuna* (Jackson: University of Mississippi Press, 2012), 51–78; Robin F. A. Fabel, *The Economy of British West Florida, 1763–1783* (Tuscaloosa: University of Alabama Press, 1988), 29–38; Daniel L. Schaefer, "Plantation Development in British East Florida: A Case Study of the Earl of Egmont," *Florida Historical Quarterly* 63 (1984): 172–183; Daniel L. Schaefer, "'Yellow Silk Ferret Tied Round Their Wrists': African Americans in East Florida, 1763–1784," in *The African American Heritage of Florida*, ed. David R. Colburn and Jane L. Landers (Gainesville: University of Florida Press, 1995), 71–103; Daniel L. Schaefer, "'A Swamp of an Investment?' Richard Oswald's British East Florida Experiment," in *Colonial Plantations and Economy in Florida*, ed. Jane Landers (Gainesville: University of Florida Press, 2000), 11–38; Daniel L. Schaefer, *William Bartram and the Ghost Plantations of East Florida* (Gainesville: University of Florida Press, 2010); David Hancock, *Citizens of the World: London Merchants and the Integration of the British Atlantic Community, 1735–1785* (Cambridge, UK: Cambridge University Press, 1995), 143–171; Mark Quintanilla, "The World of Alexander Campbell: An Eighteenth-Century Grenadian Planter," *Albion* 38, no. 2 (2003): 229–240; Mark Quintanilla, "Mercantile Communities in the Ceded Islands: The Alexander Bartlet and George Campbell Company," *International Social Science Review* 79, 1–2 (2004): 14–26; Douglas Hamilton, "Robert Melville and the Frontiers of Empire in the British West Indies, 1763–1771," in *Military Governors and Imperial Frontiers, c. 1600–1800: A Study of Scotland and Empires*, eds. A. Mackillop and S. Murdoch (Leiden: Brill, 2003), 181–204.

6   David Eltis, Philip D. Morgan, and David Richardson, "Agency and Diaspora in Atlantic History: Reassessing the African Contribution to Rice Cultivation in the Americas," *American Historical Review* 112, no. 1 (2007): 1340.

7   Robin Law, *Ouidah: The Social History of a West African Slaving "Port," 1727–1892* (Athens: Ohio University Press, 2002), 37–38.

8   John Milner Gray, *A History of the Gambia* (Cambridge, UK: Cambridge University Press, 1940), 120–149; Kwame Daaku, *Trade and Politics on the Gold Coast,*

1660–1720: A Study of the African Reaction to European Trade (Oxford: Clarendon Press, 1970); Joshua D. Newton, "Law, Sovereignty and Naval Power in West Africa, 1750–1781," *International Journal of Maritime History* 25, no. 2 (2013): 206–211; Phyllis M. Martin, *The External Trade of the Loango Coast, 1576–1870: The Effects of Changing Commercial Relations on the Vili Kingdom of Loango* (Oxford: Clarendon Press, 1972), 81–83; Andre Delcourt, *La France et les établissements français au Sénégal entre 1713 et 1763: La Compagnie des Indes et le Sénégal; la guerre de la gomme* (Dakar: Mémoiries de l'Institut Français d' Afrique Noire, 1952).

9   That history has been especially well documented for the Gambia River district. See Gray, *A History of the Gambia,* 52–275. For English and Dutch competition on the Gold Coast during the eighteenth century, see: Harvey M. Feinberg, *Africans and Europeans in West Africa: Elminas and Dutchmen on the Gold Coast during the Eighteenth Century: Transactions of the American Philosophical Society* 79 part 7 (Philadelphia, PA: American Philosophical Society, 1989); Ty Reese, "Liberty, Insolence and Rum: Cape Coast and the American Revolution," *Itinerario* 28, no. 3 (2004): 18–37; Emma Christopher, *A Merciless Place: The Fate of Britain's Convicts after the American Revolution* (New York: Oxford University Press, 2010), 129–148, and Newton, "Law, Sovereignty, and Naval Power."

10   Joshua D. Newton, "Slavery, Sea Power and the State: The Royal Navy and the British West African Settlements, 1748–1756," *Journal of Imperial and Commonwealth History* 41, no. 2 (2013): 171–193.

11   The Province of Senegambia increasingly attracts attention from researchers, after more than a half-century of neglect. Until very recently, the colony drew most substantial mention in Eveline C. Martin, *British West African Settlements, 1750–1821: A Study in Local Administration* (London: Royal Colonial Institute, Longmans, Green Publishing, 1927); H. A. Wyndham, *The Atlantic and Slavery* (London: Oxford University Press, 1935), 51–58; and Gray, *A History of the Gambia,* 234–275. For the current rediscovery, see Christopher Leslie Brown, *Moral Capital: Foundations of British Abolitionism* (Chapel Hill: Omohundro Institute of Early American History and Culture, University of North Carolina Press, 2006), 274–277; Joseph Inikori, "Gentlemanly Capitalism and Imperialism in West Africa: Great Britain and Senegambia in the Eighteenth Century," in *Africa, Europe, and Globalization: Essays in Honor of A. G. Hopkins,* ed. Toyin Falola and Emily Brownell (Durham, NC: Duke University Press, 2011), 213–235; Joshua D. Newton, "Naval Power and the Province of Senegambia, 1758–1779," *Journal for Maritime Research* 15, no. 2 (2013): 129–147; Matthew Dziennik, "'Till These Experiments Be Made': Senegambia and British Imperial Policy in the Eighteenth Century," *English Historical Review* 130 (2015): 1132–1161; Paul Lovejoy, "Forgotten Colony in Africa: The British Province of Senegambia," in *Slavery, Abolition, and the Transition to Colonialism in Sierra Leone,* ed. Paul E. Lovejoy and Suzanne Schwarz (Trenton: Africa World Press, 2015), 109–125; Bryan Rosenblithe, "Britain's Vital Extremities: British Africa and the Coming of the American Revolution," in *The American Revolution Reborn,* ed. Patrick Spero and Michael Zuckerman (Philadelphia: University of Pennsylvania Press, 2016), 150–167.

12   Christopher Lloyd, *The Navy and the Slave Trade: The Suppression of African Slave Trade in the Nineteenth Century* (London: Longmans Green, 1949); Eltis, *Economic Growth and the Ending of the Atlantic Slave Trade*; Tara Helfman, "The Court of Vice Admiralty at Sierra Leone and the Abolition of the West African Slave Trade," *Yale Law Journal* 115 (2006): 1122–1156; Wayne Ackerman, *The African Institution (1807–1827) and the Antislavery Movement in Great Britain* (Lewiston, ME: E. Mellon Press,

2005); Keith Hamilton and Patrick Salmon, eds., *Slavery, Diplomacy and Empire: Britain and the Suppression of the Slave Trade, 1807–1975* (Sussex: Sussex Academic Press, 2009); Robin Law, "Abolition and Imperialism and the British Suppression of the Atlantic Slave Trade," in *Abolition and Imperialism in Britain, Africa, and the Atlantic,* ed. Derek R. Peterson (Athens: Ohio University Press), 150–174; Padraic X. Scanlan, *Freedom's Debtors: British Antislavery in Sierra Leone in the Age of Revolution* (New Haven, CT: Yale University Press, 2017).

13   Reverend John Lindsay, *A Voyage to the Coast of Africa in 1758, containing a succinct account of the expedition to, and the taking of the island of Goree, by a squadron commanded by the Honorable Augustus Keppel* (London, 1759), 7–62; George Duke, *The Life of Major-General Richard Worge, Colonel of the 86th Regiment of Foot, and Governor of Senegal in Africa; with an Account of the Settlements of Senegal and Goree* (London: Parker, Furnivall and Parker, 1844); A. J. Marsh, "The Taking of Goree," *The Mariner's Mirror* 51, no. 2 (1965): 117–130; James L. A. Webb, Jr, "The Mid-Eighteenth-Century Gum Arabic Trade and the British Conquest of Saint-Louis du Senegal, 1758," *Journal of Imperial and Commonwealth History* 25 (1997): 37–58.

14   See, from among innumerable examples, *England's Glory. A collection of loyal songs, sung at the theatres, Vauxhall, ranelagh, the musical societies and co. On the astonishing Victories obtain'd by His Majesty's Forces, by Land and Sea* (London, 1762), 41.

15   Malachy Postlethwayt, *In Honour to the Administration. The Importance of the African Expedition Considered: with copies of the Memorials, as drawn up originally, and presented to the ministry, to induce them to take possession of the French forts and settlements in the river Senagal, as well as others on the coast of Africa—the whole as planned and designed by Malachy Postlethwayt: to which are added observations, illustrating the said memorials, for the peculiar benefit and advantage of all British African and West-African merchants and British planters, as well as the kingdom in general: with reasons for Great Britain's keeping possession of the French African settlements, if possible; humbly addressed to the British ministry* (London, 1758); Kate Hotblack, *Chatham's Colonial Policy: A Study in the Fiscal and Economic Implications of the Colonial Policy of the Elder Pitt* (London: Routledge, 1917), 41–42.

16   See most recently, Nancy F. Koehn, *The Power of Commerce: Economy and Governance in the First British Empire* (Ithaca, NY: Cornell University Press, 1994), 149–164; Helen Dewar, "Canada or Guadeloupe? French and British Perceptions of Empire, 1760–1763," *Canadian Historical Review* 91, no. 4 (2010): 637–660. The tenth article of the definitive treaty of peace reads as follows. "His Britannic Majesty shall return to France the island of Goree, in the condition it was in when conquered; and his most Christian Majesty cedes, in full right, and guaranties to the King of Great Britain, the River Senegal, with the forts and factories of St. Lewis, Podor, and Galam; and with all the rights and dependencies of the said River Senegal."

17   The exception now is Rosenblithe, "Empire's Vital Extremities," 154–157, which emphasizes the role of merchants and men with knowledge of the nearby Gambia trade in encouraging the return of Gorée.

18   *London Chronicle,* January 13, 1763; *Gazeteer and London Daily Advertiser,* January 18, 1763; *London Evening Post,* February 8, 1763; *London Evening Post,* March 8, 1763.

19   *Public Advertiser,* September 5, 1763; *An Address to Sir John Cust, bart. Speaker of the House of Commons; in which the character of Lord Bute, Mr. Pitt, and Mr. Wilkes, appear in a new light …* (London, 1763).

20   The best overview of the subject remains Stein, *The French Slave Trade in the Eighteenth Century;* although also see David Geggus, "The French Slave Trade: An Overview," *William & Mary Quarterly,* 3rd Series, 58, no. 1 (2001): 119–138, especially 122–123. The public controversy over the relative importance of Gorée in the Atlantic slave trade may be traced in Dibril Samb, ed., *Goree et L'Esclavage: Actes du Semainaire, sur Goree dans la Traite atlantique: mythes et realites* (Dakar: Université Cheikh Anta Diop de Dakar, 1997); and in Ralph A. Austen, "The Slave Trade as History and Memory: Confrontations of Slaving Voyage Documents and Communal Traditions," *William & Mary Quarterly,* 3rd Series, 58 (2001): 229–244. For the growing importance of Anomabu to France and its challenge to British power there, see Newton, "Slavery, Sea Power, and the State," 183–187; and Randy Sparks, *Where the Negroes Are Masters: An African Port in the Era of the Slave Trade* (Cambridge, MA: Harvard University Press, 2014), 35–67. Île-Saint-Louis was even less important as an entrepôt for the slave trade. In most years during the first half of the eighteenth century, it sent even fewer African captives to the Americas than Gorée. In some years, it appears, Île-Saint-Louis exported no one.

21   *The Annual Register or a View of the History, Politics, and Literature of the Year 1762* (London, 1763).

22   Walter Rodney, *History of the Upper Guinea Coast, 1545–1800* (Oxford: Clarendon Press, 1970), 152–170; David Eltis, "The Relative Importance of Slaves and Commodities in the Atlantic Trade of Seventeenth-Century Africa," *Journal of African History* 35, no. 2 (1994): 237–249.

23   Joseph Inikori has pursued this subject most persistently. See his *The Chaining of a Continent: Export Demand for Captives and the History of Africa South of the Sahara, 1450–1870* (Mona, Jamaica: Institute of Social and Economic Research, University of the West Indies, 1992), 47–50, and his *Africans and the Industrial Revolution in England* (Cambridge, UK: Cambridge University Press, 2002), 385–388. More recently, see, Robin Law, Suzanne Schwarz, and Silke Strickrodt, eds., *Commercial Agriculture, The Slave Trade, and Slavery in Atlantic Africa* (Woodbridge, UK: James Curry, 2016).

24   James L. A. Webb, *Desert Frontier: Ecological and Economic Change along the Western Sahel, 1600–1850* (Madison: University of Wisconsin Press, 1995), 97–131; Webb, "The Mid-Eighteenth-Century Gum Arabic Trade," 38–41; Inikori, *Africans and the Industrial Revolution in England,* 397–399; Maxine Berg, "In Pursuit of Luxury: Global History and British Consumer Goods in the Eighteenth Century," *Past and Present* 182 (2004): 137–140. Gum senegal and Gum Arabic are sometimes conflated in the secondary literature. Textile manufacturers in Europe were quite certain, though, that the former served their purposes better than the latter. See, for example, *Journals of the House of Commons* 26 (1750–1754): 442–443.

25   Andre Delcourt, *La France et les établissements français au Sénégal entre 1713 et 1763,* 179–346; Webb, "The Mid-Eighteenth-Century Gum Arabic Trade," 41–43; Inikori, *Africans and the Industrial Revolution in England,* 397–398.

26   Webb, "The Mid-Eighteenth-Century Gum Arabic Trade," 43–46; Berg, "In Pursuit of Luxury," 137–141. For one of the many contemporary chronicles that narrate the history of this expedition, see John Almon, *A Review of Pitt's Administration* (London, 1763), 83–85.

27   A. P. Wadsworth and J. de Lacy Mann, *The Cotton Trade and Industrial Lancashire, 1600–1780* (Manchester: Manchester University Press, 1931), 156–157, 244–247; Alan J. Kidd, "Samuel Touchet (c. 1705–1773), merchant and politician," *Oxford*

Dictionary of National Biography online edition; and *Letter to a Merchant at Bristol, concerning a Petition of S- T-, Esq; To the King, For an Exclusive Grant to the Trade of the River Senegal* (London, 1762), 5–16.

28 *Letter to a Merchant at Bristol* 15–43, citation on page 40. A full summary of the debate on these petitions in Parliament appears in *The London Magazine, or Gentleman's Monthly Intelligencer* 34 (1765): 122–124. The debate over the proposed monopoly is narrated well in Joseph Inikori, "Gentlemanly Capitalism and Imperialism in West Africa: Great Britain and Senegambia in the Eighteenth Century," 223–229.

29 Christopher L. Brown, "The British Government and the Slave Trade: Early Parliamentary Enquiries, 1713–1783," in *The British Slave Trade: Abolition, Parliament and People*, ed. Stephen Farrell, Melanie Unwin, and James Walvin (Edinburgh: University of Edinburgh Press, 2007), 31–38; William Pettigrew, "Free to Enslave: Politics and the Escalation of Britain's Transatlantic Slave Trade, 1688–1714," *William & Mary Quarterly*, 3rd Series, 64, no. 1 (2007): 3–38; Pettigrew, *Freedom's Debt: The Royal African Company and the Politics of the Atlantic Slave Trade, 1672–1752* (Chapel Hill: Omohundro Institute of Early American History and Culture, University of North Carolina Press, 2013); Martin, *The British West African Settlements, 1750–1821*, 43–56; Frederick Madden, with David Fieldhouse, eds., *Imperial Reconstruction, 1763–1840: The Evolution of Alternative Systems of Colonial Government. Select Documents on the Constitutional History of the British Empire and Commonwealth, Volume III* (New York: Greenwood, 1987), 493.

30 Pierre Boulle, "Eighteenth-Century French Policies toward Senegal: The Ministry of Choiseul," *Canadian Journal of African Studies/Revue Canadienne des Etudes Africaines* 4, no. 3 (1970): 305–320. Nicholas Tracy, "The Gunboat Diplomacy of the Government of George Grenville, 1764–1765: The Honduras, Turks Island and Gambia Incidents," *Historical Journal* 17 (1974): 711–731; Martin, *British West African Settlements*, 61–63; Brown, *Moral Capital: Foundations of British Abolitionism*, 262–274; Rosenblithe, "Empire's Vital Extremities," 161–165; Madden, ed., *Imperial Reconstruction, 1763–1840*, 491–499.

31 Madden, ed., *Imperial Reconstruction, 1763–1840*, 497–499; Martin, *British West African Settlements*, 80–102; Gray, *History of the Gambia*, 234–275; Wyndham, *Atlantic and Slavery*, 51–58.

32 This (too) brief sketch draws principally from J. D. Hargreaves, "Assimilation in Eighteenth-Century Senegal," *Journal of African History* 6, no. 2 (1965): 177–184, George E. Brooks, Jr., "The Signares of Saint-Louis and Goree: Women Entrepreneurs in Eighteenth-Century Senegal and Goree," in *Women in Africa: Studies in Social and Economic Change*, ed. Nancy J. Hafkin and Edna Bay (Stanford, CA: Stanford University Press, 1976), 19–44, James H. Searing, *West African Slavery and Atlantic Commerce: The Senegal River Valley, 1700–1850* (Cambridge, UK: Cambridge University Press, 1993), 93–106; and Brooks, *Eurafricans in Western Africa: Commerce, Social Status, Gender, and Religious Observance from the Sixteenth Century to the Eighteenth Century* (Athens: Ohio University Press, 2003) 206–221, 258–261. Also see, Searing, "The Seven Years' War in West Africa: The End of Company Rule and the Emergence of the *Habitants*," in Mark. H. Danley and Patrick J. Speelman, eds., *The Seven Years War: Global Views* (Leiden: Brill, 2012), 271–279.

33 George Duke, *The Life of Major-General Richard Worge*, 96–97. For additional detail on British adjustment to Île-Saint-Louis and Wolof political realities immediately after the occupation, see Searing, "The Seven Years War in West Africa," 280–286.

34   Madden, ed., *Imperial Reconstruction, 1763–1840,* 499–501.
35   Charles O'Hara to the earl of Dartmouth and Board of Trade, [n.d.] 1765 and July 26, 1766, National Archives, Kew, UK (NA) CO/267/1; Charles O'Hara to the Earl of Hillsborough, August 1, 1772, NA CO/268/4. Also see Martin, *British West African Settlements, 1750–1821,* 70–88. A more extensive description of O'Hara's ambitions appears in Matthew Dziennik, "'Till These Experiments Be Made,'" 1144–1148.
36   Charles O'Hara to earl of Dartmouth and Board of Trade, [n.d.] 1765, NA CO/267/1.
37   Charles O'Hara to the Earl of Hillsborough, August 1, 1772, NA CO/268/4.
38   Before the Seven Years' War, between 1750 and 1755, Britain had imported, according to contemporary estimates 477 tons of gum senegal. Less than two decades later, between 1768 and 1773, British merchants imported roughly 4,000 tons. Inikori, *Africans and the Industrial Revolution in England,* 396.
39   According to the *Trans-Atlantic Slave Trade Database,* 61 French ships boarded captives at Île-Saint-Louis from 1659 to 1759. Compare this with the 155 British ships that exported slaves from Île-Saint-Louis between 1759 and 1776. Because the records of the French slave trade in the eighteenth century are among the most complete, it is unlikely that the number of French slave ships voyages from Senegal would be much higher than the database reports. David Geggus, "The French Slave Trade: An Overview," *William & Mary Quarterly,* 3rd Series, 58, no. 1 (January 2001): 121; James Pritchard, David Eltis, and David Richardson, "The Significance of the French Slave Trade to the Evolution of the French Atlantic World before 1716," in *Extending the Frontiers: Essays on the New Transatlantic Slave Trade Database,* ed. Eltis and Richardson (New Haven, CT: Yale University Press, 2008), 205–227.
40   Boubacar Barry, *The Kingdom of Waalo: Senegal before the Conquest* (New York: Diasporic Africa Press, 2012), 136–137, 139–140, 144–145, first published as Barry, *Le Royaumme du Waalo: Le Senegal avant le Conqueste* (Paris: Karthala, 1985).
41   I base these conclusions on the available slave ship data in the *Transatlantic Slave Trade Database,* which, for these purposes, is more reliable for general trends than exact numbers. Of the 155 British slave ship voyages that embarked from Île-Saint-Louis, 106 had been sent to Senegal from London. Yet, of the 2058 British slave ship voyages sent to all African ports in these same years, London launched only 371 (or 18 percent) of the total. For the London slave trade in the last half of the eighteenth century, more generally, see James A. Rawley, "The Port of London and the Eighteenth-Century Slave Trade: Historians, Sources, and a Reappraisal," *African Economic History* 9 (1980): 85–100.
42   See, for example, the evidence presented in Greg E. O'Malley, "Diversity in the Slave Trade to the Colonial Carolinas," in *Creating and Contesting Carolina: Proprietary Era Histories,* ed. Michelle Lemaster and Bradford Wood (Columbia: University of South Carolina Press, 2013), 245.
43   "A Petition Present. By the Inhabitants of Senegal Request. For a Redress of the Injustice Done to Them by His Excellency. Gov. O'Hara at Difft. Times. Senegal, August 22, 1775," NA CO/267/1. Excerpts from this petition are republished in *France and West Africa: An Anthology of Historical Documents,* ed. J. D. Hargreaves (London: Macmillan, 1969), 76–83.
44   The broader context for rights-claiming by British subjects who were not British is well explored in Hannah Weiss Mueller, *Subjects and Sovereign: Bonds of Belonging in the Eighteenth-Century British Empire* (New York: Oxford University Press, 2017), particularly chapters 3, 4, and 5.
45   Searing, *West African Slavery and Atlantic Commerce,* 114–120.

46   Martin, *British West African Settlements,* 88–89.

47   The final years of the colony, with a particular attention to the failures of
      administration, are detailed in Lovejoy, "Forgotten Colony in Africa," 116–119.

48   Searing, *West African Slavery and Atlantic Commerce,* 115; Brooks, *Eurafricans
      in Western Africa,* 272–274, J. P. Schotte, *A Treatise on the Synochus Atrabiliosa, a
      Contagious Fever, Which Raged at Senegal in the Year 1778 …* (London, 1782).

49   The considerations that led the Shelburne ministry to abandon the Senegambia
      venture are described in Inikori, "Gentlemanly Capitalism and Imperialism in West
      Africa," 229–234.

50   Stein, *The French Slave Trade in the Eighteenth Century,* 39–40.

6

Rebellion of the Puppet Nabob: Mir Qasim's Desperate Campaign against the East India Company

Sudipta Sen

The art of political substitution

"Nabob" is an English corruption of the Hindustani word *nawab,* derived from Arabic, which in its elementary form simply denotes a person who stands-in for another. During the long period of Mughal rule in India, it also came to mean someone invested with authority to rule on behalf of the emperor. A nawab was therefore a person of wealth and ostentation, but also one who stood in for the legitimate ruler, or in other words, a substitute. After the British East India Company's political ascendancy in Bengal in the latter half of the eighteenth century, the word was Anglicized to "nabob," and acquired a somewhat different meaning. In something of a parody of the original Perso-Arabic title, it now became associated with "vague stories of untold wealth and oriental luxury, of wild extravagance and incredible vice, of pomp and power."[1] A nabob was frequently not an Indian at all, but a British servant of the Company who had acquired a private fortune in India, often through murky and nefarious means. It conjured up images of Robert Clive and Warren Hastings and their fabulous rise to riches, and also invoked the vast wealth acquired by other Britons in the decades after the Battle of Plassey in 1757.

The manner in which the nabobs enriched themselves was often described as "shaking the pagoda tree." The pagoda in this case referred to a gold coin current in the southern part of the Indian peninsula, where many European adventurers had profited from financial speculation and country trade following the period of the first Carnatic Wars (1768–80).[2] The legend of a tree that bore gold coins became a literary trope in the next century. In many nondescript Victorian novels the "pagoda tree" represented the hopes of young fortune-seeking British gentlemen drawn to "lacs and crores of rupees, maunds of cotton, pekuls of indigo" and many other sources of Asian wealth.[3] The myth of the Pagoda tree was double-edged. The same men who were lauded in Britain for their part in the conquest of India were at the same time seen as infected with a taste for oriental profligacy.

It is no coincidence that the term "nabob" first appeared in the same era in which the political legitimacy of actual Indian nawabs was being undermined. The diminution of the latter and the seemingly counterfeit nature of the former were two sides of the same coin. In the struggle between the British and the French in India waged through their respective trading companies, the art of political substitution became a highly refined stratagem. The term "nabob" thus also came to be applied to native rulers who had been set on the throne by Europeans, almost as pretentious as Europeans portrayed in native regalia.

An early and outstanding example of such newly minted and suspect native authority can be found in the three depositions and installations of the nawab of Bengal carried out by officials of the Company between 1757 and 1764. First, Mir Jafar was rewarded for betraying his rightful ruler Siraj ud-Daulah at the Battle of Plassey by being put in his place by a grateful Robert Clive. Three years later, however it was the traitor's turn to be betrayed, and Mir Jafar was deposed in favor of his son-in-law, Mir Qasim. In 1764, for reasons described in this chapter, the Company changed its mind again, and switched the ruler of Bengal one more time.

Those contemporary observers, already ill-disposed toward the political spoils and financial gaming of the East India Company's overseas servants in India, popularized the unsavory spectacle of political puppetry in India. In his lengthy parliamentary invective against Hastings, Edmund Burke valiantly defended the dignity of native Indian potentates and the legitimacy of their sovereign status. According to Burke, Hastings preyed on the "tattered remains of the nabob's grandeur" to further his ends:[4]

> The Nabob had represented to Mr. Hastings, that he was now of age; that he was an independent sovereign prince; that being independent and sovereign in his situation, and being of full age, he had a right to manage his own concerns himself; and therefore he desired to be admitted to that management: and indeed, my lords, ostensibly, and supposing him to have been this independent prince, and that the Company had no authority, or had never exercised any authority over him through Mr. Hastings, there might be a good deal said in favour of this request. But what was the real state of the case? The Nabob was a puppet in the hands of Mr. Hastings.[5]

We can follow the evolution of the phrase "puppet nabob" from this period onward, it featured routinely in British histories of the conquest of Bengal, and was regurgitated in exams at English grammar schools. For example, John Cassell in the *Illustrated History of England*, a book that went through multiple editions, remarked approvingly upon the Marquis of Wellesley's policy at the turn of the nineteenth century of using military force to compel native rulers to accept subsidiary alliances, which he described as the means used to create new "puppet princes" in India.[6] Ernest Foster, in his *Heroes of the Indian Empire*, explained that much of the suffering native subjects experienced in Bengal during the early rule of the East India Company took place because the nabob had been allowed to 'retain his outward semblance of authority,' and also because native officials were permitted to reside at the court and to monitor the collection of the revenue on behalf of the British.[7] This dual arrangement, Foster wrote, resulted in the people suffering great oppression at the hands of the tax collectors, who not only fleeced them in the name of the "puppet Nabob," but also intercepted revenues that rightfully belonged to the Company.[8]

The deposition and substitution of rulers became a political maneuver of great importance to the British in India. The practice eventually resulted in the creation five hundred or more princely states that existed under the paramount power of the East India Company, and later, the Raj.[9] The subsequent history of titular rulers in British India provides the thematic context for this chapter. This is a study of the short reign of Mir Qasim, who was placed on the throne of Bengal by the British after his father-in-law, Mir Jafar, installed in 1757 by Robert Clive as the first "puppet," turned out to be feeble, ineffective, and hopelessly addicted to opium. Qasim, conversely, proved to be much more ambitious and independent minded than the British had bargained for. Rather than a tool in the hands Company officials, Mir Qasim nursed his own political ambition. He opposed the Company factors and the interference of their Indian agents in local markets, and abolished all taxation on trade putting Indian merchants on an equal footing with British private traders. He abandoned the old capital at Murshidabad for a new one at Munger on the river Ganges in the present-day Indian state of Bihar, farther away from Company surveillance and control. He even raised his own independent army.

But if Mir Qasim was unlike other puppet nawabs such as Mir Jafar, he was also quite unlike the traditional nawabs of Bengal. He did not really attempt to establish a new dynasty. Instead, he was a soldier of fortune, a fiscal-military man peculiar to his times who tried to adapt to the changing political climate in India during a turbulent period of European overseas expansion and the frantic duel for territorial supremacy between France and England.

In the end, Mir Qasim's reach exceeded his grasp. At the Battle of Buxar in October 1764, the combined military forces of Mir Qasim, Mughal Emperor Shah Alam II, and Shuja ud-Daulah, the ruler of Awadh, were defeated by the troops of the British East India Company. The importance of this event has long been noted by contemporary and later historians of India.[10] Along with Clive's victory at Plassey in 1757, and the defeat of the French and their native allies at the Battle of Wandiwash in 1761 (which effectively ended the French challenge), the Battle of Buxar laid the foundation of Britain's Indian Empire.[11] The following year (1765) the Company reaped the immense spoils of their military triumph when the emperor was forced by the terms of the Treaty of Allahabad, to cede the office of revenue collection (*diwani*) in the three great eastern provinces of the Mughal Empire: Bengal, Bihar, and Orissa, to Clive and the East India Company. Mir Qasim turned out to be an inadvertent agent of empire and its eventual victim. He ended up, so to speak, on the "wrong side" of world history.

The nabob as puppet

The Company official who was chiefly responsible for the installation of Mir Qasim on the seat of the nawab in Bengal was Henry Vansittart. Vansittart had been a member of the Council in Madras, and had taken part in the defense of Fort St. George against the French in 1759. In the same year he was appointed to replace Clive as President of the Calcutta Council and Governor of Bengal upon the latter's departure for England. After taking up his office in Fort William, Vansittart found that under Mir Jafar, Clive's chosen protégé, the financial affairs of Bengal had fallen into complete disarray. To the British, Mir Jafar seemed to embody their archetype of the "Oriental Despot." In the formal memorial detailing the reasons for his deposition, Company officials described Mir Jafar as "extremely tyrannical and avaricious, at the same time very indolent."[12] He was said to have surrounded himself with people who were either "abject slaves and flatterers" or were the "base instruments of his vices," so that the affairs of the government could not be "properly conducted."[13] Colonel John Caillaud, commander of the Company's Bengal army, wrote to John Zephaniah Holwell, surgeon and senior Company official: "The more I see of the Nabob, the more I am convinced that he must be ruined."[14]

Soon after his accession, Vansittart realized that Mir Jafar could not be relied upon. As he later detailed in his letter to the proprietors of the East India Stock, payments to the troops were in arrears, and the two million rupees promised by the nawab as payment for his accession had not been delivered to the treasury in Calcutta. Meanwhile, neighboring strongmen such as the Raja of Birbhum, only three day's march from the nawab's seat at Murshidabad, were threatening to take advantage of the situation.[15] In this letter, in which Vansittart sought to vindicate his decision to depose Mir Jafar in favor of Mir Qasim, he summed up the bargain that had been struck between Mir Jafar and Clive after Plassey in the following manner: "An alliance was made with the Nabob of the provinces, by which the Company became his protectors, and the sole defenders of the country, instead of being a factory of merchants trading under his permission and good pleasure."[16]

Vansittart claimed that by deposing Mir Jafar and replacing him with Mir Qasim, he was simply putting Clive's original plan, according to which the nawab was to provide the financial support for the Company's defense of Bengal, back into operation.[17] Later, Hastings would write to Colonel Caillaud that it had been a sound policy of the British never "to leave the Nabob without a subject for his jealousy to feed on and inculcate in him a due sense of dependence on the English alliance."[18]

During the heyday of the Raj, when annals of the British conquest of Hindustan had become a standard subject of historical romance, such promises made to native rulers would not be seen as insidious or unjust but simply as a necessary response to the French threat. Sir Alfred Lyall in his biography of Warren Hasting in the series *English Men of Action* argued that it was actually Joseph François Dupleix, Governor-General of the French East India Company, who first made such alliances with native rulers in order to further his designs against his British rival following the peace of Aix-la-Chapelle in 1748. Dupleix's "system" consisted of "acquiring a dominant influence in the political disputes of the native princes by maintaining a force drilled and armed on the European model," which could intervene decisively in native power struggles. However, according to Lyall, Dupleix's strategy proved to be inherently unstable, because it fostered "complicated and very unscrupulous intrigues with the native competitors for rule in the Indian peninsula." "The English were compelled, very reluctantly" Lyall wrote, from motives of self-defense, "to contract alliances and to join in the loose scuffling warfare that went on round them; [but] they soon proved themselves better players than the French at the round game of political hazard."[19]

Installing the second nawab

During the second half of the eighteenth century, East India Company officers and factors understood the value of ceremony and pageantry that accompanied the position of the nawab in Bengal. This was an era where the distinction between gifts, bribes, tribute, and revenue was of little consequence in the pursuit of profit and political advantage. Every governor from this period including Clive, Vansittart, and Hastings was later accused of corruption and subject to parliamentary scrutiny for overindulging in native customs of sumptuary hospitality. At the time however, not only were presents seen as necessary for dealing with the nawabs of Bengal, the Company had an ongoing inventory of valuables and trifling items intended for lesser deputies as well in the various branches of local administration. These expenses had become routine by the mid-nineteenth century listed under the head of "Durbar Charges" intended to keep the officers of the native court happy, so that they would not interfere with the trade of the Company or the private dealings of Company servants.[20]

In 1759, when the British officers received Mir Jafar at Fort William, Calcutta, the entertainment and gifts to the nawab exceeded the sum of 50,000 Rupees. Among these were fifteen pairs of brass candlesticks, china, liquor, an East African slave boy, rose water, wax candles, cigars, coffee, and vinegar.[21] These customary gifts continued after Mir Qasim replaced Mir Jafar on the seat of Bengal. On a single trip to Murshidabad for an audience with Mir Qasim, Governor General Vansittart spent close to 11,000 rupees, which included the sumptuous offering of forty gold and sixty-nine silver coins.[22]

And yet the token formality of such gestures, where the uniformed Company officers seemed to play the role of supplicants to humor an Oriental potentate, belies the political and administrative exigency in Bengal where the collection of revenue and tribute was falling short of burgeoning military expenditures. Equally importantly, Mir Jafar, despite his promises, was actually trying to wrest a measure of political autonomy. Events leading up to the accession of Mir Qasim reveal that the military leaders of the Company were quite prepared for a new outbreak of hostilities, despite the depleted state of the nawab's own army stationed at Murshidabad.

It was not clear how Mir Jafar might respond to the Company's decision to remove him from office, nor was it obvious that his replacement, and son-in-law, Mir Qasim would simply acquiesce to the Company's terms and conditions. Governor Vansittart, convinced of the "manifest danger" of the revenue and trade of Bengal being ruined, resolved to also purge the counselors and confidants who had led Mir Jafar astray. The removal of the nawab's favorite courtiers, as the governor knew quite well, could not be accomplished without "some degree of violence" (or at least the naked threat of it). In view of this, when he marched to Murshidabad, he brought along a detachment of Europeans and native sepoys under the command of Colonel John Caillaud, under the pretense of sending them to join the garrison at Patna in Bihar.[23]

What followed was a very strange ceremony. Colonel Caillaud, with two European battalions and six companies of native soldiers, crossed the river between three and four in the morning, and surrounded the palace before day-break. Vansittart then sent a letter and envoy to the nawab claiming that he was "extremely desirous to prevent any disturbance or bloodshed."[24]

Mir Jafar, it was said, worked himself into a state of "great rage" at this intrusion and effrontery, and was only pacified by the repeated entreaties of Warren Hastings and Stephen Lushington.

The situation remained in a doubtful state for about two hours. Finally, the nabob, realizing that he was indeed a hostage, sent a message to Mir Qasim, informing him that he was ready to relinquish the grand seals and other insignia of his office, and ordered the *nahbat* (musicians stationed above the entrance of a palace) to play and announce the changing of the guard. He formally requested Mir Qasim to take charge of the government, pay all arrears due to the troops, and send regular revenue to the Mughals in Delhi. He also asked that his life be spared and that he be treated with dignity and allowed to enjoy a respectable pension.[25]

And so the reign of the first "puppet nawab" ended. Vansittart notes in his account of the affair that all the zamindars, merchants, and other notables residing in the city arrived immediately, and proclaimed their loyalty and acknowledgments to the new ruler. This was a remarkably sedate "revolution," and by the evening, "everything was as perfectly quiet" as if there has been no change. "The people, in general" he wrote, "seem much pleased with this revolution; and we were perfectly happy in its being brought about without the least disturbance in the town, or a drop of blood spilt."[26] A participant in the negotiations, Laurence Sulivan, wrote about the deposition of the late nawab as having taken place with the "general consent of all the Great People, as well as highly satisfactory to the Inhabitants in general."[27] There was no bloody coup, thanks to the "masterly abilities" of Vansittart.

Mir Jafar had tried to disentangle himself a few times from the clutches of the British company without success.[28] His attempt to maintain an army of 80,000 men proved utterly beyond his means; his soldiers became increasingly desperate about the arrears in their pay, and eventually mutinied, threatening his very life. If the account of Ghulam Hussein Salim is to be believed, the nawab's unpaid soldiers besieged the nawab in his palace, and cut off his food and water.[29] To add to his misery, the fugitive Mughal prince, allied with the former province of Awadh and the French commander Jean Law, crossed into the Bengal territory, and prepared to march on Patna. In response, the nawab had little recourse but to turn once more to Robert Clive, and ask for help from the military forces of the Company. Clive did rescue him, but by then, negotiations were already underway with Qasim. Once superseded, Mir Jafar cut a forlorn figure. He was allowed by Mir Qasim to leave the palace unharmed, but his pension was restricted to family heirlooms, and his retinue reduced to the women and children of his large harem.

Contemporary British accounts of Mir Jafar's departure seem to suggest that he was almost relieved at his removal. According to Governor Vansittart, the deposed nawab, who had once harbored "great expectations of rendering himself as powerful and arbitrary as his old master" the great Alivardi Khan (nawab of Bengal from 1740 to 1756), was now pretty easy, and seems to be reconciled to the loss of a power, which he owns to have been rather a burthen than a pleasure, and too much for his abilities to manage, since the death of his son; and the enjoyment of the rest of his days in security, under the English protection, seems to be the chief object of his wishes.[30]

Looking into the matter of Mir Qasim's succession a little further, one detects in the British accounts of the period an admission that Mir Jafar did not agree with the plan of replacing him with his son-in-law. Ghulam Hussein, an eyewitness and participant in many of these events, and author of the *Seir-ul-Mutakherin*, states bluntly that Mir Jafar never accepted Mir Qasim as his successor. However, ultimately, he had little say in the matter. By 1760, he was seen by East India Company officials as debauched, decrepit, and corrupt, and was taken into custody by the Company's military forces and brought to Calcutta.[31] No matter which version of the story we accept, it appears that the first "puppet nawab" was forced to abdicate under duress.

An abortive and turbulent reign

When Mir Qasim took over the reins of administration in Bengal the finances of the province were in a state of great disarray, the treasury amounted to less than fifty thousand rupees. By all accounts, the new nawab immediately undertook an overhaul of the financial affairs of Bengal with unprecedented urgency and diligence. He was under tremendous pressure to procure money for the Company, but he was also keen to rebuild his own armed forces. He did not hesitate in pursuing a ruthless policy of extracting money from all available sources.[32] As he began to dismantle Mir Jafar's old administration, he persecuted former courtiers of the Murshidabad palace, many of them merchants who had become wealthy on favors rendered by the former nawab. Mir Qasim also went after stalwart zamindars (landholders) in the realm, and asked them to submit detailed accounts of their landed estates, trying to detect undisclosed sources of profit.[33] Under threat of such a forcible audit, many rich courtiers deserted Murshidabad, and some moneyed families of long standing were ruined. Using the power of his office, Mir Qasim was able to borrow at a favorable rate of interest large sums of money from the eminent family of bankers, the Jagat Seths.

A remarkably frugal man, Mir Qasim scrupulously curtailed the luxurious lifestyle expected of a nawab. The house he built in Munger to serve as his palace still stands on a hill overlooking the Ganges riverfront. Given its function, it is a remarkably modest piece of architecture, more reminiscent of contemporary merchant's houses in the city of Calcutta, than the lavish palace he left behind in Murshidabad. Although he was a devout Shiite Muslim, Mir Qasim removed gold and silver decorations from the major Shiite Muslim shrines in his capital. He reduced expenditures during the festival of Muharram. He also asked the Company to cut back on his own allowance fixed at about Rs. 25,000 a month, asking instead for the very modest sum of Rs. 2,000, although he also complained repeatedly to the governor general that the Company was not allowing him the necessary revenue and resources to uphold his office, especially in comparison with the luxuries afforded to the last nawab, Mir Jafar.[34]

Mir Qasim's search for a secure revenue base was driven partly by the fiscal and military anxieties of the Company itself, which was increasingly strapped for money. There was a growing demand for native troops, as military skirmishes with both the French and local powers seemed inevitable in the near future. Mir Qasim in this regard vindicated his selection as the ruler of Bengal. He complied with all his engagements to the Company, ceding the prosperous districts of Burdwan, Midnapore, and Chittagong, and paying a bulk of the arrears in pay to the Company troops. A few days after his accession he sent a supply of one hundred thousand rupees to Patna. He also gave the Company a sum of Rs. 500,000 toward the impending showdown with the French forces in Pondicherry, and a part of this money was immediately dispatched by boat at the height of the monsoon to Fort St. George, Madras. However, despite such overtures, rumors soon became rife about Mir Qasim's underlying hostility toward the British and their agents. While Governor Vansittart endorsed Mir Qasim as a capable man who was willing to do the Company's bidding, many senior officers of the Company disagreed and did not like Vansittart and his dealings with the nawab. Mir Qasim was aware of this and did not trust many of the British officials he dealt with, with the possible exception of his friend, the governor.[35]

As his political benefactors soon discovered, Mir Qasim did not care much about the prescribed set of etiquettes in dealing with Company chiefs. In 1761, he entered into a lengthy dispute with the chief of the factory in Patna, William Ellis, over allowing British agents access from their factory to the gates of the city. Mir Qasim was particularly displeased with the naib of Patna, Ramnarayan, who had been instructed by Clive to keep an eye on the activities of the nawab ever since the accession of Mir Jafar. Knowing full well that Ramnarayan enjoyed the support of the Council and was backed by army officers John Carnac and Eyre Coote of the 39th regiment, Mir Qasim carefully prepared a series of grievances against him. His complaints included a demand for revenues in arrear, misplacement of documents, improper etiquette, misappropriation of taxes, and even the instigation of rebellion in the provinces.[36] Ramnarayan appealed to the British, but in a series of calculated moves, Mir Qasim refused the audience of Carnac and Coote, removed the naib, and took control of the fort and city of Patna (known at that time as Azimabad). Patna had been a stronghold of the East India Company's forces during the period of Mir Jafar's administration. In 1761, by wresting the city away from the Company, Mir Qasim made it clear that he wished to free himself almost entirely from the clutches of the British.

Soon after, Mir Qasim resolved to bring the frontiers of his province under his direct command, especially in the region of Bihar. Much of this was undertaken for purely fiscal reasons, but it also helped him stamp his authority over arrogant zamindars many of whom had designs to join the nawab of Awadh or the Mughal troops of the young emperor Shah Alam II, and break their allegiance. Mir Qasim placed garrisons at all the major forts in Bihar, such as Bettiah and Rohtasgarh, and appointed his own men to strategic posts. He terrorized local landlords, and had certain key revenue officers executed on the mere suspicion of corruption.[37]

It was said that no local ruler or landlord felt safe in Mir Qasim's regime.[38] His summary punishments, unusually severe methods of interrogation, and the pace at which he attempted to restructure his finances and his military, all point to his fear that a conflict with the British was inevitable. There is no doubt—as his enemies would grudgingly acknowledge—that he was a capable fiscal administrator. Soon after his accession, if some contemporary British accounts are to be trusted, he had raised the revenues of Bengal, Bihar, and Orissa by 26 percent.[39]

Because of the harsh steps he took to against administrative corruption in Bengal, Mir Qasim has been portrayed, justly or unjustly, as a mistrustful and vengeful man. Many of his methods of interrogation rivaled those of the first nawab of Bengal, Murshid Quli Khan, who had terrorized the zamindars of Mughal Bengal during the early eighteenth century. In 1762, for example, Mir Qasim besieged the city of Bettiah for three months and took the raja of Bettiah prisoner. He brought the raja to the city of Patna, where he died in captivity after a period of four months.[40] He made an example of certain prominent and powerful zamindars who had refused to comply with his demand for money, such as the raja of Krishnanagar who was confined and physically tortured.[41] Mir Qasim was convinced that he was surrounded by enemies—some of them in his own camp. As his letters make it clear, he kept up a correspondence with the French, the Nawab of Awadh Shuja ud-Daulah, and also the Mughal emperor, although he did not fully trust any of these potential allies against the British.

A fort in Munger

Already by 1761 disputes between Mir Qasim and the British had escalated over the issue of inland trade and collection of market duties. In all his dealings, the nawab resolved to treat British officials much like his own petty officers. His utter disdain for agents of the Company infuriated the likes of Ellis, Hay, and Aymatt, who complained bitterly to the governor and the Council at Calcutta about this high-handed behavior.[42] Sensing that Murshidabad, the old capital, was no longer safe, Mir Qasim named his uncle Mir Turab Ali Khan the Deputy nazim in Murshidabad and, in 1762, left for good. Mir Qasim "bade farewell to the country of Bengal," and with all his effects—elephants, horses, and treasures including cash and the collected jewelry of the harem—moved his court to Munger (Monghyr, in contemporary British accounts) in Bihar situated on the southern bank of the river Ganges.[43]

Munger had always enjoyed the reputation of being an impregnable fortress. Afghan Suris who had fought against the Mughal Empire made it one of their chief centers of command. In the sixteenth century, a descendent of the Afghan Emperor Sher Shah, Islam Shah controlled the area, until it was seized by another Afghan military adventurer, Sualiman Karnani. His son Daud Karnani became involved in a disastrous military encounter with the Mughal Emperor Akbar, who defeated the Afghans and occupied Bihar in 1574. During the disturbances that followed the Mughal conquest of eastern India, Akbar dispatched Raja Todar Mall to pacify Bengal. Todar Mal took over Munger as his headquarters and extended the line of fortification all the way to the hills.[44] During Aurangzeb's bid for the throne, one of his rival brothers Shah Shuja turned nearby Rajmahal into his capital, but he also strengthened the fort of Munger by deepening the moat, and raising still more fortifications toward the hill side.

From the start, Mir Qasim treated this old and redoubtable stronghold as a military bastion and not merely as an administrative center. He immediately set about strengthening the walls of the fort facing the Ganges so that it would be able to withstand a cannonade from the river.[45] In other ways, he prepared to defend himself against attack. Most of the artillery in Murshidabad was transferred to Munger, and at least a hundred new cannons were purchased.[46] Mir Qasim's new residence, built some distance away from the main fort, was surrounded by a temporary earthen "breastwork" raised high enough to allow musketeers to fire over it from a standing position.

Mir Qasim appointed his favorite general the Armenian Gurgin (Gregory) Khan, a former trader from Isfahan who had acquired considerable skills in the military arts, to refashion the nawab's army on the British model.[47] He established a large arsenal for the manufacture of firearms and the training and settlement of gunsmiths (their descendants still make firearms in Munger).[48] By the time Governor Vansittart, along with Hastings, visited Munger in 1762, British attitudes toward Mir Qasim had changed considerably. Some accounts suggest that after the nawab "entertained" the governor with a parade of his troops amounting to sixteen thousand cavalry and twenty-five thousand infantry, Vansittart warned Mir Qasim that impressive as his army was, it would only be effective against native enemies and that any engagement with Europeans forces would be ill-advised.[49]

Visitors to Munger today can still see Mir Qasim's residence overlooking the river Ganges, right across from the British Residency, now a complete ruin. The sparse style of the architecture, its remarkable lack of grandeur, its neoclassical fluted columns and the sparse insignia of a lotus in full bloom suggests the preferences of a man who had little use for ostentation. From his hilltop, Mir Qasim could keep a hawk-eye on the British. This was also a place from where he might either withstand or escape an attack. The forbidding tunnels that he had dug from the banks of the river all the way to the fort, their entrances now shuttered by iron grates, were designed to allow for a swift getaway but might also permit reinforcements and resupply for a besieged garrison.

Mir Qasim rebuilt and secured the old town of Munger as well, and had a particularly keen eye for architecture in the European style. Old walls were strengthened and new walls protecting the city were erected. He tried to administer the countryside as best as he could from this military post. He took the audience and attendance at his court seriously, and sought to emulate the Mughals in dispensing justice by hearing cases two days a week. He would often take the time to consult with qazis before coming to difficult decisions. Contemporary observers, Maharaja Kalyan Singh, author of *Khulasat-ut-Tawarikh*, and Ghulam Hussain, author of *Sair-ul-Mutakharin*, both praised the nawab for his interest in the law and legal administration.[50]

Did Mir Qasim understand and deliberately repudiate his assigned role as a "puppet"? Were these gestures simply a ruse to defy the authority of his European masters? Or did he revert back to an older tradition of rule that he believed his father-in-law Mir Jafar had abandoned? If we look closely even at his early letters, we can see that he was making a distinction between the nawab's old exchequer and the portion of the land revenue stipulated in his treaty with the East India Company.[51] He believed that such a dual arrangement could not be sustained for long. The fiscal administration of the country was already in crisis, abetting the insubordination of petty zamindars.[52]

A defiant stance

Much has been written on the military conflict between Mir Qasim and the British that does not warrant repetition here.[53] There is little doubt that the search for added revenues led him to examine the management of internal trade in Bengal. He complained repeatedly against Company servants and their native agents, the *gumāshtahs*, misconstruing the privileges stipulated under the grant (*farmān*) of the Mughal Emperor Farruksiyar, which stated that only export and import trade of the Company should be free of duties, and not inland or private trade.[54] Mir Qasim was right in his assessment. Later Vansittart would write: "My opinion of the inland trade from the very beginning was this; that the firmaun gave us no sort of right to it … in inland trade it leaves us with an equal footing with the natives of the country."[55] However, this was the most lucrative aspect of the service in India for new recruits from the British Isles. Their meager salaries hardly justified the risk of disease and death they courted for their passage to these distant posts.

Mir Qasim noted with particular chagrin the flagrant abuse of handwritten passes or *dastaks* by Europeans of every description, who evaded tolls and duties at the main trading routes, passages along major rivers, and at the various marketplaces, simply by presenting the colors and flags of the Company.[56] His list of demands to Vansittart makes it clear that he saw the usurpation of the privileges of internal trade as a root cause of the administrative disorder in the countryside and the growing resentment of local traders and zamindars toward the British and their Indian henchmen.

Mir Qasim's objections were succinct. He stated that Company factors should not oppress the peasants, evade duties or forcibly buy below and sell above market price at the bazaars at their will. He was vehement on the point that the Company's Indian agents should never be above censure from the officers of the nawab. He also enjoined that chiefs of factories should not take over the manufacture and distribution of salt, which was a privileged commodity reserved for the nawab.

He wanted to forbid the Company servants to purchase land or lend money, and thus stop interfering in the collection of revenue and the distribution of credit. He wanted the agents of Company factors to refrain from obstructing the work of weavers. He pointed out that Company officials and their native agents were setting up their own private estates, revenue farms, granaries, and markets for which they had no written authority. Moreover, the intrusion of European agents in the indigenous trade of salt, betel leaf and betel nut, and tobacco, he pointed out, compromised the majesty of the nawab in the eyes of his subjects more than anything else.[57]

Governor Vansittart found many of these grievances to be justified. He would later remark that one of the primary causes of the war between the nawab and the Company was the disruption of the internal trade in salt, betel nut and tobacco, thanks to the licentious behavior of Company servants.[58] Mir Qasim estimated that the loss of revenue from the British private traders evading internal duties came to Rs. 250,000 per annum.[59] When Vansittart reported on the nawab's remonstrance to the Council, only Warren Hastings supported him. Mir Qasim's frustration on this matter became clear during his recapture of the city of Patna from the British when he marched in and seized the gates of the city and laid the markets to waste.[60] The lines had already been drawn before this move. Mir Qasim had placed guards at all the outposts along the river Ganges to try and intercept soldiers of the Company that might try to escape.[61] He had also given orders to cut down all the mulberry trees that supplied the worms for the Company's extensive and lucrative trade in silk textiles.[62]

The price of survival

In 1763, the Company deposed Mir Qasim and declared war on him as a political usurper. Mir Jafar was brought out of retirement and instated once again by the British in Murshidabad. Mir Qasim was defeated in a pitched battle fought by the creek of Adhua Nala on August 2, 1763, after which he took refuge in the fort of Rohtas. Both Patna and Munger were stormed and taken by Company troops later that year. Mir Qasim fled with his remaining treasure and army to Awadh in the west where he was received by his rival the nawab wazir of Awadh, Shuja ud-Daulah. Despite a history of mutual distrust, they joined forces and rallied the reluctant Mughal Emperor Shah Alam II to also take the field against the British forces. In the Battle of Buxar on October 23, 1764 Company forces under the command of Hector Munro routed the combined armies of this Indian alliance.

Mir Qasim's fate had already been sealed. On the eve of Buxar, secret correspondence shows that the Mughal emperor was already asking Captain Carnac for advice on how to deal with the "unfaithful" Mir Qasim after he was deposed.[63] Mir Qasim was now almost a prisoner in the camp of Shuja, who stripped him of his possessions, but refused to hand him over to the Company. Mir Qasim eventually managed to escape into the territory of the Ruhella Afghans with a small retinue, using his family jewels to buy his way out. The Afghans gave him refuge for a while, but they did not entertain his renewed efforts to gather support against the British, and eventually threw him out. Mir Qasim then took shelter with rajas of Gohad in central India, and then further in the west in Jodhpur, Rajasthan. In 1774 he once again tried to apply for service in the Mughal court, with little success. He died shortly afterwards 1777 at Kotwal, in a little-known village near Delhi.

Mir Qasim's opposition to the British culminating in his defeat and exile is not easy to place in the category of either traditional or primary forms of resistance or patriotic nationalism. Such distinctions are perhaps misleading in the wider context of the European war that had engulfed the Indian subcontinent in the 1760s, which involved the French, and British and occasionally the Dutch. Mir Qasim's fight for political survival was merely one episode in the history of the protracted struggle for political supremacy.

For indigenous participants who were drawn into the war, this was an era of mounting anxiety when political and military fortunes could swing precariously. The European companies had demonstrated that with money and discipline, rural militias could be turned into bands of drilled musketry, and a concerted investment in artillery training could give political entrepreneurs new opportunities and advantages. Trade, warfare, tribute, extortion, and plunder were now the routine tools of petty state-building, all pointing to a form of predatory accumulation that was a direct result of the pervasive European military presence in India. As the status of traditional rulers who had reigned directly or indirectly through the Mughal imperial writ was diminished by the exposure of their military weakness, and as older forms of political reciprocity and loyalty were breaking down, new forms of fiscal and military enterprise had to be invented for the political survival of the traditional ruling classes as well as the new soldiers of political fortune.

Some historians might see the regime that Mir Qasim attempted to craft as a latter-day version of a fiscal-military state that had already sprung up in the Indian subcontinent even before the advent of European companies. Many such regimes would eventually be absorbed into the variegated body politic of the Company Raj.[64] A logical consequence of this argument is that the British were successful in conquering parts of the Indian subcontinent not because of their superior military power or diplomatic acumen, but because they were able to incorporate the methods of territorial expansion and revenue extraction practiced for centuries by Indian regimes during the long period of Mughal imperial rule.[65] Leaving alone the question whether a singular definition of the fiscal-military state—derived no doubt from John Brewer's persuasive analysis of the term—is applicable in equal measure to the late-seventeenth-century British state and mid-eighteenth-century Indian regimes, I find the term by itself useful but ultimately inadequate in describing the exigent nature of regimes eventually dismantled by the East India Company, especially in northern India.[66] Neither Mir Jafar nor Mir Qasim, whose regimes were very short-lived and turbulent, could have fundamentally overhauled the old style of revenue management and taxation to sustain the exponential growth of the East India Company's Bengal Native Army. These were transient military experiments foisted on a revenue base that could not support them. Moreover, excessive and uneven taxation had a deleterious effect on their relationship with dependent zamindars, and thus their hold upon the traditional seats of power and produce in the rural countryside became even more precarious.

Mir Qasim's unsuccessful reign provides a glimpse into the price of political survival in the age of British expansion in India. His unusual cruelty toward detractors, his constant suspicion, his uneasy complicity with the machinations of the Company and his subsequent, almost racial enmity toward the British, and equally, his futile, last ditch attempts at reconciliation are all indications of a breakdown rather than the extension of traditional tenets of political culture. Fleeing from Munger to Patna, he ordered the slaughter of one hundred and fifty British prisoners with the help of one of his commanders, the German Walter Reinhardt, alias Sumru.[67] Later he would write to Warren Hastings and try to absolve himself from the crime, suggesting that the massacre was secretly arranged by Mir Jafar to drive a permanent wedge between him and the British, "so that the path of compromise with the English might be closed."[68]

Mir Qasim understood better than many of his contemporaries that warfare and trade conducted by the Company were two sides of the same coin, and he wanted to carve out an independent revenue base for his newly reconstituted army along similar lines. However, the maintenance of a large and permanent army was inordinately expensive at this time in northern India. The Company during this same period saw a steep rise in military expenditure. In 1760, the Company's native army comprised only eighteen thousand horse and foot. This was still not considered sufficient for military readiness vis-à-vis its other European rivals. Between 1760 and 1763, few recruits arrived from England.[69]

The fight with Mir Qasim, beginning with the march of Major Adams and ending with the victory of Hector Munro at Buxar in 1764, marked a long and exhausting campaign where the army had to operate at a considerable distance from Calcutta. After Shuja ud-Daulah invaded Bengal with the support of the Mughal emperor, the Company's forces were stretched thin. They had to defend a considerable stretch of the country while also protecting both banks of the Ganges, garrisoning the forts of Munger and Patna, securing the passes, and guarding the frontiers. Eventually they were reinforced by the arrival of a regiment from Bombay, Munro's regiment from Madras, and marines taken from the King's Indian Ocean squadron.

As a far-flung empire with many strategic possessions, the British enjoyed certain marked logistical advantages over the native powers of India. However, they found the campaign against Mir Qasim very costly, and the penurious Mir Jafar reinstated in Murshidabad had little to offer. Mir Qasim's plunder of Murshidabad, Patna, Dacca, and other places was estimated to have cost the Company upward of a million rupees.[70]

Contemporary accounts of the Battle of Buxar suggest that Mir Qasim was regarded as an unpredictable and formidable adversary. Despite heavy military setbacks at Suti and Adhua Nalla, he managed to secure the support of the nawab of Awadh, Shuja ud-Daulah, and to live and fight another day. Moreover, in February 1764, there was a defection in the Company's troops from the European battalion. Non-commissioned officers and private soldiers, along with some cavalry officers, a total of 170 soldiers, crossed enemy lines and went over to Mir Qasim's side, although some of the British soldiers were later persuaded to return to the ranks. Colonel Richard Smith wrote: "In my own opinion, Bengal never was so near a crisis."[71] Alexander Champion, who marched with John Carnac in this skirmish, notes in his journal that rumors were being spread by Mir Qasim to create disaffection among the Company's native troops as well.[72] Mir Qasim also resorted to guerilla tactics. Without directly engaging the enemy, he tried to disrupt the supply of grain for the Company troops by intercepting boats on the river.[73] Six years after the Battle of Buxar when Mir Qasim was still a fugitive, rumors of him returning with a large armed force, or making an alliance with the Marathas to attack the British, were still taken very seriously.[74]

Mir Qasim fantasized about returning to his throne even during the final days of his exile. In one of his last letters, written to the nazim of Deccan, he asked for his help in reclaiming his lost seat in Bengal. He complained that the Afghan invader Ahmad Shah Abdali, his supposed ally, was preoccupied with affairs back home, and unable to assist him. Political adversity had taken its toll: "Misfortune has pursued me, but no one gives me comfort after four years solitude."[75] He lamented that no power in India could help him regain his authority; the Marathas and Sikhs were "a worthless race" and the rajahs "all taken up with their own affairs." Toward the end of the letter his demeanor borders on resignation: "What can I do? What expedient can I device? Wherever I make an alliance I am deserted and betrayed. It is this vicissitude, the wheel of fortune."[76]

Perhaps he was loath to admit it, but the only viable political tool that remained in much of India was making a treaty of strategic friendship with the East India Company. However, with the departure of the French as a legitimate threat to British interests, such a treaty would have been a proof of his ultimate political capitulation, which he was clearly unwilling to accept.

The commonplace idea that local rulers who entered into political alliances with the Company amounted in the end to nothing more than pretenders or hapless victims has a long genealogy, based on viewing the history of Britain's conquest of India as a fait accompli. These accounts share a familiar dénouement, where along with battles and treaties, the manipulation of native rulers became part of a historical retrospective, or, as Ranajit Guha pointed out in a perceptive essay, a discourse of "conquest foretold."[77]

The rising political mastery of the British in India in such narratives thus also implies a projected mastery over the subcontinent's political destiny, where rulers such as the nawabs of Bengal would no longer be respected as truly sovereign agents of history. In this regard the figure of the ruler as puppet was not merely a conceit, but rather an acknowledgment of the power of the puppeteer as kingmaker and empire-builder. Mir Qasim, the puppet nawab, had to exit the political stage as soon as he had stepped beyond his designated role in the expanding theater of empire in Bengal.

Notes

1   Percival Spear, *The Nabobs: A Study of the Social Life of the British in Eighteenth Century India* (New Delhi: Oxford University Press, 1998), 43.

2   See W. H. Davenport Adams, *Episodes of Anglo-Indian History: A Series of Chapters from the Annals of British India, Showing the Rise and Progress of Our Indian Empire* (London: Marlborough and Co., 1879), 86–87.

3   Theodore Edward Hook, *Gilbert Gurney* (London: R. Bentley, 1850); See also Hook's earlier novel, *Sayings and Doings*, where the wealthy Sunderland family is depicted seated at the dining table talking about the lives and adventures of Company men during the "olden times in which the shaking of the pagoda-tree was an operation more generally performed," T. E. Hook, *Sayings and Doings, or Sketches from Life* (3 Volumes, London: Henry Colbourn, 1825–30), 1: 74.

4   *The Works of the Right Honourable Edmund Burke* (8 volumes, London: Henry G. Bohn, 1854–7), 7: 323.

5   Ibid., 326.

6   John Cassell, *Illustrated History of England* (8 Volumes, London: W. Kent and Co., 1861), 5: 374.

7   Ernest Foster, *Heroes of the Indian Empire; or, Stories of Valour and Victory* (London: Cassell and Co., 1886), 49.

8   Ibid.

9   On the legality of conquest, deposition and the history of unequal treaties see Sudipta Sen, "Unfinished Conquest: Residual Sovereignty and the Legal Foundations of the British Empire in India," *Law, Culture & the Humanities* 9 (June 2012): 8–9.

10 See Holden Furber, *Rival Empires of Trade in the Orient, 1600–1800* (Minneapolis: University of Minnesota Press, 1976), 171.

11　G. J. Bryant, "The War in the Carnatic," in *The Seven Year's War: Global Views*, ed. Mark H. Danley and Patrick J. Speelman (Boston: Brill, 2012), 97–103; and Furber, *Rival Empires of Trade,* 169.

12　"Causes of Deposition of Mir Jaffer," in *Proceedings, November 10, 1760,* in *Selections From Unpublished Records of Government for the Years 1748–1767,* ed. James Long (Calcutta: Office of Superintendent of Government Printing, 1869), 222–223.

13　Ibid., 223.

14　Caillaud to Holwell, February 27, 1760 cited in Henry Dodwell, *Clive and Dupleix: The Beginning of Empire* (Reprint, New Delhi: Asian Educational Services, 1989), 194.

15　Henry Vansittart, *A Letter to the Proprietors of the East-India Stock* (London, 1767), 15.

16　Ibid., 21.

17　See Abdul Majed Khan, *The Transition in Bengal, 1756–75: A Study of Saiyid Muhammad Reza Khan* (Cambridge, UK: Cambridge University Press, 2007), 42.

18　Ibid., 35.

19　Alfred Lyall, *Warren Hastings* (London: Macmillan, 1889), 6–7.

20　See "Bengal Consultations," December 20, 1754, for presents sent to the nawab of Hugli to stop him from favoring the French in *Selections from Unpublished Records,* ed. Long 51.

21　Ibid., Inventory submitted by Robert Clive, Calcutta, October 30, 1759.

22　Ibid., Proceedings of November 25, 1760, "Governor's traveling expenses to Moorshedabad."

23　Vansittart's Remonstrance to the Board of Calcutta, in John Zephania Holwell and Henry Vansittart, *India Tracts: An Address to the Proprietors of East-India Stock; Setting Forth, the Unavoidable Necessity, and Real Motives, for the Revolution in Bengal, 1760* (London, 1764), 64.

24　Henry Vansittart, *A Narrative of the Transactions in Bengal, from the Year 1760 to the Year 1764* (London, 1766), 1: 118–119.

25　Ibid., 122.

26　Ibid.

27　Laurence Sulivan to Robert Wood, June 17, 1760, India Office Records (IOR), Home Miscellaneous Series (HM), British Library, London, UK, 96: 179–180.

28　According to Scrafton, a contemporary observer, Mir Jafar "burnt with desire to free himself from our yoke." See Luke Scrafton, *Reflections on the Government of Indostan: With a Short Sketch of the History of Bengal* (London, 1770), 104.

29　See Ghulam Husain Salim, *Riyaz-us-Salatin*, trans. Abdus Salam (Calcutta: Baptist Mission Press, 1902), 384.

30　Vansittart, *Narrative of the Transactions,* 119.

31　Seid Gholam Hosseyn Khan Tabatabai, *The Seir Mutaqherrin, or, Review of Modern Times,* trans. Nota Manus (Lahore: Oriental Publishers, [1789] 1975), 2: 695.

32　Nandalal Chatterji, *Mir Qasim: Nawab of Bengal, 1760–1763* (Allahabad: Indian Press, 1935), 42.

33　Hosseyn, *Seir Mutaqherrin,* 2: 696.

34　Chatterji, *Mir Qasim,* 36.

35　Khan, *The Transition in Bengal,* 42.

36　Chatterji, *Mir Qasim,* 70–71.

37　Hosseyn, *Seir Mutaqherrin,* 2: 711.

38　This has been recorded by the contemporary chronicler Karam Ali in the *Muzaffarnama,* MSS Khuda Bakhsh Library Patna, f. 334; see also Shayesta Khan, ed., *Bihar and Bengal in the 18th Century: A Critical Edition and Translation of the Muzaffarnama* (Patna: Khuda Bakhsh Oriental Public Library, 1992), 324–325.

39 See the account of Anthony Lambert, *The Asiatic Annual Register* (London, 1804), 5: 33.

40 See the account of the Italian Capuchin missionary Marco della Tomba who came to Bengal in 1757 and witnessed the political upheavals following the accession of Mir Qasim, *Gli Scritti del Padre Marco della Tomba* (Florence, 1878), 63–64.

41 Karam Ali, *Muzaffarnama*, f. 334; he also intimidated the zamindars of Bhojpur, see Khan, *Bihar and Bengal in the 18th Century,* 324–325.

42 Narenda Nath Raye, *The Annals of the Early English Settlement in Bihar* (Calcutta: Kamala Book Depot, 1928), 207.

43 Hosseyn, *Seir Mutaqherrin,* 2: 711.

44 See L.S.S. O'Malley, *Bihar and Orissa District Gazetteers: Monghyr* (Revised edition, New Delhi: Logos Press, 2007), 233.

45 Salim, *Riyaz-us-Salatin,* 385.

46 Chatterji, *Mir Qasim,* 135.

47 According to Karam Ali, the recruitment of Armenian gunners in the nawab's army was a mistake. Armenians in India were essentially part of an old trade network and not professional soldiers. They proved to be ineffective during the fight against the East India Company's army; Khan, *Muzaffarnama,* f. 332.

48 The arsenal would later be turned into a foundry by the British.

49 Rajat Kanta Ray, "Colonial Penetration and Initial Resistance: The Mughal Ruling Class, the English East India Company and the Struggle for Bengal, 1756–1800," *Indian Historical Review* 12, no. 1–2 (July 1985–January 1986): 25.

50 Hoseyn, *Seir Mutaqherrin,* 2: 718.

51 In his letters, Mir Qasim uses the Persian expressions *ilāqā-i nizāmat-i khārij,* which can be translated as "territory under the land revenue administration" or *ilāqa-i sarkār-i nizāmat,* "territory belonging to the head of the administration" meaning the territory belonging to the nawab himself. It is important to note here that he deliberately distinguished his own revenues as separate from the share of the revenue promised to the East India Company, for which he uses the expression *khārajāt-i kampani,* i.e., "revenues of the Company." See *Letters Persian,* British Library MSS, Add. 5634, f. 2.

52 Ibid., 2–3; here Mir Qasim uses the phrase *ajab halat* or "strange situation" in which both the revenue administration and the merchants have become corrupt. The breakdown of the old system of revenue collection and the subsequent political chaos has been noted by Karam Ali; see Khan, *Muzaffarnama,* f. 324.

53 See, for instance, Benoy K. Chowdhury, "Political History: 1757–72," in *The History of Bengal (1757–1905),* ed. Narendra Krishna Sinha (Calcutta: University of Calcutta, 1967), 38–39.

54 Vansittart, *Letter,* 83.

55 Ibid., 80.

56 See Sudipta Sen, *Empire of Free Trade: The East India Company and the Making of the Colonial Marketplace* (Philadelphia: University of Pennsylvania Press, 1998), 84.

57 Ibid., 83–86.

58 See Vansittart, *Letter,* 75–76.

59 N. K. Sinha, *Economic History of Bengal* (Calcutta: K. L. Mukhopadhyay, 1961), 1: 11; Ghulam Hussein Salim in the *Riyaz-us-Salatin* also notes that the English were defrauding the nawab of his legitimate dues, see Salim, *Riyaz,* 387–388.

60 See *Fort William India House Correspondence: India Records Series* (Delhi: National Archives of India, 1760–5), 3: 482.

61 Karam Ali, *Muzaffarnama,* f. 346.

62 Ibid., f. 336.

63 *The Indian Correspondence of Brigadier-General John Carnac,* July 1–28, 1764, Microform 5/7, Reel 4, National Library of Wales, Aberystwyth, UK.

64 The notion that early British rule in India did not really transform much of the indigenous society and polity which it absorbed has a long genealogy. More than half a century ago Robert Eric Frykenberg made a strong case for British rule in the Carnatic as simply a trapping for what remained essentially a set of Indian regimes and institutions that continued to operate with a large measure of autonomy. See R. E. Frykenberg, "'Company Circari' in the Carnatic: The Inner Logic of Political Systems in India," in *Realm and Region in Traditional India,* ed. Richard Fox (Durham, NC: Duke University Press, 1977), 117–159.

65 For a succinct and illuminating discussion of the debate regarding the indigenous roots of the East India Company's fiscal military state in India, see C. A. Bayly, "The British Military-Fiscal State and Indigenous Resistance in India, 1750–1820," in *An Imperial State at War: Britain from 1689–1815,* ed. Lawrence Stone (London: Taylor and Francis, 1994), 322–323.

66 A fuller treatment of this point requires an extended discussion of the implications of John Brewer's much-cited discussion of the rise of the fiscal-military state in late-seventeenth-century England, which is beyond the immediate purview of this chapter. See John Brewer, *The Sinews of Power: War, Money and the English State, 1688–1783* (London: Routledge, 1989). For a lively interchange on the implications of Brewer's study see Christopher Storrs edited, *The Fiscal-Military State in Eighteenth-Century Europe: Essays in Honour of P. G. M. Dickson* (Farnham: Ashgate, 2009), 2–5; and also, P. G. M. Dickson, *The Financial Revolution in England: A Study in the Development of Public Credit, 1688–1756* (Farnham: Ashgate, 1967).

67 Later this became known as the "Patna Massacre." There was a monument erected in the vicinity of the spot at which the English were held captive. It overlooked the well in a courtyard where the mutilated bodies of the soldiers and officers were thrown. For a discussion of the significance of the monument itself see Rebecca Brown, "Inscribing Colonial Monumentality: A Case Study of the 1763 Patna Massacre Memorial," *The Journal of Asian Studies* 65 (February 2006): 91–113. Upward of seventy Europeans including "gentlemen" were recorded as having been slain during this event in contemporary accounts, which include the diaries of an unknown soldier and Surgeon Fullarton. See James Talboys Wheeler, *Early Records of British India: A History of the English Settlements in India, as Told in the Government Records, the Works of Old Travellers and Other Contemporary Documents, from the Earliest Period Down to the Rise of British Power in India* (London: Trübner, 1878), 323–325.

68 See S. H. Askari, "An Unpublished Persian Letter of Mir Qasim," *Bengal: Past and Present* 57–60 (1939): 17–22.

69 Vansittart, *Letter,* 96–98.

70 IOR, HM, Volume, 196, 88.

71 See letter from Colonel Richard Smith to Orme, relative to the Campaigns of 1764 and 1765; the Swinton family records, Kimmerghame, Allen County Public Library, Fort Wayne, Indiana.

72 See the private journal of Alexander Champion, January 6–May 14, 1766, IOR HM 198: 1–326.

73 Ibid., 764: 20–22.

74 See Military Advices from Bengal, February 17 and March 18, 1770, ibid., Volume 102 (14), 559–562, 587–589.

75 Ibid., Volume 202, 33. This is the substance of a letter of Kasim Ali (Mir Qasim) to the Nazim of the Deccan (this is an enclosure to Captain Harper's letter).

76 Ibid.

77 Ranajit Guha, "A Conquest Foretold," *Social Text* 54 (Spring 1998): 85–99.

7

A Tale of Two Treaties: Negotiating with the Indians in Bengal and Florida in 1765

Robert A. Olwell

Threads of empire

In the latter half of 1765, a treaty was negotiated between a group of British officials, supported by a body of regular troops, and an assemblage of Indian potentates. The signatories to the resulting document promised that they would maintain a "perpetual peace" and a "perfect, sincere, and … lasting friendship," and solemnly declared that they "shall hereafter be looked upon as one people."[1] This particular ceremony, however, did not take place beside the River Ganges outside the city of Allahabad (Prayagraj) in August—although the signers of that famous accord also mutually pledged "perpetual and universal peace, sincere friendship, and firm union."[2] Instead, it occurred three months later, and over eight thousands miles away, at Fort Picolata beside the St. Johns River in northeastern Florida.

Nor was the similar language used in the Treaty of Allahabad and the Treaty of Picolata the only thing that the two treaty negotiations had in common. Among the goods the British distributed to the Indians who assembled in Florida were shirts made of "Printed Calicoes" and "Coloured Cottons."[3] Earlier in the eighteenth century, furious lobbying and rioting by manufacturers and weavers in Britain's domestic textile industry had induced Parliament to strictly limit the East India Company's importation of cloth into the country and forced the Company to turn to the colonial re-export trade as an alternate outlet for this commodity.[4] Consequently, it is very likely that the "trade shirts" that were presented to the natives in Florida, and whose like were being worn throughout Southeastern American "Indian country" by the middle of the eighteenth century, had been woven and sewn in Bengal by other Indian hands.[5]

East Indian-made shirts on American Indians' backs are one example of the ties of trade and politics that linked the British world together in the mid-eighteenth century. But the connection between British-America and British-Asia was indirect. Cotton cloth, tea, and other Asian commodities were first shipped to Britain before being reshipped across the Atlantic to the American colonies. Nor, at least until its doppelganger was raised over the camp of the Continental Army on the first day of 1776, did the red-and-white-striped flag of the East India Company ever fly in

America.[6] Although thousands of people sailed each year to and from Britain bound for the far corners of British world, few individuals, even in the course of their entire lives, sojourned in both the American and Asian ends of the empire.[7]

Although global in scope, the eighteenth-century British Empire was structured and largely operated on a core–periphery, or hub-and-spoke, model. With few exceptions, the lines of trade, culture, information, and migration ran from each colonial region to and from the British metropolis, rather than across the imperial rim, from periphery to periphery.[8] Only from the perspective of the metropole could one readily take in the vastness of the British world. In a single afternoon, strolling the streets surrounding the Royal Exchange in London, a person might call in it at the East India, Jamaica, Virginia, Carolina, and New England coffeehouses, and through engaging in conversation with their assorted clientele and perusing their stacks of colonial newspapers and letters, measure out the life of the empire in coffee spoons.[9]

In a somewhat less hypothetical, and less caffeinated, alternative, British-based ministers, merchants, and mapmakers could sort through the dispatches they received from colonial correspondents to gather the diverse threads of the empire into their hands and attempt to weave them into a single imperial tapestry. In this way, it might fairly be said that the new conception of Britain in the decade after 1763 as a global, multi-ethnic, and centralized imperial state was another article manufactured in the metropole from imported colonial raw materials for re-export to the periphery.[10]

Indians, both east and west, played a key role in this process of metropolitan imagining and empire making. By the terms of the Treaty of Paris, France ceded Canada, the eastern half of "Louisiana" (the Mississippi River watershed), and its outposts in Alabama to the British. In the same treaty, the British exchanged Havana, which they had captured in 1762, for Spanish Florida. Thus, after February 1763, all of North America east of the Mississippi became British territory. Within this huge expanse, King George simultaneously acquired as his new subjects, the perhaps two hundred thousand people who lived there. But Native Americans had not been invited to Fontainebleau Palace when the Treaty of Paris was being negotiated. They did not consider themselves the subjects of any one but themselves.

Britain's rise to empire occurred in a more convoluted, if also far more spectacular, fashion on the other side of the world. In the course of the Seven Years' War and its aftermath, by adroit military and diplomatic maneuvers, the British East India Company had gained a martial and political ascendency over Bengal. By the terms of the Treaty of Allahabad in August 1765, the Mughal emperor, Shah Alam II, ceded the *diwani*, the authority to collect taxes, from the perhaps twenty million inhabitants of his provinces of Bengal, Bihar, and Orissa to Robert Clive acting on behalf of the company. When it took on this new role, the East India Company's principal character in northeastern India transformed from "trader to sovereign," or, one might say, from merchant to magistrate. If this change did not mark, in Lawrence Henry Gipson's words, "the real beginning ... of the British raj," it was the first step in that direction.[11] Over the next half-century, the company would gradually acquire similar powers over the rest of the subcontinent. Following the "Great Mutiny" of 1857–1858, this authority was assumed by the British government, which subsequently directly governed India.

In the eighteenth century, no ships sailed between St. Augustine and Calcutta, but the two ports and two halves of the empire were nonetheless indirectly linked through ties of kinship and trade. For example, Francis Levett sailed to East Florida in the late 1760s to act as the agent for the earl of Egmont who had staked claim to a vast estate there. Levett eventually came to possess twenty thousand acres in the colony himself and was appointed a member of the Governor's Council and an assistant judge.[12] Meanwhile, his brother John, who had departed Britain for India at about the same time, prospered as a merchant and eventually became an alderman in Calcutta.[13] Henry Strachey, Clive's private secretary at Allahabad, returned to Britain as a wealthy "nabob" and used some of the "loot" he brought back with him to purchase a seat in Parliament; along the way he also became the absentee proprietor of a thousand Florida acres.[14]

Alexander Wedderburn, perhaps best known to Americans for the blistering philippic he directed at Benjamin Franklin in front of the King's Privy Council in January 1774, acted as Clive's attorney in Britain, and also claimed a twenty-thousand-acre Florida land grant. Alexander's brother David has the distinction of being the only person I have so far discovered to have sojourned in both Florida and India during the 1760s. David, a lieutenant colonel in the British army, first went to Florida in 1765. Soon after his arrival he attended a conference with the Choctaw and Chickasaw Indians in Mobile. But Wedderburn's self-professed ambition was "making rich" somehow and somewhere in the empire, and finding little immediate prospect for riches in Florida, he returned to Britain, traded his army commission for a far more lucrative one in the armed forces of the East India Company and departed for India. By 1771, he was writing from Bombay to Alexander to boast that he had "two houses, two carriages, six horses, and fifty-three servants." He died fighting in the company's service two years later.[15] Included in the inventory of his estate compiled after his death was a warrant for twenty thousand acres in Florida.[16]

But if engagement in South Asian or Southeastern American affairs includes those who merely owned shares in the East India Company and also applied for land in Florida, the roster of men with a stake in both places increases greatly in both number and prominence. For example, although Sir Alexander Grant never left Britain, in the decade of the 1760s, he claimed twenty thousand acres in Florida, owned East India Company shares, and pulled strings to secure positions in India for his nephews and younger cousins.[17] Another of his cousins, James Grant, was appointed the first Royal Governor of East Florida in 1763 and served there until 1771.

By the middle of the eighteenth century, East India shares or annuities were a standard part of most wealthy Britons' investment portfolios.[18] Acquiring a land grant in Florida was a less common, and far more speculative adventure (although if the claim was not developed, it cost relatively little). However, for a few years in the mid-1760s, staking a claim in the colony also briefly became the "fashion" among the British elite. A list of men who applied to the Privy Council for land grants in Florida in these years forms a virtual "who's who" of the British establishment: George Grenville, Charles Townshend, Lord Temple, the earl of Dartmouth, Alexander Wedderburn, Admiral Edward Hawke, the earl of Egmont, and many others.[19] Most of these men also held East India shares.

But the most significant example of how ties of business and kinship could link Florida and India together in these years is the case of the brothers Johnstone. George Johnstone served as the first royal governor of West Florida from 1763 to 1767, at the same time that his brother John was a prominent trader in India and a member of the Calcutta Council; their younger sibling, Patrick, perished in the infamous "Black Hole of Calcutta" in 1756.[20]

When, at the request of Director Laurence Sulivan, the East India Company's board of directors removed John from the Calcutta Council in early 1764, George delayed his departure from London to take up his post in Florida to organize a shareholder's revolt on his brother's behalf at the corporation's annual meeting in London. The Johnstone faction allied itself with other dissident shareholders, including a bloc headed by Robert Clive. The malcontents wanted the company to follow a far more dictatorial policy in India than the conciliatory one advocated by Sulivan and Henry Vansittart, the company's resident governor in Calcutta. When the dissidents gained control of the board of directors in April 1764, they immediately voted to replace Sulivan as chairman, reinstate John Johnstone to the Calcutta Council, and empower Clive to return to India with a broad authority to act as he pleased. Their allied aims accomplished, the erstwhile allies departed Britain, Clive bound for Calcutta (and the Treaty of Allahabad) and George Johnstone for Pensacola (and his governorship).

Anglo-Indian wars

In the years surrounding these events in London, affairs in Bengal and in the "Indian county" of the North American interior followed a remarkably similar path. Like the strange, if entirely accidental, resemblance between the flags of the Continental Army and the East India Company, a few scholars of North America and South Asia have, quite coincidentally, denoted the violence that took place between 1763 and 1765 in their particular hemisphere as an "Anglo-Indian war."[21] But an examination of the causes of these conflicts reveals sufficient similarities to suggest that their simultaneous outbreak may have been more than mere coincidence and that perhaps the concept of a global "Anglo-Indian war" in these years might be analytically useful.

In the spring of 1763, the main grievances of native rulers in both American Indian country and in Bengal concerned the closely related questions of sovereignty and trade. In the wake of their military and political triumphs (against the French and their native allies in both hemispheres), influential Britons in both Asia and America advocated a new policy of "free trade" and sought to disregard or dispense with the previous customs or agreements made with the natives. From his headquarters in Montreal, General Jeffrey Amherst, commander-in-chief of all the king's forces in America and the newly appointed governor-general of Canada (his nephew and heir, William, would serve as governor-general of India in the next century), viewed the American Indians as a conquered people, and saw his task as one of reducing them to submission. In August 1761, following the conquest of Canada, Amherst ordered an abrupt end to the, by now six decades old, practice of providing European goods to Indian leaders. Rather than wait for handouts, he wrote, the Indians henceforth would have "to Supply themselves [entirely] by barter." Amherst confidently expected that besides saving the British exchequer money, the Indians' need to obtain via trade items which they had previously received as gifts and tokens of British goodwill, would serve to "keep them more constantly employed" and hence give them less opportunity to be troublesome.[22]

But in ways that Amherst did not fully appreciate, the plan to impose market principles, and a new labor regime, on Indian Country, drastically undermined the political position of native leaders. In most North American Indian societies, leadership and authority were both symbolized and enacted through the practice of gift giving, or the distribution of goods. Although contact with Europeans and access to Western manufactures had greatly altered both the nature and quantity of these gifts, European guns, kettles, blankets, and "printed calicoes" still served much the same purpose that deerskins, pearls, and sashes made of shells had in prior centuries. The great majority of the "presents" that Indian headman received from European officials were immediately passed out among their people. It was this ability to, quite literally, "deliver the goods," that validated a leader's position in Indian eyes. The Algonquian term *Werowance*, which the English usually translated in purely political terms to mean lord, or king, actually had an economic connotation, translated literally, it meant something closer to "he is rich."[23] Amherst, who never understood the prestige–goods political economy of the natives, described Indian leaders' requests for the continuation of present-giving as "begging."[24]

If they had nothing to give to their people, American Indian leaders feared that their status and authority would be diminished. One Native headman complained that if he returned from a meeting with the British empty-handed (perhaps significantly, the term he actually used was "naked"), the "people … will [get] a handle of it and laugh at us."[25] Britons who were more familiar with Indian customs knew that access to trade goods conveyed political power. In 1759, a British Indian agent argued for a temporary trade embargo as a means of "destroying … [the] Credit & Influence" of a particular Creek leader regarded as hostile to British interests. The man's inability to supply his people with wares, either as gifts or through trade, soon produced "such a Clamour against him from his own Warriours, & other People, even the Women of that Town, that he was forced to quit," the agent later reported with satisfaction.[26] Amherst's decision in 1761 to abruptly cease providing Indian headmen with "presents" (the Indians themselves probably thought of the custom as a form of tribute) threatened to put all Indian leaders in a similar predicament.

Amherst also advocated removing the locus of trade from native villages, where headmen could use their ability to invite or expel traders as another source of influence and power, to British forts or trading posts. In this way, he argued, not only could prices be better regulated, but Indians' access to guns, ammunition, liquor, and other "dangerous" commodities could be more easily controlled or curtailed. Forcing natives to carry their deerskins or beaver pelts to the trading post, where each Indian would be given an individual account, would not only bypass and undercut the authority of Indian headmen, but might also encourage each native "customer" to put his own private economic interests before those of the larger community. For natives, the prospect of obtaining goods on credit also raised the frightening possibility of being forced into debt peonage if they could not repay their debt.

In Bengal meanwhile, a somewhat similar process was developing, albeit on a far grander scale (Bengalis outnumbered the inhabitants of American Indian country approximately one hundred fold). Operating out of their entrepôt in Calcutta, British "free-traders" like John Johnstone evaded or openly defied the licenses and fees through which the nawab of Bengal, Mir Qasim, sought to control their activities and also raise revenue. In the minds of Johnstone and his partners, one of the fruits of the East India Company's victory at the battle of Plassey in 1757 and its subsequent rise to supremacy in Bengal (in 1760, the company had deposed the previous nawab and set up Mir Qasim in his place) was to open up the Bengali market to British trade.[27]

Faced with this economic threat to their political position, and finding their complaints brushed aside and ignored, both American Indian headmen and the nawab of Bengal decided to take up arms in defense of their interests, striking almost simultaneously in the spring of 1763 on opposite sides of the world. In a remarkable demonstration of coordination, American Indians attacked and destroyed British military-trading posts hundreds of miles apart in the Great Lakes region in late May and early June 1763. By early July, British troops and traders had been killed or forced to withdraw from the entire area lying north of the Ohio River. The only remaining British outposts in this vast territory were the small garrisons at Detroit and Pittsburgh both of which were closely beset by native war parties.[28] In Bengal, the "Anglo-Indian war" began when Mir Qasim ordered his army to seize the British trading factory at Patna in June 1763. He also captured fifty Britons, who he later ordered to be killed when he was forced to retreat (the so-called "Patna massacre").[29]

In North America, the "Anglo-Indian war" of 1763 did not spread south of the Ohio River. This may have been due to the fact that without the charismatic example of Neolin, a Lenni Lenape prophet, and his most important recruiter and military leader, Pontiac (or Obwandiyag), an Ottawa headman, who before the war had traveled extensively among the Indians in the Great Lakes region urging unity, native groups in the southeast remained mutually divided and suspicious.[30] But the fact that they did not join in the coordinated attack should not be taken as evidence that the natives south of the Ohio did not share in the same sense of grievance over the new terms of engagement that the British were promulgating. In May of 1760, for example, angry Creeks suddenly turned upon and killed eleven British traders in their towns.[31]

Another likely reason that "Pontiac's Rebellion" did not spread southward was the fact that much of the region was still recovering from a brutal war. The Cherokee, one of the most powerful native groups in the Southeast, had begun the Seven Years' War as allies of the British. But, dissatisfied with their share of the spoils from the capture of Fort Duquesne (modern Pittsburgh) in 1758, and infuriated by the murder of twenty Cherokee by Virginia frontiersmen, they were "seduced" (and supplied) by the French posted at Fort Toulouse (in what is now central Alabama) and decided to change sides. Throughout 1759 and 1760, Cherokee war parties attacked western settlements from Virginia through the Carolinas and ambushed the colonial forces sent to combat them.

In the summer of 1761, an army comprised of British regulars and colonial militia, commanded by Colonel James Grant (later governor of East Florida), marched into the heart of Cherokee country and laid waste to their principal towns and corn fields. In December, the Cherokees and the British met in Charlestown and negotiated a treaty in which the Cherokee leaders renounced their alliance with the French, acknowledged the sovereignty of the English, and ceded a large part of their territory (now western South Carolina).[32] In 1762, four Cherokee headmen were taken to London to meet, and pay fealty to, King George.[33] The Creeks, Choctaw, and Chickasaw may have taken a measure of satisfaction from witnessing the humbling of the Cherokee, but the lesson that British military power had taught their rivals was likely not lost on them either.

In the spring and summer of 1763, British officials and officers north of the Ohio River responded to native attacks by mustering their military forces to relieve the besieged garrisons and seeking to suppress the "rebellion." Ultimately, the outcome of the "Anglo-Indian war" in North America did not hang upon a scorched earth campaign into Indian country as with the Cherokee, or upon the outcome of a single decisive battle (as at the Battle of Buxar in Bengal in October 1764, when the army of the East India Company defeated the combined forces of Mir Qasim, the Nawab of Awadh Shuja ud-Daulah, and the Mughal Emperor Shah Alam II), but upon American Indians' difficulty in sustaining the war once their initial supply of weapons and ammunition became exhausted (the conflict having, of course, brought a complete end to trade). In the fall of 1764, the British brokered a peace and negotiated the terms of subjection within the empire with various Indian nations at conferences held throughout the region. The Indian leaders who attended at these conferences did not go home empty-handed. Rescinding their previous policy, the British had liberally lubricated the proceedings with the distribution of thousands of pounds worth of presents.

"A congress held in a pavilion"

These events formed the prelude to the "congress" that was held at Fort Picolata in November 1765. The leading British representatives present were James Grant, Royal Governor of the newly established British colony of East Florida, and John Stuart, royally appointed Indian Superintendent for the Southern District of North America. The native representatives present were thirty-one headmen from thirteen Creek Indian towns. The chief spokesmen for the Indian delegation were Tallechea, representing the "white" or "peace" towns, and Captain Aleck, spokesman for the "war towns."

After three days of talks and ceremony, a treaty was duly ratified. In the articles of the treaty, both sides promised to do "full and ample justice" to each other. The Indians agreed to put to death any Indian who slew a "white man," while among the "English," anyone accused of killing an Indian would "be tried in the same manner as if he had murdered a white man." The last, and longest, article of the treaty described a "boundary line" to divide that part of Florida belonging to the "English" from the "hunting grounds reserved" for the Indians. At the bottom of the document, Governor Grant and Superintendent Stuart signed first and affixed to their signatures, large, red wax, seals. Beneath, their names listed beside those of their respective towns, the thirty-one Indian "chiefs" made their marks and affixed smaller drops of melted wax.[34]

It will surprise no one to learn that the "perpetual peace" pledged in the treaty proved illusory. Most treaties made between Anglo-Americans and Indians were honored far more in the breach than in the observance. The Picolata treaty itself offers a rather blatant example of this. Soon after the congress adjourned, Governor Grant ordered that the survey of the boundaries of the agreed-upon cession be postponed. Belatedly convinced that the land he had acquired for European settlement was "too narrow," Grant hoped to amend the agreement so to obtain a larger cession without having to negotiate an entirely new treaty. The dimensions of the "Picolata purchase" would not be definitively determined until a court ruled on that matter more than two centuries after the treaty was signed.[35]

The specific articles of the Picolata treaty are not the only things about the congress that proved to be less than "perpetual." None of the parties in whose name the treaty was made have stood the test of time. Eighteen years after 1765, the British colony of Florida was no more. Fifty years after that, the two Creek "nations" described in the text would likewise be erased from the map, their people forcibly removed from lands they had long inhabited. Even the "ancient" Spanish blockhouse where the meeting took place: a stone tower, sixteen-foot square, thirty feet high, with walls two feet thick, has long since disappeared. Its precise location is today unknown.[36]

But while Fort Picolata did once actually exist, the rest of the world described in the Picolata treaty was not really "lost." Instead, the treaty describes a world that might have been, an empire in prospect. On both sides of the negotiating table, the makers of the Picolata treaty hoped to construct a new political realm in which Indian "nations" would form subordinate but self-governing units within a British American Empire. In this American "Raj," both Britons and Indians would benefit. Ordinarily, nations make treaties, but at Picolata in November 1765, a treaty was instead used to help define a nation and to construct an empire.

The documentation for reconstructing the 1765 Picolata Congress is unusually rich. Alongside the text of the final treaty itself and the "official transcript" of the talks that proceeded its ratification, one can add the letters of Governor Grant and Stuart as well as a careful description of the ceremonies written by John Bartram, the newly appointed "King's Botanist for the Floridas" who was a witness to the event.[37] There also survives an extremely rare visual record of the proceedings in the form of an engraved powder horn made by (or, more likely, for) Lieutenant William Sharp, a junior officer in the British army who was among those in attendance (see Figures 7.1 and 7.2).[38]

However, before viewing the Picolata Congress as a performance, the stage must be set. The negotiations at Picolata took place in a "Pavilion … 9 paces long & 4 wide;" covered on top, back, and half of each side with "pine branches." The scene within, as depicted on Lieutenant Sharp's powder horn and as described by the elderly Bartram, was a blend of European and Creek concepts of symbolic power. One half of the pavilion resembled a European-style chamber, with pine boughs forming a ceiling and three walls. In this "room," in chairs behind a table, sat the representatives of British authority: the governor and the superintendent. Immediately to the governor's right elbow, a clerk sat, quill in hand, to transcribe the proceedings. The clerk was depicted on the powder horn as hatless, perhaps to suggest his lowly status. Behind the seated governor, superintendent, and clerk, the powder horn's engraver etched the standing

Figure 7.1 British and Indian Leaders smoking a calumet (peace pipe), detail of Lieutenant William Sharp Powderhorn. Credit: Royal Ontario Museum.

Figure 7.2 The "Pavilion," the roof made of pine branches and the hatless clerk, detail of Lieutenant William Sharp Powderhorn. Credit: Royal Ontario Museum.

figures of a number of other men, perhaps British officers, or some of the "curious gentlemen" who Bartram claimed had accompanied Grant to the congress.

The other half of the pavilion reflected Indian concepts of order and power. According to Bartram's account, this end of the pavilion, covered above with pine branches but open on every side, was "wrap[p]ed round with blankets for ye indian chiefs to sit upon." The space in the center of this circle, directly in front of the table, formed a stage where a speaker could stand before the governor and the superintendent but also before the other attending "headmen" and their retainers. The arrangement revealed the importance that Indians placed on oratory as the basis of political authority.

The distinction between the primacy of the written text for the British, and the Indians' focus on spoken words would have been obvious to all in attendance. Perhaps observing the clerk's quill moving as he spoke (and the interpreters translated), Captain Aleck noted that "both red men and white men spring from the same God, but though the white people are more sensible and can write, yet the red people are very sincere in what they say and speak from their hearts." Likewise, while for the British, the treaty was made "official" by the signing ceremony, the speeches and verbal promises made before, and the "presents" that came after, were probably more significant in confirming the agreement in Indian eyes.

The conference opened with appropriate ceremonials. Bartram carefully described the approach of the Indian delegation: "They marched with an easy pace, sometimes dancing, singing & shouting." Although Bartram did not think it worth describing, the British no doubt had offered a "dance" of their own, as the red-coated soldiers of the ninth regiment marched onto the meeting ground, drums beating, and presented their arms. After smoking "the pipe of peace," the two sides took turns making speeches. To emphasize a point, or to indicate peaceful intentions, speakers would occasionally pause to drop "a string of beads," each duly noted by the watching clerk.

Both parties at the Picolata Congress were relative newcomers to Florida. The British had acquired the colony not by conquest but by the terms of the Treaty of Paris (in exchange for returning Havana to Spain). By the time Governor Grant arrived in St. Augustine to establish the British government in July 1764, both the city and colony had been almost completely evacuated by the Spanish. Sixteen months later, at the time of the Picolata Congress, the town contained less than a thousand people; almost half of them soldiers. Outside of St. Augustine, and apart from a small military outpost at Fort St. Marks (near modern Tallahassee), there were no British soldiers and very few Britons of any kind in all of Florida.

The Creeks asserted, with perhaps greater justice, that they were the rightful conquerors and possessors of Florida. Their people had fought against the Spanish since the late seventeenth century, as allies of the English during imperial wars, but on their own at other times. The Indians gathered at Picolata may have viewed the Spanish evacuation of Florida as marking their final victory in very long war. Even before 1763, Creek war parties had moved with impunity through all of Florida that lay outside the range of the cannon of St. Augustine and Fort St. Marks. At Picolata, Governor Grant appeared to acknowledge the merit of the Creek's claims when he conceded that "the peninsula of Florida" had been "conquered by the white and red people jointly together."[39]

The identities with which two parties at Picolata were clothed were also newly tailored and in some cases still fit awkwardly. The term "Creek," for example, resembled the long-tailed coats that many of the Indian headmen were depicted as wearing in the powder horn engraving because it also was of British manufacture.[40] The identity was first coined by Carolina traders at the end of the seventeenth century to denote a group of Muskogean Indians hostile to the Spanish in Florida and thus open to British offers of alliance and trade.[41] They were first described in British colonial records by their location (in modern south central Georgia) as the "Ochese Creek Indians." This was eventually simplified to the "Creek Indians." The name stuck even after most members of the group migrated westward in the early eighteenth century. There, they were divided into the "lower towns" along the Chatahoochee River (on the modern Georgia–Alabama border), and the "upper towns" along the Coosa and Tallapoosa Rivers (in modern central Alabama). None of the Indian speakers at Picolata identified themselves as Creek. Nor, for that matter, did they refer to themselves as "Indians." Instead, they spoke simply of those they represented as the "people," or more interestingly perhaps, as the "red men."

But most often, when Indian speakers at Picolata described themselves or others in their party, they spoke of the towns represented: "of Cowetaws" or "of Latchawie." This close identification with the town expressed the speakers' understanding of southeastern Indian political realities. In the mid-eighteenth century, every Creek village was an autonomous polity, accustomed to making its own decisions as regards trade, treaty, or war.[42] The British were well aware of the significance of towns among the Indians. In a letter written before the congress, Governor Grant noted that Indian "towns … may be considered as so many different Republiks which form one State, but each of … [which] has Separate Views & Interests."[43]

The Treaty of Picolata reflected this duality between "different Republiks" and "one State." To British eyes, the operative words may have come at the head of the text: "Upper and Lower Creek Nations." For Indians however, the more significant words probably came later, when the headmen each signed alongside the names of their respective towns. Where the British read an agreement between one kingdom and two nations, the Creeks may have seen a treaty between fourteen, independent, signatories. Perhaps, it was hoped these separate towns were becoming a "nation" by virtue of the treaty itself. In fact, none of the upper Creek towns had sent representatives to the Picolata Congress. Thus, their inclusion in the treaty text was an act of presumption on the part of the British. The fact that none of the Indians present objected suggests that they felt that only towns (or their representatives) could bind themselves in such matters.

For the British as much as the Creeks, the question of "national" identity was a complicated one. It is unlikely, for instance, that anyone present at Picolata would have thought of themselves to themselves as being "British." The kingdom of "Great Britain" was created in 1707 from the merger of two kingdoms, or as eighteenth-century authors commonly described it, two "races": the English and the Scots. The flag that flew from Fort Picolata during the conference embodied the "invented" character of the British nation as it simply combined the English cross of St. George and the Scottish cross of St. Andrew. However, although the "act of union" had occurred almost sixty years before, cultural distinctions between English and Scots remained very strong in 1765.[44]

The prominence and predominance of Scots in positions of influence in the British government and military establishment in the 1760s was a subject of great and vitriolic discussion in England. In the English opposition press, Scottish officials and officers were depicted as parasites on the body politic, and as posing a danger to traditional "English" liberties. At Picolata, James Grant and John Stuart may have officially represented the king of Great Britain, but on the streets of London, or Charleston, and probably even St. Augustine, they were also instantly marked, and likely identified themselves, as Scots. Likewise, a good number of the traders who lived and traveled among the Creek were "North Britons." By the early nineteenth century, many prominent Creeks would be the children of "acts of union" between Scottish traders and Indian women, and bear names like McIntosh or McGillivray.[45]

Indian speakers at Picolata employed an outdated vocabulary when they referred to those on the other side of the negotiating table as "English." They also, less commonly, spoke of "white people," but never of "British." When, in the treaty text itself, the Indians pledged themselves to "do full and ample justice to the English" it is unlikely that they were reserving the right to kill Scotsmen. Instead, their usage suggests that the term "English" served the same function for Indians as the misnomer "Creek" did for the British. Moreover, its inclusion in the treaty text indicates that the British both knew of and conceded to the Indians' use of "English"—much as the Indians acceded to the British use of the term "Creek."

The newest, largest, and most contingent identities being performed and inscribed at Picolata were closely related and to a considerable degree interdependent. Beyond the boundaries of their individual towns, Indian headmen may have sought to create a more cohesive "Nation." For the British, the "Creek Nation," once created, could take its place within an emerging concept of "Empire" that would extend far beyond the borders of the "Kingdom of Great Britain" to incorporate and control millions of diverse peoples from around the globe.[46]

The enormity of the British triumph in the Seven Years' War had profound repercussions on both sides of the Atlantic. The Spanish evacuation of Florida and the simultaneous departure of the French from their outposts at Fort Toulouse in central Alabama and Fort Condé at Mobile ended the multi-lateral politics which the native peoples of the Southeast had operated within for most of the preceding century. The reach of Carolina's Indian traders and their British-made trade goods had long stretched from Charlestown to the Mississippi.[47] But, before 1763, the British had never claimed political sovereignty over the trans-Appalachian region. Likewise, the Creeks, who had for half a century had carefully maneuvered for advantage in a "middle ground" between three rival European states, now found themselves declared by the terms of a treaty that they had not signed, to be the "subjects" of the British king, and living in a world in which the British had an economic and political monopoly.

In the late spring of 1763, as the terms of the Treaty of Paris became known, Indians throughout the trans-Appalachian region responded with anger. In the Northwest, British attempts to unilaterally assert their sovereignty and dictate the terms of trade provoked the so-called "rebellion" of Pontiac.[48] In the Southeast, a British observer reported that the Creeks had declared with fury "that we [i.e., the British] have no right to possess the lands that were never given to us; and they will oppose all our attempts in that way."[49] In the face of Britain's newly expansive territorial claims, and in the absence of any other European empires to use as a counter-weight, the usually independent Creek towns had a powerful incentive to act together to form a united front.

Meanwhile in London, imperial gears were also turning. Realizing the possibilities and duties of empire, as well perhaps as responding to the news of Pontiac's rebellion, the government issued a royal proclamation in October 1763, which established the new colonies of Quebec in the north and East and West Florida in the South, and, what was most important for Native Americans, declared the vast region lying between the crest of the Appalachians and the Mississippi River, closed to colonial speculators and settlers and "reserved" to the "several Nations or Tribes of Indians ... who live under our Protection."[50]

The next year, the Board of Trade concocted an elaborate plan to organize and govern the king's new Native American subjects. According to the plan, every Indian town was to select, with the approval of the superintendent, a "beloved man ... to take care of the mutual interests both of Indians & Traders." The collected town representatives of each "nation" would in turn "elect a Chief of the Whole Tribe" to act "as Guardian for the Indians and protector of Their Rights." Once this political structure was in place, Indian superintendents were instructed to seek "the consent and concurrence of the Indians ... to ascertain and define the precise and exact boundary and limits of the lands which it may be proper to reserve to them and where no settlement shall be allowed."[51]

The so-called "plan of 1764" proposed the creation of an imperial political system in the trans-Appalachian region that would consist of separate and subordinate Indian "nations" each with a semblance of representative government able to politically defend their "interests" not wholly unlike that claimed by the older colonies lying along the Atlantic sea board. As Dan Richter has noted, the plan envisaged the sort of indirect imperial rule that was simultaneously being negotiated by agents of the East India Company on the other side of the globe.[52] Pontiac's war (the Anglo-Indian war's western theater, in our reimagining) had exposed the limits of British military power in the American interior. If the British hoped to exercise control, and extend their imperial rule, over the region, they realized that could only hope to do so with the "consent and concurrence" of its local rulers and peoples.

When Stuart was informed of the plan in December 1764, he responded with enthusiasm and a long letter of detailed suggestions.[53] Eleven months later, at Picolata, it appears that Stuart and Grant may have sought to put the plan into practice. When the preamble to the Picolata treaty described the document as an agreement between King George III and the representatives of the "Creek Nations," it suggested that the political unity of the towns the plan called for was an accomplished fact. More likely, Stuart may have hoped that the treaty would help make it so. Likewise, when the Indian spokesman Tallachea was described in the treaty text as the "Head Beloved Man of the Nation," or "Head Ruler of the Lower Creeks," the British were seeking to set him upon a figurative throne, as "Chief of the Whole Tribe," that the plan of 1764 had constructed.

At the conclusion of the Picolata Congress, the British sought to formally inaugurate their "informal empire." One by one, Stuart brought chosen Indians before Governor

Grant who hung silver "medals about their necks" while the "drums beat and the guns fired from the fort." The superintendent then carefully explained to the recipients "the duties of their office." Not all the headman who attended the congress received medals, nor were all medals equal. Tallachea, Estime, and Captain Aleck were made "great medal chiefs" while four other Indians were given smaller medals.[54]

But the British presumed too much. Tallachea, in his own words, never claimed to be "Chief of the Whole Tribe." Instead, he spoke in plurals: of the "kings and Headmen of the nations." Similarly, none of the other Indian speakers apparently viewed Tallachea as their newly anointed "Chief." In a single speech, Captain Aleck's description of Tallachea was translated alternately as "headman of all the towns," "head man of the white towns," and as "the headman of all the white towns." Most often, Tallachea was described as the "the mouth," that is, the spokesman, or chief negotiator, rather than the leader, of "the Nation."

However, while the Creeks may have rejected the hierarchical political system that the British sought to impose upon them, they may have found the concept of a unified "nation" appealing or at least useful. The very process of negotiating a physical boundary to Creek territory may have served to enhance the concept of the Creek nation as a polity with fixed geographic limits. This notion of a territorially defined state differed from the customary Native American practice of delineating the parameters of the "nation" primarily through alliances, trade, and war. (Such culturally rather than geographically determined conceptualizations can be seen on rare Indian-made "maps" that consist of circles representing towns or groups connected by lines representing linkages.)[55] However, the headmen of the towns may now have realized that if they hoped to defend their lands against the assertive claims of the "Great King" over the ocean, and the encroachment of his much closer "white" subjects, they would need to learn how to act in unison and to use Western-style maps with geographically drawn and surveyed borders.[56]

Historically, Creek unity had been constrained by the lack of any coercive mechanisms with which to rein in dissent. Individuals, groups, or towns that disagreed with the decisions of the majority simply pursued their own course, or broke away to form new settlements. Latchaway, the Creek village closest to Picolata was one such independent "republic." The inhabitants of Latchaway had migrated into central Florida in the mid-1750s. As Stuart noted in July 1764, the Indians at Latchaway consisted of "Lower Creeks who have detached themselves from their Nation."[57]

At Picolata, the headman of Latchaway, Ahaya (or the Cowkeeper) was conspicuous by his absence. Although he claimed to be ill, the Cowkeeper may have feigned sickness, and deliberately remained aloof from fear that he would be treated disrespectfully by the other Creek headmen or pressed to confederate Latchaway with the rest of the Creek "nation." Instead, the Cowkeeper sent Wioffke (Long Warrior) to observe the proceedings on his behalf. Long Warrior, who described himself as "not accustomed to speak[ing] in public," made only one brief speech in which he sought to secure his village's economic independence by asking the governor to send a "licenced [trader] to Latchawie." But if the arrival of a resident trader promised autonomy to Latchaway and other such towns, restriction of trade was also a weapon that could be used to rein them in. In this vein, Stuart reported that two years after the Picolata Congress,

Creek "deputies … [had] requested that Traders might not be suffered to go to the detached Creek villages … by which means they would be obliged to return and join the nation."[58]

But even if they were capable of regulating the trade as closely as these Indians wished, the British had their own reasons not to do so. Governor Grant in St. Augustine found the Cowkeeper a useful ally for the colony (in capturing escaped slaves for example) and encouraged the independent ambitions of his community. Two months after the Picolata conference had concluded, Governor Grant entertained the Cowkeeper (and "sixty [of his] attendants") in St. Augustine and made him a "great medal chief," thus recognizing Latchaway as being politically distinct from the other Creek nations.

A chair for a throne

If the surviving documentation of the proceedings at the making of the Treaty of Picolata is remarkably rich, contemporary accounts of what happened at Allahabad, despite the far greater historical significance with which that treaty has been regarded, and the far larger number of people impacted by its terms, are amazingly scanty. There is, for example, as far as I can discern, no surviving record of what was said by either party before the treaty was ratified. Nor was any visual image of the event made until 1774, when Benjamin West made some preliminary sketches for a painting commissioned by Lord Clive. The project was halted upon Clive's death (by suicide) later that year, and the painting was not finished until 1818, more than fifty years after the event it commemorates.

The contemporary silence regarding what precisely happened at Allahabad in 1765 was no accident. Neither Robert Clive, who, as governor-general of the East India Company, represented British interests, nor the Mughal Emperor Shah Alam II may have wanted to preserve or publicize a precise record of the proceedings at Allahabad. Rather than the legitimating rituals of nation or empire building as enacted on the St. Johns River in November, to the mutual satisfaction of all present, publication of the details of the meeting between the governor-general and the emperor on the River Ganges the preceding August could serve no one's interest.

The British met the Indians at Allahabad not in the guise of allies or co-conquerors, but as victor and vanquished. The emperor had allied himself against the company in the "Anglo-Indian war" of 1763–1765. When the anti-British coalition was decisively beaten at the Battle of Buxar in October of 1764, the Mughal emperor was left to the mercy of the East India Company's forces and had no choice but to sue for terms. The proceedings at Allahabad were thus conducted in an atmosphere of defeat and humiliation. After he marched his troops to a field outside the walls of the imperial capital of Allahabad, Clive did not call upon the palace, but instead summoned the emperor to come to him. A tent had been erected near the army camp, and within, an improvised throne had been set up for the emperor to sit upon.

A sense of the world-turned-upside down atmosphere of the meeting is provided by a later description of the setting. The "throne" devised for the emperor, it was said, "did not stand, like the famous throne of his ancestors, on six massive feet of solid gold inlaid, with rubies, emeralds, and diamonds, but was placed atop a pair of simple dining tables." Nor was the throne itself made "of solid gold emblazoned with priceless gems," instead, it was just an ordinary dining "chair … covered with embroidery."[59]

Clive had endeavored to allow the emperor to retain a shred of dignity, by allowing him to sit upon an improvised throne for example. Ostensibly, the treaty also allowed Shah Alam II to retain his sovereignty by placing the Company under his authority. By the provisions of the Treaty of Allahabad, the emperor, in return for a monetary allowance, granted to the East India Company the authority to collect taxes in his richest province. He also made Clive a nawab, or subordinate prince. However, since the emperor was in no position to refuse Clive's demands, the treaty terms were less a negotiation than a diktat that made the emperor the subject of his new British subjects. It was all completed quickly in a ceremony as make-shift as the emperor's throne: "After two copies of the treaty … were drafted, signed, and sealed, Lord Clive placed a Bible in the Nawab's hand, and the Nawab put a Koran in Clive's hand and the two embraced."[60] An Indian contemporary later remarked bitterly that a "business of so much importance, which at other times would have required the sending of vice-ministers and able envoys, was done and finished in less time than would have been taken up in the sale of a jackass."[61]

An even more embarrassing scene ensued as Clive prepared to leave. According to a witness, "the Emperor addressed him with tears in his eyes" and declared, "You have arranged the Company's affairs to your satisfaction, but have done nothing to consolidate my position …. and you now wish to abandon me, amidst a treacherous and treasonous people." The observer reported that at hearing these words (probably in translation) Clive appeared to be "distressed and somewhat ashamed."[62]

What the emperor desired was for the company to use its military resources to restore him to his rightful throne in the Red Fort, or imperial palace, in Delhi, which was then occupied by the Marathas, a powerful Hindu Empire, centered in Northern India. (It was the Mughal Empire's misfortune in the mid-eighteenth century to be threatened by rising powers on two fronts.) Clive, however, concurred with the company's dread of becoming ensnared in a prolonged war in the Indian interior, and so adhered to its directive "never to engage in a march to Delhi."[63]

What Clive and the company desired was to maintain the new post Allahabad status quo as long as possible. If they had no interest in restoring the emperor to his throne and independent power base in Delhi, neither did they want to depose him. With the memory of the "Patna massacre" of October 1763 still fresh in their minds, British officials and traders in India were well aware of the tenuousness of their position in the Bengal countryside. By reducing the Mughal emperor to a ward of the company, dependent on Calcutta for his security and income, they hoped to gain control of what was still "the only legitimate fountain of … dominion" in the eyes of most Bengalis.[64]

Once the ink was dry on the Treaty of Allahabad, the British could gain nothing from publicizing the fact that Clive had reduced the Mughal emperor to tearful pleas. Nor, of course, would the emperor benefit from such a public transcription of his humiliation. Immediately after the conclusion of the treaty proceedings, the emperor sought to escape his predicament by going over Clive's head. Shah Alam II wrote directly to King George III, one sovereign to another. In the letter, the emperor intimated that the revenue-collecting rights in Bengal that he had granted to the East India Company were meant as a down payment for future services to be rendered to him by company's troops (meaning the recapture of Delhi). Clive promised the emperor that he would deliver the letter, but instead he had it quietly destroyed. Likewise, the money that the emperor provided to accompany the letter, meant as a present for the king, was simply added to Clive's enormous "reward."

Nation making and empire building

As this chapter makes abundantly clear, bringing "together what it is conventional to keep apart," that is, attempting to tie together events that were occurring simultaneously in the eastern and western ends of the British Empire, is a hazardous, and perhaps foolhardy, enterprise.[65] As an astute, and contemporary, student of the empire, Edmund Burke, once noted, there was a great difference between the "cutchery court" in Calcutta and the "grand Jury of Salem."[66] The same might be said about the difference between a "beloved man" of the Creeks and the "Lord of the Universe" in Bengal.[67] If one wanted to detail the many attributes that the Indian in North America and South Asia did not share, the list would have no end.

But there were also commonalities. Although the treaties of Picolata and Allahabad employed the same clichés about peace, friendship, and comity, and Native Americans may have worn Bengali-made calico shirts, the most important thing that the Indians at the two gatherings had in common was the party seated at the opposite side of the negotiating table. On both sides of the globe in the 1760s, the British were busily endeavoring to legitimate their new imperial rule, not with the courts of Europe—that had been done by the terms of the Treaty of Paris—but at the local level, with the indigenous inhabitants whose lives now came under their sway.

However, parallel purposes required alternative tactics. While the events in Indian Country in American and Asia in the years 1763–1765 seem in many ways to be following the same track, the trains were moving in opposite directions. In Florida, the imperative to legitimate the basis of their authority over Indian Country engaged British officials on the scene in a process of "nation building" in which subordinate, but also semi-autonomous, Indian nations would be constructed to take their place within the larger imperial structure.

In India, at least in the mid-eighteenth century, the only method by which the East India Company could legitimize its new, post-Buxar, ascendancy to the local population, was under the auspices of the Mughal emperor. Therefore, while with hindsight, we might fairly say that through the Treaty of Allahabad the British were "unmaking" the Mughal Empire, and laying the foundations of their own empire in India, this project was not articulated at the time and probably not yet foreseen. Instead, while Clive and his associates were subverting the subcontinent's traditional order, they were also declaring that nothing had changed.

It is perhaps an ironic commentary on the difference between historical outcomes and historical designs, that of all the polities that were being constructed, propped up, or conceived at Picolata and Allahabad in 1765, only one has survived to this day. Apart from Canada, the sun set on the Britain's American Empire in 1783. The Creek Nation, at least as it was defined by the Treaty of Picolata (and subsequent others with Britain and the United States), was dispossessed and its peoples forcibly "removed" to Indian territory (Oklahoma) in 1833. In India, the last Mughal emperor, long a mere figurehead, was deposed following the Great Mutiny in 1858. The same year saw the end of the East India Company's rule. Even the British Raj, the seeds of which were being planted at Allahabad, and which replaced the company after 1858, came to an end with the independence and partition of India in 1947.

Only the Cowkeeper's figurative "declaration of independence" of his village from the rest of the Creek Nation, indicated by his refusal to attend the Picolata Congress, engendered a nation that still endures. In 1765, the headmen of the older creek towns disdainfully called the Cowkeeper and his villagers, "ishti semoli," meaning "wild men," or renegades.[68] But only six years later, the British would begin to denote this people by a name that, like them, survives to this day: "Seminoles."[69]

Notes

1   The text of the 1765 Treaty of Picolata is printed in James W. Covington, ed., *The British Meet the Seminoles: Negotiations between British Authorities in East Florida and the Indians, 1763–1768* (Gainesville: University of Florida Press, 1961), 35–37.

2   From the text of the Treaty of Allahabad as printed in the appendix to William Bolts, *Considerations on India Affairs; Particularly Respecting the Present State of Bengal and Its Dependencies* (London, 1772).

3   From a list of goods distributed to Indians attending the Picolata Congress, National Archives, Kew, UK (NA) CO/5/540/247.

4   For the Calico Acts, see Peter Linebaugh, *The London Hanged: Crime and Civil Society in the Eighteenth Century* (London: Verso, 2003), 19–20, and Jonathan Eacott, *Selling Empire: India in the Making of Britain and America, 1600–1830* (Chapel Hill: Omohundro Institute of Early American History and Culture, University of North Carolina Press, 2016), 72–117; for the importance of the American colonies as an outlet for South Asian textiles in the eighteenth century, see K. N. Chaudhuri, *The Trading World of Asia and the English East India Company: 1660–1760* (Cambridge, UK: Cambridge University Press, 1978), 12–13.

5   For Native Americans as a market for South Asian cloth, see Eacott, *Selling Empire,* 147 (and note 38); the fact that, by the mid-eighteenth century, most Native American men in the Southeast were wearing cloth shirts did not mean that they looked (or wished to look) like Europeans; Nicholas Cresswell, an Englishman who lived among the Indians in Kentucky in the mid-1770s, noted that the "Indian fashion" was for men to wear "calico shirts… without buttons at neck or wrist and in general ruffled and a great number of small silver brooches stuck in it," *The Journal of Nicholas Cresswell, 1774–1777* (New York: Dial Press, 1924), 103, 120, 109; the "Indian fashion" was to gather the shirt at the waist by a belt. Below, or beneath, their shirt tails men wore a breachclout and leggings; in cold weather they might also use a wool blanket as a cloak or mantle; the three Cherokee "kings" who visited London in 1762 were depicted in English paintings and engravings in this sort of costume

described "as their own country habit:" see Troy Bickham, *Savages within the Empire: Representations of American Indians in Eighteenth-Century Britain* (Oxford: Clarendon Press, 2005), 31.

6   The Grand Union flag, the first standard of the Continental army, looked exactly like the ensign that had flown from the masts of East Indiamen since 1707. Both flags had a Union Jack in the canton and thirteen red and white stripes on the fly; most vexillologists believe the duplication was coincidental; certainly the reputation of the East India Company in both American and British opposition circles as a corrupt and tyrannical monopoly makes a deliberate appropriation unlikely; see Mark Leepson, *Flag: An American Biography* (New York: St. Martins, 2005), 15–16.

7   There were exceptions, of course; besides David Wedderburn (described below), among the bi-hemispheric I have uncovered are Thomas Dale, governor of Virginia from 1611 to 1616, who later served as a soldier for the East India company; Jean Pierre Purry, who did military service for the Dutch East India company before establishing a Swiss settlement in South Carolina in 1732; Thomas Thistlewood, who briefly sojourned in India before settling in Jamaica in 1750; see Alison Games, *The Web of Empire: English Cosmopolitans in an Age of Expansion, 1560–1660* (Cambridge, MA: Harvard University Press, 2008); Arlin Migliazzo, *To Make This Land Our Own: Community, Identity, and Cultural Adaptation in Purrysburg Township, South Carolina, 1732–1865* (Columbia: University of South Carolina Press, 2007); and Trevor Burnard, *Mastery, Tyranny, and Desire: Thomas Thistlewood and His Slaves in the Anglo-Jamaican World* (Chapel Hill: University of North Carolina Press, 2004).

8   A useful discussion of the core–periphery model of metropolitan-colonial relations, and its use by historians can be found in Amy Bushnell and Jack Greene, "Peripheries, Centers, and the Construction of Early Modern Empires, An Introduction," in *Negotiated Empires: Centers and Peripheries in the Americas, 1500–1820*, ed. Christine Daniels and Michael Kennedy (New York: Routledge, 2002), 1–13; in a study of the wine trade, David Hancock argues for a decentralized Atlantic economy based on local networks; see David Hancock, *Oceans of Wine: Madeira and the Emergence of American Trade and Taste* (New Haven, CT: Yale University Press, 2009).

9   Brian Cowan, *The Social Life of Coffee: The Emergence of the British Coffeehouse* (New Haven, CT: Yale University Press, 2005), 169, 165.

10 For the role treaty making played in the creation of empire include Seliha Bellmessous, ed., *Empire by Treaty: Negotiating European Expansion, 1600–1900* (New York: Oxford University Press, 2015); for North America in particular see, Colin Calloway, *Pen and Ink Witchcraft: Treaties and Treaty Making in American Indian History* (New York: Oxford University Press, 2013).

11 H. V. Bowen, "British India, 1765–1813: The Metropolitan Context," in *Oxford History of the British Empire*, volume 2 [The Eighteenth Century], ed. P. J. Marshall (New York: Oxford University Press, 2001), 530–551; Lawrence Henry Gipson, *The British Empire before the American Revolution* (15 volumes, New York: Knopf, 1936–70), 9: 345.

12 Earl of Egmont to James Grant, April 19, 1769, McPherson-Grant Papers, Ballindalloch Castle, Scotland (MGP) 32/264; Charles Loch Mowatt, *East Florida as a British Province, 1763–1783* (Berkeley: University of California Press, 1943), 60–61, 163–164.

13   See David Hancock, *Citizens of the World: London Merchants and the Integration of the British Atlantic Community, 1735–1785* (Cambridge: Cambridge University Press, 1995), 151; Willem G. J. Kuiters, ed., *The British in Bengal, 1756–1773: A Society in Transition Seen through the Biography of a Rebel: William Bolts (1739–1808)* (Paris: Indes Savantes, 2002), 194.

14   For Strachey's background, see his entry in the *Oxford Dictionary of National Biography* online edition; for his Florida holdings, see Daniel Schaefer, "'A Swamp of an Investment'?: Richard Oswald's British East Florida Plantation Experiment," in *Colonial Plantations and Economy in Florida*, ed. Jane Landers (Gainesville: University of Florida Press, 2000), 30; according to the Oxford English Dictionary, the word "loot" entered English in the eighteenth century derived from a Hindi word meaning to rob.

15   For the Wedderburns, see Emma Rothschild, *The Inner Life of Empires: An Eighteenth-Century History* (Princeton, NJ: Princeton University Press, 2011), 129.

16   Ibid., 129–130; for his application for a land grant in Florida, see James Munro, ed., *Acts of the Privy Council: Colonial Series* (6 Volumes, Hereford: His Majesty's Stationery Office, 1908–12), 4: 814.

17   List of the Grantees of East Florida, MGP 30/249; Hancock, *Citizens of the World*, 53–56.

18   See Hancock, *Citizens of the World*, 260–272.

19   Mowatt, *East Florida as a British Province*, 59–60.

20   For the Johnstones, see Rothschild, *The Inner Life of Empire* and Robin Fabel, *Bombast and Broadsides: The Lives of George Johnstone* (Tuscaloosa: University of Alabama Press, 1987), 17–24.

21   For example, for North America Keith Widder, *Beyond Pontiac's Shadow: Michilimackinac and the Anglo-Indian War of 1763* (East Lansing: Michigan State University Press, 2013); for South Asia Pitirim Sorokin, *Social and Cultural Dynamics* (4 volumes, New York: American Book Company, 1937–41), Volume 3.

22   Quoted in Fred Anderson, *Crucible of War: The Seven Years' War and the Fate of Empire in British North America, 1754–1766* (New York: Vintage, 2000), 470.

23   For a discussion of the operation of the "prestige goods economy" in Native North America, see Daniel Richter, "Tsenacommacah and the Atlantic World," in *The Atlantic World and Virginia, 1550–1624*, ed. Peter Mancall (Chapel Hill: Omohundro Institute of Early American History and Culture, University of North Carolina Press, 2007), 29–65.

24   Colin Calloway, *The Scratch of a Pen: 1763, and the Transformation of North America* (New York: Oxford University Press, 2006), 69.

25   Quoted in Joshua Piker, *Okfuskee: A Creek Indian Town in Colonial America* (Cambridge, MA: Harvard University Press, 2004), 139.

26   Ibid.

27   See P. J. Marshall, *The Making and Unmaking of Empires: Britain, India, and America, c. 1750–1783* (New York: Oxford University, 2005), 153–154.

28   See Richard Middleton, *Pontiac's War: Its Causes, Course, and Consequences* (New York: Routledge, 2007).

29   The "Patna massacre" was added to the "Black Hole of Calcutta" as a native atrocity that could be used to justify the British domination and subjection of India; see Rebecca Brown, "Inscribing Colonial Monumentality: A Case Study of the 1763 Patna Massacre Memorial," *Journal of Asian Studies* (February 2006), 91–113.

30   On Neolin and Pontiac, see Richard White, *The Middle Ground: Indians, Empires, and Republics in the Great Lakes Region, 1650–1815* (New York: Cambridge University Press, 1991), 269–305.

31   Piker, *Okfuskee*, 52–63.

32   On the causes, course, and consequences of the Anglo-Cherokee war, see Tom Hatley, *Dividing Paths: Cherokees and South Carolinians through the Revolutionary Era* (New York: Oxford University Press, 1995), 119–140.

33   The South Carolinians may have intended the journey to Britain as a ritual humiliation (in the manner of a Roman Triumph), but the "Cherokee Kings" instead became the toast of London high society; their portraits were painted, engravings made, and they were lionized as noble savages; see Alden Vaughn, *Trans-Atlantic Encounters: American Indians in Britain, 1500–1776* (New York: Cambridge University Press, 2006), 165–175.

34   The manuscript of the treaty is in NA CO/5/540/157–168; a printed version can be found in James W. Covington, ed., *The British Meet the Seminoles: Negotiations between British Authorities in East Florida and the Indians, 1763–1768* (Gainesville: University of Florida Press 1961), 18–41; unless otherwise indicated all quotes are taken from the latter text.

35   The decision settled two related cases: "The Seminole Indians of the State of Florida v. the United States," and "the Seminole Nation of the State of Oklahoma v. the United States." The litigation began in 1950 was finally decided on June 28, 1968; See Louis De Vorsey, Jr., *The Indian Boundary in the Southern Colonies, 1763–1775* (Chapel Hill: University of North Carolina Press, 1966), 202; http://digital.library.okstate.edu/icc/v19/iccv19p187.pdf

36   A description of Fort Picolata in 1765 can be found in John Bartram, *Diary of a Journey through the Carolinas, Georgia, and Florida, 1765–1766* in *Transactions of the American Philosophical Society*, ed. Francis Harper, 33 Pt. 1 (1942): 34–35, 51; by 1773, when John's son William passed by the "ancient" Fort on his celebrated travels, he found it "dismantled and deserted," William Bartram, *Travels Through North & South Carolina, Georgia, East & West Florida* (Philadelphia, 1791); reprint edition (New York: Penguin, 1988), 87; an image of the Fort made in 1763, as well as an account of recent archaeological efforts to find its location can be found online at www.anthro.fsu.edu/…/picolata/fort02.jpg

37   See James Grant to James Wright, August 29, 1765; James Grant to William Knox, December 9, 1765; and James Grant to William Knox, January 12, 1765, in James Grant Letterbook, MGP; John Bartram's account of the Picolata Congress was published John Bartram, *Diary of a Journey through the Carolinas, Georgia, and Florida*, 34–35, 51; see also Kathryn E. Holland-Braund, "'The Congress Held in a Pavilion': John Bartram and the Indian Congress at Fort Picolata, East Florida," in *America's Curious Botanist: A Tercentennial Reappraisal of John Bartram, 1699–1777*, ed. Nancy E. Hoffmann and John C. Van Horne (Philadelphia, PA: American Philosophical Society, 2004), 79–96; and Robert Olwell, "Incidental Imperialist: John Bartram's Florida Travels, 1765–1766," in *European Empires in the American South*, ed. Joseph P. Ward (Oxford: University of Mississippi Press, 2017), 188–217.

38   Lieutenant Sharp's powder horn is now in the collection of the Royal Ontario Museum, Toronto, Canada who generously granted permission for the use of these images.

39   In another context however, the British used the Indian's argument of possession by right of conquest to invalidate colonial Spanish land grants that had been sold at fire-sale rates by departing *Floridanos* to British speculators. The speculators,

John Gordon and Jesse Fish, claimed to have purchased ten million acres from the departing Spanish in 1763. The British had agreed to honor Spanish land grants, and Gordon and Fish followed proper Spanish procedure in obtaining the land, so the Gordon–Fish claims posed an obstacle to settling the colony. Gordon–Fish offered to sell their lands—at a profit—to the crown. Instead, the government invalidated their claims, in part by a dispossession by conquest argument. But Gordon–Fish were invited to pursue a legal remedy. (Ordinarily, the crown was immune to prosecution.) The result however was a "bleak house" like train of litigation that lasted far longer than the colony, in fact, until after the American acquisition of Florida in 1819. See Mowatt, *East Florida as a British Province, 1763–1783,* 53–54.

40   For the origins of the term "Creek," see, Verner W. Crane, "The Origin of the Name of the Creek Indians," *Mississippi Valley Historical Review* 5 (1918): 339–342.

41   "Muskogean" refers to a Native American language group which includes the Alabama, Appalachee, Choctaw, Chickasaw, and Creek-Seminole people; see Lyle Campbell, *American Indian Languages: The Historical Linguistics of Native America* (New York: Oxford University Press, 1997), 147–149.

42   For the "centrality of Creek towns" in Creek culture, identity, and politics in this period see Piker, *Okfuskee,* 7–9.

43   James Grant to the Board of Trade, December 1, 1764, Lansdowne Papers (microfilm), PK Yonge Library, University of Florida, Gainesville.

44   A useful discussion of the problem and problematics of British national identity in the eighteenth century is Linda Colley, *Britons: Forging the Nations, 1707–1837* (New Haven, CT: Yale University Press, 1992); I should add that while it is unlikely that any white person would have identified themselves as "British," there is evidence that Africans living within the British Empire were doing so by this time; see Vincent Caretta's introduction to Vincent Caretta, ed., *Unchained Voices: An Anthology of Black Authors in the English-Speaking World of the Eighteenth Century* (Lexington: University of Kentucky Press, 1996).

45   For the term "Scots Indian" as well as a discussion of their role see Claudio Saunt, *A New Order of Things: Property, Power, and the Transformation of the Creek Indians, 1733–1816* (Cambridge, UK: Cambridge University Press, 1999).

46   For Florida's place within post-1763 British dreams of empire see Robert Olwell, "Seeds of Empire: Florida, Kew, and the British Imperial Meridian in the 1760s," in *The Creation of the British Atlantic World,* ed. Elizabeth Mancke and Carole Shammas (Baltimore, MD: Johns Hopkins University Press, 2005), 263–282.

47   See Kathryn Holland Braund, *Deerskins and Duffils: Creek Indian Trade with Anglo-America, 1685–1815* (Omaha: University of Nebraska Press, 1993).

48   See Gregory Evans Dowd, *War under Heaven: Pontiac, the Indian Nations, and the British Empire* (Baltimore, MD: Johns Hopkins University Press, 2002).

49   Quoted in Steven Hahn, *The Invention of the Creek Nation, 1670–1763* (Omaha: University of Nebraska Press, 2004), 265.

50   From the text of the Proclamation as found at http://www.ushistory.org/declaration/related/proc63.htm

51   See Daniel K. Richter, "Native Americans, the Plan of 1764, and a British Empire that Never Was," in *Cultures and Identities in Colonial British America,* ed. Robert Olwell and Alan Tully (Baltimore, MD: Johns Hopkins University Press, 2006), 269–292.

52   Ibid., 285.

53   Clarence Carter, ed., "Observations of Superintendent John Stuart and Governor James Grant on the Proposed Plan of 1764 for the Future Management of Indian Affairs," *American Historical Review* 20 (1915): 815–831.

54 Estime, although silent at the conference, may have been recognized as a "great medal chief" because he led the delegation from Coweta, which was traditionally considered to be the "mother town" of the Lower Creeks, and as such accorded something of a influential role; see Hahn, *Invention of the Creek Nation,* 10–47.

55 A delegation of Catawba Indians presented one such map, drawn on a deerskin, to Governor Francis Nicholson of South Carolina in 1721; the original has been lost but Nicholson had a copy of it made on paper and sent to the Board of Trade in London; the map is now in the collection of the Library of Congress, a digital image of it can be seen at https://blogs.loc.gov/maps/2016/11/celebrating-native-american-cartography-the-catawba-deerskin-map/

56 My argument here is closely informed by Hahn *The Invention of the Creek Nation.*

57 John Stuart to the Board of Trade, July 21, 1764, NA CO/323, volume 18; Library of Congress, Washington, DC, Photostat.

58 John Stuart to James Grant, October 3, 1767, James Grant papers (microfilm) 22671, reel 13, Library of Congress.

59 John Clark Marshman, *History of India from the Earliest Period to the Close of the East India Company's Government* (Reprint of the 1876 edition, Cambridge, UK: Cambridge University Press, 2010), 162.

60 Mirza Sheikh I'Tesamuddin, *The Wonders of Vilayet: Being the Memoir, Originally in Persian, of a Visit to France and Britain,* trans. Kaiser Haq (Leeds, UK: Peepal Tree Press Ltd., 2001), 18–19.

61 Quoted in Marshman, *History of India,* 162; another account of the treaty ceremony can be found in Robert Travers, "A British Empire by Treaty in Eighteenth-Century India," in *Empire by Treaty,* ed. Bellmessous, 146–148; Travers notes that, as befit protocol, Shah Alam II only served as "executor" to the Treaty of Allahabad, which was actually signed on his behalf by the nawabs of Awadh and Bengal.

62 Mizra Sheikh I'Tesamuddin, *Wonders of Vilayet,* 19.

63 Quoted in Rajat Kanta Ray, "Indian Society and the Establishment of British Supremacy, 1765–1818," *Oxford History of the British Empire,* volume 2 [The Eighteenth Century], ed. Marshall, 511.

64 Ibid., 510.

65 Marshall, *The Making and Unmaking of Empires,* 1.

66 Edmund Burke, quoted in ibid., 3.

67 "Lord of the Universe" was one of the titles of the Mughal emperor, see Ray, "Indian Society and British Supremacy," 510.

68 The origins of the word "Seminole" are debated, another source often suggested is the Spanish word "cimarrón" (meaning wild or untamed).

69 A letter to General Thomas Gage, written on December 14, 1771, in which John Stuart referred to the "Seminoles or East Florida Creeks" is the earliest known use of the term "Seminoles" to denote the Muskogean Indians living in Florida; cited in Patricia Riles Wickman, *The Tree That Bends: Discourse, Power, and Survival of the Maskoki People* (Tuscaloosa: University of Alabama Press, 1999), 197; In 2006, a 1774 letter from British East Florida's Governor Patrick Tonyn to "The Cowkeeper, the founder of the Seminole Tribe of Florida," was purchased and put on display at the Ah-Tah-Thi-Ki Museum in the Seminole Nation's Big Cypress Reservation in the Florida Everglades. Tina Osceola, the museum's director, described Cowkeeper as "the George Washington of the Seminole Tribe of Florida," *Miami Herald,* June 5, 2006.

8

The East India Company's "Ancient Form of Government" and the Exigencies of Empire: Bengal 1765 to 1773

P. J. Marshall

Introduction

In any assessment of the place of the Seven Years' War in the development of empire, the British stake in India, above all in Bengal, seems to be the clearest case of a transformation that followed success in the war. During the course of war, the East India Company began a marked increase in its territorial possessions in India, making gains in the south and especially in Bengal, where rights over an area immediately around Calcutta were obtained in 1757 and three major districts passed under its control in 1760. In 1765, shortly after the ending of the war, spectacular additions were made when Robert Clive accepted for the Company from the Mughal emperor the grant of the office of *diwani* or revenue administrator of the whole of the provinces of Bengal and Bihar. This grant was interpreted by the British as giving them sovereign authority over a huge population, which they usually estimated as up to twenty million people, and over a great extent of land. "The Company had acquired," in Clive's words, "an empire more extensive than any kingdom in Europe, FRANCE and RUSSIA excepted."[1] Control of Bengal had, in Warren Hastings's view, given the Company "the dominion of an extensive kingdom, the collection of a vast revenue, the command of armies and the direction of a great political system." The Company's "ancient form of government," which was instituted for the export of Indian commodities to London, was now, he considered, entirely inappropriate for the scope of its new responsibilities.[2]

Within a relatively short space of time the Company's "ancient form of government" was indeed displaced. The new territories remained under the administration of

An earlier version of this chapter was previously published as: P. J. Marshall, "The Shaping of the New Colonial Regime in Bengal," in *Bangladesh: History, Politics, Economy, Society and Culture – Essays in Honour of Professor Alamgir Muhammad Serajuddin*, ed. Mahmudul Huque (Dhaka: The University Press Limited, 2016), 15–40. This revised version is printed here with the permission of the University Press Limited.

the Company's servants in India who continued to receive instructions from the directors in Leadenhall Street, but on great issues of war and peace or of India's connection with Britain, the Company had been put under the supervision of the national government and made accountable to parliament. There was, however, a clear consensus that problems of time and distance and lack of detailed knowledge meant that no metropolitan authority, be it Company or state, could closely manage the government of India. A strong local executive, headed by a governor general, who was effectively a government appointee, was therefore established to whom a large measure of discretionary power was entrusted. Local Company rule came to be through a bureaucracy dominated by Europeans at its higher levels. This rule was effectively autocratic. It did not depend on the consent of those over whom it ruled, be they resident Europeans or the indigenous population for whom any form of representative government was deemed to be entirely unsuitable. In its scale and in the nature of its population, empire in India was thought to differ from empire in any other part of the world and to require a system of imperial governance that was both new and unique to it.[3]

This chapter will be concerned with the period between the grant of the *diwani* in 1765 and the passage of Lord North's Regulating Act in 1773. That act can be seen as marking a significant stage both in the growth of state intervention in the management of British India and in the creation of a strong executive in Bengal. The government of Bengal was to be placed under a new Supreme Council of four councilors and a governor general. The men who were to fill these offices were named in the act and for a period of five years they were only removable by the crown. They were to receive their orders from the directors of the Company, but copies of their dispatches home which related to "the management of the revenues" or "civil or military affairs and government" were to be submitted to ministers.[4] The first governor general was to be Warren Hastings, who had been the Company's governor of Bengal since 1772. Hastings was already showing that he had high ambitions for his office. Throughout what was to be a long career he did not submit easily to direction from home and in retrospect the autonomy of future governors general as undisputed heads of the government of British India can be seen to have owed much to him.[5]

The terms of the 1773 Regulating Act may have given a clear indication of how a new system of British Indian governance was likely to develop, but in the years between the granting of the *diwani* and the passing of the act there had been strong opposition to any trend toward either greater state involvement in India or the creation of an autocracy in Bengal. For many contemporaries the Company's ancient form of government seemed preferable to both.

There was much debate in the 1760s and early 1770s about the respective rights of the crown or the East India Company to the new provinces in India. Arguments hinged on questions as to whether any territory acquired by British subjects automatically belonged to the crown or whether grants from Indian rulers had given the Company a right of property over its new acquisitions. Although there was some vigorous dissent, the consensus appears to have been that new Indian provinces were crown possessions and therefore an integral part of the British Empire. That the Company must be accountable to parliament for its stewardship of them was unquestioned;

whether they should be directly managed by the crown or left to the management of the Company was, however, another matter altogether. There were a few who urged that the crown should appoint viceroys to preside over the government of Bengal.[6] Adam Smith believed that the Company had proved itself to be incapable of governing an empire, and since he considered that the "crown, that is …, the state and public of Great Britain," had an undoubted right to the revenue of the Indian provinces, he implied that the crown should take over their management.[7] The overwhelming bulk of opinion seems, however, to have considered that to replace the Company with a royal administration was impractical and many denounced any attempt to do so as a ministerial plot to seize the wealth of Bengal and the patronage that flowed from appointments there in order to free the executive from dependence on parliament. This was the staple of parliamentary opposition whenever proposals for reforming the Company were being discussed. The dangers of government intervention in Indian affairs were constantly invoked by the radical press. Richard Price, truest of True Whigs, thought that "nothing more unfavourable to the security of public liberty has been done since the REVOLUTION" than the limited extension of government control over the Company involved in Lord North's Regulating Act.[8] Whatever their opponents may have thought, Lord North and his ministers were only too aware both of the practical difficulties and of the political sensitivities of direct involvement in India and left the direction of Indian policy with the Company for as long as they felt that they could.

There was also strong public aversion to any authoritarian system of government in Bengal. It was widely alleged that both Robert Clive when he returned to Bengal in 1765 and his successor Harry Verelst, governor from 1767 to 1769, had tried to establish such a government, using the powers which they had improperly assumed to amass great fortunes for themselves while persecuting their fellow servants, dismissing them from the service and driving them out of India. Clive's most inveterate enemy was John Johnstone who had been forced out of the service in 1765 when Clive charged him with corruption. Back in Britain, he fought a vigorous campaign to defeat attempts to prosecute him and did all he could to discredit Clive. He was supported in this effort by his brother George, usually known as Governor Johnstone (he was royal governor of West Florida from 1763 to 1767), and by other Scottish connections.[9] In 1769 the Johnstones took up the cause of William Bolts who had just been forcibly deported from India at the orders of Verelst.[10] In January 1772, Bolts published his *Considerations on India Affairs* in three volumes, a highly polemical exposure of the Company's misrule in Bengal that alleged that since the grant of the *diwani*, trade had been controlled in the interest of senior Company servants and justice had given way to "despotism supported by military violence."[11]

Historians have tended to dismiss the Johnstones, Bolts, and their allies as people who sought to cover their own misdeeds by assailing men like Clive and Verelst, who, whatever their imperfections, had a sense of Britain's imperial mission in India. The self-serving incentives behind their campaigns can hardly be denied, but they also put forward a clear view of how British India should be governed. As George Johnstone put it, "despotic authority in a few" must not be allowed to replace "*limited* authority in many." In other words, the Company must revert to its old constitution of presidents and Councils.[12] They envisaged the Company's trading settlements as communities of British subjects similar to those around the Atlantic. "Because British subjects going out and settling in the East-Indies ... carry with them the rights and priviledges not only of men but of the British constitution," their "freedom and property" must be secured against "the tyrannies and oppressions that have been exercised of late by the superior servants of the East India Company."[13] Eventually, the "happy effects of a moderated government may extend to the native inhabitants of the country by due degrees."[14]

In 1764 the directors had given wide discretionary power to Robert Clive when he returned to India. He had accordingly accepted the *diwani* on his own authority. Such powers were not, however, granted to his successors and the directors tried to restore an older model of an Indian government of checks and balances. Ambitious governors were in theory, if by no means always in practice, as cases such as Streynsham Master, John Child, and Gerald Aungier, abundantly demonstrated, restrained by the need to secure the agreement of their Councils and the obligation to act strictly according to rules and precedent. Strictness in record keeping was enjoined so that what was done in Asia would be accountable to authority at home.[15]

The directors also tried to ensure that major decisions of policy were taken by them rather than by men in India. Their most striking intervention was their order in 1771, which seemed to generations of historians to be a major turning point in the development of British government in India, that the Company should "stand forth" as *diwan* of Bengal, that is, that its European servants should directly involve themselves in the administration of the province to what was assumed to be an unprecedented degree.

Frustrated expectations

In the years immediately after the grant of the *diwani* the government of Bengal raised increasingly acute problems that intruded themselves more and more on public attention in Britain. What had promised to be a great asset for the Company and for Britain seemed to be turning into a serious liability. There was a strong sense of frustrated expectations.

Long the most valuable of all the East India Company's concerns, it was assumed that Bengal after the acquisition of the *diwani* would play an even more dominant role in the Company's affairs and that great wealth would pass from the Company to the national exchequer. Robert Clive and others anticipated that the *diwani* revenue would put immense surpluses at the Company's disposal. Not only would these pay for greatly increased cargoes of Bengal's own goods, but they would also provide for larger shipments of China tea and sustain the other Indian Presidencies, Madras and Bombay, whose territorial resources were limited. Engaged in an unsuccessful war against Mysore, Madras began to make huge demands on Bengal. In September 1768, however, Clive's successor Harry Verelst told him that the accounts on which he had based his confident estimates were overinflated and that "we are short of your Lordship's calculations by millions."[16] At the same time Verelst warned a director of the Company that what could be actually realized from Bengal "will fall greatly short of what your and the nation's expectations may be."[17] Within a year or two it was becoming apparent that Bengal's resources could by no means be stretched to meet all the demands being made on them. The Company's administration in Bengal could not meet their own costs, let alone provide for China or the other Presidencies.

To a degree that came to be seen as utterly scandalous, control over spending on the Bengal army and on civil expenditure, especially on huge building projects, appeared to have broken down, so that "every rupee of the revenue is eaten up in costs civil and military."[18] Furthermore, Bengal's financial problems were being transferred to Britain, since to supplement their inadequate funds the Bengal Council felt that they had no alternative but to borrow money from the European community in Bengal in exchange for bills of exchange payable in London at rates that the directors regarded as exorbitant. Bills for over £1,500,000 were drawn on London in 1771–1772.

Verelst and his colleagues soon became convinced that the financial crisis facing them was symptomatic of something much deeper. Bengal's resources had not merely been overestimated, they were actually disappearing. In September 1768, Verelst wrote of "a declining and exhausted country."[19] "We see, we feel the increasing poverty of the country," he told his colleagues in his farewell message to them.[20] At the same time George Vansittart, brother of the former Governor Henry Vansittart, reported that "since the government has fallen into the hands of the English every part of the country has been visibly on the decline. Trade, manufacturing, agriculture are considerably diminished."[21] Verelst's successors were soon reporting that famine in western Bengal was producing "mortality and beggary" that "exceeds all descriptions."[22] Accounts of "an universal famine" in which "the greatest part of the inhabitants have died" began to appear in the London press.[23]

The Company's servants in Bengal found political explanations for the decline of the province. After receiving the grant of the *diwani*, Clive had left matters largely under the nawab's authority. The nawab's chief minister or naib, Muhammad Reza Khan, directed a largely unchanged revenue system with only remote British supervision. This so-called "double government" was diagnosed as the source of Bengal's problems. The nawab's officials were unable to prevent misuse of power by Europeans while they themselves committed great oppressions. They were said to be "generally adventurers from Persia, educated in the manner and principles of a government where tyranny, corruption and anarchy are predominant." They brought with them a "numerous train of dependents and underlings, … whose demands as well as the avarice of their principals, are to be satisfied from the spoils of the industrious ryott."[24]

A powerful rhetoric was being developed of the inevitable corruption of any Indian entrusted with power.[25] Under what was held to be a despotic regime there could be no spirit of public service; office was simply an opportunity for exploiting others. Just rule required that the Company's European servants should directly intervene in the government of the province. The Company had been content for too long, Verelst argued, to leave responsibility for the government of Bengal in indigenous hands while they continued to act "on the spirit of mere merchants," seeking to maximize commercial profit and revenue yields without extending "an adequate protective power over the people who pay."[26] This could not continue.

Verelst and his colleagues had attributed the tribulations of Bengal to misconceived systems of government and to the failings of Indians entrusted with power. Others were to attribute them directly to the misdeeds of the Company servants themselves. A rhetoric of white "Nabob" depravity was coming to match the rhetoric of native depravity. This was largely the achievement of the Johnstones and of Bolts and others such as Alexander Dow, who, in 1772, published a third volume of his *History of Hindostan*, which contained much highly polemical material about the misgovernment of the Company's servants. In 1771, newspaper paragraphs began to describe the catastrophic effects of the Bengal famine as having been greatly exacerbated by monopolies established by Company servants who profited from forcing up the price of rice.[27] Allegations that millions had died because of British avarice produced a huge wave of popular revulsion.

The spectacular success of those who were campaigning against Clive and his successors in using the press to appeal to a wider public was highly embarrassing for the directors. The damaging effects to be expected from such publicity were deplored in a letter to Clive by George Colebrooke, then chairman of the Company. "I have my doubts whether drawing attention to the Company's affairs, does not excite in them a further curiosity and lead to inquiries in the Ho[use of Commons]. These inquiries if ever set on foot, serve to gratifie the resentment of some but seldom end in giving the Company any relief, or affording them any effectual advantage."[28]

In 1767 the Company had bought off government inquiry and interference by offering an annual payment to the state of £400,000. Now, the public's indignation aroused by the revelations about India led to new calls for parliamentary inquiries in which the Company's enemies, most obviously the Johnstones, would take the lead. Such inquiries were likely to lead to renewed efforts to pass measures that would increase government oversight and make inroads into the Company's cherished privileges.

Colebrooke's successor as chairman was said in June 1771 to be "particularly uneasy at their situation abroad and thinks it may be an object of a very speedy inquiry at home."[29] There were ominous indications that ministers were taking what seemed to be an untoward interest in India. Their main concern for some years was of an attack by the French, probably in alliance with a disaffected Indian power. The Company's preparations against such a possibility were deemed inadequate, and it was thought to be both wantonly alienating its Indian allies and needlessly provoking the hostility of others. By 1771, tensions with France had eased somewhat, although ministers were still receiving alarming accounts of French military preparations in Asia.[30]

The attention of the ministry was shifting to what seemed to be the very serious state of affairs in Bengal, the pivot on which British power in India depended. Lord North, the prime minister, was said "to feel the necessity of taking some steps immediately for the preservation of so important an object."[31] Since "the very critical and dangerous situation of our affairs in India will probably make it necessary to bring them under the consideration of parliament" in the next session, North told Clive in the autumn of 1771 that he wished urgently to consult with him to remedy his "very imperfect knowledge."[32] To stave off parliamentary or ministerial intervention, or at least to exercise some control over it, the directors felt that they must show themselves to be capable of coping with Indian problems. If others were not to force their nostrums on the Company, they must bring forward their own reforms.

Standing forth

Both contemporaries and historians have been dismissive of the capacity of Court of Directors to take effective charge of their new territorial empire. According to Clive they had "neither the abilities nor resolution to manage such important concerns as are now under their care. Of this the world in general seems to be very sensible."[33] When, in 1773, Lord North denounced the directors as being "so incapable of governing" their Indian possessions, he was repeating what had become conventional wisdom.[34] Many criticisms of the directors' failings were entirely justified. They were bitterly and destructively factional and many pursued personal concerns with little apparent regard to the corporate interests of the Company. The financial debacle that overwhelmed the Company in 1772 owed much to their mismanagement. Nevertheless, too much can be made of the directors' supposed ignorance of India or their lack of engagement with the problems of Bengal.

The most powerful figure in the Court in this period was the redoubtable Laurence Sulivan. He was an old India hand, even if his service did not have much relevance to post-*diwani* Bengal—he had resided in Bombay and had returned to England in 1753, but he was a man of great industry who had assiduously kept abreast with developments in India.[35] A number of other men with direct experience of Bengal became directors. Edward Holden Cruttenden had been a member of the Council there until 1760. He was a director from 1765 to 1768 and again in 1770 and 1771. Luke Scrafton, closely associated with Clive in Bengal, was a member of the Court from 1765 to 1768. He was said to have "the direction of Indian correspondence."[36] Robert Gregory, a very rich Bengal private merchant, served as director from 1769 to 1772. Two ex-governors were directors for single years: Henry Vansittart spent huge sums to secure votes in the 1768 Company election before taking sail in the commission of supervisors who were to be lost at sea. Harry Verelst received "the most earnest solicitations" to stand for the Direction in 1771, shortly after his return from India, and he was appointed to "one of the most important public departments belonging to the direction of their affairs," that is, he became a member of the powerful Committee of Correspondence, usually reserved for directors of long standing.[37]

Returned servants were widely consulted by the directors. Clive was regarded by many as the ultimate source of wisdom on all Indian matters. He complained of "the little attention deployed of late by the Court of Directors upon my advice and opinion,"[38] but there is clear evidence that he was frequently consulted on a number of topics.[39] His old friend, but now disillusioned critic, Robert Orme, thought that he "still persists in keeping Bengal under his own management, which I think the public will not allow—and which no one but he would dare to think they would."[40]

Lesser men were also consulted. In March 1771, then Chairman Sir George Colebrooke asked Thomas Rumbold and Francis Sykes for information about Bengal bazar duties and whether they could be abolished.[41] To a critic of the Company's leadership, Colebrooke, Chairman from 1769 to 1771 and from 1772 to 1773, exercised an "over-ruling influence in every the minutest article" of the Company's affairs. He was only rivalled by the "*territorial* and *plausible* knowledge" of Sulivan as "the great mover of this machine."[42] He had no Indian experience and his preoccupation with the huge speculative operations in stocks and commodities that were to ruin him made it difficult for contemporaries to take his claims to statesmanship seriously. But he was very assiduous in seeking information about Bengal which he entered into "a kind of *compte rendu* or a book, ... containing not only what I had actually proposed to the Company but what I thought still remained to be done to add to the prosperity of the Bengal Provinces."[43]

There were close connections between directors and men still serving in India who had been appointed by their patronage. Such links were much condemned. It was thought that they were the means whereby servants exercised an undue influence over policy-making at home. That no doubt could be the case, but they were also an important channel of information. Servants abroad wrote copiously to individual directors, explaining the situation in Bengal as it seemed to them and outlining the ambitions for which they sought support. Verelst indeed complained that the directors seemed to be more influenced by private accounts of individuals than by the proceedings and dispatches sent home by the servants in their official capacity.[44]

Indian notables also transmitted information to Britain which could have significant effects. Nabakrishna (known to the British as "Nobkissen"), who had served Clive as "Political Banian," told him in 1772 that he knew "all the Company's concerns" and was willing to brief him on them.[45] He wrote frequently to Clive and to his former secretary Henry Strachey. The director Robert Gregory was said to keep in close contact with Muhammad Reza Khan's great enemy Nandakumar, who wrote by every ship, telling him "every thing as it happens."[46] His influence on the Company's decision to "stand forth" as *diwan* was crucial, as will be shown. Reza Khan himself communicated with his "many friends" in Britain, including Sulivan.[47]

There was thus no sharp divide between Leadenhall Street and Calcutta, between the directors making policy at home and the servants in Bengal executing it or disregarding their orders, as the case might be. London and Bengal were linked in many ways. Orders emanating from London were based on information from Bengal and were strongly influenced by men who had served there, either as members of the Court or as its informants. A consensus was developing both in London and in Calcutta about the failings of the "double government" and the need for the Company's servants to take a more active role in the administration of the *diwani* lands.

The instructions drafted in 1769 by the directors for the commission of three supervisors being sent to India clearly show both their determination to "enforce a due obedience to orders" on their servants in Bengal and to involve themselves more directly in the administration of the province. The instructions were the outcome of many meetings of the Committee of Correspondence at which recent dispatches from Bengal, the views of Clive, and "accounts of revenue and charges" were closely studied.[48]

The supervisors were told that the *diwani* revenues must be put on "a just and honorable footing," both to benefit the Company and to ensure that "the inhabitants and tenants" were spared from "extortions and oppressions." To achieve this, the deployment of the Company's servants should be extended. There should be "a Resident, with a Council or proper assistants at the chief places of collection" where they would "conduct and regulate the mode and charges of collection, and reform all abuses." A survey of the resources of the *diwani* lands was to be instituted. Inquiries were also to be undertaken into the administration of justice and reforms were to be devised which would ensure that "the properties" of the "natives" would be "less precarious and their possessions more permanent."[49]

In attempting judicial reforms, the directors evidently felt themselves to be treading on uncertain ground and so Colebrooke, who was then Chairman, and Henry Vansittart, then a director, consulted the lord chancellor in person. They asked for his views on whether the Company could exercise "some legal power within the provinces" independent of the courts established by royal charter in their settlements. What they proposed was to act in the name of the nawab to reform the indigenous courts and establish "moderate and wholesome laws." The chancellor, Lord Camden, "entirely approved of the design" and made the astonishing suggestion that "a proper code of laws" should be "framed here for those essential purposes."[50] Such a view reflects the confidence of contemporary British common lawyers in the underlying similarity of all human law and that, as Lord Mansfield put it, "there are ways of knowing foreign laws as well as our own."[51]

The instructions for the supervisors suggest that the role of the Company in Bengal was being envisaged in new ways. Its primary concern of course remained the extraction of revenue, but in asserting its obligation to regulate the courts and its right to do so, it was potentially intervening much more widely in the government of the province, investing itself with the role of a just ruler caring for its subjects rather than being simply a holder of contractual revenue rights. The implication that just rule depended on European not on native agency was clear. The commission of supervisors, including two directors, Vansittart and Scrafton, were lost at sea with their instructions. Copies, however, reached Bengal and, when all hope for the commission had to be abandoned, the Bengal Council treated the supervisors' instructions as sanctioning its own policy of closer European involvement in the administration of the revenue.[52]

In August 1769, a significant increase in British intervention in the administration of Bengal was launched by Verelst's Select Committee. European Company servants, called supervisors, were to be appointed to the Bengal *diwani* districts. The scheme was strongly opposed by Muhammad Reza Khan, whose control over the revenue system was obviously at stake, and Verelst insisted on caution. The supervisors were initially charged only with gathering information; they were to leave the collection of the revenues to the Naib's officials. After the departure of Verelst, members of the Council forced a policy of more active European involvement on his successor. They were determined to break the hold of Muhammad Reza Khan over the revenue administration in the expectation that "we shall attain a certain knowledge of the country and that the revenue will be greatly increased."[53] Revenue Councils were to be stationed at Murshidabad and Patna and Muhammad Reza Khan's district officials, *amils* and *faujdars*, were to be withdrawn, leaving the European supervisors in full control. "A desperate blow" was said to have been "given to the black government; whose rapacity has greatly distressed the country as its wealth has corrupted the Company's servants." "Unanswerable proofs" were appearing of "the propriety and necessity of having the revenues of the country collected by the Company's servants."[54] Muhammad Reza Khan remained as Naib, but by the beginning of 1771 "the administration of the districts had passed completely out of [his] control."[55] Thus the Bengal administration had moved a considerable way towards assuming the full powers over the revenue system that the directors were to order in 1771.

By the time these orders were received, there was a new governor in place in Bengal. In April 1771 the directors ordered a break in the usual succession of governors from among the senior members of the Bengal service. Warren Hastings, an old Bengal servant, was to be transferred from Madras, where he was acting as second in Council, "to the same situation in the Council of Fort William and to succeed the government in case of the death or absence" of the present incumbent, John Cartier.[56] Shortly afterwards, the Court decided that Hastings was to become governor with immediate effect.[57] It was an appointment which seems to have enjoyed wide support. According to George Dempster, a supporter of the Johnstones, he was "chosen for his good sense and integrity."[58]

In retrospect Hastings's tenure of the governorship of Bengal—governor general after the 1773 Regulating Act—can clearly be seen as a significant milestone in the transformation of that office into what it was to be throughout the later history of British India. Governors general and later viceroys were to be vested with great powers and with a wide discretion in using them. Hastings quickly staked his claim both for powers and for discretion. He pointed out that there had been a rapid succession of governors whose standing was little more than that of any other member of their Councils. He announced that he intended to serve not for some three years as had become conventional but for as long as his health and the wishes of the directors allowed. Furthermore, he urged that the governor should "have the privilege of acting on his own separate authority on such urgent cases as shall in his judgement require it, notwithstanding any decision of the Council."[59] It is most unlikely, however, that the directors would invest him with such powers. Although the right to overrule his Council had been granted to Clive and his Select Committee in 1764, in March 1768 the directors had withdrawn it and in 1771 they had sided with the Council in a conflict of authority with the Select Committee. In a climate of frenzied hostility to what were alleged to be the arbitrary powers wielded by Clive and Verelst and their Select Committees, any augmentation of the governor's powers would be extremely contentious. Even though he was to exercise a remarkable ascendancy over his Council of fourteen, amounting according to his critics to a "despotick" influence which reduced his colleagues to "cyphers,"[60] Hastings had to be content with the tacit superiority wielded by long custom by governors of Bengal.

Even so, the appointment of Hastings was clearly intended to be a stage in imposing reform on Bengal, albeit reform within the parameters of the Company's ancient form of government. He was not given executive discretion, but the directors invested him from time to time with special inquisitorial powers to bring offenders to book. Their perennial fear was that their Councils overseas would combine together to conceal malpractices from them. An outsider of integrity acting on his own was intended to break through such combinations. In May 1771, Hastings was ordered to investigate overcharging in the provision of silk.[61] Because Muhammad Reza Khan was presumed to have bought support in the Council, Hastings was to act in secrecy on his own in dismissing him and bringing him to book. In December, the Committee of Correspondence ordered that Hastings be given "extraordinary powers" to uncover and root out abuses.[62] He was sent a personal secret letter instructing him to investigate allegations that the members of the Council had monopolized grain during the famine.[63] Rumours of this leaked out and George Johnstone raised the matter in the Court of Proprietors on March 18, 1772, asking for the secret instructions that gave Hastings "uncommon arbitrary power" to be made public. The Chairman, Sir George Colebrooke, refused, but, recognizing the sensitivity of the issue, assured the Court that the special powers would only last for a short time and that while they would enable Hastings to "do a great of good," they could "do no harm."[64] The role of inquisitor into past misdemeanors was not one that appealed at all to Hastings. "These retrospections and examinations are death to my views," he wrote.[65]

He had much grander plans for his office. Even before he knew of his appointment, he had written a characteristically powerful letter to a great national politician, Lord Shelburne, setting out the dire defects as he saw them of the Company's system. It had not been reshaped to the needs of "a military and territorial power" and was "ready to fall to pieces ... unless it be preserved by the timely intervention of some superior power."[66] Strengthening of the powers of the Bengal government was not, however, to be attempted until the 1773 Regulating Act.

Having a governor in place in whom they had confidence was no doubt a necessary pre-condition for the directors' orders that their government in Bengal should assume full responsibility for the administration of the province. These orders, dated August 28, 1771, were primarily directed against Muhammad Reza Khan. He must be removed and put on trial. The directors presumably thought that only an outsider would be immune from his influence. The immediate stimulus for bringing down the Khan was a letter written to Robert Gregory by Hazari Mal, brother-in-law and executor of the estate of the great north Indian businessman, Amirchand ("Omichund"), who had played a prominent role in pre-Plassey Bengal. Hazari Mal was a major revenue farmer and banker in his own right, closely associated with Nandakumar. He accused the Company servants of engrossing "the whole trade of Bengal" and the administration of Muhammad Reza Khan of committing "inhuman and horrid oppressions."[67] There can be no doubt that Nandakumar, who maintained very close contact with Gregory, had instigated this demarche against his rival Muhammad Reza Khan. Verelst, now a director, who as governor had given Muhammad Reza Khan strong support and called him his "worthy friend," seems to have been powerless to deflect the attack on him.[68] The accusations were said to have been fed to the Johnstones, Bolts, and Dow and so at the height of public indignation about the famine the directors could not risk the damaging publicity that would ensue if they ignored them.[69] On receiving his orders, Hastings duly dismissed the Khan and placed him in confinement, to the outrage of many of his colleagues. He then started to implement the changes that he himself deemed necessary for the Company to be able to exercise its full powers as *diwan*.

In their dispatch the directors ordered the Company's servants "to take upon ourselves the entire care and management of the revenues." The office of Naib was to be abolished. New regulations for the revenue administration of Bengal must be instituted which would "ensure to us every possible advantage, and free the ryotts from the oppressions of the zemindars and other petty tyrants."[70] Hastings interpreted his instructions as a mandate for making sweeping changes of his own devising. The Company's Council at Calcutta was now to have direct responsibility for the revenue administration. The revenue secretariat and the treasury, called the *Khalsa*, were transferred from the nawab's capital at Murshidabad and placed under British management at Calcutta. Henceforward, Hastings wrote, "the whole power and government of the province will center on Calcutta, which may now be considered as the capital of Bengal."[71] A committee, consisting of the governor and four other councilors, traveled out of Calcutta to make settlements with Indian revenue payers. New courts were set up to administer civil justice, which was the responsibility of the *diwan*. Although the powers of the nawab as Nazim were not included in the 1765 grant, Hastings believed that the Company already exercised control over "political and military affairs by prescription."[72] This control was now to be formalized by allowing the appointment of a naib for the Nizamat, held by Muhammad Reza Khan, to lapse and by creating new courts for criminal justice subjected to Company supervision.

The order to "stand forth" and Hastings's reforms that followed came to be seen as a decisive turning point in the history of British India. The ancestors of the future Indian Civil Service seem to have been given full administrative responsibility. James Mill in his *History of India* of 1817 wrote that "a total change in the management of the revenues more deeply affected the condition, individually and collectively, of the people of India, than it is easy for the European reader to conceive. It was an innovation by which the whole property of the country, and along with it the administration of justice, were placed upon new foundations."[73] In what is still the fullest account of Hastings's early administration, M. E. Monckton Jones wrote in 1918 of a change of "epoch-making importance," although she recognized that the orders to "stand forth" and the way in which these orders were implemented were not new initiatives but were the culmination of increasingly interventionist policies drawn up over some years in both Britain and Bengal.[74]

Whether a revolution had been brought about in how Bengal was governed is open to question. The directors' expectations for "standing forth" were that great benefits would ensue primarily from a change of personnel. Their dispatch ordered the removal of "petty tyrants," that is corrupt and self-serving Indians, who as intermediary collectors or as officials, in their view, syphoned so much out of the revenue for their own benefit as well as perverting the course of justice. They were to give way to upright and disinterested Europeans. Huge sums of misappropriated money would thus go into the Company's treasury, while the cultivators would be freed from oppression and extortion. Men with Indian experience did not necessarily accept such simplicities. One of the most reflective of the senior servants, George Vansittart, compared his capacities for administering Bihar with those of the dismissed naib there, Shitab Rai. He had "the vanity to consider myself better acquainted with the state of the Bahar province than any other European." While conceding that the Naib had a more "exact knowledge" and that his "application to business has been at least as constant as mine,"

Vansittart calculated that "a more steady impartiality, a greater desire to realize the revenue and a more earnest solicitude for the country are the advantages I think on my side." He concluded that the most that could be expected was that the Bihar revenues would at least be "as well managed" by the European servants as by the naib.[75]

Whatever qualities Vansittart and some other high-minded Company servants might impute to themselves, many, including preeminently Warren Hastings himself, were unwilling to entrust power over Bengal districts to inexperienced and corruptible Europeans. Hastings told Clive that appointing supervisors, that is taking "the internal administration of the provinces out of the hands of their former government" and placing it under the Company's "own agents," had produced a "general licentiousness."[76] Hopes that the Company's servants could accurately assess the revenue yield of the districts they ruled, deal directly with the peasantry, or preside effectively over courts were illusory. In reality the Company had little alternative but to try to work the systems that it had inherited. If it got rid of one level of Indian intermediaries, the naibs and their officials, it still had to do deals with those revenue payers that the directors had denounced as "petty tyrants" and to employ experienced Indian administrators at lower levels.

A recent assessment has cogently argued that Hastings's revolution of 1772 was essentially, a revolution in rhetoric, "an exercise in political legitimation" intended to put a brave and acceptable face on "the vagueness and uncertainty with which he and his colleagues confronted the daunting tasks of Indian governance."[77] Nevertheless, the Company's determination to "stand forth" as *diwan* had at least one major consequence: it enabled Hastings to stand forth as governor of Bengal and to invest his office with what was to prove an enduring significance.

The making of the Regulating Act

Whatever the eventual effect of these decisions upon matters in Bengal, they seem to have attracted little public attention in Britain and did nothing to ease the pressure in London and Westminster for the Company directors to enact further reforms. Denunciations of the Company's rule rose to a crescendo with the publication of Bolts's *Considerations* at the end of January 1772 and the next month with the first reference made in the House of Commons to abuses in Bengal made by George Johnstone, who with "very affecting details of the cruelties exercised by the Company's servants in India," presented a petition on behalf of one of Bolts's Armenian associates.[78] For the first time, specific accusations were also levied at Lord Clive. A non-party Commons Select Committee tasked with exposing wrongdoing tried unsuccessfully to persuade the House to censure Clive for misconduct.

There was still, however, uncertainty about the government's ultimate intentions. For the moment, ministers waited for the Company to bring forward proposals. Lord North was willing "to leave every thing to Providence and the Directors," Clive reported.[79] Laurence Sulivan, on behalf of the directors, sponsored a bill to establish a new court in Bengal for the punishment of abuses, to be staffed by judges appointed in Britain.[80] Plans were laid to send out another commission to supervise the governments in the Indian Presidencies. But neither measure came to anything. The bill attracted little support and was dropped and it proved very difficult to induce men of any standing to accept places on a commission to go to India. Before the commission could be filled, the severity of the great financial crisis that faced the Company finally forced the government to act.

In the autumn of 1772 mounting difficulties—falling sales of Asian goods, a great oversupply of unsold tea, dividends paid at an unsustainable level, and the huge sums charged to the Company by bills issued in India—coincided with an international credit crisis. In September, the Company gave notice that it would have to postpone paying the annual dividend. Stock prices fell sharply on that news and there were rumors that the Company would be forced to stop payments altogether. On October 5, Lord North decided that the government could no longer avoid taking the initiative in referring Indian matters to parliament. The consequences for the national economy if the Company failed were too serious to be contemplated. Money would have to be lent to the Company to see it through its difficulties, but the price of financial aid must be a thorough reform of the Company's affairs. North was still willing to consider proposals from the Company, but the crisis had undermined the capacity of the Company to formulate them. Its leadership was totally discredited, Sulivan and Colebrooke being among those who were put out of the Court of Directors. A mutinous Court of Proprietors became very hard to manage. The government therefore felt that it had no alternative but to impose its own reforms and appointed a Secret Committee to investigate the Company.

The Committee's inquiries and the government's proposals were at first concerned with the Company at home, with its finances and with its constitution, but they soon went on to consider how Bengal should best be governed. The Committee's sixth report focused on how Bengal's revenue was being administered. The seventh report looked into the administration of justice in Bengal, hearing much evidence about the deficiencies of indigenous courts and noting Hastings's attempts to reform them. There were obvious reasons for the government to be concerned with the Bengal revenues, since, were they to fail, the effect might be to bring down both the Company and the government. A concern for the proper administration of justice, however, suggests a wider view. Of course, the prosperity of Bengal and therefore its capacity to pay taxes were, like anywhere else in the world, presumed to depend on the security that the law afforded to individual property. But beyond that it was clear that establishing good government in India was coming to be regarded as a desired object for its own sake. It was increasingly seen as the duty of the British state to compel the Company to rule its subjects justly. The extent to which Lord North and his colleagues accepted this obligation became clear when he finally produced his proposals that became the Regulating Act of 1773.

During the turmoil in the Company's affairs at home Hastings prided himself that he and his colleagues were doing their duty without unduly concerning themselves about "new ordinances from the Court of Directors" or about what might eventually emerge from parliament.[81] He must, however, have been apprehensive that he might be superseded in any new arrangement. He certainly feared that codes of law fashioned in Britain would be foisted on him. Such anxieties turned out to be groundless. He was eventually to be confirmed in his position in Bengal as governor general of a new Supreme Council and the reforms which he had been enacting since 1772 were to be endorsed.

Proposals for a Supreme Council in India arose from mounting concern about what seemed to be the lack of coordination between the Company's Presidencies in resisting the French and in dealing with Indian states, especially with the Marathas, whose expansion seemed to be threatening all three of them. Now on the fringe of politics, William Pitt, Earl of Chatham, thought "putting under circumspection and control the high and dangerous prerogative of war and alliances so abused in India" was very necessary.[82] At this point Clive seems to have been influential. He advised that Hastings should be a member of any supervisory commission, but that if no commission was sent, the Company should revert to the much criticized mechanism of a small committee like that through which he himself had governed Bengal. The new committee should be given powers over the other Presidencies. Clive fed such a plan to Lord North, and the government adopted it.[83] The committee came to be known as the Supreme Council and the individual at the head of it as the governor general. Clive had come to think well of Hastings and he suggested that the Council should be headed by him with two other Company servants and two "gentlemen of respectable character from England."[84] Sulivan, who also gave his ideas "to the fountain head," supported both the appointment of a governor general, which he described as "a fixed and favourite point," and the choice of Hastings.[85]

In May 1773, the government proposed that affairs in India should be managed by a governor general and a Supreme Council with four or five councilors. Hastings was proposed as the first governor general. Lord North believed that "the publick … may rejoice in the activity and resolution with which the present Governor appears to have acted." He told the Commons that the parliamentary Secret Committee had reported that the way revenues were collected under Hastings's administration seemed to be "founded in equity and humanity" and that the new courts that he had established "were calculated to give those people all that is necessary to make them happy."[86] Under Hastings's scheme the new courts were to use what was assumed to be existing Hindu and Islamic law, not a code devised for them in Britain.

Hastings had done much to enhance his reputation by the dispatches and the personal letters in which he described to influential people how he had implemented his instructions to "stand forth" as *diwan*. Penned with consummate skill, they did indeed convey an impression of "activity and resolution." Hastings persuasively depicted what he had achieved as a great program of reform. He won much applause for doing so. In April 1773, the Secret Committee of the Court of Directors assured him of their "entire approbation of your conduct" and of their "firmest support in accomplishing the work you have so successfully commenced." They looked forward to "the deliverance of Bengal from oppression" and to "every advantage which the Company or the nation may justly expect."[87] In the House of Commons even George Johnstone, who thought "all the regulations [Hastings] has made are defective," still felt compelled to add: "Yet the principle he has laid down [is] true, just, equitable. [It shows] more of the legislative spirit that ought to actuate a Governor than you will find in the whole records of the India House."[88] Most important of all, Lord North had been persuaded. While the Company was still conducting elaborate inquiries from former servants as to how the revenues of Bengal might be collected, Hastings's dispatches were describing a well-designed system of revenue and justice, which appeared already to be effectively in operation.[89] In the view of one of Hastings's closest friends in Britain, his writings had carried the day for a man who "for want of a strong personal interest" was otherwise unlikely to have been chosen. He now had the "prospect of a long government."[90]

The new system

Hastings's tenure as governor general was certainly to be a long one: he was not to leave Bengal until February 1785. But the terms on which he held his great office were, it quickly seemed to him, calculated not to empower him but to frustrate the high ambitions for public service with which he had embarked upon his governorship. He complained of a consistent lack of support and at times of downright hostility from ministers and the Court of Directors in Britain. For eleven years, he told the directors in 1783, "I have invariably had to contend not with the ordinary difficulties of office, but with such as most unnaturally arose from the opposition of those very powers from which I primarily derived my authority, and which were required for the support of it."[91] Under the terms of the Regulating Act, something of the old principle of authority subject to checks survived: the governor general was given four colleagues on the Supreme Council and was bound by the views of the majority. Hastings notoriously faced opposition from a hostile majority both at the beginning and in the last years of his tenure; nor could the Bengal Supreme Council effectively exercise the powers given to it in the act to control the other Presidencies. In the memoir that he wrote on his retirement from Bengal in 1785, Hastings described British India as "a dominion held by a delegated and fettered power." The governor general must, he insisted, have "a power absolute and complete within himself and independent of actual controul." He reflected that a weak governor and Council overseas might be acceptable under "an arbitrary monarchy" at home, but that "the rule of a province so remote from a free state like that of Great Britain ... cannot be too simple and unrestrained."[92]

The deficiencies of the Regulating Act's provisions came to be widely accepted, even if for many people the corollary that Warren Hastings should have been entrusted with wider discretionary powers did not necessarily follow. In 1783, Henry Dundas, who was to be the dominant figure in the metropolitan management of India for the rest of the century, introduced a bill which would have placed the "whole civil and military government" of Bengal and of the other Presidencies under a "Governor General and Captain General of all the British settlements in India" with power to overrule his Council.[93] In presenting his bill, Dundas explained that exceptional powers should be entrusted to an exceptional person who would be above all temptation to abuse them. He was universally understood to be referring to Lord Cornwallis. In what appear to be notes for his speech, Dundas elaborated arguments as to why "in a distant country [far] from the seat of government the executive operations should be quick and strong." As justification, he invoked the received wisdom about oriental despotism. Those who objected that "the powers of the Governor General [were] too despotick" should reflect that "the original government of the Hindoos" had been despotic and that of "the Musselmen" had been "despotick and military."[94] Pitt's India Act of 1784 did not go as far as Dundas had proposed: in a Council reduced to four, the governor general was to have the "casting vote" to break ties but could still be overruled three to one.[95] When Cornwallis accepted the governor generalship in early 1786, the act was, however, amended to enable him to overrule his Council in emergencies. Greater powers for the governor general would, the act asserted, "tend greatly to the strength and security" of British India.[96] The powers of future governors general were to remain essentially those vested in them by the act of 1786.

That the governor general should have sweeping powers was a proposition that by 1786 aroused little criticism. Edmund Burke, however, was a notable exception. For him, the 1786 act marked the introduction of "despotism and arbitrary government" into India under the guise of British authority. Claims such as those made by Dundas of the superiority of arbitrary power placed in the hands of a single person were contrary to all "our theories and knowledge of human nature." These were "principles," Burke told the Commons, "which would have shaken every fibre in the frame of their ancestors." "Arbitrary government," he declared, was invariably "weak and imperfect."[97] What was needed for the government of British India, he argued, was not a free rein but stricter limits upon the capacity of men overseas to do harm.

This was the principle behind Charles Fox's India Bill of 1783. Fox had said that he was willing to make any changes desired in that bill, so long as "the seat of government was established at home not in India."[98] Burke was later to pay tribute to the old "mercantile constitution of the Company." It was a fundamental part of that constitution "that their whole government shall be a written government," that is, based on dispatches sent from India and orders sent from London. This meant that "it was in the power of a man sitting in London to form an accurate judgment of every thing that happened upon the Ganges" and to detect the "wickedness" of Company servants overseas. Burke described this as "perhaps the best contrivance that has ever been thought of by the wit of men for the government of a remote, large, disjointed empire."[99] By the time he spoke, however, this was very much a minority opinion.

Ancient and modern

This chapter has tried to show that to the despair of Clive and Hastings, men of soaring ambition, contemporaries were generally reluctant to abandon the "ancient form of government" of the East India Company, either at home or in Asia. The great expansion of empire had not necessarily rendered it anachronistic. With greater responsibilities, the need to enforce discipline from home and to check abuses in India seemed indeed to become more urgent. The initial response to the acquisition of the *diwani* was to refurbish the old system of government by the directors at home and by Councils in India. Most historians have dismissed such efforts as doomed to inevitable failure: India was too important to Britain to be left in the hands of a trading Company and the rule of an imperial domain required a strong executive with streamlined decision-making. The terms of the Regulating Act did indeed signal the tentative adoption of such principles: it included measures that began to entrench government supervision over crucial Indian issues, while the new office of governor general was eventually to be given wide discretionary powers. Yet close study of the years between 1765 and 1773 suggests that the old system showed considerable vitality and that it was to be undermined by the course of events rather than by any sense of its inherent weaknesses.

The strength of inhibitions about any measure of direct government intervention in Indian affairs meant that the initiative in wrestling with the problems of ruling Bengal remained with the directors. They could not be accused of being passive in the face of their new responsibilities. In the instructions relating to Bengal drafted in 1769 for the commission of supervisors and the orders issued to "stand forth" as *diwan* in 1771, the Company responded with some vigor. The directors were still trying to devise further reforms in 1772. Their credibility as reformers was, however, completely destroyed by the financial storm that engulfed the Company in the fall of that year, leaving reluctant ministers with no alternative but to devise their own solutions. The reforms of the Regulating Act were in part intended to bolster the directors' authority, but governments, especially after another Indian crisis in the early 1780s, were to give progressively stronger institutional form to their influence over Indian policy.

The story of the rise of the governor general as head of an autocratic executive in India is a more complex one. That men overseas would inevitably try to defraud the Company and that their power to do so must be strictly controlled was a deeply entrenched principle for the Company's governance of its settlements throughout its history. Authority was vested collectively in Councils whose proceedings must be exactly recorded so that they could be closely scrutinized at home. Wrongdoing was to be deterred by the threat of detection and punishment. These principles survived the transformation of the Company into a territorial ruler. Indeed, stories of abuses in Bengal in the later 1760s served to reinforce them. The concentration of power in the hands of Clive's Select Committee was reversed. Mechanisms for bringing delinquents to book were strengthened. As governor, Hastings was invested with special powers to expose abuses. Both the court proposed in the 1772 bill and Supreme Court established by the 1773 act were primarily intended to hear complaints "for any crimes, misdemeanours, or oppressions" by the Company's servants.[100]

The wording of the act of 1786 formally signaled that a concern for "strength and security" had replaced fear of abuse as the dominant criterion for shaping British Indian government. Power was to be concentrated in the hands of a governor general rather than being diffused through a regime of checks and balances under close scrutiny from home. Such a shift would probably have been hard to avoid once possession of the *diwani* had turned the Company into a major Indian territorial power competing with other Indian territorial powers. The successful conduct of diplomacy and war no doubt required quick and decisive decision-taking. What could be seen as a response to practical necessity for conducting the Company's foreign policy was also deemed to be applicable to the internal government of Bengal. Here it was reinforced by the strength of certain assumptions indicated in this chapter. Developments in Bengal after 1765 were interpreted as confirming the wisdom of the ancients and of travel writers about despotism in India. In the words of Robert Travers, "Asiatic despotism" became "a kind of prefabricated, all-inclusive form of self-justification" for the Company.[101] It was used to explain how the rich resources of Bengal had been dissipated by the unchecked rapacity of Indians brought up in the service of despotic systems. This meant that Clive's attempt to preserve an indigenous regime had been a failure. The Company's European civil servants must therefore 'stand forth' as the effective rulers of the province. In spite of all the abuse heaped on white nabobs and the doubts of men like Hastings about the capacity of Europeans to discharge administrative roles, they were assumed to have the potential for disinterested public service and there was increasing confidence that power could safely be entrusted to them. Demotion of Indian office-holders took place on a large scale in the 1780s.[102] Asiatic despotism not only rendered Indians unfit for responsible offices, but dictated how the mass of the population should be governed. They had been accustomed to it for centuries, it was said, and had no desire for any other form of rule. The new British order should therefore be an authoritarian one dispensing justice from on high by white bureaucrats in the manner to which the local people were accustomed.

That the governor general should be the key figure in this new order owed more than a little to the personal influence of Warren Hastings. From his appointment in 1772 he envisaged himself as a statesman presiding over a great empire and he had the literary capacity to project his vision in a convincing way to contemporaries. Naming Hastings as the first governor general seemed the safest course in 1773. The ten tumultuous years of subsequent service may have left him with a somewhat equivocal personal reputation, but it also firmly established both the importance of his office and the need to enhance its powers for the future holders of it.

Notes

1   *Lord Clive's Speech in the House of Commons, 30th March, 1772* (London, 1772), 57.
2   Letter to G. Colebrooke, March 7, 1773, G. R. Gleig, *Memoirs of the Life of the Right Hon. Warren Hastings* (3 volumes, London: Richard Bentley, 1841), 1: 290.
3   The sharpness of the caesura between the ancient form of government of a trading Company and the new regime of a territorial empire has, however, been questioned in a powerful recent study by Philip Stern. Stern invites us to see continuities between the great expansion of empire and the concerns of the East India Company going back to the later seventeenth century, which in his view provided "a crucial foundation for the political and ideological conditions that made the Company's territorial empire in India conceivable." Taking account of continuities will, he argues, give us "a more continuous, gradual, and contingent account" of the creation of what was to become the British Raj. Philip Stern, *The Company-State: Corporate Sovereignty and the Early Modern Foundations of the British Empire in India* (New York: Oxford University Press, 2011), 7, 186. This chapter is intended in part as a response to Stern's call to reconsider the continuities in the history of the East India Company before and after the great world wars of the mid-eighteenth century and it will try to explore the implications of his fruitful insights. It will stress that although most later historians of the British Raj saw a system of Indian government with a powerful local executive subject to state supervision from Britain as both inevitable

and appropriate—inevitable since they considered that India could effectively be governed in no other way and appropriate since an authoritarian regime was assumed to be well suited to the nature of Indian society—contemporaries saw matters very differently. Putting the wealth of Bengal and all the valuable offices arising from its government at the disposal of the state would create an over-mighty British executive fraught with danger to the balance of the constitution, while to entrust governors in India with unfettered power would be a recipe for misgovernment and oppression. There seemed therefore to be compelling arguments in favor of prolonging the ancient form of government of the Company into the new age of empire. Replacing it was a process fraught with difficulties and, as this chapter will try to show, contingent on unforeseen events. There was no planned or purposeful drive toward state supervision at home or an autocratic executive in India.

4   13 Geo. III, cap. 63, secs 9, 11.
5   See my assessment of him in "The Making of an Imperial Icon: The Case of Warren Hastings," *Journal of Imperial and Commonwealth History* 27 (1997): 1–16.
6   For example, *A Plan for the Government of Bengal and for the Protection of the Other British Settlements in the East Indies* (London, 1772), 10–12; *The Measures to be Pursued in India ... farther considered* (London, 1772), 13–15.
7   Adam Smith, *Wealth of Nations*, Book V, chapter iii.
8   *Additional Observations on the Nature and Value of Civil Liberty and the War with America* (London, 1777), 49.
9   See the recent study of the Johnstone brothers by Emma Rothschild, *The Inner Life of Empires: An Eighteenth-Century History* (Princeton, NJ: Princeton University Press, 2011).
10 On Bolts, see Willem G. J. Kuiters, *The British in Bengal 1756–1773. A Society in Transition Seen through the Biography of a Rebel: William Bolts (1739–1808)* (Paris: Les Indes Savantes, 2002).
11 *Considerations on India Affairs* (3 volumes, London, 1772), 1: viii.
12 George Johnstone, *Thoughts on our Acquisitions in the East Indies; particularly respecting Bengal* (London, 1771), iv, 24.
13 Printed "Reasons" for opposing a bill sponsored by the Company in 1772 to give its servants stronger powers to deport Europeans, India Office Records, British Library, London (IOR) A/9, ff. 245–246.
14 Johnstone, *Thoughts on our Acquisitions,* 27.
15 Stern, *Company-State* 11; Miles Ogborn, *Indian Ink: Script and Print in the Making of the English East India Company* (Chicago, IL: University of Chicago Press, 2007), 76–83.
16 Verelst to Clive, September 22, 1768, Ames Library of South Asia, University of Minnesota, Minneapolis, India Office Library microfilm, Neg, 4373.
17 Verelst to T. B. Rous, September 25, 1768, ibid.
18 R. Barwell to R. Leycester, September. 30, 1771, India Office Library, British Library, London (IOL) MS Eur. D 535/1, 158.
19 To Directors, September 26, 1768, Harry Verelst, *A View of the Rise, Progress and Present State of the English Government in Bengal* (London, 1772) Appendix, 112.
20 To Council, December 16, 1769, ibid., 120.
21 To H. Vansittart, September 29, 1769, IOL Eur. F. 331/18, 82.
22 Select Committee to Directors, May 9, 1770, Bisheshwar Prasad, ed., *Fort William-India House Correspondence* (Delhi: National Archives of India, 1961), 6 (1770–1772): 203.

23   For example, *General Evening Post*, March 22–23, 1771.

24   Select Committee's Resolutions, August 16, 1769, Verelst, *Rise and Progress*, Appendix, 224.

25   Robert Travers, *Ideology and Empire in Eighteenth-Century India: The British in Bengal* (Cambridge, UK: Cambridge University Press, 2007), 67.

26   To Council, December 16, 1769, Verelst, *Rise and Progress*, Appendix, 122.

27   For example, "Letter from Bengal, February 1771" in *Public Advertiser*, September 17, 1771.

28   January 8, 1771, IOL MS Eur. G 37/61/1, f. 6.

29   A. Wedderburn to R. Clive, June 1, 1771, IOL MS Eur. 37/61/4, f. 42.

30   See material in The British National Archives, Kew, SP/78/282–3.

31   A. Wedderburn to R. Clive, October 29, 1771, IOL MS Eur. G 37/62/2, ff. 24–25.

32   Ibid., f. 27, and also A. Wedderburn to R. Clive, November 17, 1771, IOL MS Eur. G 37/62/3, f. 23.

33   To H. Verelst, November 7, 1767, IOL MS Eur. F 218/90, f. 31.

34   H. V. Bowen, *Revenue and Reform: The Indian Problem in British Politics 1757–1773* (Cambridge, UK: Cambridge University Press, 1991), 178.

35   Sulivan's career is treated in full in L. S. Sutherland, *The East India Company in Eighteenth-Century Politics* (Oxford: Clarendon Press, 1952). See also George McGilvary, *Guardian of the East India Company: The Life of Laurence Sulivan* (London: Tauris Academic Studies, 2006).

36   George Colebrooke, *Retrospection: Reminiscences Addressed to my Son Henry Thomas Colebrooke* (London: Privately Published, 1898), 134.

37   Letter to [Comte de Verelst], April 25, 1771, IOL MS Eur. F 218/81.

38   Memorandum of November 24, 1772, IOL MS Eur. E 12, f. 119.

39   For example, "Subjects for Lord Clive's Opinion. Transmitted to Lord Clive by Mr Rous," December 1767, IOL MS Eur. G 37/9/13. He was interviewed on Bengal affairs on May 5, 1769, by the Committee of Correspondence (IOR D/24) and subsequently sent them a memorandum (IOL MS Eur. F 128/141, ff. 35–43).

40   To J. Dupré, May 30, 1770, IOL Orme MSS OV 202, f. 39.

41   Letters of March 8, 1771, IOR E/1/215 224.

42   *A Letter to Sir George Colebrooke, Bart, on the Subjects of Supervision and Dividend. By an Old Proprietor and Former Servant of the East India Company* (London: 1772), 4.

43   Colebrooke, *Retrospection* 209. This was presumably what was called "the Chairman's Remarks on Bengal Affairs." (Secretary to R. Gregory, February 24, 1771, IOR E/1/215, 220).

44   To T. B. Rous, September 25, 1768, Ames Library of South Asia, University of Minnesota, IOL microfilm, Neg. 4373.

45   Letter of April 14, 1772, IOL MS Eur. G 37/63/3, f. 12.

46   F. Sykes to W. Hastings, February 6, 1774, British Library, London (BL) Add MS 29134, f. 298.

47   F. Sykes to W. Hastings, undated [1773], BL Add MS 29194, f. 118; Sulivan to Hastings, December 20, 1774, BL Add MS 29135, f. 402.

48   See minutes of the Committee between May 3 and August 4, 1769 (IOR, D/24). Henry Vansittart attributed the instructions to the Chairman, Colebrooke (letter to Colebrooke, July 22, 1769, IOL MS Eur. D 822, f. 4.

49   IOR H/100, 409–10, 417–18, 422.

50   Committee of Correspondence Minutes, June 22, 1769, IOR D/24, unpaginated.

51 Judgment in Fabrigas *v.* Mostyn, T. B. and T. J. Howell, compiled, *A Complete Collection of State Trials* (34 volumes, London: Hansard, 1816–26), 20: 231.

52 Council to Directors, September 8, 1770, IOR E/4/29, 315–22. Orders to a similar effect had been sent by the directors on June 30, 1769, N.K. Sinha, ed., *Fort William-India House Correspondence* (Delhi: National Archives of India, 1957), 5: 211–213.

53 Richard Barwell to T. Rumbold, August 29, 1770 and to Roger Barwell, August 25, 1770, IOL MS Eur. D 535/1, 1, 13–14.

54 R. Kyd to H. Verelst, September 13, 1770, IOL MS Eur. F 218/93, f. 69.

55 Abdul Majed Khan, *The Transition in Bengal: A Study of Saiyid Muhammad Reza Khan* (Cambridge, UK: Cambridge University Press, 1969), 259.

56 Court Minutes, April 9, 1771, IOR B/86, 457.

57 Directors to Council, April 25, 1771, Prasad, ed., *Fort William-India House Correspondence*, 6: 111.

58 Letter to E. Burke, August 4, 1772, L. S. Sutherland, ed., *The Correspondence of Edmund Burke* (Cambridge, UK: Cambridge University Press, 1960), 2: 322.

59 Letter to Directors, November 11, 1773, Gleig, *Hastings Memoirs*, 1: 372, 373.

60 R. Barwell to T. Rumbold, March 3, 1773, IOL MS Eur. D 535/2, 140; W. Wynne to H. Strachey, July 21, 1773, IOL MS Eur. F 128/105, f. 87.

61 Secret Committee to Hastings, May 8, 1771, IOR E/4/621, 47–8.

62 December 12, 1771, IOR D/27, 64.

63 Letter of December 18, 1771, IOR E/4/621, 217–22.

64 The same account of the proceedings in the General Court appeared in many newspapers. For comment on them, see *Public Advertiser*, March 24 and 27, 1772.

65 Letter to F. Sykes, March 2, 1773, Gleig, *Hastings Memoirs,* 1: 283.

66 Letter of July 16, 1771, BL Add MS 88906/3/12, ff. 131–137.

67 Copy of letter of October 10, 1770, authenticated by Gregory, BL Add MS 29132, f. 385.

68 See his letter to T. Burgess, January 3, 1775, IOL MS Eur. F 218/81.

69 Sykes to Hastings, undated, BL Add MS 29194, f. 118.

70 Prasad, ed., *Fort William-India House Correspondence*, 6: 123.

71 Hastings to J. Duprè, October 8, 1772, BL Add MS, 29125, f. 156.

72 To Unknown, July 8, 1772, BL Add MS 29125, f. 102.

73 James Mill, *A History of British India*, 4th edn. (6 volumes, London: Baldwin, Craddock, and Joy, 1840), 3: 521.

74 M. E. Monckton Jones, *Warren Hastings in Bengal* (Oxford: Clarendon Press,1918), 118.

75 To Hastings, May 23, 1772, IOL MS Eur. F 331/21, 49–50.

76 Letter of November 12, 1772, IOL MS Eur. G 37/9/15, ff. 29–30.

77 Travers, *Ideology and Empire,* 103, 106.

78 *General Evening Post*, March 3–5, 1772.

79 Letter to H. Strachey, November 7, 1772, George Forrest, *The Life of Lord Clive* (2 volumes, London: Cassell, 1918), 2: 396.

80 Text in Sheila Lambert, ed., *House of Commons Sessional Papers of the Eighteenth Century* (145 volumes, Wilmington: Scholarly Resources, 1975), 22: 389–402.

81 Letter to J. Graham, July 26, 1773, BL Add MS 29125, f. 231.

82 Letter to Shelburne, June 17, 1773, W. S. Taylor and J. H. Pringle, eds., *Correspondence of William Pitt, Earl of Chatham* (4 volumes, London: J. Murray, 1838–40), 4: 276–277.

83　　A number of manuscript versions of his memorandum "laid before Lord North," dated November 21, 1772, survive. See IOL MS Eur. E 12, pp. 173–218 and IOL MS Eur. F 128/141, ff. 14–28. It is summarized in John Bruce, *A Historical View of Plans for the Government of British India* (London: J. Sewell and J. Debrett, 1973), 55–71.

84　　Draft [1772], IOL MS Eur. F 128/141, f. 110.

85　　Undated letter to Hastings, BL Add MS 29194, f. 84.

86　　Speech of May 3, 1773, BL Egerton MS 246, ff. 33–34, 42.

87　　Letter of April 16, 1773, Gleig, *Hastings Memoirs* 1: 255.

88　　Speech on June 2, 1773, BL Egerton MS 249, ff. 190–191.

89　　Letters of P. Michell to H. Verelst, March 19 and of Committee of Directors, March 29, 1773, IOL MS Eur. F 218/24.

90　　F. Sykes to Hastings, November 8, 1773, Sophia Weitzman, ed., *Warren Hastings and Philip Francis* (Manchester: Manchester University Press, 1929), 208.

91　　Letter of March 20, 1783, Gleig, *Hastings Memoirs,* 3: 84.

92　　*Memoirs Relative to the State of India,* new edn. (London, 1787), 154, 157–158, 160.

93　　An abbreviated text of the bill is in P. J. Marshall, *Problems of Empire: Britain and India 1757–1813* (London: George Allen and Unwin, 1968), 120–125. For the full text, see Lambert, ed., *Sessional Papers,* 35: 109–168.

94　　National Archives of Scotland, GD 51/3/11/4.

95　　24 Geo. III, cap. 25, sec. 21.

96　　26 Geo. III, cap. 16, sec. 7.

97　　Speech of March 22, 1786, P. J. Marshall, ed., *The Writings and Speeches of Edmund Burke, Volume 6, India: The Launching of the Hastings Impeachment* (Oxford: Oxford University Press, 1991), 6: 68–69.

98　　Speech on January 16, 1784, *The Parliamentary Register: or History of the Proceedings and Debates in the House of Commons* (45 volumes, London, 1780–1796), 22: 298.

99　　Speech, February 15, 1788, Marshall, ed., *Burke Writings and Speeches,* 6: 295–298.

100　　Lambert, ed., *Sessional Papers,* 22: 392; 13 Geo. III, c. 63, sec. 14.

101　　Personal communication, May 9, 2012.

102　　P. J. Marshall, "Indian Officials under the East India Company in Eighteenth-Century Bengal," in P. J. Marshall, *Trade and Conquest: Studies on the Rise of British Dominance in India* (Aldershot: Variorum, 1993), Ch. 5.

9

Varieties of "Patriotism" in the Post-1763 British Empire: The Strange Career of Charles Lee

David L. Preston

Boston, August 1775

Standing upon Prospect Hill with a spyglass pressed to his eye, a discerning patriot general conspicuously inspected the British works fortifying Boston and the Charlestown peninsula. He expected the soldiers manning the opposing lines to fire upon him at any moment, once they observed the telltale Pomeranian dogs that were always by his side. The British were indeed on the lookout for a man they considered a traitor. Major General Charles Lee was a native Briton and had been an officer of nearly thirty years of service in the British Army. Now, as one red-coated officer averred, "There is not a Soldier or Officer in the Garrison, and especially [in] his old Regiment (44th) but would be happy to get a Shot at Him." From Lee's perspective, fighting for English liberty against "a band of ministerial assassins" was just the sort of "patriotic" cause he had long dreamed of serving; but his decision to resign his royal commission and accept a general's commission from a rebel congress came at an immense personal and emotional cost.[1]

"What a tryal is a civil war," Lee wrote, contemplating how the imperial crisis had sundered old friendships and loyalties. Among the British soldiers garrisoning Boston were two of his old friends, Generals Thomas Gage and John Burgoyne. A few months before, Lee wrote and published personal letters addressed to both of them, explaining his principled stand for liberty and imploring them to reconsider the morality of their own involvement in the war on the opposing side. Thirteen years earlier, Burgoyne and Lee's friendship had been forged in combat in Portugal; and seven years before that, Lee and Gage had fought for king and empire against the French and Indians in the woods of North America. In 1755, Lee was a young lieutenant in the 44th Regiment of Foot, one of two battalions sent under the command of Major General Edward Braddock to expel the French from the Ohio Valley. Gage, a man whom Lee both admired and loved, was then lieutenant colonel of the regiment. Gage led the vanguard of Braddock's army on the bloody July day it was routed by Indian and French foes at the Battle of the Monongahela. Now, Major General Charles Lee commanded the left wing of an army whose commander, General George Washington, had served as Braddock's aide-de-camp at the Monongahela. Brigadier General Horatio Gates, another former British officer present at "Braddock's Defeat," was now serving as Washington's adjutant general. In the summer of 1775, this trio of Monongahela veterans, Washington, Lee, and Gates, were besieging an old comrade-in-arms, Thomas Gage, who was now commander-in-chief of all of His Majesty's forces in North America as well as the royal governor of Massachusetts.[2]

The divergent roads taken by these men between 1755 and 1775 are an important reminder that the American War of Independence was also an imperial civil war whose combatants were bitterly divided over the meanings of loyalty and identity. The imperial crisis of the 1760s and 1770s severely strained or severed human connections and affective ties among many Britons and British Americans. When Henry Laurens of South Carolina received word of the Declaration of Independence, for example, he expressed "a Tear of affection for the good old Country and for the people in it whom in general I dearly love." Laurens described his heart as "full of the lively sensations of a dutiful Son, thrust by the hand of Violence out of a Father's house into the wide world."[3] Yet, the emotional gravity of those decisions has often been erased from history books by the assumption that American independence was both natural and inevitable.

This chapter, however, will begin with the presumption that the Americans' violent resistance to the royal government was "unnatural," a term that many contemporaries used to describe the conflict, and therefore merits both examination and explanation. The story of Charles Lee's personal odyssey from a royal to a rebel officer is an exceptional yet revealing case study. Focusing upon Lee's individual choice also humanizes the larger historical processes often reduced to dry abstractions; and it presents the larger imperial or institutional developments on a human scale as a *lived* experience. Why did Lee, British born and possessed of a respectable fortune, with deep social and political ties to the establishment, and a personal acquaintance with King George III, decide to become a rebel? And what can his decision reveal about the nature and fate of the post-1763 British Empire?

In most histories of the American Revolution, Lee is depicted as a comic figure: an eccentric ex-British officer nicknamed "Naso," for his exceptionally large nose; a volatile man, whom the American Indians named "Boiling Water" for his turbulent personality; and a misanthrope who cared more for his Pomeranians, Spado, and Sappho, than for people. There is evidence for such views. For example, Continental Army chaplain Jeremy Belknap of Massachusetts described him as "a perfect original, a good scholar and soldier, and an odd genius; full of fire and passion, and but little good manners; a great sloven, wretchedly profane, and a great admirer of dogs."[4]

Along with his personal oddities, there were other serious factors that have shaped Lee's posthumous reputation. His public and private criticisms of George Washington following the Battle of Monmouth Court House in 1778 led to his being cashiered from the Continental Army. The discovery in the mid-nineteenth century, that while a prisoner of the British in 1777, Lee provided Sir William Howe with suggestions on how to defeat the Americans, raises fundamental questions about his commitment to the revolutionary cause. Previous biographers—John Alden's work remains the finest—have largely concerned themselves with the narrow question of whether Lee was a patriot or a traitor.[5]

This chapter explores the question of loyalty and identity in the post-1763 British world through an analysis of Lee's strange and tortuous career. His experience powerfully illuminates the tensions that caused the political bands binding the British world together to fray. Lee's choice to take up arms against his king was shaped by a potent mixture of several discernible ingredients: his connections to English radicals, his significant career as a political writer, his background as a trans-Atlantic soldier, and his Enlightened quest for a virtuous republic. This chapter also benefits from a series of Charles Lee's letters unknown to previous scholars, which shed new light on Lee's thinking and raise anew the fundamental questions of why he decided to separate from Britain, and whether he viewed that separation as irrevocable.

Along with many Britons and British Americans, Charles Lee gloried in the triumphant conclusion of the Seven Years' War. He believed that the Peace of 1763 presented Great Britain with the "glorious task of giving laws and peace to nations, protecting the weak and injured," and also an obligation of not "trampling on the rights of her dependencies." Obtaining victory in a global struggle of unprecedented extent, duration, and magnitude required an astonishing increase in the ability of the British state to command the peoples' loyalty and to mobilize their support for the war effort. While the material demands of the war were often complained of—the colonial American experience offers sufficient evidence—the British state's massive mobilization of men and logistical resources represented an astonishing achievement. Between 1754 and 1763, Scots, Irish, English, Welsh, New English, New Yorkers, Pennsylvanians, Virginians, Carolinians, Hanoverians, Prussians, Portuguese, Iroquois, Cherokees, Catawbas, Mahicans, Jamaicans, and Bengalis became the human means used to achieve British imperial ends, however the participants' own motives and goals may have differed.[6]

But Lee's expectations of a glorious future for the British Empire soon tarnished. By 1769, Lee declared that Britain had descended from "the summit of glory, opulence, and strength to the lowest degree of poverty, imbecillity, and contempt."[7] Lee's wildly inflated hopes of 1763 were bound to end in some kind of disillusionment or disappointment, but in a broader sense, Lee's odyssey expressed critical shifts in many subjects' relationships to the imperial state and the monarchy. Older notions of loyalty and allegiance became unhinged, and new ones were not yet solidified.

The years between 1763 and 1775 are replete with examples of changed understandings of allegiance: French Canadians, former foes, accepted British rule, while British Americans, formerly loyal subjects, bristled under new imperial innovations. Native peoples in the Ohio Valley, British subjects according to the terms of the Treaty of Paris, fought against their new "father" and his army in Pontiac's War in 1763 and 1764. Boston mobs carried emblems of Hanoverian arms through the streets on Pope's Day, but also breathed damnation to the king's troops when they arrived in 1768. Meanwhile, Scottish Highlanders—who twice fought against the Hanoverian monarchs earlier in the eighteenth century—increasingly filled the ranks of the British Army and the administrative posts of the expanded empire.[8]

Charles Lee's political and personal transformations illuminate in microcosm the problematics of loyalty in the post-1763 British world. What did being the subject of a king mean in the society, culture, and landscape of Britain and America? To what degree did the monarch serve as a point of reference for personal and national identity? Linda Colley has argued that following the loss of America, during the wars of the French Revolution, George III and the British monarchy became "more celebrated, more broadly popular and more unalloyedly patriotic than it had been for a century at least." Previous Georgian kings, foreign-born and German-speaking, were "too aloof, too unconcerned [with the public], and too [politically] controversial to be invariably or broadly popular."[9] But rather than loyalty to the king, Colley suggests that the most formative aspects of eighteenth-century British identity were ideas such as Protestantism, the pursuit of empire, or encounters with the "other." Most historians of the British American colonies in the late colonial era have similarly detected only a superficial allegiance to the monarchy, emphasizing instead late-colonial America's proto-revolutionary and republican characteristics.[10]

But a royalist counterattack has recently been launched. Brendan McConville, while noting that the idea of "what it was to be an American *subject*, in love with king and country, has been lost to us," argues that "for the people of that time, it was a consuming attachment." Similarly, Julie Flavell's study of colonial Americans in London offers intriguing evidence of colonists' strong affection for the monarchy. McConville provocatively asserts that the colonists (to whom the king was an ideal rather than a reality) were "more overtly monarchical than England itself." Maya Jasanoff's authoritative work on loyalists amplifies those ties and affections among colonists for the monarch and the monarchical world that he framed. By contrast, if the familiarity and close contact that many Englishmen had with their king did not actually breed contempt, it may have produced an "apathy" that could quickly turn to open hostility—a portrait that resonates with Charles Lee's experience.[11]

However, recent scholarship has begun to question the depiction of Britons as largely indifferent to the monarchy. Bob Harris and Christopher Whatley note that while historians of Jacobitism have deeply explored the concept of loyalty, "relatively little work … has been done on the promotion of Hanoverian monarchy and on the use of celebration and festivity to bolster its popularity and indeed its rule." Harris and Whatley assert that royal celebrations compromised "a very important and vital part of the political calendar in many parts of Britain throughout George II's reign." Hannah Smith has similarly argued that the "culture of loyalty" remained strong in Britain, and that previous scholars have underestimated the charismatic significance of the royal court in the eighteenth century.[12]

If, as this work suggests, we must give more credence to the strength of monarchical attachments among both colonists and Britons in the third quarter of the eighteenth century, how can one explain Thomas Jefferson's 1777 remark that the people of Virginia cast off the monarchy and became republicans "with as much ease as would have attended their throwing off an old and putting on a new suit of clothes," or, for that matter, Charles Lee's own decision, made one year earlier, to exchange his own red uniform for a blue one?[13]

"The spirit of the citizen has always predominated"

Born in 1732 into a prominent English gentry family in Cheshire, Lee was predestined for an army life. His father, John Lee, was colonel of the 55th Regiment and a veteran of the '45, having campaigned against the highland Scots and Prince Charles Edward

Stuart. It is significant that John sent his young son to Switzerland for his schooling. At this time, the Swiss were renowned for their republican form of government. Later, Charles would frequently remark that he "was bred up from infancy with the highest regard for the rights and liberties of Mankind." As a student, Lee's favorite subject was classical history. During the revolution, one contemporary remarked that "it is upon the model of the antient heroes Lee always has formed himself; nor is there an academic, much less is there an officer, so perfectly versed in classic lore."[14]

Lee's education imprinted many Enlightenment ideals firmly upon his character. Above all, there was "my divine and incomparable master Rousseau," as Charles wrote in a letter to a friend. He "could not help comparing" the differences between the countries of Europe and praising the general prosperity and happiness of republican Switzerland against the poverty and misery of absolutist France. Citing Montesquieu, he concluded that the greatest merits of the Venetian and Genoese republics were that "they have no king. They have no court." For the cosmopolitan young Englishman, the ideals of the Enlightenment and of classical antiquity, not British Protestantism, were his guiding principles and "sacred fuel."[15]

When Lee told a staff officer that "altho' I was bred in the army the spirit of the citizen has always been predominant," he expressed a central tension in his life: between the discipline and monarchical culture of the army and the liberty and independence of the citizen. Lee began his military career at the age of fourteen in 1746, when his father purchased an ensign's commission for him in his own regiment. One year after his father's death in 1750, Lee used some of his inheritance to obtain the rank of lieutenant in the regiment (which was renumbered from the 55th to the 44th in 1749).[16]

Lee's service during the Seven Years' War may have caused him to be "cynically dispos'd" toward incompetent leadership and toward his fellow man in general. Lee was directly involved in two of the worst British disasters of the conflict: Braddock's Expedition in 1755 and the Battle of Ticonderoga in 1758. On July 9, 1755, he barely missed the Battle of Monongahela, in which two-thirds of the British soldiers engaged were killed or wounded in the space of four hours. Stationed in the rear division (out of the fight), Lee nonetheless witnessed the return of the dazed and demoralized survivors, aided in the destruction of the army's supplies, and perhaps the burial of General Braddock, and joined in the humiliating retreat back to Virginia.[17] Braddock's death spared him from Lee's scorn, but the young officer acerbically referred to the earl of Loudoun, who assumed command, as a "damn'd beastly poltroon." His opinion of Loudoun's successor was far harsher. At the debacle at Ticonderoga in 1758, General James Abercromby sacrificed his troops by repeatedly ordering costly and futile frontal assaults on the French fortifications, thus incurring over 2,000 casualties in a single day, including Captain Charles Lee, who was wounded in action. The experience unleashed Lee's penchant to criticize his superiors and refusal to allow any perceived wrong to be "passed over in silence." Afterward, Lee excoriated "our Booby in Chief." "I really did not think that so great a share of stupidity and absurdity could be in the possession of any man," he marveled. The conduct of the Ticonderoga campaign, Lee wrote, proved Abercromby to be a "blockhead" who was "so far sunk into Idiotism as to be oblig'd to wear a bib and bells."[18]

Lee finally tasted the fruits of victory in 1759 when he participated in the conquest of Fort Niagara, at the junction of Lake Ontario and the Niagara River. Afterward, Lee led a small party across Lake Erie and down the Allegheny River to link up with the British garrison at Fort Pitt (Pittsburgh). Lee also served under General Jeffrey Amherst in the final conquest of New France in the 1760 Montreal campaign, a monumental feat of arms in which three separate British armies converged on the last remaining French stronghold. Lee's service in America impressed a number of important ideas in his mind that would gestate over the next decade. He was enraptured with the natural splendor of America, and praised the fighting capacities of the colonists. Lee's independence and willingness to test boundaries were evident in his dealings with Native Americans whom he encountered. Lee claimed that while stationed in the Mohawk Valley in 1756, he married an Iroquois woman named Bright Lightning and that the Six Nations adopted him with the name "Boiling Water"— one that his English friends found entirely fitting and which they continued to employ for him long after the war. He may have encountered Bright Lightning the year before, when she accompanied her father Kaghswaghtaniunt during Braddock's Expedition. Regardless of the truth of Lee's claim, he immersed himself in Native culture, and observed diplomatic conferences between Iroquois allies and the British superintendent of Indian Affairs, Sir William Johnson. Lee absorbed the lesson of Braddock's disaster, and argued that the British Army should adopt light infantry tactics and follow the methods of American Indians and colonial rangers. During the Ticonderoga Expedition, one soldier reported seeing Captain Lee in "his Indian dress, which he seems very fond of."[19]

In 1761, Lee returned to England and was promoted to the rank of major in the newly raised 103rd Regiment of Foot. The next year, Lee and his regiment formed part of the expeditionary force sent to defend Britain's ally Portugal from a Spanish invasion (Britain having declared war on Spain in January 1762). Count Wilhelm of Schaumburg-Lippe, Lee's commanding officer and patron (and an illegitimate grandson of George I), was one of the most famous military theorists and artillerists of the eighteenth century. Lee's most celebrated exploit during the campaign was a raid on a Spanish camp, in which he "fell upon their rear in the night, made a considerable slaughter, dispersed the whole party, destroyed their magazines, and returned with scarce any loss." In a letter to William Pitt, Schaumburg-Lippe praised Lee for making "so brilliant a stroke [that it] speaks for itself," and the feat achieved greater renown after it was included in James Entick's 1765 *Compleat History of the Late War*. Colonel John Burgoyne fought alongside Lee during the war in Portugal, creating a shared bond between the two officers. However, while in Portugal, Lee also became embroiled in a dispute with the commander of the British contingent, and his old commander from America, the earl of Loudoun, over the legality of the colonelcy that Lee accepted in the Portuguese Army.[20]

The scrape with Loudoun was perhaps one reason why Lee's fame and battlefield exploits did not spare him when the British Army was demobilized at the war's end. The 103rd regiment was disbanded and Major Lee was put on half-pay—an inactive status that conveyed economic and professional oblivion. He was but one of many meritorious officers who were left without a place in the reduced, postwar, army. However, in

1763, Lee was at a juncture in life—he was thirty-one—where he desperately desired recognition and reward, and his subsequent disenchantment with those in power may have stemmed from a resentment toward superiors who seemed oblivious to his talents. Like everyone else in that world, Lee pulled what strings he could. The earl of Thanet, Lee's most powerful patron, wrote that he had spoken to king, "who has promis'd to promote [you] to the first vacancy" in regimental command. While he waited impatiently for a colonel to resign or drop dead, Lee sought employment under a different monarch, the king of Poland, Stanislaus II. Carrying letters of introduction from Count Schaumburg-Lippe and British diplomats, Lee traveled to Poland and was appointed aide-de-camp to the king.[21]

Lee's quest for martial fame and honor abroad may have been motivated primarily by his own "disappointed ambition" and his sense of being "absolutely proscribed" in the British ranks, although he maintained that a zeal for liberty was the mainspring of his actions. Lee's dwindling family network also made it possible for him to leave England. After his mother's death in 1765, the sole surviving member of his immediate family was his sister, Sidney. Lee had a significant fortune—accounted to produce more than £1,000 in annual income in the mid-1770s—but he nonetheless expressed concern that his standing as a gentleman might slip: "It is wretchedness itself not to be able to herd with the class of men we have been accustomed to from our infancy," he confided to his uncle Sir Charles Bunbury. He claimed that he would rather "find respectable employment" as an officer abroad rather than remain "idleing at Home" on half-pay status.[22]

In late 1766, Lee's impatience and impertinence induced him to strike a fatal blow to his hopes of resuming his career in the British military. Appearing before King George III to deliver a letter of recommendation from the king of Poland, he took advantage of the opportunity to remind the king "of his promise in my favor to L[or] d Thanet three years ago." According to Horace Walpole, when George III demurred, the disgruntled half-pay major told his sovereign that "I will never give your Majesty an opportunity of breaking your promise to me again." Clearly, Lee never developed the right blend of self-effacement and self-promotion that was recommended when soliciting favor from powerful patrons.[23]

Along with his personal and professional frustration, another powerful influence on Lee's evolving attitude about the state of the British Empire was his engagement in radical politics. Lee's participation in political debate pre-dated 1766. Immediately upon his return to England from Canada (and prior to his departure to Portugal), Lee had contributed to the sensational debate over the terms of the prospective peace, hinging on the question of whether Britain should retain Canada or the West Indies' sugar island of Guadeloupe. In a pamphlet entitled *The Importance of Canada Considered in Two Letters to a Noble Lord*, Lee advocated retaining Canada and returning Guadeloupe to France. Having seen for himself the strategic importance of the Ohio Valley and the Great Lakes, as well as the formidable strength of the region's Native nations, Lee was convinced that Sir Jeffrey Amherst, the British commander in Montreal, was mismanaging Britain's new Native American subjects. Lee's judgment was not without merit considering how Amherst's policies would contribute to the outbreak of Pontiac's War in the spring of 1763.[24]

When he returned from Portugal, Lee's caustic pen took aim at a host of establishment figures. Prime Minister George Grenville and the dukes of Bedford and Newcastle were assailed as an "order of coxcombs." William Pitt was also attacked when he accepted the peerage of the earl of Chatham in 1766. Friends warned Lee that his views, while "honest and patriotic," were "not politic," but their warnings went unheeded. Throughout his life, Lee never quite learned, as one friend enjoined, that "common prudence should teach us to hold our tongues" nor how to separate the political from the personal. Sir Horace Mann, a contemporary, believed that Lee's many good qualities or worthy ideas were too often overshadowed by "the rankest malice that the most indecent terms could express against every individual who differed from him in politics."[25]

In London, Lee's closest political associates were a network of veteran officers who were "friends of America," as Benjamin Franklin described the trio of Robert Monckton, Horatio Gates, and Charles Lee after he dined with them in 1768. Monckton, who served with Gates in the capture of Martinique in 1762, would decline an offer to command the British Army in America in 1773. Lee claimed to have a "brotherly affection" for Gates, whom he had known during Braddock's Expedition, and who also became a rebel officer in 1775. Their 1768 dinner conversation with Franklin hinged on American affairs, particularly the army's presence in the colonies, their prospects for western settlement, the recently published *Letters from a Farmer in Pennsylvania* by John Dickinson, and the limits of Parliament's authority. Lee himself described his cohort as "that audacious faction who dare to think for themselves," and mentioned Colonel Isaac Barré—a fellow veteran of the American War, member of Parliament, and vociferous advocate for the American "Sons of Liberty"—as also among their number. A 1764 document names Lee as president of a gentleman's organization called the "American Club," which criticized Amherst's conduct as Pontiac's War continued to rage.[26]

Lee's political views and published writings reflected the major themes of the radical Whig tradition: ministerial corruption (or the "pecuniary influence" upon British politics), the decline of virtue, and the crown's drift toward absolutism (Lee praised the English radical John Wilkes during the height of his confrontation with the crown). His correspondents and favorites ranged from Rockingham Whigs like Edmund Burke to opposition leaders like Isaac Barré and to Whig writers such as the famed historian Catherine McCauley. While such oppositional views did not necessitate a break with the king, the inherent suspicion and distrust of authority they contained probably did not help matters.[27]

Perhaps of even greater import was Lee's infatuation with the example of ancient Rome and with the downfall of the Roman Republic. As historian Gordon Wood has observed, the widely held fascination with the ideology of classical republicanism (evidenced by a use of classical analogies and eponyms) worked to undermine the old monarchical order: "It ate away at it, corroded it, slowly, gradually, and steadily." During the Revolution, Lee likened his victorious troops to the "*decima Legio*"; hailed members of the Continental Congress as "senators"; compared the British government to "the rascally Senate of Tiberius"; and spoke of worshipping the "Goddess Liberty" in her American temple.[28]

Lee and other members of the "American Club" were interested in America for reasons that were personal as well as political. Led by Walter Patterson, one of Lee's acquaintances from the Ticonderoga campaign, a group of veterans including Lee claimed land on Île St. Jean (modern Prince Edward Island) in Canada and successfully lobbied the British government to declare the island a separate colony from Nova Scotia. But Lee's 10,000 acres on Île St. Jean remained undeveloped and unprofitable, his 20,000 acres in East Florida were in a similar state, and his attempts to gain land on the New York frontier fell through. In many respects, Lee's postwar land schemes or hopes paralleled those of another fellow veteran officer, George Washington, who likewise found the fruits of imperial victory difficult to grasp.[29]

Enlightenment soldier of fortune

Already estranged from his king, Lee's estrangement from Britain took root during a "peregrination and progress" he made through Europe between 1764 and 1772 as he searched for military employment and advancement. His travels reinforced many of his Enlightened views. On his tour, he visited Germany, Prussia, Poland, Russia, Austria, Turkey, France, and Italy. So numerous were Lee's audiences with various European monarchs that he compared himself to Lord Peterborough, an English officer who had campaigned in and visited the courts of Europe at the end of the previous century. In making the comparison, Lee might have pondered the possibility that he might one day break with *his* king, as Peterborough did with William III (an event that led to Peterborough's imprisonment in the Tower of London in 1697).[30] In the course of his self-imposed exile, Lee refashioned himself into a citizen of the world and a soldier of fortune in the cause of republican liberty and virtue.

As Lee's loyalty to king, constitution, and even country eroded, his support for the colonists' resistance to Parliament grew. Lee closely followed news of the Stamp Act crisis while in Constantinople in the spring of 1766, writing to his beloved sister Sidney of his prayer that God would "prosper the Americans in their resolutions, that there may be one Asylum at least upon the earth for men." Before long he was writing that "his country is every part of the Empire," an understanding that resonated with many colonial Americans' own extended view of a pan-Atlantic "Greater Britain." Contemplating Britain in 1772, he concluded that liberty "seems to be worn out in this Hemisphere," and, just as Thomas Paine would famously argue in 1776, he began to view America as its last refuge in the world. Later, when he defended his decision to fight for America, Lee asserted that he felt himself at home among men "who prefer their natural rights to the fantastical prerogative of a foolish perverted head because it wears a Crown."[31]

Lee's familiarity with the "foolish" crowned heads of Europe may have bred much of his contempt for George III in particular and for monarchy generally. He stood face-to-face with George III, Prussia's Frederick II, the Holy Roman Emperor Joseph II, and Poland's Stanislaus II and was not awed. Lee's conversations with kings often centered on America. For example, he wrote that he had talked to Frederick the Great for "more than half an hour, and what was fortunate, upon the topick I am best acquainted with:

American affairs." Lee boasted of his ability to gain entrée to kings and their courts, and he was clearly successful in this milieu. In 1769, the king of Poland appointed Lee as a major general in his service (which later gave him claim to an equal rank in the American Army). But, as he also confessed to Sidney, "the life of a Courtier is not the best adapted to my disposition."[32]

Close contact with other European rulers also allowed Lee to compare Britain's monarch with his contemporaries. In 1771, for example, he anonymously published an article entitled "The Character of the Present Emperor of Germany," which implicitly contrasted Emperor Joseph II of Austria and George III to the latter's disadvantage. Lee praised Joseph II for his "generous notions of the rights of mankind," and his disdain for the "wantonness, pride, ambition, avarice and folly of the optimates or monarchs" of other realms. Lee predicted that Joseph II would "one day make a figure, at least comparatively with the [other] sad automata of sceptered herd."[33]

Lee's observations of the other end of the social scale in Poland, Russia, and Germany similarly horrified him. European despotism had reduced the common people to "mere moving clods of stinking earth," he wrote. The sight provided him with a vivid picture of Britain's future if it continued its descent toward autocracy. Lee made the parallel between absolutism and poverty explicit in his 1771 pamphlet entitled *An Epistle to David Hume* in which he excoriated Hume's *History of England* for its alleged defense of the Stuart monarchs. Lee invited Hume and "other Monarchical writers" to visit Poland in order to reap the "fruits which their blessed labours entitle them." In sum, Lee wrote, "I have, if possible, since my passage through Germany, and my residence here [in Poland], a greater horror of slavery than ever."[34]

Most of Lee's venom was reserved for the successive British ministries of the 1760s and early 1770s. Like many colonial Americans, he had initially faulted the king's ministers, not the king, as the source of Britain's postwar problems. Lee hurled invectives such as "damnable administration," "dens of thieves the L[ord]s and Commons," and "hellhounds of an execrable Ministry" at the British government. The fall of the Roman Republic was perennially his favorite analogy. It must have been at least some consolation to the Romans, he mused, that "it was Julius Caesar, a man with more than mortal talents, who was their subverter." But when a "clod" like the duke of Grafton or a "reptile" like Lord North could so easily usurp Britons' liberties, what did that say about Britain's vaunted virtue? Soon, Lee's seething contempt for the ministry was accompanied by a growing alienation from his countrymen. In 1769, he wrote of "that abominable seat of corruption and folly my native Country." Two years later, while in Italy, he declared to Sir Charles Davers, "As to England, I have foresworn it, [only] America has a chance of emerging from ministerial oppression [and] on this I fix my hopes."[35]

In 1773, Lee decided to follow his hopes and move to America. Few in Britain noticed his departure, save for the earl of Dartmouth, who later recalled to Jeffrey Amherst that he "happened to hear a little of General Lee before he left England." "I have always considered him as a madman," Dartmouth continued, but, he added prophetically, "madmen are sometimes capable of giving a great deal of trouble to those who are more in their senses than themselves," especially if they fall in with "people little less mad than themselves."[36]

Virtuous treason

Lee had not departed from England intending to join a rebellion. He planned only to retire to his peaceful American asylum. Every true republican needs a farm, so Lee had purchased a small plantation (he named it "Prato Rio") in the Great Valley of Virginia, only a few miles away from the estate of his old army friend Horatio Gates (who had emigrated for similar motives the year before). But his arrival in Philadelphia in late 1773 closely coincided with the final rupture between Britain and the American colonies occasioned by the Boston Tea Party and Parliament's subsequent passage of the Coercive Acts. Lee could not sit idly on the sidelines in the midst of such a crisis. Within weeks, he had plunged into the maelstrom, meeting with patriot leaders in Boston, New York, Philadelphia, and Williamsburg, arguing for resistance to British measures and against moderation. Informed of these activities, Lord Dartmouth took note of how "Lee associates only with the enemies of government, [and] he encourages the discontents of the people by harangues and publications, and even advises [them] to arms." Dartmouth instructed General Gage to watch Lee closely and pursue every legal means to stop him.[37]

As colonists prepared for the ever more real possibility that the British would resort to force to win the argument with the colonies, experienced military men were in short supply. Lee's military expertise and fame made him a welcome source of wisdom and reassurance to Americans unsure of their own martial abilities. When he visited Boston in August 1774, he was hailed as one of the "greatest military characters of the day." The Boston radical Thomas Young praised Lee as a man of "rank, sense, spirit and patriotism," adding "Never Man parted us with a more general regret than General Lee."[38] But Lee was given a cold shoulder from an old friend. While in Boston, Lee wrote a personal letter to General Gage (now also the governor of Massachusetts) expressing his "eagerness to embrace Mr. Gage." Gage however did not reply, and they did not meet.[39]

By late 1774, Lee's soldierly bearing and reputation as a military hero thrust him in the middle of conversations that broached the possibility of an imperial civil war. Lee was part of an inner circle of radicals, including John and Samuel Adams of Massachusetts; Patrick Henry and Richard Henry Lee of Virginia; Benjamin Franklin, Benjamin Rush, and Robert Morris of Pennsylvania; and Alexander McDougall of New York, who did not shrink from the prospect of violent resistance. Benjamin Rush recalled a dinner party at Thomas Mifflin's house during the meeting of the First Continental Congress in Philadelphia in September 1774. Mifflin's guests included George Washington, the two Adamses, and other delegates, but the star of the evening was Charles Lee. John Adams, who first met Lee in this period, was impressed by the Briton's military acumen. Adams later wrote that, at this time, "I had read as much on the military Art and much more of the History of War than any American Officer … General Lee excepted." That fall in Philadelphia, the two men became, and remained, friends. Adams later remarked that "the cordiality between him and me continued till his death."[40]

Lee soaked up all the attention and expressed pleasure at his new life and destiny. "I us'd to regret," he wrote his new friend Patrick Henry, "not being thrown into the

World in the glorious third or fourth century of the Romans"—taking it for granted that Henry would know that he meant the third and fourth centuries of the Republic. But Lee was now looking forward rather than backward in time, and envisioned "a mighty empire establish'd of Freemen whose honour, property, and military glories are not to be at the disposal of a scepter'd knave, thief, fool, or Coward; nor their consciences to be fetter'd by a proud domineering Hierarchy." Here, in America, would rise the meritocratic republic that would properly honor and advance men like Lee, whose virtues and worth had been disregarded by the corrupt regime he had left behind.[41]

When the war began in April 1775, Lee cast his lot with his new friends and his new cause without hesitation. The political friendships and connections he had made in the Congress, particularly among the influential Virginia and Massachusetts delegations, as well as his extensive military experience, made Lee a strong candidate for high command. On the same day that the Congress appointed George Washington as commander-in-chief of the Continental Army, Lee was named as one of his four major-generals. Of the army's five highest-ranking officers, Lee was the only one not American born. The fact was not thought to be significant, except to Lee, who bristled at being outranked by Artemas Ward (of Massachusetts), who he thought "an old church-warden." Observers like Samuel Adams, however, were "more and more satisfied in the Appointment of General Lee. He is certainly an able officer and I think deeply embarked in the American Cause."[42]

Before joining Washington on his journey from Philadelphia to Cambridge, Massachusetts to assume their commands in the Continental Army, Lee sought to make it clear to both American and British audiences that he acted not from motives of personal ambition but from political principles by publicly resigning his commission in King George's army. On June 22, 1775, he wrote to Lord Barrington, the Secretary of War, "in the most public and solemn manner, that I do renounce my half-pay from the date hereof." Perhaps a residual attachment to the king, and maybe even a slight hope for reconciliation, can be deduced from Lee's promise that "whenever it shall please His Majesty to call me forth to any honorable service against the natural hereditary enemies of our Country, or in defence of his just rights and dignity, no man will obey the righteous summons with more zeal and alacrity than myself." By contrast, Lee averred, the policy being pursued by the present administration was detrimental to liberty, the empire, and the king's honor. To most British observers, both the timing of Lee's resignation (after his appointment to the major generalship) and his equivocations as to when he would give or withhold his loyalty only made his claim to be acting purely upon principle appear more suspect. "Has he not drawn himself into a bad scrape by appearing in open rebellion before he gave up his commission, though on half-pay?" Horace Mann noted, "His own letter [to Barrington] seems to imply his doubts on that subject."[43]

If Lee indeed entertained any "doubts" about the path he had taken, he was not alone. In the summer and fall of 1775, the Continental Congress itself wavered between voting for military preparations (and appointments) and seeking a reconciliation. It had not only created a Continental Army, but also drafted an "Olive Branch petition" that proclaimed loyalty to the king and appealed to him to resolve the imperial crisis. Men on both sides of the lines outside of Boston expressed regret at the prospect that they would soon face old friends as foes on the battlefield. Major Andrew Bruce of the 38th Regiment, upon learning of Lee's presence in the "enemy's" camp, exclaimed to an American courier, "General Lee! Good God sir! Is General Lee (there)? [I] served two years with him in Portugal. Tell him, sir, that I am extremely sorry that my profession obliges me to be his opposite in this unhappy affair. Can't it be made up? Let me be of you to use your influence, and endeavor to heal this unhappy breach!"[44] Both Lee and Horatio Gates mourned the fact that their old friend Thomas Gage was taking an active hand in the repression of the colonies. As Gates had written to Lee in 1774, "I have read with wonder & astonishment Gage's Proclamations, surely this is not the same man you and I knew so well in days of yore."[45]

In the summer of 1775, Lee published a series of letters addressed to his "quondam friend Gage," as well as to British officers Earl Percy and John Burgoyne, that powerfully humanized the dissolution of imperial bonds. The letters were reprinted in Philadelphia, New York, and in multiple other colonial cities. In his letter to Earl Percy, Lee proclaimed that an English soldier should have "a greater degree of reverence" for his country's liberties than for the obedience due to a monarch. He defined his true country as not only Britain itself but "every part of the empire," and added that America's cause was "the Cause of mankind" (a phrase that anticipated a basic theme in Paine's *Common Sense*). In many ways, these public, yet still deeply personal, "olive branch petitions" are among Lee's most revealing writings.[46] To be sure, Lee intended that his "private" letters be published. He expected them to establish his own loyalty to the American cause and to justify his own actions by charging British officers still serving the king with participating in an unjust and immoral war. But the sentiments of feeling and friendship that Lee expressed to Burgoyne and Gage were not disingenuous, they are borne out in all of Lee's other private correspondence regarding them.[47] The letters illustrate the nature of the imperial civil war that was confronting everyone on both sides of the Atlantic. Although American colonists like Eunice Paine believed that Lee's letter to Burgoyne "gain'd him the Esteem of Generous Souls," Lee was not entirely seeking to publicly vindicate himself. He was also justifying and counting the cost of his new allegiance as he severed ties with old British friends. In November 1775, for example, Lee sent a personal note to General William Howe, requesting that, as a favor, he convey a letter to Lee's old patron in England, Lord Thanet.[48]

Writing a letter was "a duty I owe to the friendship I have long and sincerely professed for you," Lee told Burgoyne. He spoke of the "esteem and affection" that cemented their friendship. Lee claimed that he was astonished that Burgoyne, Gage, and William Howe had been "seduced into so impious and nefarious a service by the artifice of a wicked and insidious court and cabinet" and impugned their motives as being guided by ambition and avarice. How else could it be that Howe would make war upon the very people among whom his elder brother George had fought and died in the Seven Years' War? "Gracious God! [How] is it possible," Lee asked, that "Mr. Howe should be prevailed upon to accept of such an office![?]"[49]

Lee's letter repeated the colonists' constitutional argument against Parliamentary taxation, and accused the British government of having a "regular plan … to abolish even the shadow of liberty from amongst us." Were Parliament to succeed in its repression of the colonies, he wrote, it must inevitably work the subversion of the whole empire. A Parliamentary victory would only worsen the twin evils that he identified as poisoning British politics: "inadequate representation of the subject, and the vast pecuniary influence of the crown." Lee also cautioned his old friends that the British could not hope to defeat a numerous and spirited people who had fought so well in the last war: "As to the idea that Americans are deficient in courage, it is too ridiculous and glaringly false to deserve a serious refutation." But Lee provided a refutation nonetheless. Noting General James Grant's recent boast to the House of Commons that he could conquer America with a mere 5,000 regulars, Lee laid on the delicious irony that in 1758, Grant's command (and perhaps his life) had been "saved from destruction by the valour of a few Virginians" in a desperate battle against the French and Indians at Fort Duquesne during General John Forbes's Expedition. Lee closed by wishing Burgoyne well, and hoping that his talents and services might soon be used against Britain's "natural" enemies. For his part, he declared that he would fight for the "last asylum of persecuted liberty" even against his esteemed friends if they chose to wage an "inexpiable war against America."[50]

Burgoyne seemed sincerely moved by Lee's appeal to their friendship. He replied that "when we were last together in service I should not have thought it within the vicissitudes of human affairs that we should meet at any time, or in any sense, as foes. The letter you have honored me with, and my own feelings, continue to prove we are still far from being personally such." Burgoyne's substantive answer to Lee was both historical and constitutional. He argued that he was upholding the sovereignty of King-in-Parliament, and following in the footsteps of the "immortal Whigs" who had defended English rights in the past. Burgoyne explained to Lee that these sentiments were shared by "the great bulk of the nation." Burgoyne also invoked an older notion of personal obligation to the monarch that motivated many British officers in America. "A King of England never appears in so glorious a light as when he employs the executive powers of the state to maintain the laws," Burgoyne declared, and during those times, he continued, "His Majesty is particularly entitled to our zeal and grateful obedience, not only as soldiers but as citizens." In closing, he offered to meet Lee between the lines to discuss matters further.[51]

As Lee explained to Benjamin Franklin (who helped to publish the correspondence in Philadelphia), his letters to Burgoyne pursued a rhetorical strategy of forcing Burgoyne (and other Britons) to choose between the bonds of friendship and kinship they felt toward the colonists, and their narrow duty to the current government. "Declare great affection for the Mother Country" (or for friends like Burgoyne), he wrote, and "assure 'em that unless they give up immediately the Ministry and Ministerial system, you are determin'd to dissolve the connection." However, the ties of blood and the bands of military brotherhood proved more brittle than those of duty to the army or loyalty to the king. In the end, Lee's correspondence with Gage and Burgoyne resulted in nothing but the severing of their friendship. Lee may have assuaged his conscience by writing the letters, but his British correspondents were unmoved. Gage, in fact, thought that the publication of the letters revealed Lee's insincerity and he condemned Lee's "shabby Answer" to Burgoyne.[52]

In the end, of the roughly 3,500 commissioned officers in the king's army in 1775, only three Englishmen (Lee, Horatio Gates, and Richard Humpton) and two Irishmen

(Edward Hand and Richard Montgomery) resigned their commissions to join the American rebellion. Lee referred Burgoyne's invitation for a personal meeting to the Massachusetts Provincial Congress. Believing that it might send a hesitant signal to the population and unduly raise suspicions of Lee's own devotion to the cause, the Congress forbade it. Lee and Burgoyne, like many Britons and British Americans, never saw each other or corresponded again.[53]

As the Siege of Boston continued, Washington, Lee, and Gates (one American and two Britons) formed a triumvirate whose collective military talents shaped the formation of the Continental Army and significantly bolstered American fortunes. Washington's overall leadership molded the Continental Army's character, while Lee functioned like an executive officer supervising and encouraging the soldiers; as adjutant general, Gates was responsible for the army's basic administration and organization. James Warren, president of the Massachusetts Provincial Congress, reported to Samuel Adams in August 1775 that "Genl. Washington, Lee, Gates & the Character of the Gentlemen with them are greatly esteem'd & unlimited confidence is placed in them."[54]

At the close of 1775, Lee's radicalism exceeded that of Washington (who was still toasting the king's health each night at his headquarters), and anticipated Thomas Paine, another citizen of the world who would depict America as an asylum for liberty. In fact, Benjamin Franklin noted the political congruity between the two Englishmen, commenting to Lee that Paine's "sentiments are not very different from your own." When he met Paine in New York City in early 1776, Lee was mesmerized by the "genius in his eyes." He warmly approved of *Common Sense*, declaring it a "masterly, irresistible performance" that would "give the coup-de-grace to Great Britain."[55]

But, as we have seen, Lee had been thinking along these lines before he read Paine's famous anti-monarchical pamphlet. In the fall and winter of 1775, Lee unhesitatingly denounced George III as a "tyrant," and referred to "Our damn'd Tyrant of St. James" in the letters he wrote to the revolutionary leadership. He dismissed monarchy in general as "nonsensical," and blasted the concepts that "the king can do no wrong – [or that] his Person is to be considered as Sacred." To Lee, such ideas were "beastly Barbarisms shocking to common sense." Lee hoped that Americans would soon eschew the "fulsome nauseating cant [that] may be well enough adapted to barbarous Monarchies" and "pompous Aristocracies," but which was unequal to the "true dignity" contained in the simple republican title of "citizen."[56]

The most influential product of Lee's pen was his 1775 masterpiece, *Strictures on a Pamphlet Entitled "A Friendly Address to All Reasonable Americans on the Subject of Our Political Confusions,"* which appeared in seven editions and became one of the most popular and widely disseminated pamphlets of the American cause to appear before 1776. Its circulation and importance rivaled John Dickinson's far better remembered *Letters from a Farmer in Pennsylvania.* Lee's pamphlet demolished the arguments made by Myles Cooper, a New York clergyman and loyalist, in his "Friendly Address" of the same year. His refutations of Cooper anticipated many of the arguments later made by Paine in *Common Sense.* In response to Cooper's claim that Americans could not hope to defeat the military power of Britain, Lee drew important contrasts between the British Army that had won the Seven Years' War and the current army, which he characterized as "unfit for real service." Moreover, he argued, there was no British general comparable to a military genius like James Wolfe who could orchestrate the conquest of an entire continent. While New France might have been conquered by one victory at Quebec in 1759, Lee believed that it was "impossible to calculate" the number of victories the British would have to win in order to subdue the thirteen colonies. It was inconceivable, Lee wrote, that "7,000 very indifferent troops, composed of the refuse of an exhausted nation, few of whom have seen action of any kind, should be able to conquer 200,000 active vigorous yeomanry." Moreover, he added, even during the Seven Years' War, Americans' martial virtues had compared favorably with that of the redcoats: "While your Militia were frequently crowned with success, these regulars were defeated or baffled for three years successively in every part of the Continent." Lee's reputation and experience as a British officer lent credibility to his timely pamphlet, which helped bolster colonists' confidence and deflected the American loyalists' argument that military resistance was futile. Benjamin Rush later remembered that Lee "was useful in the beginning of the war by inspiring our citizens with military ideas and lessening in our soldiers their superstitious fear of the valor and discipline of the British Army."[57]

While strengthening American resolve, Lee was also casting doubts upon the possibility of reconciliation. By the middle of 1775, Lee was publicly telling Americans that any hopes for peace that were based upon a belief in the "magnanimity of the British nation, and the known goodness and virtue of the king" were doomed. In early June 1776, Lee stopped in Williamsburg, Virginia (en route to Charles Town, South Carolina, to help defend that city against a British attack). While there, Lee heard the Virginia Convention resolve that "the United Colonies [are] free and independent states absolved from all allegiance to, or dependence upon, the Crown or Parliament of Great Britain"—a resolution that the Continental Congress eventually voted on and later included in the Declaration of Independence. Witnessing and participating in such a historic moment seemed the fulfillment of Lee's dream of reliving the "glorious" days of the Roman Republic, as he wrote to Patrick Henry shortly after the Declaration's passage.[58]

How did Lee mark his personal declaration of independence from Britain, even as the colonies individually and collectively declared independence in 1776? His departure from Britain for America in the fall of 1773 is one tempting moment. But Lee himself saw Parliament's passage of the Coercive Acts the following spring as a watershed. He then told Edmund Burke bluntly, that "unless the Boston bills (and I may add the Quebec [Act]) are repealed, the empire of Great Britain is no more." But the event that struck Lee, and many Americans, with irrevocable force was King George III's speech to Parliament on October 26, 1775. In this speech, the king proclaimed that the colonists were in "open rebellion" and engaged in a war for independence. Referring to the "Olive Branch petition" issued by the Continental Congress in July, the king noted that conspirators had treacherously expressed their "attachment to the parent state and the strongest protestations of loyalty to me, [even] whilst they were preparing for a general revolt."[59]

Lee wrote to Robert Morris of New York that "until the appearance of the King's speech," he had been a "strong advocate for dependence," that is, retaining the imperial tie. But the speech, in his view, "absolutely destroys all hope of reunion ... We must be Independent or Slaves." He believed that *"from the date of the King's speech* [and] the address [from Parliament] that echo's it back" a divorce between Britain and the colonies had "taken place to all intents and purposes." The king's decision to levy war upon his own subjects had broken the social compact. For his own part, Lee believed that he was engaged in a "brave, virtuous kind of treason." "There are times," he wrote in a letter that revealed much about his own feelings, "when we must commit treason against the laws of the State for the salvation of the State."[60]

The zenith of Lee's military career in the American Revolution came with his role in helping to defeat the British Expedition against Charles Town, South Carolina, in late June 1776. The nadir came less than six months later, after Lee witnessed the near-destruction of the Continental Army in the New York Campaign during the fall. The ease with which the British Army crushed the Continental Army in battle on Long Island, at Kip's Bay, and Fort Washington, shattered Lee's faith in the ability of American militia to face up to the British on the battlefield, let alone win the war. In stark contrast to his earlier statements of the steadfastness of the colonial "yeomanry," he now asserted that the "militia from the incompetency of their officers, or some vice in its constitution, manifestly does not answer the purpose," and that only the creation of a regular, well-disciplined, army could stave off defeat.

Lee commanded a detachment of the fast dwindling Continental Army during the ensuing retreat across New Jersey in November and December 1776. Although Washington ordered him to rejoin the main army's encampment across the Delaware River, Lee delayed obeying that order, claiming that if he remained in northern New Jersey he could attack the flanks of the British and Hessian forces as they moved toward Philadelphia. At the same time, Lee returned to his former pastime of verbally lacerating his commanding officer. He indirectly criticized Washington when he reported to the president of the Massachusetts Council that it was "indecision in our military councils" that had led to the disasters around New York.

When he replied to a flattering letter he had received from Joseph Reed, Washington's own aide, which suggested that Lee could more effectively lead the Continental Army, Lee tacitly agreed, obliquely referred to Washington as a "decisive blunderer," and wrote of his "fatal indecision of mind which in war is a much greater disqualification than stupidity or even want of personal courage." Thinking the letter a dispatch intended for him, Washington opened it, but magnanimously passed over Lee's remarks, saying nothing of them in his subsequent pleas with his renegade subordinate to hasten to rejoin the main army.[61]

On the night of December 12, 1776, Lee was warmly ensconced in a tavern at Basking Ridge, New Jersey, a few miles from the much-less cozy encampment of his troops. In a letter composed to his old friend Horatio Gates, he wrote: *"Entre nous*, a certain great man is most damnably deficient."[62] The letter was never sent however, for early the next morning, it, and Lee himself, were captured by a British cavalry patrol that had learned of his presence in the tavern, and his lack of sufficient guards.

The ecstatic response among Britons to the news of Lee's capture perhaps reveals their own anxieties about an "unnatural" war waged against fellow subjects. In Britain, most newspapers had earlier dismissed Lee's "desertion" and his acceptance of a general's commission in the Rebel army as the actions of a disgruntled and vainglorious half-pay officer. Rather than a principled warrior fighting for liberty, Lee was depicted as a brazen opportunist, a despicable turncoat, or even a madman, such as in the "Ode to General Lee" that appeared in the *General Evening Post*, which described him as:

Ambition's dupe, a lawless Faction's tool,
Must live a madman, must die a fool.
Here read thy character, thy peril, Lee;
A traitor's name, a traitor's destiny.[63]

Now, in something of a contradiction, but with typical metropolitan condescension, Britons asserted that Lee, the ex-British officer, had been "the most active and enterprising of the Enemy's Generals," and that with his capture, the rebellion would be rapidly extinguished. A junior officer who had assisted in taking Lee prisoner hailed it as a "most miraculous Event," and predicted that "this Coup de Main has put an end to the Campaign. We shall not cross the Delaware."[64]

Lieutenant Colonel William Harcourt, commanding officer of the party of the 16th (Queen's) Light Dragoons that had taken Lee, was hailed in prose and poetry and became a popular hero. Lee's capture was prominently featured in most British histories of the American War for the next few decades, and illustrated in Edward Barnard's *New, Impartial, and Complete History of England* (London, 1790). Monuments to Harcourt were erected in St. Michael's Church at Oxford and St. George's Chapel at Windsor Castle (the latter features a relief of Lee surrendering). Harcourt was ordered home and rewarded with the post of aide-de-camp to the king.[65]

As a prisoner of war, Lee received a very different treatment. He became a figure of fascination and horror, condemned by all who saw him as "a traitor who had betrayed his king and comrades." Ambrose Serle, Lord Howe's secretary, visited Lee and judged him a "rogue" and an "unprincipled man." Captain John Bowater, the Royal Marine officer, responsible for guarding Lee on HMS *Centurion*, at anchor in New York harbor, could not contain his visceral contempt for both Lee and Americans in general. Bowater wrote to the earl of Denbigh, "It requires a pen of a Littleton, & the pencil of a Hogarth, to delineate the person & Character of this atrocious Monster, who … is not only my Prisoner, but my Companion. He is as perfect in Treachery as if he had been an American born."

For a time, the British debated whether to try Lee as a traitor, a deserter, or both. (Although one British officer, with a sense of humor and a memory of the political career of the opposition gadfly John Wilkes, facetiously predicted that "I hear that he means to be a Candidate for Middlesex, at the next Election, [and, by and by,] I shall not be surprized to see the Garter upon him.")[66]

Lee's case is very revealing about British attitudes regarding loyalty. Recent work on British public opinion during the American Revolution suggests that there was a broad consensus of support for the war effort. Although the outbreak of fighting in 1775 provoked much political and popular controversy, most of the loyal addresses submitted in the war's first years were framed in terms of standing by the king at a time of national crisis.[67] As Ilya Berkovitch has shown, *ancien regime* armies had deep reservoirs of loyalty and motivation that bound the rank and file of the army to the king. Far from being the unprincipled, unthinking mercenaries of American propaganda, many redcoats were sincere patriots and royalists. George Washington "might be a good man," one soldier told an American civilian, "but he was most damnably misled to take up arms against his sovereign." Captain Robert Prescott called service in the war with America "a Duty we owe to God, to our Country, to our King, [and] to our own Honour."[68]

During his eighteen-month captivity, Lee's own perspective on the Revolutionary War changed. Perhaps the hatred and contempt that was heaped upon him from fellow British officers led him to reconsider his actions. He was undoubtedly concerned about the possibility of being tried for desertion or treason and executed, as some demanded. Whatever his motives, Lee endeavored to explain his actions to his captors (and perhaps to himself). In letters written to two British officers, Lee asserted the purity of his motives:

> I do therefore most solemnly declare by all that is sacred and solemn (that as far as I know myself) I do believe that no personal consideration had the least share in actuating me to take up arms in the present cause. If in my cooler moments, I have any thing to upbraid myself with, it is perhaps an intemperate and ferocious zeal for liberty.[69]

But the other correspondence Lee wrote while in captivity reveals that his once "ferocious zeal for liberty" was spent. A newly discovered cache of his letters in the Papers of James Grant reveals just how fundamentally and rapidly he changed as a result of twin disasters of the New York Campaign and his own humiliating capture. Immediately after he became a prisoner, Lee set about ingratiating himself with his former colleagues in the British Army, such as James Grant, William Howe, and William Erskine. Lee requested an audience with General James Grant only six days after his capture, and requested permission to address Admiral Lord Howe with "some matters of importance not only to myself but the whole continent." Lord Howe's brother, and British Commanding General, William, rejected Lee's letters and pointedly returned them, addressed to Lieutenant Colonel Lee, to remind him of his rank in the British Army and the possible charge of treason. Now, Lee provided the Howes with all that he knew of the Continental Army's current condition and locations, from the upper Hudson Valley to the Delaware Valley. To be sure, such candid relations of military intelligence by high-ranking prisoners were not unusual in the eighteenth century, but this new documentation of Lee's "co-operative" attitude so soon after his capture in December 1776 reflects upon subsequent events.[70]

In March 1777, Lee wrote a lengthy document to the Howe brothers that outlined strategies by which Britain could defeat the American revolutionaries. Lee no longer believed that the American rebels could militarily win the War of Independence. "America has no chance of obtaining the ends She proposes to herself," he began. He proposed a campaign against the Middle Colonies, although he warned that simply taking Philadelphia would have no meaningful effect. He rather urged a broader war in order to "unhinge … the whole system or machine of resistance," by which he meant disuniting the thirteen colonies, isolating the Congress, and gaining loyalist support. It remains hotly debated whether Lee's motives were treasonous (this time to America) or whether this was a ruse designed to mislead the Howes, as biographer John Alden sympathetically, but unconvincingly, argues. The document itself was not discovered until the 1850s. Had its contents been made known in the 1770s, it is likely that Lee would have taken his place alongside Benedict Arnold in the American Hall of Infamy.

Lee's sincerity is reflected in his pledge to the Howe brothers that he would henceforth work zealously to find an "accommodation" between Britain and the colonies. He made good on that promise when the British government dispatched a peace commission, headed by the earl of Carlisle, to negotiate with the Congress following France's entry into the war in 1778. The commissioners were authorized to concede to all of the colonies' demands except independence. When the commissioners sought to use Lee as an instrument of reconciliation, he agreed to help, apparently unable to see how his actions might appear duplicitous to the American rebels. Released by the British in early 1778, Lee appeared before the Continental Congress and urged them to receive the British commissioners and pursue a political compromise—the very thing he had ardently denounced as an utter impossibility before his capture.[71] Rather than viewing Lee as a harbinger of peace, his old friends among the Whigs sensed something suspicious, even sinister, about him. Benjamin Rush, a close ally in 1775–1776, recalled that Lee had always shown an unhealthy disposition "for negotiations and conferences with general officers belonging to the British army," an ironic reversal of his 1775 correspondence with Burgoyne that was supposed to have established Lee's revolutionary credentials. Other Americans denounced Lee for "suffering himself to be made a pawn of by the Howes" during his captivity. In the end, the Carlisle peace commission came to nothing. Perhaps its only substantive result was to return Lee to his freedom and to his former place and rank in the Continental Army.[72]

The final act of Lee's revolutionary career was in some ways perfectly consistent with his long veneration of republicanism, his habitual defiance of his superiors, and his inability to temper his behavior to his political circumstances. When he returned to the camp of the Continental Army in the spring of 1778, Lee found not an ideal republic, united by a spirit of public virtue and common cause, but a community filled with suspicion and torn by jealousies. Over the winter of 1777–8, Washington had faced down severe threats to his command from both Congress and from rival officers such as Thomas Conway and Lee's old comrade Horatio Gates, the victor of Saratoga the previous fall.

During the eighteen months of Lee's captivity, Washington's abilities (both political and military) had matured. The army had also changed. Lee's opinion of the troops he commanded was still shaped by the near-collapse of the Continental Army in the fall 1776. But during his captivity, he had missed the army's remarkable victories at Trenton and Princeton, its hard-fought and very credible conduct during the Philadelphia campaign in the fall of 1777, and its refining experience at Valley Forge that winter. Having never seen them, Lee believed that it was "talking Nonsense" to claim that Americans could trade volleys with disciplined British regulars. But Washington and his officers, notably Baron Von Steuben and his systematic drill system, had built a

Continental Army that now had the experience, the training, and the confidence to do precisely that.

The Lee of 1775, boosting the morale of apprehensive and untried American troops, was no longer necessary, and to a large degree no longer wanted. In a sense, Lee's return to camp in 1778 was an unwelcome reminder to American veterans of how uncertain and insecure they had once been. One army chaplain remarked to Washington that Lee's capture had been a blessing in disguise for it enabled Americans to show the British "that we can maintain the war without the presence of General Lee."[73]

In June 1778, Lee commanded the vanguard of the American Army with orders to attack the rearguard of General Henry Clinton's army as it retreated across New Jersey from Philadelphia. Near Monmouth Court House, Clinton instead turned and attacked Lee, and the latter ordered a retreat. General Washington, coming up the rest of the army, was furious at Lee's action (or inaction), took command, and ordered a counter-attack. The battle ended in a draw. Although Lee's conduct had been militarily sound, as the battle's foremost historians conclude, his "intemperate and foolish … insolence to Washington" sealed his fate. In the battle's aftermath, Lee and Washington exchanged a series of icy letters that culminated with Lee requesting a court martial to clear his name and exonerate his conduct. Having already repudiated his monarch, Lee regarded no man—and certainly not Washington—as above his withering criticism. But, for all of his classical knowledge, Lee could not perceive how, in his absence, Washington had become more than a mere man. Like an eighteenth-century Cincinnatus, Washington had become the ideal of the citizen–soldier, and for many Americans, had begun to embody the Revolution itself.[74]

The trial was a contest between Lee and Washington and its outcome was therefore a foregone conclusion. The military tribunal found Lee guilty of disrespect, insubordination, and of "making an unnecessary, disorderly, and shameful retreat." But the lenient penalty—suspension for one year and retention of rank—revealed the strong political pressures at play. Although the seriousness of the charges did not seem to fit the mildness of the punishment, Congress refused to investigate, lest doing so seems to imply a rebuke of Washington. An embittered Lee withdrew to his farm in the Shenandoah Valley, where poverty, poor health, and of course his dogs were his only companions. When his army suspension expired, he lobbied Congress for a new command but was utterly ignored. He died of a fever in a cheap Philadelphia tavern in 1782, virtually friendless, nearly penniless, utterly disillusioned in his quest for a classical republic, and only dimly remembered by his countrymen. So it was how Charles Lee ended his days, like the loyalists, as one of "liberty's exiles," even as the American revolutionaries were increasingly transfixed, with nearly monarchical devotion, by the rising sun of Washington's republican majesty.[75]

Notes

1   L. H. Butterfield, ed., *Diary and Autobiography of John Adams* (4 volumes, Cambridge, MA: Belknap Harvard University Press, 1961), 3: 325; Harold Murdock, "Letter of Harry Farrington Gardner, 1775," *Colonial Society of Massachusetts Transactions* 26

(1927): 292–295 at 293; Lee to Benjamin Rush, December 12, 1775, and Lee to General Thomas, July 23, 1775, in *The Charles Lee Papers* (4 volumes, New York: Collections of the New-York Historical Society, 1871–4), 1: 226, 198 [hereinafter cited as *CLP*]; Richard Frothingham, *History of the Siege of Boston and of the Battles of Lexington, Concord, and Bunker Hill*, 3rd edn (Boston, MA: Little, Brown, and Co., 1872).

2   Lee to Benjamin Rush, December 12, 1775, *CLP* 1: 227; see David L. Preston, *Braddock's Defeat: The Battle of the Monongahela and the Road to Revolution* (New York: Oxford University Press, 2015), for the relationships among the battle's veterans between the French and Indian War and the American Revolution; and Andrew Jackson O'Shaughnessy, *The Men Who Lost America: British Leadership, the American Revolution and the Fate of Empire* (New Haven, CT: Yale University Press, 2013) for biographies of the leading British commanders.

3   Henry Laurens to John Laurens, August 14, 1776, in David R. Chesnutt et al., eds., *The Papers of Henry Laurens* (16 volumes, Columbia: South Carolina Historical Society, University of South Carolina Press, 1968–2002), 11: 228.

4   Journal of Dr. [Jeremy] Belknap, October 21, 1775, *Massachusetts Historical Society Proceedings* (June 1858): 82–83; *The Journal of Nicholas Cresswell, 1774–1777* (New York: Dial Press, 1924), 246; Benjamin Rush to David Hosack, August 15, 1810, in L. H. Butterfield, ed., *The Letters of Benjamin Rush* (2 volumes, Philadelphia, PA: American Philosophical Society, 1951), 2: 1058; "Biographical Anecdotes of the Late General Lee," *Universal Magazine*, February 1, 1785, 60–62.

5   John Richard Alden, *General Charles Lee: Traitor or Patriot?* (Baton Rouge: Louisiana State University Press, 1951); Samuel White Patterson, *Knight Errant of Liberty: The Triumph and Tragedy of General Charles Lee* (New York: Lantern Press, 1958); John Shy, in widely known essay, argued that Lee's main significance to the Revolutionary War was his call for Americans to take the "radical alternative," that is, wage a guerrilla war (or as it was termed in the eighteenth century, a "partisan war") against the British. I find Shy's argument unconvincing, however, and the evidence that Lee called for any such thing is extremely tenuous. John Shy, "American Strategy: Charles Lee and the Radical Alternative," in *A People Numerous and Armed: Reflections on the Military Struggle for American Independence*, rev. edn, ed. John Shy (Ann Arbor: University of Michigan Press, 1990), 133–162. Philip Papas, *Renegade Revolutionary: The Life of General Charles Lee* (New York: New York University Press, 2014) is a finely crafted biography that is updated with recent historiography, but does not supersede Alden's original research.

6   Lee to Lady Blake, May 2, 1769, *CLP* 1: 72. For the war's global dimensions see Franz Szabo, *War, State and Society in Mid-Eighteenth-Century Britain and Ireland* (New York: Oxford University Press, 2006); Fred Anderson, *Crucible of War: The Seven Years' War and the Fate of Empire in British North America, 1754–1766* (New York: Alfred A. Knopf, 2000).

7   Lee to Lady Blake, May 2, 1769, *CLP* 1: 72.

8   Colin Calloway, *The Scratch of a Pen: 1763 and the Transformation of North America* (New York: Oxford University Press, 2006); Philip Lawson, *The Imperial Challenge: Quebec and Britain in the Age of the American Revolution* (Montreal: McGill/Queen's University Press, 1989); Kathleen Duval, *Independence Lost: Lives on the Edge of the American Revolution* (New York: Random House, 2015); David L. Preston, *The Texture of Contact: European and Indian Settler Communities on the Frontiers of Iroquoia, 1667–1783* (Lincoln: University of Nebraska Press, 2009); Daniel K. Richter, *Facing East from Indian Country: A Native History of Early America* (Cambridge, MA:

Harvard University Press, 2001); and Eric Hinderaker, *Elusive Empires: Constructing Colonialism in the Ohio Valley, 1673–1800* (Cambridge, UK: Cambridge University Press, 1999); Brendan McConville, *The King's Three Faces: The Rise and Fall of Royal America, 1688–1776* (Chapel Hill: Omohundro Institute of Early American History and Culture, University of North Carolina Press, 2006), illustration on 161; Andrew Mackillop, "*More Fruitful than the Soil": Army, Empire, and the Scottish Highlands, 1715–1815* (East Linton, Scotland: Tuckwell Press, 2000); Matthew P. Dziennik, *The Fatal Land: War, Empire, and the Highland Soldier in British America* (New Haven, CT: Yale University Press, 2015).

9   Linda Colley, *Britons: Forging the Nation 1707–1837* (New Haven, CT: Yale University Press, 2005), 195, 201, and chapter 5 generally.

10   See Jon Butler, *Becoming America: The Revolution before 1776* (Cambridge, MA: Harvard University Press, 2000); Gordon S. Wood, *The Radicalism of the American Revolution* (New York: Vintage Books, 1991); Richard L. Bushman, *King and People in Provincial Massachusetts* (Chapel Hill: Omohundro Institute of Early American History and Culture, University of North Carolina Press, 1992).

11   McConville, *The King's Three Faces*, quotes on 8, 11, 50, 138; Julie Flavell, *When London Was Capital of America* (New Haven, CT: Yale University Press, 2010); Maya Jasanoff, *Liberty's Exiles: American Loyalists in the Revolutionary World* (New York: Alfred Knopf, 2011).

12   Bob Harris and Christopher A. Whatley, "'To Solemnize His Majesty's Birthday': New Perspectives on Loyalism in George II's Britain," *History: Journal of the Historical Association* 83 (July 1998): 397–419; Hannah Smith, *Georgian Monarchy: Politics and Culture, 1714–1760* (Cambridge, UK: Cambridge University Press, 2006); and Andrew C. Thompson, *George II* (New Haven, CT: Yale University Press, 2011). For other works that have informed my argument, see Clarissa Campbell Orr, "New Perspectives on Hanoverian Britain," *Historical Journal* 52, no. 2 (2009): 513–529; James Livesay, *Civil Society and Empire: Ireland and Scotland in the Eighteenth-Century Atlantic World* (New Haven, CT: Yale University Press, 2009); Bob Harris, *Politics and the Nation: Britain in the Mid-Eighteenth Century* (New York: Oxford University Press, 2002); J. C. D. Clark, "Protestantism, Nationalism, and National Identity, 1660–1832," *Historical Journal* 43, no. 1 (2000): 249–276; Kathleen Wilson, *The Sense of the People: Politics, Culture, and Imperialism in England, 1715–1785* (Cambridge, UK: Cambridge University Press, 1998); Marilyn Morris, *The British Monarchy and the French Revolution* (New Haven, CT: Yale University Press, 1998), 1–12.

13   Jefferson to Benjamin Franklin, August 13, 1777, quoted in Wood, *Radicalism of the American Revolution*, 109.

14   Fragment of a Letter to the Public (no date, probably 1774), *CLP* 1: 149–150; "Anecdote of General Lee, When in Portugal," *Morning Chronicle and London Advertiser*, September 5, 1775; Stuart Reid, *1745: A Military History of the Last Jacobite Rising* (New York: Sarpedon, 1966).

15   Lee to Miss Robinson, December 15, 1775, *CLP* 1: 230–231.

16   Lee to Daniel of St. Thomas Jenifer, May 6, 1776, *CLP* 1: 474; National Archives, Kew, UK (NA) WO/64/11, f. 133 (44th Regiment officer list).

17   Lee to Benjamin Rush, September 19, 1775, *CLP* 1: 208 (cynically dispos'd). There is no evidence that Lee fought at the Monongahela, as he is not mentioned on any of the officer lists or orderly books describing Braddock's advanced force that engaged the French and Indians on July 9, 1755; he would have remained in the rear division led by Colonel Thomas Dunbar. See Preston, *Braddock's Defeat*, 273, 411, note 9.

18 Lee to Sidney Lee, September 16, 1758, *CLP* 1: 7–8 ("poltroon," "booby"); "Narrative of 1758 Campaign," *CLP*, 1: 13; René Chartrand, *Ticonderoga 1758: Montcalm's Victory against All Odds* (Oxford: Osprey, 2000); for Lee's having been wounded at Ticonderoga, see NA WO/1/1, f. 202.

19 Preston, *Braddock's Defeat* 109; Lee to Sidney Lee, June 18, 1756, *CLP* 1: 8. Lee's marriage claim is doubtful, as neither Lee's subsequent correspondence nor any other contemporary accounts ever mention it. On Lee's friends, see Charles Davers to Gates, June 30, 1770, Horatio Gates Papers, New York Historical Society, New York, New York (HGP). Richard Mather to Thomas Mather, June 28, 1758, in Lothrop Withington, "Pennsylvania Gleanings in England," *Pennsylvania Magazine of History and Biography* 31 (October 1907): 474–482, 476 (Indian dress); Douglas R. Cubbison, *All Canada in the Hands of the British: General Jeffery Amherst and the 1760 Campaign to Conquer New France* (Norman: Oklahoma University Press, 2014); see Preston, *Braddock's Defeat*, chapter 6, on British military adaptations following 1755.

20 Lee to Sidney Lee, February 6, 1767, *CLP* 1: 51–52; on Lee's Portuguese service, see Lee to Shelburne, July 10, 1762, Colonel Cosnan to Lee, December 6, 1762, Lee to Colonel Cosnan, December 8, 1762; British Library, London, UK (BL) RP 5707/4 Box 134 946D; James Lunt, *John Burgoyne of Saratoga* (New York: Harcourt Brace, 1975) quote at 42–43; Lee to William Pitt, November 20, 1764, NA PRO 30/8/48; John Entick, *A Compleat History of the Late War, or Annual Register of Its Rise, Progress, and Events, in Europe, Asia, Africa, and America* (2 volumes, London: David Steel, 1765), 2: 478; Patrick Speelman, "Strategic Illusions and the Iberian War of 1762," paper presented at Omohundro Institute of Early American History and Culture's Conference: "Contest for Continents: The Seven Years War in Global Perspective," October 2009, manuscript in author's possession.

21 Lee to Sidney Lee, July 4, 1761, *CLP* 1: 33. On the politics of officers' commissions, see John Shy, *Toward Lexington: The Role of the British Army in the Coming of the American Revolution* (Princeton, NJ: Princeton University Press, 1965); J. A. Houlding, *Fit for Service: The Training of the British Army, 1715–1795* (New York: Oxford University Press, 1981); and Stephen Brumwell, *Redcoats: The British Soldier and War in the Americas, 1755–1763* (Cambridge, UK: Cambridge University Press, 2002).

22 Lee to Sidney Lee, March 28, 1772, *CLP* 1: 110, Lee to Sidney Lee, April 3, 1765, *CLP* 1: 51; Lee to Sir Charles Bunbury, December 7, 1764, *CLP* 1: 36; Lee to Sidney Lee, April 3, 1765, *CLP* 1: 38; for Lee's income, see Edward Langworthy, *Memoirs of the Life of the Late Charles Lee* (London, 1792), reprinted in *CLP* 4: 117–167 (income described at 124–145).

23 John Duran, ed., *The Last Journals of Horace Walpole during the Reign of George III from 1771–1783* (2 volumes, London: John Lane, 1910), 1: 404–405 (quote at 405).

24 Charles Lee, *The Importance of Canada Considered in Two Letters to a Noble Lord* (London, 1761); Helen Dewar, "Canada or Guadeloupe?: French and British Perceptions of Empire, 1760–1763," *Canadian Historical Review* 91 (December 2010): 637–660; Calloway, *The Scratch of a Pen*, chapter 2.

25 Lee to Earl Percy, 1775, *CLP* 1: 170; Thomas Wroughton to Lee, April 19, 1767, *CLP* 1: 52; Sir Horace Mann to Horace Walpole, September 16, 1775, in W. S. Lewis, ed., *Horace Walpole's Correspondence with Sir Horace Mann* (New Haven, CT: Yale University Press, 1967), 8: 129.

26 Lee to Shelburne, July 21, 1762, BL RP 5707/4 Box 134, 946D (faction); Benjamin Franklin to William Franklin, March 13, 1768, in William B. Willcox, ed., *Papers of*

Benjamin Franklin (New Haven, CT: Yale University Press, 1972), 15: 74–78 (quote on 78); Lee to Gates, May 6, 1774, HGP; For Lee's leadership of the American Club, see Richard E. Day, ed., *Calendar of Sir William Johnson Manuscripts* (Albany: University of the State of New York, 1909), 204; and James Sullivan et al., eds., *Sir William Johnson Papers* (Albany: University of the State of New York, 1925) volume 4: 341. On the importance of veterans' networks after 1763, see Stephen Brumwell, "Home from the Wars" [Army veterans in mid-Georgian Britain], *History Today* 52, no. 3 (March 2002): 41–47; Robert Scott Stephenson, "With Swords and Plowshares: British and American Soldiers in the Trans-Allegheny West, 1754–1774" (PhD diss., University of Virginia, 1998).

27 For Lee's political connections with opposition figures, see Alden, *General Charles Lee*, chapter 2; John Shy, *Toward Lexington: The Role of the British Army in the Coming of the American Revolution* (Princeton, NJ: Princeton University Press, 1965), 123; Frank O'Gorman, *The Rise of Party in England: The Rockingham Whigs, 1760–1782* (London: Allen and Unwin, 1975); Colin Bonwick, *English Radicals and the American Revolution* (Chapel Hill: University of North Carolina Press, 1977).

28 Wood, *Radicalism of the American Revolution*, 95; Lee to Patrick Henry, July 29, 1776, *CLP* 2: 177 (fourth century); Lee to Benjamin Rush, June 29, 1776, *CLP* 2: 95 ("decima Legio"); Lee to Richard Henry Lee, April 5, 1776, *CLP* 1: 380 ("dear senator"); Lee to George Colman, May 8, 1769, *CLP* 1: 82 (Senate); Lee to Thomas Gage, [1774], *CLP* 1: 134 ("Goddess"); for the importance of Roman history and precedent, see Philip Ayres, *Classical Culture and the Idea of Rome in Eighteenth-Century England* (Cambridge, UK: Cambridge University Press, 1997).

29 Henry Baglole, "Patterson (Paterson), Walter," *Dictionary of Canadian Biography*, 4: 605–11; for Lee's largely unproductive postwar land transactions, see Lee to Sir William Johnson, July 25, 1764, *CLP* 1: 34–35; "Grant of Lands in East Florida," *CLP* 1: 46–48; Walter Patterson to Lee, November 10, 1772, *CLP* 1: 112–116. See Bernard Bailyn, *Voyagers to the West: A Passage in the Peopling of America on the Eve of the Revolution* (New York: Vintage Books, 1986) for the postwar scramble for frontier lands.

30 Lee to Charles Yorke, March 27, 1765, BL Add. Mss., 35637, f. 153; Lee to Clotworthy Upton, January 18, 1772, *CLP* 1: 107; for the Peterborough comparison, see Lee letter, 1771, *CLP* 1: 96 and *CLP* 4: 176, and John P. Hattendorf, "Mordaunt, Charles, Third Earl of Peterborough, and First Earl of Monmouth," *Oxford Dictionary of National Biography* (New York: Oxford University Press, 2004) 39: 13–21.

31 Lee to Earl Percy, 1775, *CLP* 1: 171; Lee to Sidney Lee, March 1, 1766, *CLP* 1: 43; see Eliga H. Gould, *The Persistence of Empire: British Political Culture in the Age of the American Revolution* (Chapel Hill: Omohundro Institute of Early American History and Culture, University of North Carolina Press, 2000), chapter 4 and Timothy Shannon, *Indians and Colonists at the Crossroads of Empire: The Albany Congress of 1754* (Ithaca, NY: Cornell University Press, 2000) for colonial constructions of empire.

32 Lee to Sidney Lee, April 3, 1765, *CLP* 1: 37–39.

33 "The Character of the Present Emperor of Germany," *Public Advertiser*, July 27, 1771; for Lee's authorship, see Lee to Sidney Lee, August 9, 1771, *CLP* 1: 106, and John Hale to Horatio Gates, August 30, 1771, HGP.

34 Lee to earl of Charlemont, June 1, 1765, *CLP* 1: 40–41; Lee to Sidney Lee, March 1, 1766, *CLP* 1: 43; *Epistle to David Hume* [1771] 1: 102–104; see also Lee to Charles Yorke, April 27, 1766, BL Add. Mss. 35636, ff. 454–456, and John W. Werner, "David

Hume and America," *Journal of the History of Ideas* 33 (July–September 1972): 439–456.

35 Lee to earl of Charlemont, June 1, 1765, *CLP* 1: 41; Lee to Lady Blake, May 2, 1768, *CLP* 1: 72–73; Lee Letter, 1771, *CLP* 1: 97–98; Lee to Alexander McDougall, October 26, 1775, *CLP* 1: 214; Lee to Robert Morris, November 22, 1775, *CLP* 1: 219; Lee to Sir Charles Davers, December 24, 1769, *CLP* 1: 91.

36 J. C. Long, *Lord Jeffrey Amherst: A Soldier of the King* (New York: Macmillan, 1933), 224–225.

37 Dartmouth to Gage, October 17, 1774, Aspinwall Papers *Massachusetts Historical Society Collections*, 4th Series 10: 716.

38 Thomas Young to Samuel Adams, August 21, 1774, Samuel Adams Papers, volume 2, reel 1, New York Public Library, New York, NYPL.

39 *Boston Gazette*, August 22, 1774; Lee to Gage, August 6, 1774, *CLP* 1: 134; For Lee's plantation in Virginia, see "General Charles Lee House," *Magazine of the Berkeley County Historical Society* 30 (1964): 38–39.

40 George W. Corner, ed., *The Autobiography of Benjamin Rush: His "Travels through Life" Together with His Commonplace Book for 1789–1813* (Princeton, NJ: Princeton University Press, 1948), 111; John Adams mentioned other dinners with Lee, L. H. Butterfield, ed., *Diary and Autobiography of John Adams* (4 volumes, Cambridge, MA: Belknap Press, 1961), 2: 135–136, 140, 147, 151, and 3: 321 (cordiality), 446 (Lee excepted). See also Lee to Samuel Adams, July 21, 1774, in Samuel Adams Papers, NYPL.

41 Lee to Patrick Henry, July 29, 1776, *CLP* 2: 177.

42 Lee to Richard Henry Lee, July 19, 1776, *CLP* 2: 146; Samuel Adams to Joseph Warren, June 20 and 28, 1775, in Worthington Chauncey Ford, ed., *Warren-Adams Letters: Being Chiefly a Correspondence among John Adams, Samuel Adams, and James Warren* (1 volume, Boston, MA: Massachusetts Historical Society, 1917), 64, 69–70; Butterfield, ed., *Diary and Autobiography of John Adams*, 2: 323–24 (appointment).

43 Lee to Lord Barrington, June 22, 1775, *CLP* 1: 185–186; Sir Horace Mann to Horace Walpole, September 16, 1775, in *Horace Walpole Correspondence*, 8: 129; See Bushman, *King and People* chapters 1 and 4 for the monarchical language of resistance.

44 Henry Knox to Lucy Knox, c. July 1775, *Massachusetts Historical Society Proceedings* (Boston, MA: 1860), 66–67.

45 Horatio Gates to Lee, July 1, 1774, *CLP* 1: 125.

46 *General Lee's Letter to General Burgoyne Upon his Arrival at Boston* (New York: J. Anderson, 1775); *Letters of Major General Lee, to the Right Honorable Earl Percy, and Major General John Burgoyne, with the Answers* (New York: J. Rivington, 1775); *A Letter from General Lee, to General Burgoyne, Printed from the New-York Gazetteer, of July 6, to which is added, General Burgoyne's Answer, and A Copy of a Letter from General Lee, declining an Interview proposed by General Burgoyne* (Boston, MA: Draper's Printing Office, 1775), quotes at p. 4; *Letters of the two commanders in chief, Generals Gage and Washington, and Major Generals Burgoyne and Lee: With the Manifesto of General Washington to the inhabitants of Canada* (New York: James Rivington, 1775).

47 For Lee's correspondence with Gage and Burgoyne, see Lee to John Burgoyne, June 7, 1775, *CLP*, 1: 180–185; Burgoyne to Lee, July 9, 1775, *CLP* 1: 188–193; Lee to Burgoyne, July 11, 1775, *CLP* 1: 194–195; Lee to Gage, August 1775, *CLP* 1: 200–202;

Lee to Burgoyne, December 1, 1775, *CLP* 1: 222–225. See also "Letter of Edmund Quincy," *New England Genealogical Register* 11 (1857): 165 for another example of the public's reception of Lee's letter.

48   Lee to Edmund Burke, December 16, 1774, *CLP* 1: 145 (quondam); Eunice Paine to Robert Treat Paine, July 7, 1775, in Edward W. Hanson, ed., *The Papers of Robert Treat Paine* (3 volumes, Boston, MA: Massachusetts Historical Society, 2005), 75; Lee to William Howe, November 4, 1776, James Grant Papers, Library of Congress, Washington, DC, reel 35, ff. 117–118.

49   *General Lee's Letter*, 2, 7.

50   *General Lee's Letter*, 3, 6, 8; also in Lee to John Burgoyne, June 7, 1775, *CLP* 1: 180–185.

51   John Burgoyne to Lee, July 9, 1775, *CLP* 1: 188–193, quotes at 188 and 191.

52   Lee to Benjamin Franklin, December 10, 1775, in *Papers of Benjamin Franklin* 22: 294–295; Horatio Gates to Franklin, December 7, 1775, ibid., 22: 286 (Franklin's help in publication); Gage to Tryon, July 18, 1775, and Gage to Dunmore, July 26, 1775, Gage Papers, American Series, volumes 131 and 132, William L. Clements Library (Ann Arbor: University of Michigan); For Lee's correspondence with the Massachusetts provincial congress, see *CLP* 1: 193–195.

53   For loyalty in the British Army, see Ira D. Gruber, "For King and Country: The Limits of Loyalty of British Officers in the War for American Independence," in *Limits of Loyalty*, ed. Edgar Denton (Waterloo: Wilfrid Laurier University Press, 1980), 23–40 (quote at 33); Stuart R. J. Sutherland, "Richard Montgomery," *Dictionary of Canadian Biography* 4: 545–550; Paul David Nelson, *General Horatio Gates: A Biography* (Baton Rouge: Louisiana State University Press, 1976).

54   James Warren to Samuel Adams, August 4, 1775, volume 2, reel 1, Samuel Adams Papers, NYPL.

55   Benjamin Franklin to Lee, February 19, 1776, *CLP* 2: 313 (sentiments); Lee to Benjamin Rush, February 25, 1776, *CLP* 1: 325; Lee to George Washington, January 24, 1776, *CLP* 1: 259 (common sense).

56   Lee to Benjamin Rush, October 20, 1775, *CLP* 1: 213 (no wrong); Lee to Patrick Henry, July 29, 1776, *CLP* 2: 177–180, at 178 (titles). For Lee's denunciations of George III or monarchy generally in 1775–1776, see *CLP* 1: 173–174, 203, 213–214, 318–319.

57   *Strictures on a Pamphlet, entitled "A Friendly Address to All Reasonable Americans, on the Subject of Our Political Confusions," Addressed to the People of America* (Philadelphia, PA: William and Thomas Bradford, 1774), reprinted in *CLP* 1: 151–166, quotes at 156, 157, 162; Corner, Autobiography of Benjamin Rush, 156. Thomas Randolph Adams, "American Independence: The Growth of an Idea," *Colonial Society of Massachusetts Publications* 43 (1956): 4–202 (reprint of Strictures).

58   Lee to Provincial Congress of Virginia, 1775, *CLP* 1: 173 (magnanimity); Lee to Patrick Henry, July 29, 1776, *CLP* 2: 177–180. For his statements avowing the failure of reconciliation and complete independence, see *CLP* 1: 172–178, 197, 203–204, 210, 233, 255, 259, 318–319, 325, 334, 378–379, 467.

59   Lee to Edmund Burke, December 15, 1774, *CLP* 1: 145; George III's speech is contained in Merrill Jensen, ed., *American Colonial Documents to 1776, Vol. 9, in English Historical Documents* (New York: Oxford University Press, 1955), 851–852; Lee to the president of the Massachusetts Council, November 22, 1776, *CLP* 2: 303 (treason). Lee to governor at Cape François, August 30, 1776, *CLP* 2: 256; Lee to Robert Morris, January 30, 1776, *CLP* 1: 266.

60   Lee to Robert Morris, January 3, 1776, *CLP* 1: 233: Lee to Robert Morris, February
     20, 1776, *CLP* 1: 319 (emphasis added); Lee to the president of the Massachusetts
     Council, November 22, 1776, *CLP* 2: 303 (treason).
61   Lee to James Bowdoin, November 30, 1776, *CLP* 2: 324; Reed to Lee, November 21,
     1776, and Lee to Reed, November 24, 1776, *CLP* 2: 293–294, 305–306.
62   Lee to Gates, December 12, 1776, *CLP* 2: 348.
63   "Ode Addressed to General Lee," in *An Asylum for Fugitives* (London, 1776), 1:
     151–154; *General Evening Post*, March 30, 1776, cited in Lutnick, *The American
     Revolution and the British Press*, 98. It should also be noted that some opposition
     writers predicted that one day Lee and Washington would be venerated alongside
     John Hampden as defenders of English liberty.
64   Harcourt to Brother, December 19, 1776, in Edward William Harcourt, eds., *The
     Harcourt Papers* (11 volumes, Oxford: James Parker and Co., 1880), 180; Extract
     of a Letter from Cornet Tarleton of the Dragoon Guards to Lord Vaughan, 1776,
     Hardwicke Papers, BL Add. Mss. 38912, ff. 239–240; Britons who actually knew
     Lee or who had been burned by his scorn held a different view. For example, one of
     Jeffrey Amherst's friends, Joseph Yorke, wrote soon after Lee's capture that "I am not
     sorry Lee should be taken in order to have him tried, but otherwise I wish him to
     continue with the rebels, convinced he is the worst present [that] can be made to any
     Society whatever," cited in Long, *Lord Jeffrey Amherst*, 232.
65   For examples of wartime and postwar British historians and writers who celebrated
     Harcourt's valor, see *The history of the war in America, between Great Britain and her
     Colonies* (Dublin, 1779), 1: 215–217; C. Stedman, *The History of the Origin, Progress,
     and Termination of the American War* (2 volumes, London: 1794), 1: 226–227;
     "An Account of General Harcourt's Surprising the Rebel General Lee during the
     American War" [Mr. Addison], *Interesting anecdotes, memoirs, allegories, essays, and
     poetical fragments, tending to amuse the fancy, and inculcate morality* (London, 1797);
     W. Belsham, *Memoirs of the reign of George III, to the session of Parliament ending
     A.D. 1793* (Dublin, 1796), volume 1, 384–385. "William Harcourt, 3rd Earl Harcourt
     (1743–1830)," *Oxford Dictionary of National Biography*, ed. H. C. G. Matthew and
     Brian Harrison (New York: Oxford University Press, 2004), volume 16, 135–136.
     Bass, *Green Dragoon*, 19–22.
66   David Hackett Fischer, *Washington's Crossing* (New York: Oxford University Press,
     2004), 149; Edward H. Tatum Jr., *The American Journal of Ambrose Serle, Secretary
     to Lord Howe 1776–1778* (San Marino, CA: Huntington Library, 1940), 187; Captain
     John Bowater to earl of Denbigh, June 11 and 17, 1777, and September 23, 1778, in
     David Syrett and Marion Balderston, eds., *The Lost War: Letters from British Officers
     during the American Revolution* (New York: Horizon Press, 1975), 130–131, 173–174;
     The history of the civil war in America … by an Officer of the Army (London, 1780), 1:
     265–266.
67   Gould, in *Persistence of Empire*, finds only a "grudging loyalism" in Britain, but
     a popular consensus in support of the British government during the American
     War. See also Troy Bickham, *Making Headlines: The American Revolution as Seen
     through the British Press* (DeKalb: Northern Illinois University Press, 2008); Wilson,
     The Sense of the People; H. T. Dickinson, ed., *Britain and the American Revolution*
     (London: Longman, 1998); Nicholas Rogers, *Crowds, Culture, and Politics in
     Georgian Britain* (1998); Stephen Conway, *The British Isles and the War for American
     Independence* (New York: Oxford University Press, 2000); Solomon Lutnick, *The*

American Revolution and the British Press, 1775–1783* (Columbia: University of Missouri Press, 1967).

68 [Robert Prescott], *A Letter from a Veteran, to the Officers of the Army Encamped at Boston* (New York: 1774), 13, 16; Ilya Berkovich, *Motivation in War: The Experience of Common Soldiers in Old-Regime Europe* (Cambridge: Cambridge University Press, 2017); see also Matthew H. Spring, *With Zeal and With Bayonets Only: The British Army on Campaign in North America, 1775–1783* (Norman: University of Oklahoma Press, 2008), 127.

69 Lee to Captain Richard Fitzpatrick, April 4, 1778, Fox Papers, BL Add. Mss. 47582, f. 45.

70 James Grant Papers, Library of Congress, Washington, DC, reel 35: Lee to Grant, December 19, 1776, ff. 131–132 (quote), ibid., ff. 133–134; ibid., ff. 135–136; Lee to Grant, December 20, 1776, ff. 142–143; Lee to Grant, December 25, 1776, ff. 144–145; Lee to Grant, December 28, 1776, ff. 146–147; Order re: Lieutant Colonel Lee, 1776, f. 147; Lee to Giuseppe Minghini, December 28, 1776, f. 149; Lee to Grant, December 30, 1776, ff. 151–152: Lee Intelligence, 1776, ff. 153–155. It should be noted that Lee's letters did not include the year. The catalog of the James Grant Papers mistakenly gives the dates as December 1775, and archivists even penciled [1775] on some of the documents. But it is entirely clear that they were written in December 1776 while Lee was in captivity (e.g., he requests that the British send his letter to Philadelphia for his servant Giuseppe Minghini to join him).

71 On Lee's plan to end the war, see "Scheme for Putting an End to the War, Submitted to the Royal Commissioners, March 1777," *CLP*, 2: 361–366; and commentary by Shy, "Charles Lee," 153 and Alden, *Charles Lee*, chapter 11.

72 Benjamin Rush to Robert Morris, February 22, 1777, in Butterfield, ed., *Letters of Benjamin Rush*, 1: 135; Gordon to Gates, April 3, 1777, in Worthington C. Ford, ed., "Letters of the Reverend William Gordon Historian of the American Revolution, 1770–1799," *Massachusetts Historical Society Proceedings* 63 (1930): 303–613, at 339; Tatum, *Serle Journal*, 207 (suspicions of Lee in 1777).

73 Lee, "Plan of an Army," c. 1778, *CLP* 2: 388; Gordon to Washington, January 18, 1778, in "Letters of the Reverend William Gordon," 367; for the challenges to Washington's command and the Continental Army's maturation, see Ron Chernow, *Washington: A Life* (New York: Penguin, 2010), chapters 26–28.

74 Mark Edward Lender and Garry Wheeler Stone, *Fatal Sunday: George Washington, the Monmouth Campaign, and the Politics of Battle* (Norman: University of Oklahoma, 2016), 412.

75 Lee to Reed, November 24, 1776, *CLP* 2: 306; Lee to Washington, November 19, 1776, *CLP* 2: 287–288; on the continuation of monarchical infatuations in the person of Washington, see McConville, *The King's Three Faces*, 313–314; Jasanoff, *Liberty's Exiles*, 14.

10

Epilogue: The Spirit of 1773

James M. Vaughn

On the moonlit night of December 16, 1773, a large gathering of men "dressed and whooping like Indians" boarded three merchant ships that lay moored at a wharf in the harbor of Boston, Massachusetts, and dumped more than 40 tons of tea overboard.[1] By this lawless act of destruction, undertaken in the name of defending the "rights of Englishmen," Boston's "Sons of Liberty" set in train a course of events that led directly to the War of American Independence and the sundering of the British imperial world. When word of the "Boston Tea Party," as history has come to know the event, reached Britain, it brought an end to a remarkably experimental, contested, and transformative period in the history of the British Empire that began with the signing of the Treaty of Paris in 1763—the period that has been the focus of this volume.

Although Charles Lee's career transcended our concluding moment, extending well into the era of the American Revolution, it is fitting that the last chapter is focused on him. For while many aspects of Lee's story were unique, his bitter disappointment with the Empire's direction since the end of the Seven Years' War was shared by a growing number of radical dissidents across the British world from Boston to Bengal. Initially enthusiastic about Britain's global victories over France and the vast expansion of the "empire of liberty" that they seemed to promise, these radicals came to believe that ministers in London were instead pursuing a grand design to subject the peoples of the Empire to "arbitrary power," with unaccountable governments and standing armies riding roughshod over law, liberty, and property.

As the chapters in this volume demonstrate, the transformation wrought by the Seven Years' War, and the new territories and subjects brought under British rule as a result of the peace, inspired and required an outpouring of initiatives, proposals, discussions, and debates that sought to shape the Empire's evolution. Such efforts and ideas were far from the exclusive preserve of metropolitan ministers and officials. Bengali nawabs and zamindars, Senegalese merchants, Native American "beloved men," Grub Street hacks, and Quebec *habitants* all asserted their rights and interests as British subjects or as people who were newly subject to British rule. British officials on the imperial periphery and in London's corridors of power had to accommodate their demands in formulating policies for the newly expanded empire. As the Seven Years' War drew to a close, the future direction of the Empire was widely debated in the taverns and coffeehouses of London and in provincial cities throughout Britain and British America.

Imposing rule over French Catholics, Native Americans, West Africans, and South Asian Hindus and Muslims challenged long-standing notions of British identity and subjecthood. Colonial governors, company officials, and frontier officers who dealt with the demands of local populations grappled with unprecedented questions of subject status. The new and more inclusive definitions of subjecthood that began to emerge during this period were often the product of pragmatic solutions reached "on the spot" by local British authorities across the imperial world rather than of formal decisions made by courts and officialdom in Britain. The addition of the Catholic inhabitants of Quebec and Grenada to the existing Catholic populations of Ireland and Minorca induced numerous discussions and debates over the efficacy or necessity of the Empire's old religious restrictions, penalties, and test acts among British ministers and governors, who were already infused with an enlightened spirit of religious toleration. The contrast between the brutal expulsion of the Acadians from Nova Scotia in 1755 and the plans being laid for the inclusion of the Québécois and Grenadians into the imperial fold ten years later is a striking illustration of the change of mood and policy.[2] The post-1763 decade witnessed a shift of imperial governance away from anti-Catholicism and toward the incorporation of new Catholic subjects into a model of empire that was more religiously diverse and tolerant than its predecessor.

The expansion of British rule in North America over the trans-Appalachian interior and Florida, the establishment of the Crown colony of Senegambia in West Africa, and the East India Company's growing dominion in Bengal provoked wide-ranging questions and conflicts over the nature and purposes of the Empire. The terms of the Treaty of Paris transformed a largely maritime and commercial power that maintained colonies, factories, forts, and settlements along the coasts of North America, West Africa, and South Asia into a worldwide territorial empire that reached into the interior of three continents. The decade following 1763 witnessed a myriad of imperial experiments that attempted to manage this transformation and stabilize British rule in new areas and over new peoples. In Senegambia, an autocratic royal governor failed to incorporate and win the support of local elites, leading to imperial failure by the mid-1770s. After repressing Pontiac's Rebellion in the summer of 1763, British ministers and officials prohibited colonial settlement west of the Appalachian Mountains and sought, via the "Plan of 1764," to incorporate the indigenous inhabitants into the Empire by recognizing them as subordinate "nations" governed by chosen surrogates.

In Bengal, the East India Company initially used its newfound political and military power to place Mir Jafar, then Mir Qasim, and then Mir Jafar again on the throne. The Company's aim was not to assume direct control but rather to freely pursue its commercial interests under the auspices of a pliant nawab who ostensibly still governed the province. After this arrangement broke down and Clive wrested the *diwani* from the Mughal Emperor Shah Alam II, the Company began to transform itself from a trading corporation into something that more closely resembled a state, with the authority to collect taxes and an increasingly large standing army.

During the postwar decade, as the chapters in this volume demonstrate, a wide array of programs and policies were pursued to govern a British imperial world that could no longer be conceptualized as "Protestant, commercial, maritime and free."[3] Such initiatives were often the responses of local British authorities to the problems and difficulties they faced on the ground throughout the Empire. Nevertheless, while there may have been no grand imperial design conceived by ministers and officials during the war and then zealously implemented in the wake of victory, one can detect a general drift of imperial policies and plans toward what might be called "cosmopolitan authoritarianism." The British political establishment could see that the newly acquired territories were neither "Protestant," nor "commercial," nor "maritime," nor (at least in British terms) "free." But in the decade following the Seven Years' War, the ideology of British cultural and racial superiority that would come to characterize and justify imperial rule in the nineteenth century was not yet fully formed and could not be deployed.[4] Instead, in cultural and religious terms, many of the policies and programs that were proposed and sometimes implemented to consolidate imperial rule over King George III's new subjects were remarkably tolerant of diversity. British officials sought to gain and secure the cooperation of local elites—whether Bengali, Creek, or Québécois—and to incorporate them as junior partners into Britain's imperial system. Such incorporation usually took the form of allowing native rulers to retain some degree of local authority and autonomy and to maintain their laws, religions, and customs.

The animating impulse behind this form of rule was not enlightened liberalism as much as it was the need for imperial stability. The dominant view in Britain's political establishment in 1763 was that the war had utterly exhausted the fiscal and military resources of the state. Therefore, if the new imperial acquisitions were to be maintained (as they must be), they had to be made, somehow, to take care of themselves. The "Anglo-Indian Wars" of 1763–1764 in North America and Bengal showed that Britain could not simply impose its will upon native rulers and populations. Gaining the cooperation of local elites was therefore an important element in achieving imperial aims. During the postwar decade, imperial officials from Quebec to St. Augustine to Calcutta carefully attended to native cultures, often treating them with respect and even admiration. This cultural inquisitiveness was not deployed primarily for the advancement of knowledge per se, but rather as part of a strategy of rule that depended on gaining local knowledge in order to obtain local cooperation. Nevertheless, such inquisitiveness helped to shape a governing ideology that comprehended and even embraced the Empire's new cultural, ethnic, and religious diversity.

The cooperation of local elites and the maintenance of local customs were by no means intended to lay the foundation for a more politically egalitarian and participatory imperial system. For the very same concerns that informed these policies and plans—that the new Empire would prove ungovernable and that the costs of its management and maintenance would spiral out of control—also led to a program of autocratic centralization. Although there were dissident voices in London's halls of power as well as in the public sphere, the vast majority of the landed elite that ruled Britain believed that the bonds of authority were weakening and that they desperately needed to be restored throughout the British Isles and the Empire. Many ministers and officials gazed outward from Whitehall toward a post-1763 British world that seemed in upheaval from the forests of North America to the streets of London to the upcountry factories of Bengal.

Across the Atlantic, the older British-American colonies appeared to be filled with presumptuously assertive assemblies, smugglers, and restlessly expanding settlers defying or disregarding imperial authority. In Britain, Wilkesite radicals inflamed and organized popular discontent in the towns and cities, above all in the capital itself. In Bengal, the East India Company seemed incapable of controlling its own servants and securing its newly won position. Many among the Empire's ruling class were persuaded that a grand struggle between order and anarchy was underway across the British world. Hence, they proved willing to pursue innovative measures on the imperial periphery in the hope that they might reduce the expense of imperial governance, extract resources for the defense of overseas interests, and strengthen the hand of authority at home. These measures included centralizing and militarizing the Atlantic Empire and helping to transform the East India Company's growing political power on the subcontinent into an enduring territorial dominion.

Thus, during the decade following the war, at the same time that the British imperial system was becoming more religiously tolerant and culturally diverse on the periphery and at the grassroots level, it was also becoming more politically autocratic and economically extractive. Whether or not another order of things was possible— an order in which political power and participation were more widely diffused throughout the Empire's diverse lands and peoples—is a difficult counterfactual question. Regardless, there were radical dissidents who claimed that a more politically participatory and economically dynamic but nevertheless culturally diverse and religiously tolerant empire was achievable. Well-known radicals like Isaac Barré, Benjamin Franklin, and Richard Price envisioned such an alternative empire spanning the Atlantic. Less-known radicals like William Bolts, the Dutch-born former East India Company employee and independent merchant in South Asia, thought that such an alternative, inclusive empire was even possible in Bengal.[5]

Such radical voices and alternative aspirations were increasingly silenced or ignored as the British political establishment became more committed to implementing an authoritarian imperial policy. Between 1762 and 1765, the ministries of Lord Bute and George Grenville proposed to create a peacetime standing army for North America, to extend the customs service and enforce the navigation acts, and to make imperial administration in the colonies less dependent on colonial institutions and cooperation. The costs of this program were to be met in part by taxes levied on the American colonies by Parliament. The royal proclamation of 1763 prohibiting colonial settlement west of the Appalachians, the Sugar Act of 1764, and the Stamp and Quartering Acts of 1765 were each unprecedented measures of metropolitan intervention in and authority over the colonies.

In their totality, the new imperial policies sought to militarize and to politically centralize Britain's Atlantic Empire, making imperial administration and revenue-raising less dependent on colonial assemblies. British Americans' discontent with this program led in short order to the creation of a colonial resistance movement and provoked an imperial crisis that wracked the British Atlantic for over a decade. Although in the face of massive resistance the Stamp Act was repealed in 1766, other aspects of the new imperial program remained intact and Parliament confirmed its claim to wield absolute sovereignty over the Empire with the passage of the Declaratory Act.

Furthermore, during the following year, the Townshend Acts were designed to achieve the Stamp Act's objectives by other means. Their passage rekindled and expanded the colonial resistance movement. In 1770, a new prime minister, Lord North, repealed the Townshend duties on American imports except for the tea levy, which was upheld not in hope of raising revenue but in order to "maintain the principle" of Parliament's supreme authority over the colonies. Thus, the wider principles and policies of the new authoritarian imperial system remained firmly in place.

While the Grenville ministry was implementing the new Atlantic imperial program in 1764, it was also intervening in the internal affairs of the East India Company in order to back the return of Robert Clive to Bengal as governor. Clive's acquisition of the *diwani* in 1765 transformed the Company into a territorial state in northeastern India and indirectly added millions of new subjects to the British Empire. But rather than filling the Company's coffers and the pockets of its shareholders with the riches of the Orient as Clive confidently expected, the costs of managing and maintaining this dominion, combined with the loss of revenue due to war and the devastating effects of famine in Bengal during the late 1760s, pushed the Company to the brink of financial ruin by 1772. The corporation was a vital pillar of both the City of London and the British fiscal-military state. Its collapse, it was widely feared, would cause a "national bankruptcy."[6] Aiming to stabilize the Company's financial position in Britain and its imperial rule in India, the North ministry passed the Tea Act and the Regulating Act successively in May and June 1773. The latter legislation replaced Bengal's indigenous administration and created an autocratic executive in charge of all British territories in India, with a governor-general and council appointed by the Company and the Crown.

The Tea Act was designed to allow the Company to offload the large amount of tea stockpiled in its London warehouses by directly re-exporting it to the American colonies without paying the duty in Britain. Additionally, the Company was now able to consign the tea to selected merchants in America, allowing them to monopolize the profits for selling this prized commodity. The corporation would be able to sell its tea at a lower cost in the colonies and undercut smugglers while still paying the Townshend import duty, thus affirming Parliament's right to levy such a colonial tax.

When the Company shipped tea to four colonial American ports in the summer of 1773, the scene was set for a dramatic confrontation that reached its climax in Boston that December. As Benjamin Carp argues, the colonial radicals who dumped the tea in the harbor "were frightened not just because of what they saw happening in Boston, but because of what they had seen happening throughout the world. Tyranny and liberty were locked in a constant struggle, and the dissident Bostonians knew which side they supported."[7] Indeed, the protests against the Company's tea were also protests against the new authoritarian model of empire that was being promulgated from Whitehall in the decade following the war. It all seemed part of the same program. With the passage of the Tea and Regulating Acts, Parliament and the Crown had fully embraced the monopoly company's politically autocratic and economically extractive empire in Bengal. While the tea shipments were crossing the Atlantic, the "Liberty Boys" in New York declared that the East India Company's rule on the subcontinent was characterized by "a Barbarity scarce equaled even by the most brutal Savages, or *Cortez*, the *Mexican* Conqueror."[8] In the political imagination of colonial radicals, the tea symbolized an empire that was being remade along similar lines, not only in the new, post-1763 territories but also in the older colonies. For these radicals, submission to the payment of the Townshend duty on tea represented submission to an imperial state that claimed the right to govern and tax them without their consent "in all cases whatsoever," as Parliament described its unlimited authority in the Declaratory Act of 1766. When they dumped the tea in the harbor, these radicals believed they were rejecting the new imperial program and defending the existing, if embattled, "empire of liberty."

News of the Boston Tea Party confirmed the metropolitan ruling elite in its belief that there was a great struggle being waged between order and anarchy across the British imperial world. The Coercive Acts that were passed in the spring of 1774, which closed the port of Boston and restructured the government of Massachusetts Bay among other authoritarian measures, were aimed at stemming the anarchic tide. The passage of the Coercive Acts, in turn, served to confirm the suspicions of colonial radicals that ministers and officials in Britain were pursuing a grand design for arbitrary power. These radicals feared that they were on the verge of losing a titanic conflict between liberty and tyranny playing out across the Empire. When the American Revolution began one year later, it drew a line across the British world—a line that would separate Virginia and Massachusetts, as well as Florida, Minorca, and Senegambia, from Britain, Bengal, Grenada, and Quebec. By the time the smoke of revolution and war cleared, the new British world that had come into existence in 1763 was no more.

Notes

1   For the "Boston Tea Party," see Benjamin L. Carp, *Defiance of the Patriots: The Boston Tea Party and the Making of America* (New Haven, CT: Yale University Press, 2010); and Alfred F. Young, *The Shoemaker and the Tea Party: Memory and the American Revolution* (Boston, MA: Beacon Press, 1999).
2   On the expulsion of the Acadians, see John Mack Faragher, *A Great and Noble Scheme: The Tragic Story of the Expulsion of the French Acadians from Their American Homeland* (New York: W. W. Norton, 2005).
3   David Armitage coined this phrase to describe the ideology of empire dominant in Britain prior to 1763. See David Armitage, *The Ideological Origins of the British Empire* (Cambridge: Cambridge University Press, 2000).
4   For the deployment of this ideology in the British Empire beginning in the Age of Revolution, see C. A. Bayly, *Imperial Meridian: The British Empire and the World, 1780–1830* (London: Longman, 1989).
5   See William Bolts, *Considerations on India Affairs; Particularly Respecting the Present State of Bengal and Its Dependencies* (London: J. Almon, 1772).
6   Quoted in P. J. Marshall, *The Making and Unmaking of Empires: Britain, India, and America, c. 1750–1783* (Oxford: Oxford University Press, 2005), 200.
7   Carp, *Defiance of the Patriots*, 3.
8   *The Alarm*, No. 2, October 9, 1773 (New York).

Index